Sharks

This book explores the global conservation and management of sharks. There has been a rapid decline in populations of many shark species, while new science has emerged concerning the critical role they play in marine ecosystems. However, the authors show that conservation law and policy have been slow to develop, with only a small number of iconic species being protected worldwide. The increase in fishing impact – primarily through shark finning and by-catch – has led to shark conservation receiving greater international attention in recent years.

Sharks: Conservation, governance and management surveys our current knowledge and status of the law and science in relation to sharks, with a particular focus on improving frameworks for their conservation and management. Recent trends are analysed, including shark finning bans that have been put in place in several countries, the widening number of nations establishing shark sanctuaries and the growth of shark-based tourism. The efficacy of current listing processes for endangered species and fisheries regulations is also examined. Tourism is explored as an alternative to fishing and the risks and impacts associated with this industry are analysed.

Contributors include leading authorities from universities and conservation organizations in North America, Europe and Australia. A common theme is to emphasize the importance of collaborative governance between various interest groups and the need for inter-disciplinary research and management approaches that are necessary to address the decline in sharks.

Erika J. Techera is a Professor and Dean in the Faculty of Law at the University of Western Australia.

Natalie Klein is a Professor and Dean at Macquarie Law School, Macquarie University, Australia.

Sharks

Conservation, governance and management

Edited by Erika J. Techera and Natalie Klein

Routledge
Taylor & Francis Group
LONDON AND NEW YORK

earthscan
from Routledge

First published 2014
by Routledge
2 Park Square, Milton Park, Abingdon, Oxon OX14 4RN

and by Routledge
711 Third Avenue, New York, NY 10017

Routledge is an imprint of the Taylor & Francis Group, an informa business

British Library Cataloguing-in-Publication Data
A catalogue record for this book is available from the British Library

Library of Congress Cataloging-in-Publication Data
Sharks : conservation, governance, and management / edited by Erika J. Techera and Natalie Klein.
pages cm
Includes bibliographical references and index.
1. Sharks–Conservation. 2. Sharks–Conservation–Government policy. 3. Sharks–Government policy. 4. Sharks–Ecology.
I. Techera, Erika J. II. Klein, Natalie (Natalie S.).
QL638.9.S4855 2014
338.3'7273–dc23 2013049689

ISBN: 978-0-415-84476-5 (hbk)
ISBN: 978-0-203-75029-2 (ebk)

Typeset in Goudy
by Wearset Ltd, Boldon, Tyne and Wear

Printed and bound in the United States of America
by Edwards Brothers Malloy

Contents

Figures

Tables

Boxes

Contributors

Andrés M. Cisneros-Montemayor is a researcher with the Fisheries Economics Research Unit, UBC Fisheries Centre. His background is in marine biology and the economics of marine eco-tourism, and he specializes in resource economics and ecosystem modelling. Andrés continually collaborates on theoretical, applied and field studies, and has worked at venues ranging from fishing villages in Central America and Africa to the UN Headquarters in New York. His current PhD work focuses on the economics of policy strategies to aid in sustainable resource use.

Shaun P. Collin has just completed a WA Premiers Fellowship and is now an Institute of Advanced Studies Distinguished Fellow, the Deputy Director of the Oceans Institute and a member of the School of Animal Biology at the University of Western Australia. He heads the Neuroecology Group, which investigates the neural basis of animal behaviour with special emphasis on sensory systems and vision. His research team uses a range of cutting-edge techniques to investigate sensory perception in both invertebrates and vertebrates, with a strong focus on sharks.

Aurelie Cosandey-Godin is a doctoral candidate in Marine Conservation Biology at Dalhousie University and an NSERC Industrial Graduate Program Fellow with WWF-Canada. Her research focuses on the patterns, causes and management of shark, skate and ray by-catch in the Northwest Atlantic Ocean. She holds a Master's Degree in Marine Management from Dalhousie.

Brendal Davis is a research associate at Dalhousie University. Her primary focus is elasmobranch conservation and management; specifically, looking at how stakeholder input and community involvement can further advance conservation efforts. In addition, Brendal also works in the field, tracking juvenile blue sharks in the Northwest Atlantic, and teaches elasmobranch biology. She holds a Master's Degree in Marine Management from Dalhousie.

Robert Harcourt lectures in Marine Ecology and heads the Marine Predator Research Group at Macquarie University. He is an expert in marine biology, specializing in marine predators, marine science ecosystems, animal behaviour and ecology, and has published 138 scientific papers, 90 scientific reports and one book. He has made valuable contributions to ecology and conservation of large marine vertebrates including sharks, seals and whales.

Michael R. Heithaus received his PhD at Simon Fraser University in 2001. He was a postdoctoral scientist at Mote Marine Lab's Center for Shark Research before joining Florida International University's Biology Department in 2003. He is now a professor and executive director of FIU's School of Environment Arts and Society. His work focuses on the ecological role of large marine vertebrates, especially apex predators. He also investigates the importance of non-lethal effects of predators in ecosystems. He has published more than 100 peer-reviewed articles and chapters.

Jill Hepp is a senior officer with Pew's Global Shark Conservation campaign, where she works with a team of regional and country-based organizers around the world to advance policies creating shark sanctuaries, and action by RFMOs and CITES listings to reverse the decline in sharks. Before joining Pew, Hepp researched international fisheries management and wildlife trade for TRAFFIC as well as NOAA. Hepp, a Peace Corps alumna, holds a Bachelor's Degree in Biology from the University of San Diego and a Master's Degree in Conservation Biology and Sustainable Development from the University of Maryland.

Erich Hoyt is a research fellow with WDC (Whale and Dolphin Conservation), and heads its Global MPAs Programme. Based in the UK, he has authored 600 articles and reports, and 20 books, including *Marine Protected Areas for Whales, Dolphins and Porpoises* (2011, Earthscan). He co-chairs the IUCN Marine Mammal Protected Area Task Force. As co-director of the Far East Russia Orca Project and Russian Cetacean Habitat Project, he has helped manage whale research in the Commander Islands Zapovednik, Russia's largest MPA.

Charlie Huveneers has been involved in chondrichthyan research for over ten years. He completed his PhD at Macquarie University in 2002 on the biology and ecology of wobbegong sharks in relation to the commercial fishery in NSW. He then worked within SARDI as a shark ecologist investigating the diet and trophic role of pelagic species, as well as their movements and migrations using satellite technology. In 2007 he was the technical officer in charge of the day-to-day running of the Australian Acoustic Tagging and Monitoring System (AATAMS), part of the Integrated Marine Observing System (IMOS) programme during which he deployed acoustic receivers around Australia and created a national network of acoustic telemetry users. He joined the Marine Innovation South Australia initiative in 2009 through a joint position between SARDI–Aquatic Sciences and Flinders University, where he acted as shark ecologist and lecturer, respectively. In 2014, he moved to Flinders University full-time, where he leads the Southern Shark Ecology Group.

Ryan M. Kempster is a shark biologist and founder of the conservation group Support Our Sharks. Ryan began his research with an MSc in Marine Biology at Bangor University (UK) and later moved to Australia to complete a PhD at the University of Western Australia. Ryan's research focuses on the sensory biology of sharks, with the ultimate goal of refining and improving shark repellent devices to protect ocean users and reduce shark by-catch in commercial fisheries.

Jeremy J. Kiszka is a marine biologist at Florida International University (Miami). He studies marine top predator (including sharks and marine mammals) foraging and behavioural ecology, as well as the role of these large and mobile vertebrates in marine ecosystems. He is also interested in conflicts between marine top predators and human activities, including fisheries and disturbances, and how human activities may disrupt their ecological roles.

Natalie Klein is a professor at Macquarie Law School, where she teaches and researches in different areas of international law, with a focus on law of the sea and international dispute settlement. She has published most recently on maritime security, whales, tuna, sharks and the protection of citizens abroad. Her current ARC Discovery Project investigates the conservation and management of sharks. She is vice president of the International Law Association (Australian Branch) and is a fellow of the Australian Academy of Law.

Mary Lack has qualifications in agricultural and resource economics and has over 25 years' experience in Australian and international fisheries management. Mary is the director of Shellack Pty Ltd, a consulting company specializing in fisheries management and governance. She has worked and published extensively on shark trade and management, with an emphasis on the deficiencies in data collection for shark catch and trade and the need for improved and species-specific management of sharks.

Anissa Lawrence is the Executive Director of TierraMar Consulting. She specializes in strategic and institutional strengthening and policy and programme development to build and strengthen the capacity of organizations utilizing and managing coastal and marine natural resources and fisheries conservation issues across the Asia Pacific. As an experienced environmental communicator and strategist, she facilitates government, corporate, industry and community action to understand, manage and implement sustainable, workable solutions that balance business, social and environmental challenges.

Paolo Momigliano is currently undertaking his PhD in the Department of Biological Sciences at Macquarie University, working on conservation genetics of coral reef sharks in Australia and Indonesia. Before starting his PhD, Paolo worked at James Cook University and the Australian Institute of Marine Science on topics ranging from fisheries to ocean acidification. His research focuses on the use of genetic tools to answer questions relevant to conservation and fisheries management. Paolo has authored and co-authored eight scientific articles and two book chapters.

Christopher Neff has submitted his PhD for examination in the Department of Government and International Relations at the University of Sydney. His research is the first doctoral study on the 'politics of shark attacks', looking at policy responses to shark bites in Australia, South Africa and the United States. He holds a BA in Political Science from James Madison University in Virginia (1999) and a Master's Degree in Public Policy from the University of Sydney (2007).

William Robbins has researched sharks and fishes for the last 20 years. During this time he has led many projects across the Indo-Pacific, focusing on the biology and ecology of both tropical and temperate species. A number of these projects have resulted in positive legislative changes for species conservation. He now runs Wildlife Marine, an Australian-based research consultancy specializing in shark–human interactions, and providing expert advice to governments and NGOs.

U. Rashid Sumaila is a professor at the UBC Fisheries Centre. He specializes in bioeconomics, marine ecosystem valuation and the analysis of global issues such as fisheries subsidies, illegal fishing and climate change and oil spills. Sumaila is widely published, with over 140 articles in peer-reviewed journals. Sumaila has won awards, including the American Fisheries Society's 2013 Excellence in Public Outreach Award, the Leopold Leadership Fellowship and the Pew Fellowship for Marine Conservation.

Erika J. Techera is a professor of law and member of the Oceans Institute at the University of Western Australia. Her research interests focus on marine environmental law, including legal frameworks for the conservation and management of marine species and marine protected areas. She has been awarded an ARC Discovery grant with Natalie Klein, exploring how to enhance the international governance of sharks. She is a member of the IUCN Commission on Environmental Law and World Commission on Protected Areas.

Christine A. Ward-Paige is a research scientist and founder of eShark.org – a not-for-profit organization that crowd-sources data from marine explorers to fill data gaps. Her research examines the effect of human activities on the marine environment, evaluates the success of conservation strategies and identifies the need for improved management initiatives. By taking a broad-scale and long-term approach to shifts in marine ecosystems, she aims to decipher the difference between natural and human induced changes.

Elizabeth Griffin Wilson directs the Pew Charitable Trusts' International Ocean Policy programme, where she leads Pew's engagement in intergovernmental forums such as the United Nations, regional fisheries management organizations and CITES. Previously, Wilson was a manager on Pew's Global Shark Conservation campaign, and worked for both Oceana and the Atlantic States Marine Fisheries Commission. Wilson holds a Bachelor's Degree in Biology from Loyola College and a Master's Degree in Environmental Management from Duke University.

Boris Worm is a professor of marine conservation biology at the Biology Department, Dalhousie University in Halifax, Nova Scotia. His research interests focus on the ecosystem effects of fishing, associated changes in marine biodiversity and the conservation of marine species on a regional and global scale. Large predators are of particular interest to him, particularly tuna, billfish and sharks.

Acknowledgements

This book is the product of much hard work, not only by the co-editors, but each of the contributors. To produce an interdisciplinary publication is a significant challenge. Each of the contributors made a significant effort to write in a way that is accessible to those from other disciplines. We are most grateful to them all, as they were a pleasure to work with.

We acknowledge the support of our respective institutions, the University of Western Australia and Macquarie University, as well as the support of the Australian Research Council. The co-editors receive funding from an ARC Discovery Project entitled 'Improving the Global Governance of Sharks: Obstacles, Options and Opportunities'.

We thank Professor Rob Harcourt of Macquarie University for providing the stunning photograph for the cover of the book.

We are most grateful to Hiruni Alwishewa of Macquarie University for her research assistance in finalizing the volume. We also acknowledge the support of Tim Hardwick and Ashley Irons from Earthscan.

Finally, our thanks for the support from both our families, who now know more about sharks than they ever envisaged.

Erika J. Techera and Natalie Klein

Abbreviations

AAAS	American Association for the Advancement of Science
AAP	Australian Associated Press
ABNJ	areas beyond national jurisdiction
ACAP	Agreement for the Conservation of Albatrosses and Petrels
ADMCF	ADM Capital Foundation
AEAM	Adaptive Environmental Assessment and Management
AFMA	Australian Fisheries Management Authority
AFP	Agence France-Presse
AP	Associated Press
BNT	Bahamas National Trust
BRD	by-catch reduction device
CALM	Conservation and Land Management
CBD	*Convention on Biological Diversity*
CCAMLR	*Convention for the Conservation of Antarctic Marine Living Resources*
CITES	*Convention on International Trade in Endangered Species*
CMS	*Convention on Migratory Species*
CNMI	Commonwealth of the Northern Mariana Islands
COFI	Committee on Fisheries
CORAL	Coral Reef Alliance
CPOA	Community Plan of Action
CSIRO	Commonwealth Scientific and Industrial Research Organisation
CSS	Current Sightings Survey
DFO	Canadian Department of Fisheries and Oceans
DLNR	Department of Land and Natural Resources
EAST	Environment & Animal Society of Taiwan
EBM	ecosystem-based management
EBSA	Ecologically or Biologically Significant Areas
EEZ	exclusive economic zone
EPBC	*Environment Protection and Biodiversity Conservation*
EU	European Union

FAO	Food and Agriculture Organisation
FFWC	Florida Fish and Wildlife Conservation Commission
FMP	Fisheries Management Plan
FRDC	Fisheries Research and Development Corporation
GFCM	General Fisheries Commission for the Mediterranean
GFSC	Great Fiji Shark Count
HKSF	Hong Kong Shark Foundation
HSI	Humane Society International
HSS	Historical Sighting Survey
HSUS	Humane Society of the United States
IATTC	Inter-American Tropical Tuna Commission
ICCAT	International Commission for the Conservation of Atlantic Tunas
ICES	International Council for the Exploration of the Sea
ICRW	*International Convention on the Regulation of Whaling*
ICTSD	International Centre for Trade and Sustainable Development
IFAW	International Fund for Animal Welfare
IMO	International Maritime Organization
IOTC	Indian Ocean Tuna Commission
IPOA	International Plan of Action
ITQ	individual transferable quota
IUCN	International Union for the Conservation of Nature
IUCN SSG	IUCN Shark Specialist Group
IUU	illegal, unreported, and unregulated
KGBF	Kimberley Gillnet and Barramundi Fishery
LME	large marine ecosystem
LSSA	Life Saving South Africa
MAP	Mediterranean Action Plan
MCES	Micronesian Chief Executive Summit
MCT	Micronesia Conservation Trust
MoU	Memorandum of Understanding
MPA	Marine Protection Agreement
MPA	marine protected area
MSC	Marine Stewardship Council
MSY	maximum sustainable yield
NAFO	Northwest Atlantic Fisheries Organization
NGO	non-governmental organization
NMFS	National Marine Fisheries Service
NOAA	National Oceanic and Atmospheric Administration
NPOA	National Plan of Action
NPOA-Sharks	National Plan of Action for the Conservation and Management of Sharks
NRDC	Natural Resources Defense Council

NSERC	National Science and Engineering Research Council of Canada
NSW	New South Wales
NSWF	New South Wales Fisheries
OECD	Organization for Economic Cooperation and Development
PA	protected area
PISCO	Parallel Imager for Southern Cosmological Observations
POA	Plan of Action
RAC/SPA	Regional Activity Centre for Specially Protected Areas
REDMAP	Range Extension Database and Mapping project
REEF	Reef Environmental Education Foundation
RFMO	regional fishery management organization
SARDI	South Australian Research and Development Institute
SEAFO	South East Atlantic Fisheries Organization
SEDAR	Southeast Data, Assessment, and Review
SMP	Shark Meshing (Bather Protection) Program
SRI	Shark Research Institute
SSIA	Southern Shark Industry Alliance
TAC	total allowable catch
TED	turtle exclusion device
TRAFFIC	Trade Records Analysis of Flora and Fauna
UNCLOS	*United Nations Convention on the Law of the Sea*
UNEP	United Nations Environment Programme
UNESCO	United Nations Educational Scientific and Cultural Organization
UNFSA	United Nations Fish Stocks Agreement
UNRISD	United Nations Research Institute for Social Development
WCPA	World Commission on Protected Areas
WCPFC	Western and Central Pacific Fisheries Commission
WCS	Wildlife Conservation Society
WSSD	World Summit on Sustainable Development
WWF	World Wide Fund for Nature

Introduction

Erika J. Techera and Natalie Klein

A growing body of scientific research indicates that sharks play a critical role in maintaining marine ecosystem health. Furthermore, there is sound scientific evidence showing that many shark species are at risk of extinction. In this context, there has been clear recognition of the pressing need for improved shark conservation and management. Arguments in support include the biological vulnerabilities and ecological functions of sharks, ethical and conservation considerations, as well as economic values of fisheries and tourism.

In addressing these issues it has been acknowledged that law and policy cannot improve the status of sharks in isolation. Concerted multi-disciplinary effort will be essential. This book responds to the challenge by drawing attention to key scientific, economic and legal issues, as well as barriers to improving the conservation and management of sharks.

In the beginning

This book came about as a result of a number of different events. In December 2011, the co-editors held a workshop at Macquarie University in Sydney (funded through a Macquarie University Research Development Grant) exploring the way forward for shark conservation and management. Subsequently, we obtained external funding through an Australian Research Council Discovery Grant entitled *Improving the Global Governance of Sharks: Obstacles, Options and Opportunities*. Between these two events we have continued to research law and policy in relation to sharks and build networks of collaborators from other disciplines. This volume starts to bring those perspectives and that research together.

Research on sharks has lagged behind flagship marine species such as whales and dolphins. Similarly, law and policy has been slow to develop, with only a small number of iconic species being protected worldwide. Social science research in this area is only nascent and yet there are a multitude of stakeholders involved: individuals, communities, fishers, tourism operators, government agencies, conservation organizations, international institutions and states themselves.

The key aim of this book is to explore the conservation and management of sharks from a multi-disciplinary perspective. There has been a rapid decline in shark numbers, and scientific information continues to emerge of the critical role they play in the marine ecosystem. The increase in fishing impact – primarily through shark finning and by-catch – has led to shark conservation receiving some international traction in the past few years. This book explores the state of play in relation to sharks, with a particular focus on improving conservation and management. Recent trends are analysed, including shark finning bans that have been put in place in several countries, the widening number of states establishing shark sanctuaries and the growth of shark-based tourism. The efficacy of current listing processes for endangered species and fisheries regulations is also examined. Tourism is explored as an alternative to fishing and the risks and impacts associated with this industry will be analysed.

Scope and structure

A common thread running throughout the book is to draw attention to the importance of collaborative governance between various actors and the need for inter- and multi-disciplinary research and management approaches to address the decline in sharks.

The book is divided into four parts. Part I, 'Governance challenges' provides the foundation of law and governance, conservation and management. In Chapter 1, Erika Techera provides an overview of the foundation of contemporary conservation and management, law and policy. She covers such issues as ethical underpinnings, conservation concepts, sustainable development and governance, before looking at legal issues in more depth. She explains the legal foundations of current laws that seek to enhance shark conservation and management, including the law of the sea, marine environmental law and fisheries regulation.

In Chapter 2, Natalie Klein explores the current international governance framework, including relevant legal regimes, institutions and processes. Opportunities, challenges and barriers for the conservation and management of sharks are analysed, including legal issues, political issues and the reality of economic pressures. The emergence of shark-based tourism and the recent trend in establishment of shark sanctuaries are investigated as possible alternative livelihood options for those people that would otherwise be involved in fishing.

Mary Lack explores the evolution and development of the International Plan of Action for Sharks (IPOA-Sharks), the only specific global framework for sharks, in Chapter 3. The current challenges to implementation are highlighted, including the slow uptake of the IPOA-Sharks and lack of data at the species level. She notes that while the IPOA-Sharks has drawn international attention, the unintended consequence has been the isolation of sharks from regular fisheries. Possible solutions are analysed, including the need for a body to engage with target and by-catch issues separately and to identify a body to coordinate and 'champion' the conservation and management of sharks.

Part II explores 'Scientific perspectives'. Chapter 4 is written by Jeremy Kiszka and Michael Heithaus, and provides a valuable overview of the state of scientific knowledge in relation to sharks, including their biology and ecology. The ecological importance of sharks in the marine ecosystem is highlighted and risk factors explored, as well as areas where major gaps exist in our knowledge.

In Chapter 5, Paolo Momigliano and Robert Harcourt explore the science–law disconnect. The chapter begins by highlighting the status of sharks, as well as the particularly vulnerable position of some species. The authors go on to explore 'global scientific output in shark management and conservation over the past 20 years', examining possible biases, identifying that shark research is skewed towards charismatic species. They then examine whether management is evidence-based, concluding that in many cases it is not. Finally, the authors explore whether adaptive management can resolve the science–management disconnect.

Christopher Neff addresses social scientific issues by exploring the critical area of human perceptions and attitudes in Chapter 6. He notes that the 'human–shark relationship has had a profound impact on shark management and governance for centuries', most particularly in terms of perceptions about sharks and shark bites. He draws attention to the need to reconcile issues such as beach safety and shark conservation and analyses an emerging trend in the way human factors are utilized in the context of the predator policy paradox.

Part III explores the roles of different 'Actors and stakeholders'. In Chapter 7, Anissa Lawrence examines collaborations for conservation. Building on the introduction in Chapter 1, Lawrence explores the various stakeholders, as well as public–private and other partnerships, for conservation and management of sharks. In particular, she examines how government, non-governmental organizations (NGOs) and the fishing industry can work together to improve issues such as by-catch through the implementation of new technologies and equipment, through a range of case studies. Her chapter illustrates the powerful role that collaborative initiatives can play in advancing shark conservation and management.

In Chapter 8, Christine A. Ward-Paige investigates the role of the tourism industry in balancing 'human use with the requirements of the natural environment'. It is clear that shark-based tourism can provide an alternative livelihood option to fishing and the author explores the increased economic value of sharks in the tourism context. She also examines the part tourism can play in marine research by providing important data. Codes of conduct and best practice management of shark encounters and the industry are explored and the chapter concludes with recommendations for the future of this marine tourism industry.

Jill Hepp and Elizabeth Griffin Wilson explore the role of NGOs in Chapter 9. They identify a significant number of organizations working on shark conservation and draw attention to the diversity in terms of size, focus and reach of these bodies. They then turn to one particular NGO, the IUCN Shark Specialist Group (SSG), which is explored in detail in the chapter, before exploring the key issue of shark finning and the part NGOs have played in addressing the problem. The chapter concludes with comments on the next generation of shark conservation efforts.

Part IV addresses 'Risks and rewards'. In Chapter 10, Andrés Cisneros-Montemayor and Rashid Sumalia examine the economic rationale for shark conservation. They begin by reviewing the literature on the 'economic benefits currently derived from sharks in terms of fisheries and marine ecotourism' and then explore the potential of eco-tourism. This chapter analyses the economic risks and also the multiple benefits that might be achieved by protecting sharks, and concludes that achieving both sustainable eco-tourism and fisheries is feasible. In the conclusion, the authors note that 'managing our resources with a view towards ecosystem health will help ensure that we continue to obtain the economic benefits that sustain both coastal and global communities'.

Chapter 11 is co-authored by Ryan Kempster and Shaun Collin. They explore the biological knowledge and status of three species that currently have the highest level of global protection: great white sharks, basking sharks and whale sharks. Although protected at the international level, 'it is unknown whether their numbers are recovering'. New scientific information has only relatively recently revealed site fidelity for these species and it is clear that new information continues to emerge. The authors support ongoing research particularly because regardless of their harvest being banned, these three species remain at risk from habitat loss, accidental capture and even from tourism.

In Chapter 12, Charlie Huveneers and William Robbins examine 'species at the intersection'. The chapter focuses on a broad range of shark species and the potential effects of commercial and recreational fisheries, as well as wildlife tourism. The authors discuss the various management regulations and support the findings of Ward-Paige that tourism can not only reduce fishing pressure, but also help the management and conservation of a range of shark species. They also find that revenue from shark-related tourism 'can benefit multiple sectors of the economy including returns to the government'.

Part V covers a range of 'Tools and techniques'. In Chapter 13, Erich Hoyt explores the role of marine protected areas and sanctuaries. In the last few years there has been a global trend towards habitat-based conservation for sharks. Where sharks have a degree of predictable site fidelity, marine protected areas have the potential to achieve positive conservation goals by restricting fishing and providing non-consumptive opportunities such as tourism. The author draws upon his experiences with whales and dolphins to conclude that sanctuaries and protected areas may well become places for people to interact with and appreciate sharks, and support their conservation.

In Chapter 14, Boris Worm, Aurelie Cosandey-Godin and Brendal Davis explore fisheries management and regulation in detail. This chapter reviews the current state of fisheries management with respect to sharks, identifies the successes and failures, as well as 'priority actions that might help with the conservation and rebuilding of depleted populations'. They draw attention to the necessity for effective monitoring and assessment to ensure fisheries regulations are effective, and also the need to address incidental by-catch in circumstances where most sharks are threatened by this rather than directed fisheries.

The final chapter explores synergies and solutions for the future. Natalie Klein and Erika Techera examine the 'way forward', synthesizing the findings from the previous chapters and making recommendations for both in terms of areas for law reform, mechanisms to overcome management challenges and areas for future inter- and multi-disciplinary research.

In conclusion

This book contains a diversity of disciplinary perspectives provided by a range of experts from different parts of the world. In this respect it is an unusual and welcome collection of experiences and expertise. Notably, all of the contributors agree that sharks play an important role in marine ecosystems, they are under threat from anthropogenic impacts, and that, in order to improve their status, conservation, governance and management must be enhanced. This book has no doubt gone some way to identifying the issues and potential solutions for the future, although long-term advances will take time. It is to be hoped that the ideas outlined in this volume are actioned as a matter of priority.

Part I

Governance challenges

Chapter 1

Approaches to conservation and governance of marine species

Erika J. Techera

Introduction

The marine environment is a challenging area within which to work. The vastness of the oceans and their three-dimensional nature creates a complex management problem, compounded by the mobility and diversity of marine species, as well as humans whose activities impact upon them. Yet because humans depend heavily upon the oceans for food production and other ecosystem services, including assimilation of waste, climate control and carbon sequestration, it is critical that they be appropriately conserved and managed. The risks of not doing so are enormous, not only in terms of human health and well-being, but the survival of other species as well – including sharks.

Humans have interacted with the oceans for thousands of years. Historically, traditional peoples and Indigenous communities fished for subsistence purposes and developed cultural practices related to the ocean and its inhabitants. Even today it is clear that 'the close interrelationship between land and sea, mountain and shore, and river and lagoon form particularly important components of indigenous worldviews and politics' (Hviding, 2003, pp. 257–258). The impact these people had on the oceans was negligible due to low populations and lack of technology to exploit resources on a large scale. Later human oceanic exploration led to discovery, conquest and settlement of new lands. For example, the Lapita people navigated across the Pacific and settled many of the Pacific islands; the Dutch opened trading routes between Europe and Southeast Asia; the Spanish conquered South America; and the British settled the United States, Australia and New Zealand. Despite these developments, even as late as the turn of the nineteenth century there were few visible impacts on the marine environment.

It was the industrial revolution that saw the start of anthropogenic environmental degradation, initially on land and later in the oceans, resulting in the over-harvesting of marine living resources and pollution. Although commercial whaling had been undertaken since the eleventh century, mechanization and the use of factory ships began to have a negative impact in the 1800s (Roberts, 2007). The scale of that industry, and others including the mass hunting of marine mammals such as walrus for oil and fur seals for clothes, as well as the over-fishing of ocean areas close to industrialized countries, all took their toll. Simultaneously, increases in oil and gas exploration, shipping and transport have led to pollution issues. Many of the problems have been driven by technological developments. Unlike land areas, which have benefited from technology allowing more crops to be grown in smaller areas, technology has facilitated marine degradation. Equipment such as drift nets and tuna aggregation devices, as well as bottom trawling and super trawlers, have facilitated indiscriminate fishing on a massive scale. These problems have been compounded by rapid growth in human populations, resulting in expansion of markets for seafood. The growing impact that humans are having on shark populations illustrates this.

Scientific research has uncovered knowledge of these marine environmental problems, which in turn has led to law and policy responses. The bans on killing juvenile fur seals and conventions prohibiting the use of drift nets first started to appear in the 1980s. Later, whale sanctuaries were established and the global moratorium on whaling was adopted in 1986. Moves to restrict high-seas bottom trawling in 2006 are a further example of the international community's response to ocean challenges. The drastic decline in shark numbers is a more recent development, but comes as a result of the same unsustainable practices. It has been driven by environmental degradation that has harmed shark habitats, fishing methods and equipment that have resulted in sharks being taken as by-catch, and growth in populations and markets leading to the problem of shark finning. Again, albeit recently, specific laws and policies have been developed in response. Although the scientific research preceded these developments, it is clear that compared to other marine species attention has come very late for sharks. Even today, there is resistance by many people to protection measures for sharks; more often than not they are feared by humans rather than the subject of conservation efforts.

The laws and policies that are aimed at conserving and managing sharks rely upon a legal foundation comprising the law of the sea, environmental laws and natural resource regulations. These laws themselves are underpinned by concepts, principles and governance approaches that have developed over many decades. If the conservation outcomes for sharks are to be enhanced, then the frameworks and mechanisms, together with their foundations, must be analysed.

The specific details of laws for shark conservation and management are explored in the chapter that follows. The purpose of this chapter is to examine the underpinnings, approaches and tools that have been utilized. This analysis commences by examining the foundations upon which shark conservation and management have been based. This includes underpinnings of environmental law, key concepts and approaches to governance. The second focus is on law itself in terms of both the specific legal tools that are and can be used in the governance of sharks and the role of law in a broader disciplinary context. The various approaches to conservation that have been adopted and embedded in law and policy are explored, including the transition from fortress conservation to ecosystem-based management. The analysis then turns to international environmental law, which has rapidly developed in the last 40 years. What has emerged since then is a stable group of principles forming a common thread through various treaties and soft law instruments. The third section brings these foundational elements and legal tools together in the specific context of shark conservation and management. The chapter concludes with a discussion of areas where and ways in which the conservation and management of sharks might be enhanced.

Foundations

Ethical underpinnings

If current governance arrangements have not achieved their goals, it is essential to explore the foundation upon which they are built. Significantly, it has been acknowledged that environmental law has weak underpinnings and it is only recently that this has been explored (Tarlock, 1996). Environmental law is not an area of law, such as contract or tort, with a long history of legal theory at its origin; nevertheless, much of the literature in this area points to ethics as the base, with an alternative viewpoint being that science forms the foundation of environmental law (Tarlock, 1996).

The most dominant view is that approaches to environmental governance have an ethical basis and so this area is explored further here. There are fundamental differences between the treatment of the environment and natural resources by traditional communities and industrialized nations. However, as the environmental movement was largely a product of developed nations it is the ethical approaches of those countries that have dominated. Furthermore, because of these countries' influence on the development of international law, the same approaches have shaped global responses too.

In essence, these approaches are based upon a belief in the separation of humans from nature, and superiority of the former (Grima and Berkes, 1989; Colchester 1994). The origins of such separation, and the reasons why a utilitarian ethic has dominated, are both varied and complex. Some scholars point to prehistoric origins relating to the first domestication of plants and animals (Scull, 2013). Others refer to the domination of dualism, which emerged during the Enlightenment, religious and cultural influences and technological developments and processes such as urbanization (Holmes Rolston, 2012). Many commentators place the blame on Judeo-Christian beliefs (White, 1967) as

> Christianity encouraged certain special attitudes to nature: that it exists primarily as a resource rather than as something to be contemplated with enjoyment, that man has the right to use it as he will, that it is not sacred, that man's relationships with it are not governed by moral principles.
>
> (Passmore, 1974, p. 20)

There were early calls for a change in attitude. Rousseau, for example, advocated a return to living as part of the natural world, and citizen action in pursuit of the common good. Philosophers such as John Stuart Mill expressed concern about the destruction of nature and natural processes (Mill, 1965). Ralph Waldo Emerson published his essay *Nature* in 1836, in which he espoused the inclusion of humans as part of and not separate from 'nature' (Emerson, 1836). The call for a new ethical approach preceded the environmental movement itself. Aldo Leopold developed his 'land ethic' in the 1940s (Leopold, 1949) but 'no systematic ethical theory to support these ethical ideas concerning the environment' (Bosselmann, 2013). Dissatisfaction with anthropocentrism led in the 1970s to the emergence of a new field – environmental ethics – whereby 'ethics were forced for the first time to consider and articulate the value of nonhuman species of plants and animals' (Brown, 1995). Although sustainable development has marked a shift in human attitudes (Bosselmann, 2002), anthropocentric utilitarian ethics still prevail. If current environmental trends are to be reversed it will be necessary to encourage greater moral responsibilities to the environment (Solomon, 2010), and to change the ethical underpinnings of not only approaches to environmental governance, but economic development and socio-cultural concerns also. In the marine context, it will become increasingly necessary to explore sustainable and ethical fisheries to identify best practice (Lam and Pritcher, 2012).

Conservation concepts

The concept of nature conservation is of relatively recent origin, at least in western contexts. In industrialized countries, early efforts to conserve and manage land and marine areas took the form of centralized, top-down regulation. This included 'fortress conservation' pursuant to which protected areas were declared, quarantined from human inhabitants. Even in those protected areas where human occupation was permitted, more prestige was attached to those that excluded communities (Borrini-Feyerabend *et al.*, 2004). This approach embodies western conceptualizations of conservation, and the environment as provider of useful resources, goods and services for humans (Gibbs and Bromley, 1989).

The nineteenth-century Sierra Club[1] campaign to stop the reduction in the Yosemite Park boundaries arguably marked the beginning of 'fortress conservation' approaches that led to the development of protected area management. This approach quickly spread around the world, leading to the early establishment of national parks and, later, marine protected areas. This approach is based on a scientific belief that everything is in balance – therefore building a fence around an area meant that everything inside the area would be well protected (Tarlock, 1996). This has not proved to be correct as it has since been recognized that nature is not based on a permanent state of equilibrium, and geographically delimiting a conservation area will not ensure protection of species.

Conservation goals have not been achieved, leading to an exploration of more inclusive, integrated and participatory approaches. This recognition has ultimately resulted in more holistic approaches to the human use of natural resources and resulted in the emergence of a range of new management concepts.

The paradigm of ecosystem-based management has emerged only in the last 20 years, as attention turned away from conventional, sectoral and single-stock approaches to fisheries management. In essence, it involves designing management objectives and governance structures and processes based on an 'interacting system of living and non-living components in a scale-dependent context' (Hatcher and Bradbury, 2006, p. 207). Ecosystem-based management can work in combination with adaptive management – which requires regular monitoring and review of management measures – together with marine protected area management. Indeed, more sophisticated mechanisms are emerging, such as ecosystem-based marine spatial planning (Katsanevakis, 2011) and integrated maritime governance (Van Tatenhove, 2013).

However, implementation through law and policy has proved challenging in the marine environment. In western societies, as well as at the international level, natural resources such as oceans and fisheries have generally been treated as common pool resources with open access to all. The problem with this approach is that without a strong conservation ethic there is no incentive to act sustainably or environmentally responsibly, and therefore in order to protect these areas and resources strong regulatory frameworks must be implemented. This stems from the concept of the 'tragedy of the commons' as conceived by Garret Hardin, in which he argued that 'what is owned by no one is valued by no one' (Hardin, 1968). Western societies have tended to address these problems through public and private property rights (Gibbs and Bromley, 1989).

Private property rights underpin western approaches to environment and natural resource regulation. Communal ownership of property has been treated as archaic and an impediment to development (Berkes and Farvar, 1989), with the only effective methods of regulation being through state control, via markets and by the allocation of private property rights (Agrawal and Gibson, 1999). In designing laws to conserve and manage the environment, states have legislated to protect publicly owned resources (e.g. national parks), but private property owners have been given no responsibility to conserve their land or resources. With the failure of many of these approaches, attention is now turning to other approaches, as discussed below in the context of contemporary environmental governance.

Similarly, in international law the concept of freedom of the seas has dominated and has to a large extent hampered conservation. Although the law of the sea can be traced back to ancient Roman times, modern law is based upon the seventeenth-century work of Grotius, the author of *Mare Liberum*. This treatise is well known for re-introducing the doctrine of 'freedom of the seas' (Hunter *et al.*, 2010). This fundamental principle of the law of the sea meant there was no restriction on access to the ocean and its resources. Historically, the rights set out above were not balanced by any responsibilities and there was no reciprocal duty to collectively conserve the marine environment or its biodiversity. Marine resources were considered to be inexhaustible and environmental issues were not contemplated. It was only later, as marine science emerged, that responsibilities to protect and preserve the marine environment have been put in place. This has been facilitated by the adoption of the *UN Convention on the Law of the Sea* (UNCLOS) in 1984, considered further below. However, UNCLOS enshrines the doctrine of freedom of the seas, declaring the vast majority of the oceans to be the high seas – a global common open to all, with the inherent problems noted above.

The final element to be explored here is that of community-based approaches to conservation. The recent focus on community-based approaches has been driven, in part, by a loss of faith in the state, markets and progress more generally (Agrawal and Gibson, 1999). In addition, the change in focus can be seen as a reaction to the failure of exclusionary conservation practices (Berkes, 2004) and the acknowledgement of the role of public participation within the concept of sustainable development (referred to below). Participatory approaches have also been seen in other disciplines such as ecology, which has shifted towards a 'systems' views of the world, inherently involving humans, and a move away from 'expert only' approaches to conservation and management (Berkes, 2004). Similarly, although the conservation movement initially focused upon single species and narrowly defined 'wilderness' areas, there has been a recent shift to more holistic approaches. In the 1980s and 1990s, a number of non-governmental organizations (NGOs) called for greater linkages to be recognized between protected area management and the economic activities of local communities (IUCN *et al.*, 1980, 1991; World Bank, 1986); this is now reflected in new protected area guidelines (Dudley, 2008). The international community also embraced more participatory approaches. For example, in 1992 the *Convention on Biological Diversity* (CBD) moved away from centralized governance by encouraging active Indigenous involvement in conservation and the utilization of traditional practices and customary laws (CBD, 1992). This shift has also been seen in the context of marine governance: the First Congress on Marine Protected Areas in 2005 reflected a change in attitude towards community-based approaches to conservation (Borrini-Feyerabend and Lassen, 2008). Nonetheless, the challenge remains to determine the respective roles for top-down and bottom-up approaches and there is a continuing multi-disciplinary debate as to the efficacy of participatory approaches. Even among supporters there are those that note that there have been mixed results from localized projects (Berkes, 2004).

So it can be seen that contemporary approaches to conservation have been influenced by a number of different fields. Holistic, pluralistic and participatory regimes are now considered best practice. These approaches have yet to be implemented in relation to shark conservation and management, which remains quite sectoral and centralized.

Sustainable development

It was not until the environmental movement gained momentum in the 1970s that attention turned to ethical beliefs and human activities involving nature. Authors such as Rachel Carson were influential in drawing attention to anthropogenic environmental degradation (Carson, 2002) and by criticizing the technological development of destructive chemicals she implicitly challenged science for the unintended consequences of this 'progress' (Dresner, 2002). Scientific information is often regarded with suspicion, as uncertain or unreliable. This perception has resulted in, for example, the public backlash against genetically modified organisms and geo-engineering. This is perhaps a failure to understand that 'science does not produce logically indisputable proofs about the natural world' (Oreskes, 2004, p. 369). Instead, 'science can play a role by providing informed opinions about the possible consequences of our actions (or inactions), and by monitoring the effects of our choices' (Oreskes, 2004, p. 369). Significantly, science has provided the data supporting the recognition that unrestricted economic growth and industrialization have led to environmental degradation and diminution of natural resources. It was this recognition that ultimately led to the emergence of the modern concept of sustainable development in the 1980s (Jaksa, 2006).

Although the term 'sustainable development' was referred to in the 1980 IUCN World Conservation Strategy, the central idea was articulated by the World Commission on Environment and Development (Brundtland Commission) in 1987 as 'development which meets the needs of the present without compromising the ability of future generations to meet their own needs' (World Commission on Environment and Development, 1987). Determining precisely what sustainable development means has proved challenging, although it is clear that it involves integrating environmental, developmental and sociocultural concerns. To some, this balancing of triple issues is a pragmatic and flexible way to deal with the reality of decision making. To others, it signalled a move away from purely environmental protection that had been the focus since the UN Conference on the Human Environment in 1972 in Stockholm.

Regardless of the definitional issues, sustainable development has been widely accepted and endorsed by governments, NGOs and corporations around the globe. It is supported by a number of international instruments, the most significant being the *Rio Declaration* and *Agenda 21*, both of which were adopted at the UN Conference on Environment and Development held in Rio de Janeiro in 1992. The *Rio Declaration* articulates 27 principles 'to protect the integrity of the global environmental and developmental system' (Rio Declaration, 1992). The key principles that are said to make up sustainable development include inter- and intra-generational equity, the polluter pays and precautionary principle, conservation of biodiversity and public participation. *Agenda 21* complements the *Rio Declaration* by providing guidance on the implementation of these principles and sustainable development. It recognizes that population growth, technology and consumption are the drivers of environmental change. It calls upon national governments to adopt strategies, laws and policies to realize sustainable development. *Agenda 21* also recognizes the importance of participatory approaches involving all stakeholders and calls on national governments to work with international, regional and local communities to achieve sustainable outcomes by integrating environmental and economic considerations into decision making.

The Rio conference was followed by the 2002 World Summit on Sustainable Development in Johannesburg, where the principles and ideas from Rio were restated in the *Johannesburg Plan of Implementation*. The 2002 Summit advanced sustainable development by raising awareness of the importance of moving beyond broad goals to the setting of specific targets. It also focused attention on identifying new sources of finance, including the benefits of public–private partnerships.

Ultimately, sustainable development is largely operationalized through law and policy that provide the rules and regulations to protect the environment, the regulatory framework for decision making on new development activities and the mechanisms for individuals and groups to bring proceedings in relation to both public and private activities (Solomon, 2010). The legal approaches and mechanisms are explored in detail below.

Approaches to governance

Another critical concept to emerge in the last several decades is that of global (environmental) governance. The term governance has grown in international popularity in the last few decades, although its precise meaning is unclear. For example, some commentators have noted that 'almost any process or structure of environmental politics that transgresses national boundaries has been described as part of global environmental governance' (Biermann and Pattberg, 2008, p. 278). While it is clear that early regulatory efforts to address environmental problems were centralized, top-down and monistic, the term 'governance' involves recognition of the broadening of the range of actors and mechanisms. Over time, more participatory approaches have been adopted that recognize the value of pluralism and inclusivity. At the global level this includes the greater involvement of inter-governmental organizations and non-state actors such as NGOs, scientists and civil society bodies. As noted by Biermann and Pattberg (2008), this can result in both vertical and horizontal fragmentation, between levels of governance as well as parallel institutions and instruments. It is clear that such fragmentation has occurred in the context of shark conservation and management, and is hampering the achievement of positive outcomes (Techera and Klein, 2011).

Ocean areas have largely been governed in the same top-down way as land. However, there are some fundamental differences. Ocean areas are not privately owned and their governance has been based upon state entitlements and limited general responsibilities to protect and preserve derived from the law of the sea obligations. Bottom-up, participatory approaches to governance have not emerged in relation to ocean areas as they have on land.

The result of developments across a range of areas has been the emergence of a number of governance approaches. These include new environmental governance (Holley *et al.*, 2011), collaborative and cooperative governance (Arceo, 2013), integrated governance (Van Tatenhove, 2013) and global environmental governance (Speth and Haas, 2006).

The conservation and management approaches taken by states therefore have been based upon the imposition of direct controls such as the creation of national parks and through 'command and control' regulation and centralized standard setting. In relation to the marine environment this includes regulatory controls such as licences for fishing, catch limits and quotas, minimum fish sizes, equipment restrictions and other standards. Alternative theoretical approaches have been limited to the option of privatizing the commons (Ostrom, 1990). This option is particularly challenging in the area of non-stationary resources such as fisheries.

Another important aspect of governance is perhaps the most difficult to operationalize: inter-disciplinarity. Historically, science, law and economics, for example, have been discrete areas and this has translated into siloed approaches to research, management and regulation. It is only recently that a more integrated approach has been taken. Nonetheless, it is clear that truly inter-disciplinary governance approaches are still evolving. In the context of law and policy, it can be seen that scientific panels, for example, have formed important parts of international institutional arrangements under treaties for some time. An early example of this is the *International Convention on the Regulation of Whaling*, and a more recent one is the CBD. Similarly, treaties have made provision for scientific research in circumstances where other activities are prohibited; again the *International Convention on the Regulation of Whaling* is a useful example. Yet it is clear that scientific findings are not automatically being translated into law and policy. A review of the difficulty of obtaining listings for shark species under the *Convention on International Trade in Endangered Species* demonstrates this (for further details, see Chapters 2 and 3). While much environmental law is reactionary, it tends to respond only slowly in response to new scientific understanding. Thus it is clear that legal approaches to marine conservation and management are not yet sophisticated enough in facilitating inter- and cross-disciplinarity.

Legal approaches

Legal tools and mechanisms

Just as conservation concepts and governance approaches have evolved over the decades, so too have the legal mechanisms to protect the environment. Early mechanisms evolved at the national level to address the most visible environmental problems, such as air pollution in growing industrial cities. These early laws involved setting pollution standards and fining those that exceeded them. This legal approach became known as 'command and control' regulation and has been broadly used to address a wide range of environmental problems. In the last few decades, however, legal approaches have evolved dramatically with the realization that there is not only one way to manage natural resources (Berkes and Folke, 2002). In particular, it has become clear that 'command and control' mechanisms only encourage the meeting of minimum standards and do not incentivize best practice. Furthermore, they are inflexible and do not take account of the different circumstances of those being regulated, which has led to a broadening of mechanisms. The *Rio Declaration* and *Agenda 21* have also influenced the development of new mechanisms.[2] Contemporary legal tools now include economic instruments (such as taxes, grants and refund schemes) and market-based mechanisms (such as tradable permits), which are more flexible and incentivize improvement (Fisher, 2010). There has also been a turn away from enforcement based only upon government inspection, to self-regulation, monitoring and education to encourage compliance.

Another contemporary development has been the use of 'soft law' and voluntary approaches. Soft law is aspirational rather than legally binding and has featured in the development of much international environmental law. Examples of soft law include declarations (such as the *Rio Declaration*) and action plans which do not in themselves create binding norms but do set agenda and encourage states to meet the agreed goals. Voluntary mechanisms have also been used at the national level. They take the form of codes of conduct, for example, and are often developed by industry and those being regulated rather than the regulators. This bottom-up approach overcomes tensions created by government-based regulation, avoids the need for costly education programmes and improves compliance. The adoption of a combined hard and soft law framework can be seen at both the domestic and international levels. For example, most shark-based tourism frameworks include both licensing laws to control the operator, and soft law codes of conduct for participants. At the international level, we can see the combination of hard laws with enforcement mechanisms (*Convention on International Trade in Endangered Species*) as well as soft law (FAO *International Plan of Action for Sharks*).

In summary, it can be seen that pluralistic approaches adopted in other contexts and fields are also evident in the legal mechanisms and tools that have been adopted to address environmental concerns. Today, a combination of different legal mechanisms that incentivize, as well as provide a disincentive to non-compliance, have been adopted through a combination of legislative frameworks and soft law instruments.

A principled approach

While legal approaches at the international level have followed, to a great extent, national trends, there are some differences. Notably, international law is inherently centralized and Eurocentric. Core international law principles have developed over centuries, particularly in relation to the use of force. Following the establishment of the United Nations in 1945, international law quickly developed in response to an increasing range of global issues. One such field is the law of the sea, which is the most significant international law affecting governance of oceans. As will be seen in the next chapter, it is the UNCLOS that has provided a foundation for much of the current law in this area, and which created fundamental norms, including the responsibility to protect and preserve the marine environment.

The other area of international law of significance to shark conservation and management is international environmental law – a branch of law that did not exist before the 1970s. It is the development of international environmental law that has permitted a more principled approach to oceans governance to evolve. The 1972 UN Conference on the Human Environment in Stockholm marked a turning point. For the first time, global attention was directed towards addressing environmental issues. Although few binding treaties were adopted at the conference, the Stockholm Declaration was endorsed, which established a number of international environmental principles. These principles were largely affirmed in the later *Rio Declaration* and *New Delhi Declaration on Principles of International Law Relating to Sustainable Development* (2002). These principles, the most significant of which are considered below, have strongly influenced the development of binding international environmental law that followed, as well as soft law. Relevantly, the principle of prevention requires action to prevent harm before it occurs. The polluter pays principles states that after environmental damage occurs those that are most responsible for it should pay the price. The principle of transboundary harm curtails sovereignty by making one state responsible for environmental damage it causes in another. Each of these principles is relevant to advancing shark conservation and management. Perhaps most significantly, the principles include the precautionary approach which provides that lack of scientific evidence should not prevent action being taken now. There are lessons that may be learned from the management of other fisheries that may assist the implementation of the precautionary principle in relation to sharks (Bruyn *et al.*, 2013).

Bringing it all together

All of the above concepts, principles and mechanisms have influenced approaches to shark conservation and management. As will be explored in the next chapter, the law of the sea underpins many of the laws that have developed, supplemented by fisheries regulations and species conservation laws.

Law of the sea

Despite humans' longstanding exploitation of and dependence upon the marine environment, international laws relating specifically to the protection of marine living resources are relatively new. Nonetheless, the law of the sea, in relation to navigation, trade and sovereignty issues, remains one of the oldest areas of law (Pardo, 1984). Early attention to marine governance focused on, for example, the right to sovereignty over territorial waters and the freedom of the seas, with little consideration given to the issue of any reciprocal responsibilities. Prior to UNCLOS, the territorial sea was determined based upon the 'cannon shot rule' (Dupuy and Vignes, 1991).[3] The balance of the oceans fell outside national jurisdiction and was known as the high seas. The United States directly challenged the 'cannon shot' rule in 1945, claiming both fishery and mineral resources beyond the territorial sea.[4] Other claims followed and countries sought sovereignty over what had traditionally been considered the high seas. Disputes also developed between coastal and landlocked states, resulting in the UN convening a *Conference on the Law of the Sea* in an attempt to settle all of these disputes and reduce international tension. The negotiations lasted for many years, and it was not until 1982 that agreement was ultimately reached. UNCLOS was the first global framework on all aspects of oceans governance. It came into force in 1994, but by that time many provisions had become common international practice.

UNCLOS is the most significant international legal instrument in relation to marine environmental regulation. It has been described as a constitution for the oceans (Koh, 1982). It established the extent of the territorial and high seas, and created exclusive economic zones. While confirming the freedom of the high seas, for the first time it provides obligations to protect and preserve the marine environment, including pollution and fishery issues. It has subsequently been supported by a range of other treaties and plans, including regional seas conventions, protocols and subsequent action plans, marine pollution and other specific treaties, as well as multilateral fisheries agreements. It operates in conjunction with other international law, including the CBD, and facilitates measures to conserve and manage sharks. In isolation, the limited restrictions on exploitation of the high seas in UNCLOS will not ensure the future of sharks. Therefore, possible synergies between treaties, institutions and actors will need to be identified and unlocked if the status of sharks is to be improved.

Fisheries regulation

Fisheries laws are by definition laws that regulate fishing, with the aim of striking 'an appropriate balance between exploiting and conserving fish' (Gullett, 2008, p. 1). The underlying goal is the maintenance of recreational and commercial fishing and the businesses and livelihoods it supports, rather than conservation of marine living resources. However, it is clear that this must involve a balance between conservation and utilization. Therefore, fisheries management and marine species conservation are inherently linked, although originating from different starting points.

It is clear that domestic fishing rules are as old as fishing itself, with many traditional communities developing customary law relating to who could fish for what as well as where and when (see e.g. Johannes, 1978). Early national fisheries laws involved simple tools that controlled access to marine areas and the means by which fish were to be harvested. Contemporary fisheries management is more complex, involving sophisticated systems of equipment regulation, species listing, licensing, the setting of maximum sustainable yield, total allowable catch and quotas, together with area management through the establishment of aquatic reserves, for example.

International and regional fisheries regulation has been coordinated by the Food and Agriculture Organisation (FAO) since its establishment in 1945. The subsidiary body, the FAO Committee on Fisheries, was created in 1965, specifically charged with reviewing FAO programmes relating to fisheries and providing reports on fishery-related problems (FAO, 2013). In addition, it has provided an important forum for the negotiation of instruments and examination of fisheries issues. The FAO has played a key role in the development of soft law and model schemes such as the *FAO Code of Conduct on Responsible Fisheries* and *Model Port State Measures* to combat illegal, unregulated and unreported fishing. In the context of shark conservation and management, it is the FAO that has developed the soft law International Plan of Action for Sharks (IPOA-Sharks).[5]

International fisheries management has been built on the foundation of the law of the sea. UNCLOS established the jurisdictional boundaries that are relied upon to grant national control of ocean areas, including exclusive economic zones (EEZs) and territorial seas. In relation to the high seas, UNCLOS has facilitated regional approaches This has led to the adoption of a number of regional fishery management organizations (RFMOs) with agreements covering various oceans of the world, such as the Indian Ocean Tuna Commission (IOTC), Western Central Pacific Fisheries Commission (WCPFC), Northwest Atlantic Fisheries Organization (NAFO), many of which have adopted conservation management measures relating to sharks, discussed in the chapter that follows.

In terms of fisheries regulation as it relates to sharks, it will be necessary to improve all of the areas referred to above. Sustainable catch limits will need to be set based upon the precautionary principle. Regulations aimed at addressing inherently unsustainable practices – shark finning – must become more sophisticated. Finally, by-catch issues will need to be tackled through enhanced equipment regulation and utilizing improved technologies.

Environmental and conservation treaties

It was not until international attention was drawn to environmental problems that global interest turned to the necessity to protect marine habitats and conserve marine biodiversity. There was some early awareness of environmental damage to marine areas and exploitation of marine living resources, but responses were predominantly in the context of challenges to sovereignty. This can be illustrated by the *Pacific Fur Seal Arbitration* in 1893, whereby the United States attempted to apply its domestic conservation laws to protect seals on US-owned islands and areas outside its jurisdiction. The United States was unsuccessful in the arbitration and it was held that it could not apply national conservation laws in areas beyond its state jurisdiction. The arbitration confirmed the absolute freedom to fish the high seas. This case was followed by other early examples of international regulation of marine living resources, including the *International Convention on the Regulation of Whaling* (*ICRW*).[6] Many of the early international environmental treaties focused on one species only. There is no single species treaty that protects sharks; however, later developments in international environmental law have benefited them.

Later international environmental law has adopted market-based mechanisms. The *Convention on International Trade in Endangered Species* (*CITES*) seeks to protect certain species by restricting their trade. The *Convention on Migratory Species* (CMS) is an example of a treaty taking a more holistic approach to conservation by seeking to manage the whole species range. Both of these treaties use a listing mechanism to protect species, with lists that include a number of shark species. If the conservation of sharks is to be advanced then politico-legal barriers will need to be overcome in order to list more shark species. In addition, current trends in the establishment of shark sanctuaries – 'shark parks' – will need to continue.

Conclusion

Despite a recent but growing awareness of the ecological value of sharks, and the expansion of law and policy to address conservation concerns, shark numbers continue to diminish. The above analysis indicates that we already have a wealth of law and policy in place, but it has not proved sufficient to address the problem. It is also clear from the above that there is a plethora of concepts, principles and legal mechanisms available to address this problem. Existing laws for the conservation and management of sharks utilize these tools through fisheries regulation and environmental conservation treaties. However, they have not been sufficiently effective to date. Recent developments include a growing interest in shark-based tourism, which may provide an incentive for fishers to change livelihoods to non-consumptive tourism-based activities (see Chapters 8 and 9). This approach has been effective in relation to other marine species such as whales. Sharks, however, have been said to have 'negative charisma' (Dobson, 2008) and attitudes towards them no doubt need to change (see Chapter 6).

What is clear is that the solution will not be simple. A flexible range of mechanisms will be needed, which include a sophisticated combination of incentives and enforcement measures. All levels of governance and all stakeholders must work holistically both in terms of the conservation of ecosystems and the regulation of human utilization of them. Such advances may be facilitated by partnerships between public and private sectors, as well as communities and by distributing authority across centralized agencies and local communities (Berkes, 2004). Nonetheless, it is clear that international governance has a role to play where less than optimal results can be achieved at the local or national level. Conversely, in some circumstances governance is best focused at the local level. A fully networked approach may be preferable and would involve both vertical linkages between levels of government and horizontal connections between stakeholder groups (Agrawal and Gibson, 1999).

Inter-disciplinary approaches are essential – laws and policies cannot work in isolation, they must incorporate existing knowledge and encourage and facilitate review based on new scientific findings. Natural science, conservation biology and ecology must inform law and policy. Political positions must be overcome to move forward and frameworks must be supported by economic and livelihood incentives. If practices are to change from consumptive to non-consumptive exploitation of marine resources, economics is another critical field. Finally, attitudes and ethical approaches must alter to create a motivation to conserve: thus social science, including philosophy and anthropology, become important as well as the fields of psychology and behavioural science.

The chapters that follow address the conundrum of shark conservation and management from different disciplinary perspectives. Such studies are essential if the protection of sharks is to be enhanced. However, it is not enough for these disciplines to work only in parallel with law and policy – true inter-disciplinarity will be an essential component of success.

Notes

1 John Muir founded the Sierra Club in the United States in 1892 as a wilderness preservation society.

2 See, for example, *Agenda 21*, chapter 8.32, which refers to prices, markets and government policies to assist the law in achieving sustainable development.

3 The law stated that the first three nautical miles from the low-water mark formed part of a state's territorial waters. This was said to be based upon the distance a cannonball could be shot from the coast out into the ocean.

4 The 1945 Truman Proclamation: see Dupuy and Vignes (1991, p. 325).

5 Considered further by Natalie Klein and Mary Lack in the chapters that follow.

6 Although this treaty originally focused on protecting whales for the maintenance of the whaling industry rather than conservation.

References

Agenda 21 (1992) Report of the UNCED, I, UN Doc A/CONF.151/26/Rev.1.

Agrawal, A. and Gibson, C. C. (1999) 'Enchantment and Disenchantment: The Role of Community in Natural Resource Conservation', *World Development*, vol. 27, no. 4, pp. 629–649.

Antarctic Treaty, opened for signature 1 December 1959, 402 UNTS 71 (entered into force 23 June 1961).

Arceo, H. (2013) 'Moving Beyond a Top-down Fisheries Management Approach in the Northwestern Mediterranean: Some Lessons from the Philippines', *Marine Policy*, vol. 39, pp. 29–42.

Berkes, F. (2004) 'Rethinking Community-based Conservation', *Conservation Biology*, vol. 18, no. 3, pp. 621–630.

Berkes, F. and Farvar, M. T. (1989) 'Introduction and Overview', in F. Berkes (ed.), *Common Property Resources: Ecology and Community-based Sustainable Development*, Belhaven, London.

Berkes, F. and Folke, C. (2002) 'Back to the Future: Ecosystem Dynamics and Local Knowledge', in L. H. Gunderson and C. S. Holling (eds), *Panarchy: Understanding Transformations in Human and Natural Systems*, Island Press, Washington, DC.

Biermann, F. and Pattberg, P. (2008) 'Global Environmental Governance: Taking Stock, Moving Forward', *Annual Review of Environment and Resources*, vol. 33, pp. 277–294.

Borrini-Feyerabend, G. and Lassen, B. (2008), 'Community Conserved Areas: A Review of Status and Needs after Durban 2003 and CBD COP 7 2004: Preliminary Synthesis', available at http://cmsdata.iucn.org/downloads/regional_cca_reviews_synthesis.pdf, accessed 30 December 2010.

Borrini-Feyerabend, G., Kothari, A. and Oviedo, G. (2004) *Indigenous and Local Communities and Protected Areas: Towards Equity and Enhanced Conservation. Guidance on Policy and Practice for Co-Managed Protected Areas and Community Conserved Areas*, IUCN, Gland and Cambridge.

Bosselmann, K. (2002) 'Rio+10: Any Closer to Sustainable Development?', *New Zealand Journal of Environmental Law*, vol. 6, pp. 297–317.

Bosselmann, K. (2013) 'Environmental Ethics', in *Max Plank Encyclopaedia of Public International Law*, www.mpepil.com, accessed 2 April 2013.

Brown, D. A. (1995) 'The Role of Ethics in Sustainable Development and Environmental Protection Decisionmaking', in J. Lemons and D. A. Brown (eds), *Sustainable Development: Science, Ethics and Public Policy*, Kluwer Academic Publishers, Dordrecht.

Bruyn, P., Murua, H. and Aranda, M. (2013) 'The Precautionary Approach to Fisheries Management: How This is Taken into Account by Tuna Regional Fisheries Management Organisations', *Marine Policy*, vol. 38, pp. 397–406.

Carson, R. (2002) *Silent Spring*, Mariner Books, New York (first published 1962).

Colchester, M. (1994) 'Salvaging Nature: Indigenous Peoples, Protected Areas and Biodiversity Conservation', *UNRISD Discussion Paper No. 55*, UNRISD, Geneva, available at www.wrm.org.uy/subjects/nature.html, accessed 30 December 2010.

Convention on Biological Diversity, opened for signature 5 June 1992, 1760 UNTS 79 (entered into force 29 December 1993).

Dobson, J. (2008) 'Shark! A New Frontier in Tourist Demand for Marine Wildlife', in J. E. S. Higham and M. Luck (eds), *Marine Wildlife and Tourism Management: Insights from the Natural and Social Sciences*, CABI, Wallingford.

Dresner, S. (2002) *The Principles of Sustainability*, Earthscan, London.
Dudley, N. (ed.) (2008) *Guidelines for Applying Protected Area Management Categories*, IUCN, Gland.
Dupuy, R. J. and Vignes, D. (1991) *A Handbook on the New Law of the Sea*, Kluwer Academic Publishers, Dordrecht.
Emerson, R. W. (1836) 'Nature', http://oregonstate.edu/instruct/phl302/texts/emerson/nature-contents.html, accessed 15 December 2010.
FAO (2013) 'COFI Committee on Fisheries', www.fao.org/fishery/about/cofi/en, accessed 10 October 2013.
Fisher, D. (2010) *Australian Environmental Law*, 2nd edn, Lawbook Co., Sydney.
Gibbs, C. J. N. and Bromley, D. W. (1989) 'Institutional Arrangements for Management of Rural Resources: Common Property Regimes', in F. Berkes (ed.), *Common Property Resources: Ecology and Community-based Sustainable Development*, Belhaven, London.
Grima, A. P. L. and Berkes, F. (1989) 'Natural Resources: Access, Rights-to-Use and Management', in F. Berkes (ed.), *Common Property Resources: Ecology and Community-based Sustainable Development*, Belhaven, London.
Gullett, W. (2008) *Fisheries Law in Australia*, LexisNexis Butterworths, Sydney.
Hardin, G. (1968) 'The Tragedy of the Commons', *Science*, vol. 162, pp. 1243–1248.
Hatcher, B. G. and Bradbury, R. H. (2006) 'Marine Ecosystem Management: Is the Whole Greater than the Sum of the Parts?', in D. R. Rothwell and D. L. VanderZwaag (eds), *Towards Principled Oceans Governance: Australian and Canadian Approaches and Challenges*, Earthscan, Abingdon.
Holley, C., Gunningham, N. and Shearing, C. (2011) *New Environmental Governance*, Routledge, Abingdon.
Hunter, D., Salzman, J. and Zaelke, D. (2010) *International Environmental Law and Policy*, 4th edn, Foundation Press, New York.
Hviding, E. (2003) 'Both Sides of the Beach: Knowledges of Nature in Oceania' in H. Selin (ed.), *Nature Across Cultures: Views of Nature and the Environment in Non-Western Cultures*, Kluwer Academic Publishers, Dordrecht.
International Convention on the Regulation of Whaling, opened for signature 2 December 1946, 161 UNTS 72 (entered into force 10 November 1948).
IUCN, UNEP and WWF (1980) *World Conservation Strategy*, IUCN, UNEP, WWF, Gland.
IUCN, UNEP and WWF (1991) *Caring for the Earth: A Strategy for Sustainable Living*, Earthscan, London.
Jaksa, M. F. (2006) 'Putting the "Sustainable" Back in Sustainable Development: Recognizing and Enforcing Indigenous Property Rights as a Pathway to Global Environmental Sustainability', *Journal of Environmental Law and Litigation*, vol. 21, pp. 157–206.
Johannes, R. E. (1978) 'Traditional Marine Conservation Methods in Oceania and their Demise', *Annual Review of Ecological Systems*, vol. 9, pp. 349–364.
Katsanevakis, S., Stelzenmüller, V., South, A., Sørensen, T. K., Jones, P. J. S., Kerr, S., Badalamenti, F., Anagnostou, C., Breen, P., Chust, G., D'Anna, G., Duijn, M., Filatova, T., Fiorentino, F., Hulsman, H., Johnson, K., Karageorgis, A. P., Kroencke, I., Mirto, S., Pipitone, C., Portelli, S., Qiu, W., Reiss, H., Sakellariou, D., Salomidi, M., van Hoof, L., Vassilopoulou, V., Vega Fernández, T., Vöge, S., Weber, A., Zenetos, A. and ter Hofstede, R. (2011) 'Ecosystem-based Marine Spatial Management: Review of Concepts, Policies, Tools and Critical Issues', *Ocean and Coastal Management*, vol. 54, no. 11, pp. 807–820.

Koh, T. T. (1982) A *Constitution for the Oceans*, available at www.un.org/Depts/los/convention_agreements/texts/koh_english.pdf, accessed 28 December 2012.

Lam, M. and Pritcher, T. (2012) 'The Ethical Dimensions of Fisheries', *Current Opinion in Environmental Sustainability*, vol. 4, no. 3, pp. 364–373.

Leopold, A. (1949) *A Sand County Almanac*, Ballantine Books, New York.

Mill, J. S. (1965) *Principles of Political Economy: With Some of Their Applications to Social Philosophy*, University of Toronto Press, Toronto.

New Delhi Declaration on Principles of International Law Relating to Sustainable Development (2002) ILA Resolution 3/2002, Annex to UN Doc A/57/329.

Oreskes, N. (2004) 'Science and Public Policy: What's Proof Got To Do With It?', *Environmental Science and Policy*, vol. 7, pp. 369–383.

Ostrom, E. (1990) *Governing the Commons: The Evolution of Institutions for Collective Action*, Cambridge University Press, Cambridge.

Pacific Fur Seal Arbitration (United States v Canada) (1893) 1 RIAA 755.

Pardo, A. (1984) 'The Law of the Sea: Its Past and Its Future', *Oregon Law Review*, vol. 63, pp. 7–18.

Passmore, J. (1974) *Man's Responsibility for Nature: Ecological Problems and Western Traditions*, Duckworth, London.

Rio Declaration on Environment and Development (1992), Report of the United Nations Conference on Environment and Development, UN Doc A/CONF.151/6/Rev.1.

Roberts, C. (2007) *The Unnatural History of the Sea*, Island Press, Washington, DC.

Rolston III, H. (2012) *A New Environmental Ethics: The Next Millennium for Life on Earth*, Routledge, New York.

Scull, J. (2013) *The Separation from More-than-Human Nature*, http://members.shaw.ca/jscull/separate.htm, accessed 2 April 2013.

Solomon, U. U. (2010) 'A Detailed Look at the Three Disciplines, Environmental Ethics, Law and Education to Determine Which Plays the Most Critical Role in Environmental Enhancement and Protection', *Environment, Development and Sustainability*, vol. 12, pp. 1069–1080.

Speth, J. G. and Haas, P. M. (2006) *Global Environmental Governance*, Island Press, Washington, DC.

Tarlock, A. D. (1996) 'Environmental Law: Ethics or Science?', *Duke Environmental Law and Policy Forum*, vol. 7, pp. 193–223.

Techera, E. J. and Klein, N. (2011) 'Fragmented Governance: Reconciling Legal Strategies for Shark Conservation and Management', *Marine Policy*, vol. 35, no. 1, pp. 73–78.

Van Tatenhove, J. (2013) 'How to Turn the Tide: Developing Legitimate Marine Governance Arrangements at the Level of the Regional Seas', *Ocean and Coastal Management*, vol. 71, pp. 296–304.

White Jr, L. (1967) 'The Historical Roots of our Ecological Crisis', *Science*, vol. 155, pp. 1203–1207.

World Bank (1986) *The World Bank's Operational Policy on Wildlands: Their Protection and Management in Economic Development*, World Bank, Washington, DC.

World Commission on Environment and Development (1987), *Our Common Future*, an Annex to UN Doc A/42/427.

Chapter 2

The existing global legal regimes

Natalie Klein[1]

Introduction

Legal regimes for the conservation and management of shark species exist at all levels of government: local, national, regional and international. The focus of this chapter is on the international laws that regulate activities relating to shark species, including regional practice. Some national practice is also taken into account because consistency and mutual reinforcement across multiple levels of governance is required if efforts for shark protection are to be successful. It is also relevant because international law does not usually have automatic effect in national law but must be adopted through parliamentary processes. In addition, efforts undertaken at local or national levels of government may reflect best practice that can be adopted more widely and generally indicate future trends – a trickle-up effect. The global legal regimes then anticipate a trickle-down effect as key stakeholders are engaged and international benchmarks are established. Coherency and integration are essential in legal regimes. Once these elements of legal governance are achieved, the implementation of the relevant legal rules will be more feasible and effective.

The first part of this chapter provides the basic legal framework in oceans governance, highlighting the varied rights and responsibilities of states in different maritime zones. The second part focuses on the binding international rules that apply to the conservation and management of marine living resources generally and shark species specifically. There are also significant non-binding international instruments seeking to govern state action relating to shark species and these are addressed in the third part. The existing global legal regimes present both opportunities and challenges for improved regulation of shark protection. The chapter concludes with some proposals for moving forward.

General legal framework for oceans governance

All ocean areas are subject to international law. The primary roles for international law in oceans governance are to divide the oceans into different maritime zones and to set out the rights and responsibilities of states within those zones in relation to various maritime activities. The *United Nations Convention on the Law of the Sea* (UNCLOS) is often referred to as the constitution of the oceans because it sets out these international rules and these are widely accepted by all states, irrespective of whether those states have formally adopted the treaty or not.

As a general rule, the closer a maritime area is to the coast of a state, the greater authority that state has over the area to the exclusion of all other states. Moving seaward, the rights and responsibilities of coastal states are balanced with those of other states using the same areas. The areas of ocean the greatest distance from any state are the high seas and are not subject to the sovereignty of any one state. Instead, in these areas, states have exclusive authority over vessels flying their flag, or otherwise registered in their state (the rights of 'flag states'). It is important to have a clear understanding of these basic rules relating to the law of the sea, as these rules inform the actions taken by states in the conservation and management of shark species.

The ocean areas that are integrated with the coast of a state are internal waters, and in this area the coastal state has sovereignty; that is, the authority and control comparable to the powers exercised over land territory. Coastal states also have sovereignty over their territorial sea, which can extend up to 12 nautical miles from their mainland coasts and islands. Within the territorial sea, the vessels of other states are entitled to navigate through those waters but must not conduct a range of activities while in passage (UNCLOS, arts 18–19). Fishing and certain research activities are among the activities that should not be undertaken. As such, the coastal state has primary responsibility for the harvesting of coastal-dwelling shark species and also sole authority to regulate the fishing of shark species that enter into the territorial waters from other maritime zones.

Beyond the territorial sea, the next relevant maritime zone is the exclusive economic zone (EEZ), which can extend up to 200 nautical miles from the coast of a state. Where the EEZ of adjacent or opposite states overlap, a maritime boundary is required. Within the EEZ, the coastal state has sovereign rights for the conservation and management of marine living resources, as well as jurisdiction to protect and preserve the marine environment (UNCLOS, art. 56). Coastal states are required to set a maximum sustainable yield in establishing the total allowable catch of any species in its EEZ and must promote the objective of optimum utilization. Other states are entitled to access the EEZ for navigation and related uses, and each group of states must show due regard for the rights of other users in this maritime area (UNCLOS, art. 58). As with the territorial sea, the coastal state has exclusive authority to decide on the harvest and protection of shark species and may establish national laws to this effect, which can then be policed and enforced against vessels from other states.

The remaining maritime areas that are not subject to the authority of any coastal state are the high seas. All states enjoy a range of freedoms on the high seas and their authority is limited to those vessels flying their flag. The freedoms of the high seas include the right of all states to fish in these areas, although this right is now subjected to broad requirements relating to conservation and management of marine living resources under UNCLOS (UNCLOS, arts 116–120). If a vessel is in violation of these requirements on the high seas, then it usually falls to the flag state to take action against that vessel. No other state may interfere with a foreign-flagged vessel on the high seas unless the flag state has consented. As a result, states must take action against their own vessels to ensure international rules relating to shark protection are being followed when those vessels are on the high seas.

Shark conservation and management is complicated for those shark species that are highly migratory or that swim between the EEZs of different states or between the EEZ and the high seas. UNCLOS has provided only broad rules imposing duties on states to cooperate either directly or through international organizations in this situation (UNCLOS, arts 63–64).

From this overview of the general legal framework, it should be evident that global legal regimes must take into account the actions of coastal states within their own maritime zones (primarily the territorial sea and the EEZ) as well as the actions of all states on the high seas. The efficacy of the global legal regimes is therefore dependent on ensuring that there are coherent and comprehensive rules in place that account for these varied rights across maritime zones. The next part considers these existing rules in more detail.

International legal framework for fisheries management

One of the primary sources of international law is treaties, and beyond UNCLOS, states have adopted a number of treaties to deal more specifically with the conservation and management of marine living resources. These treaties are relevant generally to the protection of shark species as they set out binding obligations to be followed by all states in their decision making on conservation and management, as well as enforcement. This part considers the *1995 Fish Stocks Agreement*, the *2009 Port States Agreement*, the *Convention on Biological Diversity* (CBD), as well as the two multilateral treaties that address specific species of sharks – the *Convention on International Trade in Endangered Species* (CITES) and the *Convention on Migratory Species* (CMS). It then turns to the two non-binding international instruments intended to have the most influence on state decision making on the conservation and management of shark species, the Sharks International Plan of Action (IPOA-Sharks) as well as a Memorandum of Understanding adopted under the CMS.

1995 Fish Stocks Agreement

As noted previously, a critical issue in fisheries management is the fact that marine living resources are unaware of political boundaries and move freely across maritime zones. The 1995 *Fish Stocks Agreement* goes some way in filling gaps left by UNCLOS in relation to straddling stocks and highly migratory species. Obligations are primarily imposed in relation to fishing activities in areas outside national jurisdiction – that is, outside the EEZ of any coastal state. However, coastal states are also bound by obligations relating to cooperative mechanisms vis-à-vis highly migratory species and straddling fish stocks in their EEZ, as well as needing to adhere to the precautionary principle in decision making relating to fishing in their EEZ (*1995 Fish Stocks Agreement*, art. 6).

The requirement to apply the precautionary principle both in the EEZ and on the high seas is important in relation to the relevant shark species, as this principle accounts for the fact that there may be scientific uncertainty relating to the status of a species and demands a more cautious approach in conservation and management decisions. This approach is necessitated even where sharks are not the targeted species of any particular fishing operation.

A key feature of the *1995 Fish Stocks Agreement* is the reliance on the operation of regional fishery management organizations (RFMOs) and arrangements. Essentially, the *1995 Fish Stocks Agreement* is predicated on the existence of RFMOs to manage particular species, and anticipates the strengthening of existing RFMOs and the addition of new participants to those RFMOs. There are limitations in this approach because it means that shark protection is dependent on the existence of a relevant RFMO or arrangement, or direct action by the states concerned. The actions taken by existing RFMOs are varied and far from comprehensive, as will be discussed further below.

The *1995 Fish Stocks Agreement* further accounts for the possibility that not every state party to that agreement will necessarily be a member of a relevant regional organization and sets out a range of requirements for flag states in managing their fishing vessels (*1995 Fish Stocks Agreement*, arts 17–19). There is, of course, a gap in coverage whereby states that do not become parties to this treaty are not bound by its requirements. Thus, overall, there is useful guidance as to the requirements to be imposed on states for shark conservation and management in the *1995 Fish Stocks Agreement*, and scope within the treaty to develop mechanisms and arrangements for improved conservation and management. Establishing coherency and comprehensiveness remains an issue, however.

2009 Port States Agreement

In light of ongoing concerns about the failure of flag states to implement and police their vessels consistently, a greater role has been established for port states. This authority has been enshrined most recently in 2009 under an *Agreement on Port State Measures to Prevent, Deter and Eliminate Illegal, Unreported and Unregulated Fishing*. Pursuant to this agreement, states acquire responsibility for deciding on the entry into port, as well as inspecting fishing vessels that enter their ports, for vessels in transit or seeking to offload their catch. A key response to evidence of illegal fishing is to deny the vessel entry into port, or if the vessel has already entered port, deny the vessel a range of port services (*2009 Port States Agreement*, art. 9). The practical consequences of such decisions (e.g. requiring a longer journey by the vessel, or reducing the quality of the catch onboard) may undermine the commercial viability of the operation and dissuade the vessel from pursuing illegal fishing practices. No further enforcement action by the port state, such as arresting the vessel, its master and crew, is otherwise anticipated under the *2009 Port States Agreement* – this authority remains with the flag state instead (Klein, 2011, p. 73).

To date, the *2009 Port State Agreement* has not yet attracted sufficient support from states to enter into force and hence become legally binding.[2] Until it is widely accepted by states, its influence is minimal to non-existent. It is relevant in the global governance regime for sharks in that it reflects the role that port states could potentially play in monitoring shark catch, especially in relation to finning, and it will reinforce and broaden action that is being taken by some RFMOs to address shark by-catch and finning practices.

Convention on Biological Diversity

Critical at the international level for habitat protection is the CBD, which envisages both *in situ* and *ex situ* conservation, including the establishment of protected areas (CBD, art. 8). By focusing on the importance of maintaining ecosystems, the CBD provides a vehicle to consider the implications of over-fishing shark species to an ecosystem as a whole. As shark species are often apex predators, the excessive removal of a predator species may have consequences throughout the ecosystem and cause effects down the food chain (see further in Chapter 4). States have the authority to take a range of steps within their national jurisdiction to support biological diversity within specific areas if they wish. There is therefore scope within the agreement to provide additional protections to shark species, particularly where there is information about particular areas as important feeding or breeding grounds.

The weakness of the CBD lies in the soft language utilized in pertinent provisions, which does not establish concrete obligations on the part of states. The language is not highly prescriptive as to what steps states must take, but instead directed at empowering states if they wish to take action. There is considerable flexibility afforded to states in terms of taking action relative to resource availability (e.g. CBD, art. 6). While there can be benefits to flexibility in that states are given choices as to what steps they will take and any action may be better than no action, the possible result of gaps and inconsistencies for purposes of global governance is palpable.

Convention on the International Trade in Endangered Species and Wild Fauna and Flora

CITES provides a means for state parties to control or prohibit international trade in threatened or endangered species.

Parties to CITES decide whether species should be listed in one of three appendices. Appendix I is reserved for species threatened with extinction and strictly controls international trade in these species (including their body parts) through a system of permits (CITES, art. III). States are able to enter reservations to the listing of a species so that they are not bound by these requirements. So far, no shark species has been included in Appendix I of CITES.

For species listed in Appendix II, there is a recognized need for trade regulation through the use of import and export permits to prevent the species from becoming threatened with extinction. The regulations and requirements are still strict, but not as limiting as those set forth for species included in Appendix I. Marine species included in Appendix II may only be harvested (CITES refers to species 'introduced from the sea') when there is evidence that the specimen was so taken in a sustainable manner (CITES, art. IV(6)). Importing states are also required to ensure that the necessary permits accompany imported specimens. In the absence of compliance, the states concerned may be subjected to trade sanctions.

Three shark species were initially listed in Appendix II of CITES: the great white, basking and whale sharks. Japan, Iceland, Norway and South Korea are among a very small number of states that have filed reservations to the listing of these shark species, and so they are not bound by the Appendix II requirements.

At the 2010 CITES Conference in Doha, proposals were submitted to list an additional eight species of sharks in Appendix II, but were unsuccessful. Greater results were achieved at the 2013 CITES Conference of Parties, where states did agree to list an additional five shark species for protection under Appendix II of CITES: the oceanic whitetip; porbeagle; scalloped hammerhead; great hammerhead; and smooth hammerhead. Only a small number of states have objected to their listing (including Japan and Guyana), although other significant shark-fishing states, such as China, have not done so. The status given under CITES to these recently added species will come into effect in September 2014 (an extra year than usual was considered necessary to allow for sufficient preparation). The spiny dogfish, the sandbar shark and the dusky shark, which had been nominated for listing in Appendix II in 2010, were not included for listing in 2013.

There is a further possibility of individual states opting to list a species within its jurisdiction in Appendix III, 'for the purpose of preventing or restricting exploitation', and because 'the co-operation of other Parties in the control of trade' is required (CITES, art. II(3)). This approach would allow a state to take the initiative where it holds national concerns about the status of a particular shark species and the listing would provide a platform for ensuring the cooperation of other states that harvest the species concerned.

CITES is beneficial in the global governance of shark species because it is a key mechanism for tightly restricting international trade in a species and generally carries political weight with the states concerned. Its importance in the latter regard indicates why states are often resistant to listing species in the first instance. Instead, there has been a preference to improve regulation and management rather than introduce strict trade limitations, especially in the context of exploitable marine species with very high commercial stakes. CITES does have limitations in its operation, because it is difficult to win political support to list a species, and states may then enter reservations so they are not bound by the trade restrictions. Also, it addresses international trade, so does not necessarily prevent states from harvesting shark species from their own maritime zones for domestic consumption.

Convention on Migratory Species

The CMS is also focused on shark species that cross national boundaries, but extends to state conduct within its own maritime areas for the protection of these species. The CMS also works on a listing system comparable to CITES. There are general obligations imposed on states party to the CMS treaty to 'promote, co-operate in and support research relating to migratory species' as well as endeavouring to provide immediate protection to species in Appendix I and conclude agreements for species listed in Appendix II.

Migratory species are listed in Appendix I to the CMS if they are endangered throughout all or a significant proportion of their range (CMS, arts I(1)(e), III(1) and (2)). Once listed, states should endeavour to take steps to protect the habitat of the species concerned, prevent adverse impacts on the migration of the species and respond to factors that may further endanger the species. Three shark species are afforded Appendix I protection: the basking, great white and whale sharks.

For those species listed in Appendix I, state parties that are 'range states' are prohibited from taking the species. 'Range states' are defined in the CMS to include states that exercise jurisdiction over any part of the range of a migratory species, as well as states that have vessels registered to them that take migratory species on the high seas (CMS, art. I(1)(h)). There are limited circumstances where states may still be permitted to take the listed species, including for scientific purposes, traditional subsistence uses and if 'extraordinary circumstances so require'. The latter exception does allow for a generous scope of interpretation and may support arguments for the killing of sharks, such as the great white shark, that are considered as dangerous to local swimming beaches.

A listing under Appendix II requires range states to enter into agreements with each other for the benefit of the species, and such agreements are open to range states irrespective of whether they are parties to the CMS or not (CMS, arts IV(3), V). The four shark species listed in Appendix II are: spiny dogfish, porbeagle, shortfin mako and longfin mako. The CMS sets out what content should be addressed in each of these agreements, with the key intention of returning a species to a favourable conservation status. Further steps have been sought for the protection of some migratory shark species under the auspices of the CMS with the adoption of a non-binding Memorandum of Understanding (discussed further below).

Taken together, the binding treaties do provide an important legal framework for national efforts towards the conservation and management of sharks. However, the gaps in the regimes are clear. These start with the possibilities that states will not be bound by the treaties in the first instance or may potentially avail themselves of the option of objecting to specific provisions or listings if allowed by the treaty regimes. There is also a dependence on additional rules being adopted to implement the broadly agreed principles. While the creation of benchmarks may be helpful and should guide state conduct, the absence of additional rules potentially undermines the coherency of the global legal regime. Rather than binding treaty obligations, states have sought to fill gaps through the adoption of non-binding legal instruments, which are examined immediately below.

Non-binding obligations: the IPOA-Sharks

The creation of obligations that are not strictly binding has an important place in international law (see also Chapter 1). When obligations are not legally binding, states will not be held liable and required to make reparations in the event that their conduct has not met the standards set forth in those obligations. Instead, non-binding norms (often referred to as soft law) are intended to influence state conduct and decision making in a common direction. Soft law can represent international agreement as to what the law should be, or will be, but allows states the opportunity to make required changes according to their own priorities and resources. Non-binding obligations provide the relevant point of reference for states and as such set parameters for state action.

The most comprehensive international instrument addressing shark conservation and management is non-binding: the IPOA-Sharks, adopted by the Food and Agriculture Organisation (FAO) within the framework of the Code of Conduct for Responsible Fisheries (IPOA-Sharks, art. 10). The IPOA-Sharks covers all species of sharks, skates, rays and chimaera, with the goal of long-term sustainable management and conservation of stocks by applying the precautionary approach (IPOA-Sharks, arts 14, 16). It addresses 'shark catch', which includes directed, by-catch, commercial, recreational and other forms of taking sharks and therefore encompasses target and non-target catches (IPOA-Sharks, arts 11–12).

States are called on to assess the status of sharks and adopt regional and national Plans of Action (POAs) to conserve and manage sharks (IPOA-Sharks, arts 17–28). The IPOA-Sharks requires states to report biennially on the progress of the assessment, development and implementation of shark plans (IPOA-Sharks, para. 28). The FAO agreed in 2011 to examine the extent to which the IPOA-Sharks had been implemented, and work is ongoing in this regard.

Although the IPOA-Sharks is broader and more inclusive than the treaties addressed above, it is only voluntary, given its non-binding status, and its implementation is sporadic as uptake at the national level has been slow and inconsistent (Lack and Sant, 2011; and see further Chapter 3). Despite these problems, the IPOA-Sharks remains significant because it is the principal instrument to deal with all shark species and can be followed by all states without that state having to pursue formalities associated with becoming party to a treaty.

Non-binding obligations: CMS Memorandum of Understanding

Beyond the binding regime created under the CMS, states party to the CMS also adopted a Memorandum of Understanding in 2010 (CMS MoU). This instrument includes strengthened conservation principles for shark species specifically and calls for the development of improved management plans (CMS MoU, Section 3). The need for cooperation among governments, international organizations, non-governmental organizations (NGOs) and other stakeholders, as well as the role of states to take measures to improve the conservation status of sharks and the establishment of other management plans consistent with the CMS MoU, are all highlighted. The CMS MoU is global in its geographic scope, but only applies to the species already listed in Appendices I and II (a species list is set out in Annex I to the CMS MoU, with the criteria and procedures to amend this list agreed in 2012). There are currently 36 signatories, including the European Union.

At the 2012 meeting of signatories to the CMS MoU, a conservation plan was adopted as Annex 3 and contains a series of overall principles and five primary objectives to be attained. Each objective is then spelled out to guide state conduct across issues such as awareness raising, stakeholder cooperation, by-catch, law enforcement, ecologically sustainable management, habitat conservation and research. The steps in the conservation plan relate back to specific provisions of the CMS MoU and provide a broad sweep of actions, addressing many key concerns for shark conservation and management. While the MoU and its Annex 3 are not comprehensive because they are limited as to which species are to be subject to such conservation plans, the range of steps to be undertaken by states is extensive and in many ways parallels the IPOA-Sharks.

Overall, the non-binding agreements are important complements in global governance because they can capture the steps that should be encouraged among states in seeking to conserve and manage shark species. These details can provide important benchmarks to modify and inspire state conduct, as well as potentially creating political momentum towards more expansive binding agreements. Even where gaps and weaknesses remain in the global instruments, some of these deficiencies have been redressed through regional agreements and institutions. The latter still form part of global governance because they are addressed to a number of states, even if they are limited spatially in their application.

Regional legal framework for fisheries management

A large number of regional agreements have been reached to address fisheries management of particular ocean areas or of particular species. To date, no single regional organization has been established to manage any individual shark species. However, RFMOs have considered shark protection as by-catch or by-product of target species (commonly, tuna). While these efforts can best be described as nascent, the direction of regional approaches to shark conservation and management may further be discerned from non-binding regional plans of action thus far adopted. Both types of international agreements are assessed in this section.

Binding regional fisheries agreements

The approach of the *1995 Fish Stocks Agreement* reflects the considerable role to be played by RFMOs in the conservation and management of fish species.

Some RFMOs have focused efforts on finning, and set out requirements relating to the retention of fins vis-à-vis the shark's trunk weight. The International Commission for the Conservation of Atlantic Tunas (ICCAT), Inter-American Tropical Tuna Commission (IATTC), Indian Ocean Tuna Commission (IOTC), Northwest Atlantic Fisheries Organization (NAFO), General Fisheries Commission for the Mediterranean (GFCM), South East Atlantic Fisheries Organization (SEAFO) and Western and Central Pacific Fisheries Commission (WCPFC) each provide that 'vessels may not have on board fins that total more than 5% of the weight of the sharks' (Lack and Sant, 2009, pp. 25–29). This means that the weight of fins landed cannot exceed 5 per cent of the weight of shark trunks. The '5 per cent fin-to-body ratio' is controversial and ambiguous, and concerns have been raised about its appropriateness because of the many variables involved in assessing the ratio, and regulatory and enforcement issues (Lack and Sant, 2006, pp. 12, 14–15).

In addition, there are some measures aimed at particularly vulnerable species. In these situations, it is prohibited to retain onboard, tranship, land, store, sell or offer for sale any part of the specified shark species within the scope of jurisdiction of the RFMO. There are also additional monitoring and reporting requirements concerning what to do when specimens of the species are taken accidentally as by-catch (see also Chapter 9).

Examples in this regard include the ICCAT regulations applying in the Atlantic Ocean that do not allow retention of bigeye thresher, hammerhead and oceanic whitetip sharks (ICCAT, 2011, REC 2010-07, REC 2010-08, REC 2011-08). In 2012, ICCAT conducted a stock assessment of the shortfin mako shark within its Convention Area (ICCAT, 2012). The proposal to limit catches of the shortfin mako to current levels was not passed at the November 2012 annual meeting. Nor was a proposed ban on the retention of porbeagle sharks. ICCAT has also undertaken an ecological risk assessment for 16 shark species (20 stocks) in the ICCAT area, which makes several recommendations (Oceana, undated).

ICCAT has since moved ahead with a greater focus on sharks, agreeing at its 2012 meeting to commence a process that will amend the text of its Convention to expressly manage sharks, instead of just managing them as by-catch.

The North East Atlantic Fisheries Commission (NEAFC) prohibits shark finning, the taking of basking sharks and targeted fishing for spiny dogfish (NEAFC, 2006). The NEAFC has also adopted measures in relation to the spurdog shark (NEAFC, 2012a), the porbeagle shark (NEAFC, 2012b) and all deep-sea sharks (17 species) (NEAFC, 2012c). In the Eastern Pacific Ocean, the IATTC measures allow for zero retention of oceanic whitetip sharks (IATTC, 2011).

The WCPFC conducted a stock assessment of oceanic whitetip sharks within its Convention Area in 2012, which indicated that stocks are continuing to decline (Rice and Harley, 2012). At the December 2012 annual meeting, the WCPFC member states agreed to take additional steps for the protection of whale sharks from purse seine fishing operations. Vessels under the jurisdiction of the Convention must free whale sharks caught in their nets and must also record and report any such incidents (WCPFC, 2012).

Only the Commission for the Conservation of Antarctic Marine Living Resources (CCAMLR) prohibits targeted fishing for any sharks and provides that all by-catch shall be released alive, where possible (CCAMLR, 2006). In most other cases, steps have largely not progressed beyond monitoring or data collection and encouraging further research (Lack and Sant, 2009, pp. 25–29).

A central issue with the work of RFMOs is the limited membership; not all states that harvest a particular species are necessarily a party to the regime and will be willing to become bound by the limitations imposed upon members. Further difficulties associated with regional measures have typically included limited species coverage, non-binding obligations, lack of clarity on finning practices, and prohibiting targeted fishing operations against sharks but not addressing by-catch issues (Lack and Sant, 2008). Even if clear measures are prescribed, they are not necessarily enforced. These issues are compounded by the gaps and inconsistencies across the different organizations in the steps they are each taking in relation to shark management. As increased attention is focused on the plight of shark species within RFMOs, there is potential for more binding requirements to be adopted.

Regional POAs

A preference for non-binding legal mechanisms has also been evinced at the regional level, whereby states have agreed on regional POAs in response to the IPOA-Sharks. This approach works well in the context of regional organizations, particularly where responsibility for fisheries is primarily regulated at the regional – as opposed to national – level. This position is reflected in the 2009 decision of the Council of Fisheries Ministers to adopt a European POA in response to inadequacies in the existing range of measures and the need for a comprehensive management framework (European Community, 2009, p. 3). The geographic scope of the European POA is significant and it is also broad in that it is intended to cover both targeted and by-catch shark fisheries (European Community, 2009, p. 3). Nonetheless, the European POA is framed as a gradual response, so it can adapt to new scientific evidence as it evolves and so consistent measures can be considered with the work of RFMOs.

Regional POAs have also been adopted in West Africa, with the aim to encourage states to adopt their own national POAs that will appropriately balance utilization and conservation (Diop and Dossa, 2011), as well as in the Pacific Islands. The 2009 Pacific Island POA is not prescriptive but serves as a guide for assessing shark fisheries and determining other initiatives for shark protection (Lack and Meere, 2009). This regional POA reflects not only the IPOA-Sharks, but also measures required by the WCPFC (Techera and Klein, 2012). The Pacific POA recognizes the need for a model national POA for Pacific states and offers guidance as to the steps that need to be taken at the national level (Techera and Klein, 2012).

The advantages of the regional POAs include maintaining a focus on the need for improved conservation and management of shark species, as well as identifying relevant tools as to what steps may be taken. Yet regional POAs remain non-binding and therefore place less responsibility on the states concerned. Further, there is an ongoing risk of inconsistent measures being taken as between different regions, despite a potential need for coherency at a global level, not only for the highly migratory species but also as a matter of establishing best-practice principles.

Proposals for future development

There are opportunities available within the existing global legal regimes to improve the conservation and management of sharks. The legal agreements discussed in this chapter allow for ongoing development, particularly in terms of increasing the scope of application as well as providing greater detail on what steps states are required to take to promote conservation and management of shark species. In the absence of these developments, or as a complement, there are other options that states could pursue to enhance the global legal framework, which includes a new comprehensive treaty on sharks (as opposed to a non-binding agreement) or at least an international agreement on shark finning. Improving international law may also involve an assessment of national or regional practices and considering how those efforts may be replicated or imposed at the international level. Lessons for the global legal framework could well be learned from local practice associated with eco-tourism and the establishment of particular marine protected areas. These options are discussed in this section.

Building on what exists

There remains considerable scope to exploit the existing legal agreements further in favour of shark conservation than has been undertaken so far. One obvious path in this regard is the possibility of more shark species being listed under either CITES or CMS. Each treaty allows for a graduated response so the steps required depend on in which Appendix a species is listed. This flexibility provides options for states in taking initial steps towards better conservation of endangered or threatened shark species. The adoption of a non-binding Memorandum of Understanding on sharks within the framework of the CMS provides another avenue forward for states in initiating improved conservation and management measures.

While there has clearly been reticence for states to ban international trade in commercial marine species, the 2013 CITES Conference may indicate some shift in attitude among states in this regard. The two critical factors are compelling scientific evidence regarding the status of the species and the political willingness of states to act on that evidence. The latter does not necessarily follow from the former. Political will may be generated if there is domestic interest in democratic states in the preservation of particular species, or perhaps where states do not in fact have a strong commercial interest at stake and these states are in the numerical majority.

States that do not want to adopt measures as strong as banning harvesting in a commercially exploitable species (as might be required under CITES or CMS) may prefer to undertake management measures that allow the maintenance of economic interests while still endeavouring to promote the sustainability of the species. These steps are increasingly being taken in the different RFMOs. The actions of the RFMOs are only limited by their respective constitutive instruments and it may be the case that their terms are broad enough to encompass measures specific to shark species in the area covered by the treaty. Even if an RFMO is directed in its constitutive instrument towards the management of particular non-shark species (most commonly tuna), there are usually still options to address shark harvesting as by-catch. While these options reflect a piecemeal approach, these steps do progress state action and increase the density of the regulatory web addressing shark conservation and management at the international level.

More law (or better law?)

If the view is taken that the existing international legal agreements are inadequate, then another option is to determine if a new treaty is in fact necessary and desirable. Any such treaty could establish its own institutional structure that would be available to formulate more detailed rules as needed to meet the purposes of the treaty (a comparable example in this regard may be the International Whaling Commission under the International Convention on the Regulation of Whaling) (Herndon *et al.*, 2010). There are both advantages and disadvantages to such an approach. On the one hand, a dedicated organization may provide a means to better integrate scientific studies into rules targeted to shark management as well as provide greater international exposure to the plight of endangered and threatened shark species. On the other hand, political and economic differences can undermine the work of the organization and efforts to cooperate may stall or reach an impasse.

Even if global agreement may not be reached, states that are already in the habit of cooperating within the framework of a particular RFMO may be amenable to adopting a separate agreement that is focused on shark species among these states.

An alternative to a regionally focused agreement, or an over-arching treaty on shark conservation and management, would be an international agreement to address one of the most abhorrent practices in relation to the harvesting of sharks, namely shark finning. Widespread criticism has been directed at the practices of those in the fishing industry in cutting off the fins of sharks once caught (either as targeted species or as by-catch) and then throwing the carcass back into the sea, leaving the shark to suffer a painful death. This practice is economically lucrative as it takes less space on a fishing vessel to store shark fins rather than the whole shark and there is considerable demand, particularly in Asia, for shark fin soup.

The cruelty entailed in the practice has prompted action by a number of states and organizations. In 2011, for example, the United States adopted the Shark Conservation Act, which prohibits any person from cutting off shark fins at sea and from possessing, transferring and landing shark fins (including the tail) that are not 'naturally attached to the corresponding carcass'. This law extends 50 miles into the EEZ of the United States, and applies to all shark species, except the smooth dogfish that is harvested with a valid state licence (Techera, 2012). In 2012, the European Parliament voted to endorse the European Commission's proposal to require that fins be left naturally attached to all sharks that are brought to port (COM (2011) 798, amending EC No. 1185/2003 (566 in favour; 47 against)). The European Union had already banned the practice of discarding carcasses at sea, but instead required that fins and carcasses both had to be retained, even if separated. The requirements proved difficult to enforce and the 2012 changes will undoubtedly influence practice, given the EU's large share of global trade in shark products.

The actions of these states may well prompt a broader consensus on the particular practice of shark finning and provide the political will for an international agreement on this narrow dimension of shark harvesting. The impact on storage and transhipment for the fishing vessels concerned may potentially slow the rate of capture of shark species and promote the sustainability of shark species.

Embrace the trickle-up: practices in shark-based tourism and sanctuaries

A number of initiatives towards the conservation and management of shark species are being undertaken at the national and local levels. Steps taken by individual states may provide the impetus for other states to act, particularly in the region. These steps include completely prohibiting the harvesting of sharks, or of particular shark species, from a state's territorial sea or EEZ (examples include French Polynesia's prohibition of all shark fishing within its entire EEZ of 4.7 million square kilometres and Venezuela's prohibition of commercial shark fishing in its maritime zone in the Caribbean Sea). Beyond catch restrictions, there are a range of other practices and regulatory tools that could provide valuable lessons for other states and regions and ultimately assist in the development of global legal regimes. Two examples are considered below in this regard: shark eco-tourism and the use of marine protected areas or sanctuaries

Tourism

Shark-based eco-tourism sites are found in over 40 countries, involving at least 50 different species (see Chapter 12). The shark-based eco-tourism activities include swimming with more docile species, such as whale sharks, and diving with a range of other species such as great white, reef and bull sharks. Eco-tourism is promoted on the basis that the non-consumptive value of any fish or marine mammal over its lifetime is much greater than a one-off sale of a dead animal. These activities offer environmental, socio-cultural and economic benefits, but are not without risks, to both people and the animals. Regulatory frameworks are being developed to ensure human safety, mitigate impacts on sharks and facilitate sustainable growth of tourism (Techera and Klein, 2013).

Regulations that are being put in place include requirements, or prohibitions, around the use of berleying (or chumming) to attract sharks to particular locales and potentially modify their natural behaviour. Regulations or codes of conduct are adopted to control how humans interact with sharks as a means of protecting both species. To preserve the habitats of the sharks, and thereby maintain the economic viability of the eco-tourism operations, states and regional authorities have also designated particular areas as marine parks, or conservation areas.

The practices followed in one state could be endorsed through application in other countries, particularly if the other state is a range state for the relevant shark species. With sufficient practice and agreement among states around this aspect of shark regulation, there is potential that the rules and codes could eventually be enshrined at an international level, even if only soft law at the outset. The measures adopted to promote shark eco-tourism may ultimately have limited scope of application and practices around this industry may vary from state to state, depending on resource availability and economic interest. The potential for these steps to 'trickle-up' nonetheless reflects another means of protecting sharks and improving the overall global governance of sharks.

Sanctuaries

Beyond designating marine areas for special protection to support eco-tourism industries, there is an increasingly widespread practice of creating special maritime zones, or MPAs, to better protect the marine species located therein, including shark species. MPAs are most commonly established in one jurisdictional zone, and as such are under the exclusive control of a particular coastal state. MPAs may usefully provide protection of breeding grounds or nurseries of particular shark species and hence improve their survival rate. The inevitable challenge, however, is that many shark species will move in and out of the designated maritime areas and risk being harvested outside the protected zones.

In some instances, states have declared their entire territorial sea and EEZ to be shark sanctuaries. The most well-known of these is Palau, which has a protected area covering over 600,000 km^2 of ocean. Other Pacific Island nations have followed Palau's example and similar steps have been taken in other parts of the world. For example, in Honduras, a moratorium on shark fishing has been in place for some years and a shark sanctuary was established in 2011 (Shark Savers, 2010). The Maldives has created an Indian Ocean shark sanctuary covering its entire EEZ and totally prohibited the fishing of sharks, as well as imports and exports of shark fins (Jolly, 2010). Such blanket bans are significant conservation efforts, although such an absolute prohibition may be considered as extreme by states that instead favour sustainable utilization.

A key difficulty with these efforts is the risk that some fishing vessels will nonetheless enter these sanctuaries and take sharks, or target species that may be legally fished and incidentally catch sharks as well. The ability to police and enforce these maritime areas is important and may be beyond the resources of small island states. A further challenge is that shark species will not necessarily stay in the EEZ of the one particular state. This situation is especially acute for highly migratory shark species that pass between the maritime zones of more than one state. Nonetheless, the practice followed by individual states could gradually be picked up and followed by other states, creating a broader international practice and ultimately lead to global standards in the establishment of protected areas to enhance conservation and management efforts for shark species.

Conclusion

A central difficulty in the global legal framework for shark conservation and management is that the division of ocean space and the accompanying sovereign rights in those spaces prompt a high dependence on both the need for cooperation and for states to work individually in ways that promote the protection of shark species. The international legal framework therefore has to address how states can work together and what steps should be taken at the national level. The need for coherency is evident, but achieving that cohesiveness remains elusive.

The international treaties set out core requirements for fisheries management and have established international obligations to protect the most vulnerable shark species. These reflect some fundamental principles and concrete measures where most desirable. IPOA-Sharks and other non-binding agreements provide important guidance for states for the regulation of shark species that traverse political boundaries and also seek to inform national decision making on shark conservation and management. Integrating legal rules across international, regional and national levels of governance would enhance the conservation and management of sharks. Ensuring the rules are fully and consistently implemented and enforced would then be the next challenge.

Notes

1 Parts of this chapter draw on Techera, E. J. and Klein, N. (2011) 'Fragmented Governance: Reconciling Legal Strategies for Shark Conservation and Management', *Marine Policy*, vol. 35, pp. 73–78. The author also gratefully acknowledges the research assistance of Zack Doherty, University of Western Australia.

2 Twenty-five states must become parties to the treaty for it to enter into force.

References

CCAMLR (2006) *Report of the Twenty-Fifth Meeting of the Commission*, available at www.ccamlr.org/pu/e/e_pubs/cr/06/i12.pdf, accessed 30 November 2013.

Convention on Biological Diversity, opened for signature 5 June 1992, 1760 UNTS 79 (entered into force 29 December 1993).

Convention on International Trade in Endangered Species of Wild Fauna and Flora, opened for signature 3 March 1973, 993 UNTS 243 (entered into force 1 July 1975).

Convention on the Conservation of Migratory Species of Wild Animals, opened for signature 23 June 1979, 1651 UNTS 333 (entered into force 1 November 1983).

Diop, M. and Dossa, J. (2011) '30 Years of Shark Fishing in West Africa', *FIBA*, available at: www.lafiba.org/index.php/fr/content/.../133FiBA_Requin_EN.pdf, accessed 30 November 2013.

European Commission (2011) *Proposal for a Regulation of the European Parliament and of the Council amending Regulation (EC) No 1185/2003 on the Removal of Fins of Sharks on Board Vessels*, COM 798.

European Community (2009) *On a European Community Action Plan for the Conservation and Management of Sharks*, EU Doc COM, 40 final, 3.

FAO (1999) 'National Plans of Action: International Plan of Action for the Conservation and Management of Sharks', available at: www.fao.org/fishery/ipoa-sharks/npoa/en.

FAO (2009) *Agreement on Port State Measures to Prevent, Deter and Eliminate Illegal, Unreported and Unregulated Fishing*, FAO Doc C 2009/LIM/11-Rev.1.

Herndon, A., Gallucci, V. F., DeMaster, D. and Burke, W. (2010) 'The Case for an International Commission for the Conservation and Management of Sharks (ICCMS)', *Marine Policy*, vol. 34, pp. 1239–1248.

IATTC (2011) *Resolution on the Conservation of Oceanic Whitetip Sharks Caught in Association with Fisheries in the Antigua Convention Area*, Res C-11-10, available at www.iattc.org/PDFFiles2/Resolutions/C-11–10-Conservation-of-oceanic-whitetip-sharks.pdf, accessed 5 March 2014.

ICCAT (2011) 'Resolutions, Recommendations and Other Decisions', available at www.iccat.int/en/RecsRegs.asp, accessed 5 March 2014.

ICCAT (2012) *Shortfin Mako Stock Assessment and Ecological Risk Assessment Meeting*, Olhão, Portugal, 11–18 June 2012, available at www.iccat.es/Documents/Meetings/Docs/2012_SHK_ASS_ENG.pdf, accessed 5 March 2014.

Jolly, D. (2010) 'Maldives Ban Fishing of Sharks', *New York Times*, available at www.nytimes.com/2010/03/10/world/asia/10iht-shark.html, accessed 5 March 2014.

Klein, N. (2011) *Maritime Security and the Law of the Sea*, Oxford University Press, Oxford.

Lack, M. and Meere, F. (2009) *Pacific Islands Regional Plan of Action for Sharks: Guidance for Pacific Countries and Territories on the Conservation and Management of Sharks*, available at www.spc.int/DigitalLibrary/Doc/FAME/Meetings/WCPFC/SC6/EB-IP-03.html, accessed 5 March 2014.

Lack, M. and Sant, G. (2006) 'Confronting Shark Conservation Head On!', *TRAFFIC International*, available at www.traffic.org/species-reports/traffic_species_fish4.pdf , accessed 5 March 2014.

Lack, M. and Sant, G. (2008) *Illegal, Unreported and Unregulated Shark Catch: A Review of Current Knowledge and Action*, Department of the Environment, Water, Heritage and the Arts, Canberra and TRAFFIC, Sydney.

Lack, M. and Sant, G. (2009) *Trends in Global Shark Catch and Recent Developments in Management*, TRAFFIC International, Cambridge.

Lack, M. and Sant, G. (2011) *The Future of Sharks: A Review of Action and Inaction*, TRAFFIC International, Cambridge, and the Pew Environment Group, Washington, DC.

MCES (2011) *Resolution of the 15th Micronesian Chief Executive Summit*, 28 July 2011, available at www.pewenvironmentgroup.org/uploadedFiles/PEG/Newsroom/Press_Release/15th_MCES_Resolution_-_Establishing_the_Regional_Shark_Sanctuary_in_Micronesia.pdf, accessed 30 November 2013.

Memorandum of Understanding on the Conservation of Migratory Sharks (signed on 9 September 2010) CMS/Sharks/MOS1/Inf.1, available at www.cms.int/species/sharks/MoU/Migratory_Shark_MoU_Eng.pdf, accessed 5 March 2014.

NEAFC (2006) *Recommendation IV: A Recommendation for Interim Conservation Measures for Basking Shark in the NEAFC Convention Area in 2006*, available at www.neafc.org/system/files/rec-4_dfg-basking-shark.pdf, accessed 5 March 2014.

NEAFC (2012a) *Recommendation 5: Recommendation for Conservation and Management Measures for Spurdog (*Squalus acanthias*) in the NEAFC Regulatory Area from 2012 to 2014*, available at www.neafc.org, accessed 30 November 2013.

NEAFC (2012b) *Recommendation 6: Recommendation for Conservation and Management Measures for Porbeagle (*Lamna nasus*) in the NEAFC Regulatory Area from 2012 to 2014*, available at www.neafc.org, accessed 30 November 2013.

NEAFC (2012c) *Recommendation 7: Recommendation for Conservation and Management Measures for Deep Sea Sharks in the NEAFC Regulatory Area for 2012*, available at www.neafc.org, accessed 30 November 2013.

Oceana (undated) *ICCAT's Unmanaged Shark Fisheries*, available at http://oceana.org/sites/default/files/euo/OCEANA_ICCAT_sharks_ENG.pdf, accessed 5 March 2014.

Rice, J. and Harley, S. (2012) 'Stock Assessment of Oceanic Whitetip Sharks in the Western and Central Pacific Ocean Rev 1', www.wcpfc.int/node/3235, accessed 5 March 2014.

Shark Savers (2010) 'Honduras and the Maldives Join the Ranks of Shark Sanctuaries', *Shark Savers*, www.sharksavers.org/de/blogs-a-news/635-honduras-and-the-maldives-join-the-ranks-of-shark-sanctuaries.html, accessed 17 March 2010.

Techera, E. J. (2012) 'Fishing, Finning and Tourism: Trends in Pacific Shark Conservation and Management', *International Journal of Marine and Coastal Law*, vol. 27, no. 3, pp. 597–621.

Techera, E. J. and Klein, N. (2011) 'Fragmented Governance: Reconciling Legal Strategies for Shark Conservation and Management', *Marine Policy*, vol. 35, no. 1, pp. 73–78.

Techera, E. J. and Klein, N. (2012) 'Regulatory Tools for Shark Conservation and Management: Improving Legal Governance and Harnessing Eco-tourism' in O. P. Jenkins (ed.), *Advances in Zoology Research*, Vol. 3, Nova Science Publishers, New York, pp. 1–26.

Techera, E. J. and Klein, N. (2013) 'The Role of Law in Shark-Based Eco-Tourism: Lessons from Australia', *Marine Policy*, vol. 39, pp. 21–28.

United Nations Agreement for the Implementation of the Provisions of the United Nations Convention on the Law of the Sea of 10 December 1982 Relating to the Conservation and Management of Straddling Fish Stocks and Highly Migratory Fish Stocks, opened for signature 4 August 1995, 2167 UNTS 3 (entered into force 11 December 2011).

United Nations Convention on the Law of the Sea, opened for signature 10 December 1982, 1833 UNTS 3 (entered into force 16 November 1994).

WCPFC (2012), *Protection of Whale Sharks from Purse Seine Fishing Operations*, 5 December, Doc No. WCPFC9/2012.DP12/Rev 2, available at www.wcpfc.int/system/files/WCPFC9–2012-DP12rev2-Proposal-Australia-and-Japan-Protection-Whale-Sharks-Purse-Seine-Fishing-Operat.pdf, accessed 5 March 2014.

Chapter 3

Challenges for international governance

Mary Lack

Overview of international governance arrangements for sharks

Developments in international governance arrangements for sharks[1] have generally been reactive and in response to obvious depletion of stocks. While, it may be said, this is not uncharacteristic of fisheries management generally, it is an approach that is particularly detrimental to sharks, since they are inherently more vulnerable to overfishing than most of their teleost counterparts. Further, the emergence of shark products as widely traded fisheries commodities over the last 25 years has coincided with a period in which the need for the adoption of precautionary and ecosystem-based approaches to fisheries management generally has become widely accepted. In this environment, it might have been hoped that the mistakes leading to the need for retrospective management of species might have been behind us. However, sharks still struggle to attract the fisheries management attention they require.

Sharks as a group pose considerable challenges for effective governance. Shark species are found in all of the world's oceans and in a wide range of habitats including marine and freshwater and oceanic and coastal, and are taken by fishers in at least 150 countries. They are vulnerable to targeted and non-targeted fishing by a wide variety of gear in both artisanal and industrial fisheries. Governance is therefore required at national, regional and international levels. Currently, governance arrangements for sharks at each of these levels are piecemeal. They may relate to all or specific shark species, they vary in their rigour, comprehensiveness and effectiveness, and are variously binding and non-binding.

In broad terms, shark governance is guided and driven by:

- The *United Nations Convention on the Law of Sea* of 10 December 1982 (UNCLOS);
- The *United Nations Fish Stocks Agreement* (UNFSA);[2]
- The *Code of Conduct for Responsible Fisheries* (FAO, 1995);
- The International Plan of Action for the Conservation and Management of Sharks (IPOA-Sharks) (FAO, 2000a);

- national legislation and policy;
- the conventions of regional fisheries management organizations (RFMOs); and
- The *Convention on International Trade in Endangered Species of Wild Fauna and Flora* (CITES) and the *Convention on the Conservation of Migratory Species of Wild Animals* (CMS).

Of the list above, it is the IPOA-Sharks and its associated Technical Guidelines (FAO, 2000b) that provide the clearest guidance on the requirements for effective conservation and management of sharks. Much faith has been placed in the IPOA-Sharks to deliver improved shark governance, and it is true that it has informed actions by many states, regional fisheries organizations and other international conventions. Yet, despite a growing array of measures introduced under a range of instruments, concerns continue to be expressed for the status of many shark stocks and species (e.g. Worm *et al.*, 2013; Dulvy *et al.*, 2008).

The IUCN has assessed 1,090 Chondrichthyan species. Of those, 16 per cent are assessed as threatened, 12 per cent as near threatened and 46 per cent are identified as data deficient (IUCN, 2012). In 2008, a CMS Memorandum of Understanding (MoU) on migratory sharks was adopted and, in 2013, six commercially traded shark species were listed in Appendix II of CITES. These developments at the international level point to a failure of management at the national and regional level despite the introduction of the IPOA-Sharks. The contribution of the IPOA-Sharks to date, and its role in the ongoing efforts to ensure conservation and sustainable use of sharks, is examined below. The operation of, and challenges facing, the broader international governance system for sharks is then discussed.

The IPOA-Sharks

The IPOA-Sharks is one of a number of International Plans of Action (IPOAs) developed by the Food and Agriculture Organisation (FAO) to assist in the implementation of specific elements of the FAO Code of Conduct, which itself reflects the provisions of UNCLOS and the UNFSA. The IPOA-Sharks was developed in response to growing

> concern over the increase of shark catches and the consequences this has for the populations of some shark species in several areas of the world's oceans. This is because sharks often have a close stock–recruitment relationship, long recovery times in response to overfishing (low biological productivity because of late sexual maturity, few offspring, albeit with low natural mortality) and complex spatial structures (size/sex segregation and seasonal migration).
>
> (FAO, 2000a)

The IPOA-Sharks relates to all species of sharks, rays, skates and chimaeras (Class Chondrichthyes). It is voluntary in nature and provides guidance (see Box 3.1) on conservation and management of shark stocks in national waters and of transboundary, straddling, highly migratory and high seas stocks that are exploited by two or more countries. It is aimed at countries acting both individually and collectively through RFMOs. At the national level, it promotes the conduct of a Shark Assessment Report and the development of a National Plan of Action for the Conservation and Management of Sharks (NPOA-Sharks). It also encourages the development of Regional Plans of Action (RPOAs) by RFMOs where required. The ambitious goal of the IPOA-Sharks was that all relevant states have NPOAs in place by 2001.

Implementation and success of the IPOA

There has been ongoing concern about: the slow rate of implementation of the IPOA-Sharks; the extent to which actions purportedly taken under its name were consistent with its provisions; and, as a result, about the plan's effectiveness in improving the conservation and management of sharks. In 2002, the Shark Specialist Group of the IUCN and TRAFFIC[3] prepared a

Box 3.1 IPOA-Sharks Guidance on Plans of Action

The IPOA-Sharks suggests that plans of action should aim to:

- ensure that shark catches from directed and non-directed fisheries are sustainable;
- assess threats to shark populations, determine and protect critical habitats and implement harvesting strategies consistent with the principles of biological sustainability and rational long-term economic use;
- identify and provide special attention, in particular to vulnerable or threatened shark stocks;
- improve and develop frameworks for establishing and coordinating effective consultation involving all stakeholders in research, management and educational initiatives within and between states;
- minimize the unutilized incidental catches of sharks;
- contribute to the protection of biodiversity and ecosystem structure and function;
- minimize waste and discards from shark catches;
- encourage full use of dead sharks;
- facilitate improved species-specific catch and landings data and monitoring of shark catches; and
- facilitate the identification and reporting of species-specific biological and trade data.

report for the CITES Animals Committee on implementation of the IPOA-Sharks. That report found that: there had been a significant lack of progress made on implementation; very few countries had produced effective NPOAs and these were largely those states that already had effective shark management in place; and the large majority of those states that lacked shark management plans prior to the development and adoption of the IPOA-Sharks appeared not to have improved their capacity to manage sharks (CITES, 2002a, 2002b).

By 2005, only 10 per cent of the members of the Committee on Fisheries (COFI) had developed and implemented an NPOA-Sharks (COFI, 2005). A subsequent FAO expert consultation agreed that the IPOA-Sharks had not achieved the envisaged level of success and that concrete operational activities had been meagre and unsatisfactory. Further, it concluded that, in some instances, satisfactory implementation of the IPOA was interpreted as the mere articulation of an NPOA rather than the implementation of actions. The consultation also noted that the voluntary nature of the IPOA-Sharks was a major impediment to progress (FAO, 2006).

Five years later, similar findings emerged from an assessment of the status of shark management in the top shark-catching countries (Lack and Sant, 2011). That assessment concluded that

> shark fisheries are likely to be well managed in only a few of the Top 20 and that, although NPOAs are in place in these, there is no evidence to indicate that the NPOAs are responsible for the effective management of shark fisheries. It is possible to speculate that this management is more likely to reflect better resources and informed systems of fisheries management and governance overall. Many of the remaining Top 20 also have NPOAs, yet this analysis has failed to identify information that indicates that sharks are effectively managed. This suggests that the development of an NPOA may have become an end rather than the means.

An analysis of shark management in countries in the Coral Triangle and neighbouring countries arrived at similar conclusions (Lack and Sant, 2012).

The FAO reviewed implementation of the IPOA-Sharks in 2012 (Fischer *et al.*, 2012). The review found that 34 per cent of the 143 countries reporting shark catch in the decade to 2009 had adopted an NPOA-Sharks. The review focused on the 26 top shark-catching countries in that period, which accounted for 84 per cent of the catch. In relation to those countries, the review found that:

- 17 had adopted NPOAs and a further five had developed NPOAs and were in the process of adopting them. The NPOAs varied considerably with regard to their comprehensiveness, the detail on the nature and extent of their shark fisheries and fisheries management regimes and the extent to which they describe how the plan links to the existing legal and fisheries management systems. Most had included measurable targets and timelines, but only three NPOAs had been reviewed and updated.

- 19 had some form of specific conservation and management measures for sharks, although the type and extent of these measures varies considerably and not many have a comprehensive management regime for sharks in place. Fifteen had adopted shark finning[4] measures.
- 11 reported at least half of their shark catches to the FAO at species or genus levels, 11 report most or all of their catch at highly aggregated levels (order or class) and four report mainly at family level.

Overall, the FAO review provides no indication of the effectiveness of the conservation and management measures in place for shark species in the top 26 countries and provides no basis on which to determine whether those that have implemented NPOAs are managing their shark stocks more effectively than those that have not. Further, the review does not provide a basis to determine the relative comprehensiveness of NPOAs against the guidelines and principles of the IPOA-Sharks.

Based on the assessments undertaken to date, there is no clear evidence that the IPOA-Sharks has delivered improved management of sharks. The international community placed a lot of faith in the ability of the IPOA-Sharks to drive the necessary improvements in shark conservation and management. However, it has become increasingly clear that implementation has been slow and that, overall, this initiative has not delivered the anticipated outcomes (CITES, 2013a; FAO, 2012; Lack and Sant, 2011, 2012; Pew Environment Group, 2012; Techera and Klein, 2011; Worm *et al.*, 2013). Despite the fact that the IPOA-Sharks is a voluntary instrument, it remains surprising that, in an age of more enlightened fisheries management, the principles of the IPOA-Sharks have not delivered better outcomes.

The lack of progress in implementation of the IPOA-Sharks does not reflect on the quality of the instrument; the principles it espouses remain as relevant today as they were in 1999. The current situation does reflect a failure of countries and RFMOs responsible for its implementation. Many have paid lip service to the IPOA-Sharks, but it has taken a long time, if at all, for concrete actions to be implemented. The status of shark management at the national and regional levels is reviewed briefly below.

National management

National management arrangements for sharks, if they exist at all, are characterized by measures for a select number of target shark species, for species protected under national legislation and, to a lesser extent, by measures aimed at reducing shark by-catch. Some national measures reflect the implementation of obligations imposed by membership of regional or international arrangements.

Where national management exists, it is generally binding under fisheries legislation. However, as with fisheries management more broadly, the enforcement of such legislation is variable. National management measures may or may not be in the context of or consistent with the principles of the IPOA-Sharks.

The findings of recent examinations of available information on shark management in the top 20 shark-catching countries and countries in and around the Coral Triangle (Lack and Sant, 2011, 2012) are likely to typify the situation in many countries around the world. The findings included that there is:

- a lack of species identification in catch and trade data;
- a general failure to report shark catch to FAO in shark-specific categories;
- a general absence of specific management measures for sharks, despite sharks being targeted in a number of fisheries and by-catch of sharks, particularly rays, in some cases comprising large proportions of total catch in many others; and
- little evidence of measures being implemented at the national level to ensure compliance, where relevant, with shark reporting and management obligations to RFMOs.

Regional management

Some RFMOs have encouraged the implementation of the IPOA-Sharks by their members and have gradually improved their own management of highly migratory and straddling stocks of sharks through, for example, the adoption of some species-specific shark conservation and management measures (for species such as porbeagle (*Lamna nasus*), shortfin mako shark (*Isurus oxyrhinchus*), bigeye thresher shark (*Alopias superciliosus*) and oceanic whitetip shark (*Carcharhinus longimanus*)), the introduction of reporting requirements for shark catch and the implementation of controls on shark finning. These conservation and management measures may or may not be binding on the parties and, as is the case with national management, the extent of compliance with these measures is variable. Lack and Sant (2011) found that:

- many RFMO shark conservation and management measures, particularly those on shark finning, were ambiguous and included loopholes that could be exploited by members;
- reporting of shark catch remained voluntary in some RFMOs and that, even where reporting was mandatory, some of the major shark-catching countries did not provide data;
- there is no comprehensive, publicly available reporting on compliance with RFMO conservation and management measures; and
- there is little or no accountability, and a lack of sanctions, for non-compliance with shark conservation and management measures.

The international governance system for sharks

Other elements of the international governance system have begun to address the shortcomings in national and regional management of sharks. Actions taken under CITES and, to a lesser extent, the CMS are of particular significance. CITES (178 members) and CMS (119 members) have the potential to draw in a large number of countries catching and, in the case of CITES, trading shark. An increasing number of shark species are being added to the Appendices of both conventions (see Table 3.1). This reflects recognition that traditional

Table 3.1 Shark species listed on CITES and CMS

Species	*CITES Appendix (effective date)*	*CMS Appendix, date of listing*
Sawfishes Family Pristidae	Appendix I (2007 except for *Pristis microdon*, 2013)	
White shark *Carcharodon carcharias*	Appendix II (2005)	Appendix I/II (2002)
Basking shark *Cetorhinus maximus*	Appendix II (2003)	Appendix I/II (2005)
Whale shark *Rhincodon typus*	Appendix II (2003)	Appendix II (1999)
Porbeagle *Lamna nasus*	Appendix II (2014)	Appendix II (2008)
Scalloped hammerhead *Sphyrna lewini*	Appendix II (2014)	
Great hammerhead *S. mokarran*	Appendix II (2014)	
Smooth hammerhead *S. zygaena*	Appendix II (2014)	
Oceanic whitetip *Carcharhinus longimanus*	Appendix II (2014)	
Manta rays *Manta* spp.	Appendix II (2014)	
Manta ray *Manta birostris*		Appendix I/II (2011)
Northern hemisphere populations of spiny dogfish *Squalus acanthias*		Appendix II (2008)
Shortfin mako shark *Isurus oxyrinchus*		Appendix II (2008)
Longfin mako shark *Isurus paucus*		Appendix II (2008)

fisheries management actions for these species at the national and regional levels are inadequate.

CITES

Through a series of Resolutions and Decisions adopted since 1994, the parties to CITES have recognized the conservation threat that international trade poses to sharks and, since 2002, have expressed concern at the lack of progress in implementation of the IPOA-Sharks. In 2013, the CITES parties added a further six shark species to Appendix II (see Table 3.1). They also strengthened their Resolution on Sharks and Stingrays to highlight the need for reporting data on shark catch and trade to relevant national, regional and international authorities (CITES, 2013a), directed the secretariat to request the parties provide a summary of domestic laws and regulations that prohibit the landing of sharks or trade in shark and to collaborate with the FAO to develop a single, up-to-date source of information on RFMO measures for shark conservation and management. Parties were also encouraged to engage with the work of the CMS. Each of the 26 major shark-catching countries, with the exception of Taiwan, is a member of CITES.

CMS

CMS encourages the conclusion of legally binding agreements or of less formal, non-binding instruments, such as MoUs. An MoU on the Conservation of Migratory Sharks was developed in 2010 and has been signed by 26 of the CMS parties. However, only six of the major shark-catching countries have signed the MoU. The MoU relates to all shark species listed on the CMS Appendices (see Table 3.1), with the exception of *Manta birostris*. The signatories adopted a Conservation Plan for those shark species in 2012 that seeks to:

- improve understanding of migratory shark populations through research, monitoring and information exchange;
- ensure that directed and non-directed fisheries for sharks are sustainable;
- enforce, to the extent practicable, the protection of critical habitats and migratory corridors and critical life stages of sharks;
- increase public awareness of threats to sharks and their habitats and enhance public participation in conservation activities; and
- enhance national, regional and international cooperation.

International collaboration

Mechanisms for collaboration are in place between the three main players in the international governance of sharks, the FAO, CITES and CMS. There is an MoU in place between the CITES and CMS Secretariats and the CITES

Secretariat participated in the first meeting of the signatories to the CMS MoU where the Conservation Plan was adopted. There is also an MoU in place between the CITES secretariat and the FAO which includes, among other things, working together to consult on the scientific and technical evaluation of proposals for listing commercially exploited aquatic species in the CITES Appendices. In 2010, the CITES and FAO secretariats jointly convened a workshop to review the application and effectiveness of international regulatory measures for the conservation and sustainable use of sharks. The joint workshop concluded that harvest-related measures and trade-related measures could and should be used in tandem, where appropriate, to ensure the successful management of sharks and stingrays.

There is no doubt that the recent interventions by CITES and CMS on shark species are positive developments and indicate that at the international level, the governance system for sharks is working. However, these initiatives cover only a fraction of shark species and the potential reach of these conventions to shark species is limited. The CITES listings relate only to six commercially important internationally traded species. The status of shark species which are not traded internationally cannot be supported through CITES. The CMS MoU is, similarly, restricted to a select number of migratory shark species and the Convention does not apply to less wide-ranging shark species. Further, implementation of the provisions of the CMS Shark Conservation Plan is voluntary.

While these international initiatives provide much-needed incentives for stronger shark management, they cannot be relied upon to deliver the necessary changes required at the national and regional levels.

Impediments to implementation of effective shark management globally

Considerable effort has been devoted to determining to what extent the IPOA-Sharks has been implemented. Ultimately, the more important goal is to ensure that the management arrangements in place for sharks are improved to the point where declines in stock status have been halted, depleted shark stocks are being rebuilt and management measures preclude other shark stocks being overfished. Whether this is done in the context of the IPOA-Sharks is essentially irrelevant. The reviews of shark management conducted to date suggest that, globally, there has been increased attention paid to shark species and that there are examples of improvements in species identification, reporting and management at all levels (Lack and Sant, 2012; FAO, 2012). However, stock status remains a concern. The complexity and diversity of the biology and life history characteristics of sharks, of the fisheries in which they are taken, of the management frameworks in which those fisheries operate and in the markets for shark products continue to challenge effective governance of sharks. These factors will affect the quality of shark management regardless of whether it occurs in the context of the IPOA-Sharks.

There are over 1,000 species of chondrichthyans and they are taken in fisheries in over 150 countries from marine and freshwater habitats, in shallow coastal waters, in the deep sea and in open oceans. Not surprisingly, therefore, the life history and biological characteristics of shark species vary considerably. This variation is not consistent with a generic approach to shark management. Effective shark management will be species-based.

The nature of the fisheries in which sharks are taken varies from artisanal and subsistence fisheries to large-scale industrial fisheries. Because sharks can be taken in a wide variety of fishing gear, including trawl nets, gillnets, purse seines and longlines, they can be targeted, and are susceptible to being taken as by-catch, in numerous fisheries. Effective shark management will be tailored to the type of gear, fishery and shark catch.

Retained shark catch can be utilized for a range of markets, including for meat, fins, shark liver oil, cartilage and skin. The value of these products varies from species to species. Some shark species are caught and retained for consumption in local communities or for sale on domestic markets. Others are taken in national waters or on the high seas and fins and/or meat traded internationally. Effective shark management will take into account the nature of the markets for shark products and, in the absence of effective shark management, consumer campaigns against shark products may be required. Such campaigns have already begun to have a significant impact on consumption of shark fin, particularly in China and Hong Kong (see, for example, Horton, 2013).

While governance arrangements for sharks may be introduced at the national, regional or international level, ultimately, implementation of those measures occurs at the national level. A country can implement measures to manage shark stocks occurring in its waters in line with its domestic obligations to manage its marine resources. If it is a member of an RFMO it may need to implement other measures consistent with decisions taken by that RFMO with respect to sharks. If a state is bound by CITES, it will, for example, need to make non-detriment findings[5] for all Appendix II listed species of sharks in order to trade those species internationally. Likewise, depending on the nature of the CMS arrangement, a state may be bound to implement measures in response to the listing of shark species in the CMS Appendices. However, the capacity to implement effective shark management, and fisheries management generally, at the national level varies widely. Effective shark management will require targeted assistance to ensure that management capacity is appropriate.

Improving shark governance

It is no longer appropriate to rely on the IPOA-Sharks to generate the management actions required to deliver sustainable populations of sharks. While the guidance provided by the IPOA-Sharks remains valid, implementation of the principles of the IPOA requires additional support.

There have been suggestions that there is a need for a new, dedicated international agreement (e.g. Worm *et al.*, 2013) on sharks and/or for a new international body such as a shark commission (e.g. Herndon *et al.*, 2010). The development of a new shark agreement is, however, likely to suffer the same problems as other agreements; either there is a low level of ratification or ratification occurs but implementation is poor. Experience with the IPOA-Sharks has shown that, generally speaking, the countries that are in the best position to implement its provisions are likely to be those that have stronger fisheries management frameworks and are in fact the least likely to benefit from the IPOA. The same is likely to be true of a dedicated shark agreement.

Similarly, calls for a dedicated shark commission are unlikely to achieve the improvements in shark governance required. While superficially attractive, such a commission would have considerable overlap, in both mandate and membership, with many existing RFMOs. Many of those RFMOs would be all too willing to transfer their responsibility for ensuring sustainable shark stocks to another body. However, whether such a body could effectively manage by-catch in the RFMOs' fisheries is doubtful, particularly since RFMOs have struggled to get sufficient traction across their membership to implement effective shark management measures. Further, the funding of the existing RFMOs is already stretching the capacity and/or goodwill of their members and it is unlikely that the funds would be available to support the effective operation of an additional body.

As evidenced above, there is already a sophisticated legislative and administrative infrastructure through which better management of sharks can be pursued. Rather than extend that infrastructure, a new multi-faceted and more targeted approach to improvements in shark governance is required. This approach requires that:

- obligations exist at national, regional and international levels to ensure that shark species are not overexploited;
- the capacity exists at the national level to ensure that shark management can be implemented effectively;
- fisheries management at all levels recognizes that sharks are a fisheries commodity that warrants the same management priority as other commercial fisheries products;
- shark catch and trade data exist at appropriate levels of resolution for monitoring at national, regional and international levels;
- management of sharks moves from a generic level to a species-specific basis; and
- an effective and recognized source of advocacy for shark management that can provide reliable best practice advice on shark management, and shark by-catch mitigation in particular, for both artisanal and industrial fisheries is established.

Obligations

Obligations exist at the international level for signatories to UNCLOS and the UNFSA to ensure that marine resources, including sharks, are not overexploited. Most national fisheries legislation is couched in similar terms. The conventions establishing RFMOs usually establish a mandate with respect to certain species or groups of species. Management of sharks may be mandated under those conventions as a result of them being highly migratory species or, more commonly, through the conventions' requirements relating to management of by-catch. However, the mere existence of obligations does not ensure that they are met. This problem exists at all levels of governance and is not confined to sharks. Whether obligations are met by countries acting individually or collectively will depend on factors including:

- the availability of human, institutional or financial capacity to address the complexities involved in managing a wide range of shark species across numerous fisheries;
- the economic and social trade-offs involved in restricting shark mortality, particularly where local communities with limited alternative employment and income-producing opportunities are reliant on sharks as either food or income; and
- whether there are sanctions in place for non-compliance with regional or international measures.

These factors affect countries' willingness to agree to regional and international measures to manage shark effectively even where the obligation exists to do so. Further, even if such measures are adopted, implementation may not be possible.

Improving national capacity

As noted above, sharks are taken in more than 150 countries. However, 26 countries account for 84 per cent of the catch (see Table 3.2).

There is little doubt that if sharks were effectively managed in these 26 countries there would be a significant improvement in the status of shark stocks globally. Further, within this group several countries have well-developed fisheries management regimes and have developed shark NPOAs. Thus, while at first glance the task of improving shark conservation and management may seem daunting, it becomes more manageable if global efforts are targeted towards areas where the biggest gains are achievable. For example, focusing efforts on Indonesia and India alone would address more than 20 per cent of the shark catch.

The task is also made less intimidating if attempts to improve shark governance take an iterative approach, particularly in countries with limited fisheries

Table 3.2 Top shark-catching countries, 2002–2011

Rank	*Country*	*2002–2011 (tonnes)*	*% reported catch*	*Cumulative total %*
1	Indonesia	1,048,473	13.25	
2	India	742,074	9.38	22.63
3	Spain	585,167	7.39	30.02
4	Taiwan Province of China	438,151	5.54	35.56
5	Argentina	374,256	4.73	40.29
6	Mexico	337,804	4.27	44.56
7	United States	336,784	4.26	48.81
8	Malaysia	231,212	2.92	51.74
9	Pakistan	225,633	2.85	54.59
10	Brazil	209,912	2.65	57.24
11	Japan	203,396	2.57	59.81
12	France	199,580	2.52	62.33
13	New Zealand	175,471	2.22	64.55
14	Thailand	173,421	2.19	66.74
15	Portugal	172,465	2.18	68.92
16	Nigeria	159,023	2.01	70.93
17	Iran (Islamic Republic of)	141,212	1.78	72.72
18	Sri Lanka	135,579	1.71	74.43
19	Korea, Republic of	119,381	1.51	75.94
20	Yemen	102,233	1.29	77.23
21	United Kingdom	98,798	1.25	78.48
22	Peru	92,745	1.17	79.65
23	Australia	91,420	1.16	80.81
24	Canada	90,162	1.14	81.94
25	Venezuela, Bolivarian Republic of	82,893	1.05	82.99
26	Senegal	80,322	1.02	84.01
	Other countries	1,265,512	15.99	100.0
	Total	7,913,079		

Source: FAO Fisheries Department 2013.

management capacity, which is likely to be the case in at least half of the countries listed in Table 3.2. Where human and financial resources for fisheries management are limited and governance arrangements and infrastructure are not well developed, a more pragmatic approach to implementing the 'spirit' rather than the 'letter' of the IPOA-Sharks may be required (FAO, 2009). Lack and Sant (2012) have suggested an iterative, structured approach that could be applied in these circumstances. Such approaches can include ecological risk assessments for shark species that identify those species at most risk from fishing. This provides a clear focus for the application of available management resources.

Data

A central constraint to implementation of shark management continues to be a lack of species-specific catch data. Even where shark management measures have been implemented, assessment of their effectiveness is practically impossible in the absence of good catch data.

At the global level, there remains considerable uncertainty about the global catch of sharks and, in particular, the catch of particular species of sharks. In the decade to 2011, 147 countries reported shark catch to the FAO. During that decade, nearly eight million tonnes of shark catch was reported. Annual reported shark catch peaked in 2003 at 896,000 tonnes and has been trending downwards since then, reaching 766,000 tonnes in 2011. However, these catch figures do not provide an accurate account of global shark catch or, more importantly, fishing-induced shark mortality. The FAO figures are known to underestimate global catch because not all fishing countries are members of the FAO, some FAO members either do not report fisheries catch at all to the FAO or report shark catch under more generic fisheries headings so it cannot be separately identified, and FAO data do not include discards (see Lack and Sant, 2011). Inevitably, the FAO data also excludes any shark catch taken in illegal, unregulated and/or unreported fishing.

Various other estimates of global shark catch have been made. Most recently, Worm *et al.* (2013) estimated that the global catch and mortality of sharks from reported and unreported landings, discards and shark finning was 1.44 million tonnes in 2000 and only slightly less at 1.41 million tonnes in 2010. Earlier, Clarke *et al.* (2006) used Hong Kong auction data for shark fins to estimate that the total mass of sharks caught for the fin trade in 2000 ranged between 1.21 and 2.29 million tonnes. Thus, while the FAO data remain the most comprehensive available, it is in all likelihood a significant underestimate of shark mortality. Further, since less than 30 per cent of the shark catches reported to FAO are reported at a species level, meaningful trends in catch of particular shark species cannot be inferred from the data.

This inability to discern fishing impacts on particular species and stocks is a major impediment to effective management, particularly for those oceanic species that are taken by vessels from many countries. In some well-managed target shark fisheries, catch data are available on a species basis. However, in other fisheries, where sharks may be targeted, for example, in small-scale/artisanal fisheries that remain largely unmanaged, there is little or no catch recording either in total or on a species basis. In addition, a large proportion of shark catch is by-catch and in most cases, in both small-scale and industrial fisheries, recording of by-catch is either not required or is unreliable. Even where reporting is required, accurate species identification is lacking. Shark species identification programmes are clearly a key first step in improving the quality of shark catch data for management purposes.

Trade data can be a useful tool for identifying countries that catch but do not report shark catch and for monitoring the effectiveness of catch limits on shark species. However, there is little species-specific data on shark trade. International shark trade information is not documented to the species level in the Harmonized Tariff Schedule. Few countries report species-specific shark trade data to the FAO. This reflects both the lack of species identification in catch data and the few species-specific trade codes in place in most countries. For example, Lack and Sant (2011) found that in reporting shark trade to the FAO, 13 of the top 20 shark-catching countries provided no species breakdown, five provided very limited species breakdown and only two provided a breakdown for all major species caught. The lack of trade data has compounded the difficulties associated with successfully listing commercially fished shark species on CITES. For example, the 2013 proposals for listing of oceanic whitetip shark, scalloped hammerhead shark and porbeagle each noted the lack of species-specific trade data (CITES 2013b, 2013c, 2013d).

Species-specific management

As noted above, sharks vary in their life histories, biological characteristics, habitats and vulnerability to overfishing. The absence of accurate catch data on shark species has resulted in 'generic' shark management approaches that attempt to minimize total shark mortality. These measures include shark finning controls (see Box 3.2), shark sanctuaries and controls on the use of certain fishing gear e.g. wire leaders and size and configuration of hooks. There will remain a role for these measures. However, they ignore the fundamental differences in shark species' life history and relative vulnerability to overfishing and must, over time, be complemented or replaced by species-specific management measures that ensure that the most vulnerable species are adequately protected.

In the same way that the international community seeks to manage species of tuna rather than 'tunas', there is an urgent need at all levels of management and in all fishery contexts for sharks to be managed by species. There is some evidence of moves in this direction, particularly at the international level, with species of sharks now listed on the CMS and CITES and with a number of

Box 3.2 Shark finning controls

The 'generic' approach to shark management is well illustrated by the now widespread adoption of shark finning controls. Shark finning controls require, in broad terms, that the whole shark carcass be retained (either intact or with fins removed). These controls have been a very popular response by RFMOs, particularly the tuna RFMOs, to calls for improved management of sharks. While they may provide some disincentive for targeting sharks in multi-species fisheries and may address concerns about wastage, shark finning controls provide no species-specific protection, do not preclude the highgrading[6] of sharks and, unless strictly enforced, may have little or no impact on total shark mortality.

RFMOs having implemented species-specific conservation measures for sharks. However, there remains an apparent unwillingness to apply the same level of management rigour to most shark species as is applied to many other fish species. There are relatively few shark stocks globally, for example, for which stock assessments have been completed or for which there are binding limits on catch.

Sharks as a commercial fisheries product

Traditionally, sharks have received a lower level of fisheries management priority. This probably reflects that many shark species have been taken predominantly as by-catch to other targeted fishing operations for commercially important species. Further, until the relatively recent past, there have been limited markets for the meat of many shark species and therefore relatively few target shark fisheries have emerged as commercial fisheries.

More recently, however, markets for the meat of more shark species have been identified and the demand for shark fins has increased. These developments place sharks in a more vulnerable position. Sharks taken as by-catch that were once released alive due to lack of markets are now more likely to be retained for their fins and/or their meat, increasing the mortality of sharks. Further, the market for these products is now driving increased targeting of sharks. This is further encouraged by the deteriorating status of stocks of other target fisheries and the need for excess fishing capacity, including that used in illegal, unregulated and/or unreported fishing, to access other resources. High-value shark fins are a particularly attractive alternative.

Sharks must now be recognized as a commercial fisheries resource and managed accordingly. All the components of best practice fisheries management must be brought to bear on shark species, regardless of whether they are retained or discarded. The use of ecological risk assessments can be a useful and cost-effective mechanism for identifying priority shark species and ensuring that the relative vulnerabilities of shark species are reflected in the management approaches adopted. For those shark species or stocks that are already identified as being overfished, rebuilding strategies must be implemented. Shark species with special conservation status must be protected and fishing impacts carefully monitored.

Advocacy

To date, the FAO, through its promotion of the IPOA-Sharks, has been the recognized advocacy body for shark management. However, the nature and extent of the FAO's advocacy role is dictated by its members and available resources.

A growing number of environmental non-government organizations (NGOs) have become actively engaged in promoting and monitoring the implementation of the IPOA-Sharks, in highlighting the deteriorating status of global shark stocks and in promoting shark conservation and management measures more broadly. This has increased the profile of sharks considerably. However, there is little coordination of actions or objectives across these groups and it is likely that agreement on, and allocation of responsibilities for pursuing, core priorities for shark management improvements would be more cost-effective and productive.

There is no single recognized body that champions the cause of sharks and provides coherent and credible advice on shark conservation and management at the level of detail required to ensure that best-practice approaches are adopted. Given the lack of fisheries management capacity in many major shark-catching countries, the existence of such a body may be a cost-effective way to encourage implementation of effective shark management measures. Further, the reluctance or inability of RFMOs to address shark management issues may be reduced through the provision of external advice on the issues from a reputable body.

Actions under the Agreement for the Conservation of Albatrosses and Petrels (ACAP), developed under the CMS, provide well-regarded data, information and research on seabird by-catch mitigation and effective advocacy of management, particularly in RFMOs. The ACAP model provides a strong example of the type of advocacy and advice required to support effective shark management.

Discussion

The IPOA-Sharks and other initiatives have raised the profile of sharks in the international community. Management of sharks involves many of the same challenges as management of other fish species taken either as target catch or by-catch. One unintended consequence of the focus on sharks over the last 15 years may have been to isolate sharks from regular fisheries management. This is in fact the opposite of what is required. It is now time to ensure that, while the special needs of sharks are reflected in management, sharks are regarded as either target species that must be managed according to the same principles and methods as other commercial species, as by-catch which should be minimized or as protected species that must be conserved. An additional and increasingly recognized use of sharks is for eco-tourism purposes, acknowledging that in some instances sharks are worth more alive in the water than dead on the market.

Resources are limited and efforts to improve shark management must be better targeted to where the greatest gains can be made. This involves:

- focusing on implementation of the principles of the IPOA-Sharks in a step-wise rather than holistic way;
- tailoring initiatives to meet the needs of specific fishery and fishery management contexts;

- focusing on major catching countries where shark management is known to be lacking;
- focusing on those shark species at highest risk;
- improving data collection processes and reporting supported by programmes to assist species identification of the catch; and
- developing and advocating adoption of effective by-catch mitigation measures for sharks.

There is an increasing willingness in the international community to manage shark species. However, the vast majority of shark species and stocks remain unmanaged. Improved international governance of sharks requires a change in mindset at all levels. However, as described above, the management context for shark species is especially complex. Effective management of this group of species will involve the application of the latest fisheries management assessment methods, innovative and tailored approaches and strong enforcement. Where fisheries management capacity is lacking, support will be required. In the first instance, support to ensure the effective implementation of CITES listings for shark species will be an imperative.

Notes

1 Sharks refers to all species of chondrichthyans.
2 *United Nations Agreement for the Implementation of the Provisions of the United Nations Convention on the Law of the Sea of 10 December 1982 Relating to the Conservation and Management of Straddling Fish Stocks and Highly Migratory Fish Stocks* (in force as from 11 December 2001).
3 TRAFFIC, the wildlife trade monitoring network, works to ensure that trade in wild plants and animals is not a threat to the conservation of nature.
4 Shark finning is the removal and retention of shark fins and the discarding of the shark trunk.
5 A 'non-detriment finding' means that the country must confirm that the export of listed species will not be detrimental to the survival of the species and that the product being exported was legally obtained.
6 'Highgrading' refers to the practice of discarding already captured and dead fish in favour of higher-value fish.

References

CITES (2002a) *Report on Implementation of the International Plan of Action for Sharks (IPOA-Sharks)*, Eighteenth meeting of the Animals Committee, San Jose, Costa Rica, 8–12 April 2002, AC18 Doc 19.2.

CITES (2002b) *Update: Report on Implementation of the International Plan of Action for Sharks (IPOA-Sharks)*, Eighteenth meeting of the Animals Committee. San Jose, Costa Rica, 8–12 April 2002, AC18 Inf 10.

CITES (2013a) *Resolution Conf. 12.6 (Rev CoP16) Conservation and Management of Shark* (Class Chondrichthyes), CoP16 Com.1.10.

CITES (2013b) *Consideration of Proposals for Amendment of Appendices I and II: Proposal for inclusion of* Carcharhinus longimanus, CoP16 Prop 42.

CITES (2013c) *Consideration of Proposals for Amendment of Appendices I and II: Proposal for inclusion of* Spyrna lewini, CoP16 Prop 4.

CITES (2013d) *Consideration of Proposals for Amendment of Appendices I and II: Proposal for inclusion of* Lamna nasus, CoP16 Prop 4.

Clarke, S. E., McAllister, M. K., Milner-Gulland, E. J., Kirkwood, G. P., Michielsens, C. G. J., Agnew, D. J., Pikitch, E. K., Nakano, H. and Shivji, M. S. (2006) 'Global Estimates of Shark Catches Using Trade Records from Commercial Markets', *Ecology Letters*, vol. 9, pp. 1115–1126.

COFI (2005) *Progress in the Implementation of the Code of Conduct for Responsible Fisheries and Related International Plans of Action*, Committee on Fisheries, Twenty-sixth Session, Rome, Italy, 7–11 March 2005, COFI/2005/2.

Dulvy, N. K., Baum., J. A., Clarke, S., Compagno, L. J. V., Cortés, E., Domingo, A., Fordham, S., Fowler, S., Francis, M. P., Gibson, C., Martínez, J., Musick, J. A., Soldo, A., Stevens, J. D. and Valenti, S. (2008) 'You Can Swim But You Can't Hide: The Global Status and Conservation of Oceanic Pelagic Sharks and Rays', *Aquatic Conservation, Marine and Freshwater Ecosystems*, vol. 18, pp. 459–482.

FAO (1995) *Code of Conduct for Responsible Fisheries*, FAO, Rome.

FAO (2000a) *International Plan of Action for the Conservation and Management of Sharks*, FAO, Rome.

FAO (2000b) *Fisheries Management 1: Conservation and Management of Sharks*, FAO Technical Guidelines for Responsible Fisheries, No. 4, Supp 1, FAO, Rome.

FAO (2006) *Report of the FAO Expert Consultation on the Implementation of the FAO International Plan of Action for the Conservation and Management of Sharks*, FAO Fisheries Report No. 795, FAO, Rome.

FAO (2009) *Report of the Technical Workshop on the Status, Limitations and Opportunities for Improving the Monitoring of Shark Fisheries and Trade*, FAO Fisheries and Aquaculture Report No. 897, FAO, Rome.

FAO (2012) *Report of the FAO/CITES Workshop to Review the Application and Effectiveness of International Regulatory Measures for the Conservation and Sustainable Use of Elasmobranchs*, Fisheries and Aquaculture Report No. R984, FAO, Rome.

FAO Fisheries Department (2013) *Global Capture Production 1950–2011*, FAO, Rome.

Fischer, J., Erikstein, K., D'Offay, B., Guggusberg, S. and Barine, M. (2012) *Review of the Implementation of the International Plan of Action for the Conservation and Management of Sharks*, FAO Fisheries and Aquaculture Circular No. 1076, FAO, Rome.

Herndon, A., Gallucci, V. F., DeMaster, D. and Burke, W. (2010) 'The Case for an International Commission for the Conservation and Management of Sharks (ICCMS)', *Marine Policy*, vol. 34, no. 6, pp. 1239–1248.

Horton, C. (2013) 'Is the Shark-fin Trade Facing Extinction?', *The Atlantic*, www.theatlantic.com/china/archive/2013/08/is-the-shark-fin-trade-facing-extinction/278591/, accessed 12 August 2013.

IUCN (2012) *The IUCN Red List of Threatened Species. Version 2012.2*, available at www.iucnredlist.org, accessed 14 May 2013.

Lack, M. and Sant, G. (2011) *The Future of Sharks: A Review of Action and Inaction*, TRAFFIC International, Cambridge, and the Pew Environment Group, Washington, DC.

Lack, M. and Sant, G. (2012) *An Overview of Shark Utilisation in the Coral Triangle Region*, TRAFFIC International, London.

Pew Environment Group (2012) *Navigating Global Shark Conservation: Current Measures and Gaps*, available at www.pewenvironment.org/uploadedFiles/PEG/Publications/Report/Navigating%20Global%20Shark%20Conservation_Current%20Measures%20and%20Gaps%207%206%2012.pdf, accessed 16 May 2013.

Techera, E. J. and Klein, N. (2011) 'Fragmented Governance: Reconciling Legal Strategies for Shark Conservation and Management', *Marine Policy*, vol. 35, no. 1, pp. 73–78.

Worm, B., Davis, B., Kettemer, L., Ward-Paige, C. A., Chapman, D., Heithaus, M. R., Kessel, S. T. and Gruber, S. H. (2013) 'Global Catches, Exploitation Rates and Rebuilding Options for Sharks', *Marine Policy*, vol. 40, pp. 194–204.

Part II

Scientific perspectives

Chapter 4

The state of knowledge on sharks for conservation and management

Jeremy J. Kiszka and Michael R. Heithaus

Introduction

Sharks (Selachii) occur in all oceans, from coastal habitats (including up through some freshwater habitats) to oceanic waters, from the surface to depths of more than 3,000 metres (Priede *et al.*, 2006). Sharks also display an amazing diversity of body sizes at maturity – from 17–20 cm for dwarf lantern sharks (*Etmopterus perryi*) to 1,250–1,400 cm for whale sharks (*Rhincodon typus*), as well as feeding modes – from planktivorous whale and basking sharks (*Cetorhinus maximus*) to apex predators like white sharks (*Carcharodon carcharias*). Most elasmobranchs (sharks and rays) and the related chimaeras are characterized by relatively low fecundity and productivity, slow growth, late age at maturity, large size at birth, high natural survivorship and a long life. Such biological characteristics have serious implications for the sustainability of elasmobranch fisheries. Not surprisingly, these species generally have limited capacity to sustain and recover from heavy fishing pressure, including both direct exploitation and incidental catches (or by-catch) (e.g. Dulvy *et al.*, 2008).

A detailed understanding of the biology and ecology of sharks is critical to developing and implementing effective management measures and providing a rationale for their conservation (see Simpfendorfer *et al.*, 2011). The past decade has seen a considerable rise in studies of sharks that have greatly increased the scientific knowledge about these species from a diversity of habitats and regions around the world, including deep-sea ecosystems. Although considerable gaps remain, advances in technology and techniques and developing research infrastructure and interest in sharks worldwide are facilitating shark research. In this chapter, we provide a brief review of some aspects of the biology and ecology of sharks with the goal of providing an entry to the primary literature. A complete review is far beyond the scope of this chapter. Indeed, a number of recent volumes have been published on the biology of elasmobranchs (e.g. Carrier *et al.*, 2004, 2010, 2012 for elasmobranchs; Camhi *et al.*, 2008 for sharks of the open ocean) that contain detailed reviews of the topics that we will explore. In addition, Simpfendorfer *et al.* (2011) provide an outstanding list of research questions that are important for generating effective conservation and management outcomes and review some of the recent research in these areas.

We will not explore issues of exploitation and population trajectories directly in this chapter because they are detailed in several other chapters in this volume.

Evolution and taxonomy

Sharks (and chondrichtyans at large) have survived successive mass extinctions over the last 400 million years (Grogan *et al.*, 2012). The first evidence of the existence of sharks dates from over 450–420 million years ago, before land vertebrates existed and many plants had colonized continents. Sharks form a monophyletic group that diverged from rays 430–355 million years ago that then split into two major clades, Squalimorphii and Galeomorophii, approximately 390–310 million years ago (Heinicke *et al.*, 2009). Modern sharks, however, first appeared around 100 million years ago, with the most recently evolved families being hammerhead sharks (Sphyrnidae) (Heinicke *et al.*, 2009). Higher-order relationships of sharks are relatively well-resolved (e.g. Naylor *et al.*, 2012a) and among the approximately 1,200 species of cartilaginous fishes known, the more than 500 species of sharks are assigned to eight orders:

1 Carcharhiniformes (over 270 species). DNA analyses suggest Carcharhiniformes do not constitute a single monophyletic group. This order includes requiem sharks (Carcharhinidae), weasel sharks (Hemigaleidae), cat sharks (Scyliorhinidae), false cat sharks (Pseudotriakidae), finback cat sharks (Proscylliidae), houndsharks (Triakidae), barbelled houndsharks (Leptochariidae) and hammerhead sharks (Sphyrnidae). Carcharhiniformes constitute a group of species occurring in virtually all marine ecosystems, but also estuarine (brackish) and freshwater environments.
2 Heterodontiformes (nine species). Bullhead sharks form a single family (Heterodontidae) of bottom sharks from tropical and subtropical waters.
3 Hexanchiformes (six species). This order contains the most primitive sharks, including cow (Hexanchidae) and frilled sharks (Chlamydoselachidae).
4 Lamniformes (17 species). This order contains the Lamnidae (mackerel shark), including the extinct *Carcharodon megalodon* and the great white and mako sharks, thresher sharks (Alopiidae), basking shark (Cetorhinidae), megamouth shark (*Megachasma pelagios*, Megachasmidae), goblin shark (*Mitsukurina owstoni*, Mitsukurinidae), sand sharks (Odontaspididae) and crocodile shark (*Pseudocarcharias kamoharai*, Pseudocarchariidae).
5 Orectolobiformes (44 species). These include the whale shark (*Rhincodon typus*, Rhincodontidae), zebra shark (*Stegostoma fasciatum*, Stegostomatidae), nurse sharks (Ginglymostomatidae), blind sharks (Brachaeluridae), bamboo sharks (Hemiscylliidae), wobbegong sharks (Orectolobidae) and collared carpet sharks (Parascylliidae).

6 Pristiophoriformes (seven species). The order includes two genera of sawsharks (*Pliotrema*, with only one species *Pliotrema warreni*) and *Pristiophorus* (*Pristiophorus* spp).
7 Squaliformes (126 species). This order comprises a diversity of species occurring from tropical to polar waters, from coastal shallow to deep waters. Seven families have been identified, including gulper sharks (Centrophoridae), kitefin sharks (Dalatidae), bramble sharks (Echinorhinidae), lantern sharks (Etmopteridae), rough sharks (Oxynotidae), sleeper sharks (Somniosidae) and dogfish sharks (Squalidae).
8 Squatiniformes (23 species). These are angel sharks, represented by a single family (Squatinidae) and genus (*Squatina*). Angel sharks have a wide range from tropical to temperate waters, and one species occurs in deep waters.

Genus- and species-level relationships of sharks remain important areas of research (see Naylor *et al.*, 2012a, 2012b) and new species – including some cryptic species – continue to be described (see discussion in Heist, 2012). Substantial advances in genetic techniques and reductions in sequencing costs have greatly facilitated taxonomic work and continue to provide important insights into the evolution and diversity of sharks (Naylor *et al.*, 2012b) as well as in facilitating species identifications in trade monitoring (e.g. Shivji *et al.*, 2002; Heist, 2012). There remain, however, important unresolved issues in lower-level phylogenies, including for the Carcharhiniformes and deep-water species (e.g. *Squalus* spp.), which are facing increasing exploitation in a number of regions (Dulvy and Reynolds, 2009; Last and Stevens, 2009; Kyne and Simpfendorfer, 2010). Therefore, a major challenge for shark research and management is the improvement of knowledge on shark taxonomy, as a number of species could disappear before we even know they exist (Simpfendorfer *et al.*, 2011).

Reproductive biology and life history

A knowledge of basic life history traits and reproductive biology are critical to understanding population dynamics and effectively managing shark populations (Walker, 1998; Simpfendorfer *et al.*, 2011). Sharks display a diverse array of reproductive modes, but all species display internal fertilization (see Conrath and Musick, 2012). Embryonic nutrition is provided entirely through yolk in some species (lecithotrophic). In oviparous species, eggs may be laid one pair at a time or retained inside the female's body for some time before being laid. Most oviparous species are small and all are demersal (Musick and Ellis, 2005). Yolk-sac viviparity is more widespread taxonomically and is found in all extant orders of sharks other than the Heterodontiformes and Lamniformes (Conrath and Musick, 2012). These species use only yolk for development, but mothers retain eggs inside their bodies until they hatch. In general, species with yolk sac viviparity have fewer, larger young than oviparous species (Musick and Ellis, 2005).

In many shark species, embryos complete development within the mother and receive additional maternal resources up until birth (Conrath and Musick, 2012). In some species, maternal resources may be provided even beyond birth in the form of large livers that can serve as energy reserves until young sharks become proficient foragers (e.g. Belicka *et al.*, 2012). There are several ways in which females deliver additional nutrients to their young, including mucoid histotrophy (where embryos feed on mucus produced by the uterus) and placental viviparity (where species develop a yolk sac placenta after yolk is consumed) (Conrath and Musick, 2012). Placental viviparity is widespread in the Carcharhiniformes. In oophagy, embryos consume unfertilized eggs produced by the mother. In Lamniformes, unfertilized eggs continue to be produced throughout at least a portion of pregnancy. In sand tiger sharks (*Carcharias taurus*) the first embryo to hatch within each uterus will consume both unfertilized eggs and all other embryos within that uterus (Gilmore *et al.*, 1983). Finally, parthenogenesis[1] has been observed in captive sharks, but it is unclear whether it occurs in the wild (Chapman, 2007, 2008).

The time between reproductive events (reproductive cycle) varies across sharks (see species accounts in Compagno, 1990; Last and Stevens, 2009). Females of some species reproduce annually, while others may be on cycles of two years or more. In some species, these cycles are driven by gestation periods longer than a year, while in other species 12-month gestation periods are followed by a year of rest. Reproductive intervals may also vary among individuals of a species (Conrath and Musick, 2012).

Studies of shark age and growth have increased dramatically in the last several decades and are providing important information, including age and size at maturity and longevity, that are important for population models that form the foundation of shark management plans (for a review, see Goldman *et al.*, 2012). Unlike teleost fish, sharks tend to possess life history characteristics – large size, slow growth, late maturity, low fecundity, high inter-birth interval, long lifespan – that are characteristic of 'K-selected' species. Although all of these characteristics can vary considerably among taxa and habitats – for example, the number of young per reproductive cycle can vary from two to over 300 young (Conrath and Musick, 2012) and maximum life spans that are 15–25 years on average can reach up to 100 years – the reproductive potential of populations renders most sharks moderately to highly vulnerable to overexploitation (e.g. Dulvy *et al.*, 2008; Stevens, 2010; Conrath and Musick, 2012).

Unfortunately, we still lack basic life history data for many species and populations and continued research will be critical for developing optimal management strategies. In many cases, these data require lethal sampling of individuals or obtaining carcasses from fisheries (Heupel and Simpfendorfer, 2010). Cortés *et al.* (2012) suggest that enhancing the quantity and quality of empirical data is critical to improving the predictive power of population models, especially as models become more realistic, justifying such sampling.

Population structure and dynamics

Because of their central role in fisheries management, population structure and dynamics have been the focus of considerable research, but much work remains to be done (for a recent review, see Cortés *et al.*, 2012). Of particular importance are understanding stock–recruitment curves, or how population size influences recruitment of new individuals, and patterns of density-dependence, especially compensatory reproduction in the face of exploitation. Also critical to management and understanding population dynamics is understanding the life history stages where populations are most sensitive to increased (or decreased) mortality. For example, it has often been thought that many shark populations were limited by mortality that occurred in nursery areas and soon after birth (Kinney and Simpfendorfer, 2009). Indeed, density-dependent survival has been observed in nurseries of several species, including lemon sharks (*Negaprion brevirostris*) (Gruber *et al.*, 2001) and scalloped hammerhead sharks (*Sphyrna lewini*) (Bush and Holland, 2002).

Population models, however, suggest that population growth rates and sizes may be more heavily influenced by survival of older juveniles that have recently left nursery areas (Kinney and Simpfendorfer, 2009).

Further studies to understand the ages and locations at which population sizes are regulated as well as the factors that affect population sizes at these stages (e.g. food, predation risk, anthropogenic mortality) are important (e.g. Bush and Holland, 2002; Kinney and Simpfendorfer, 2009; Heithaus *et al.*, 2012). Shark populations exhibit considerable variation in their geographic range from highly narrow to cosmopolitan. Therefore, it is important to define the geographic extent of stocks (populations and population segments) to develop adequate management strategies. Since physical boundaries rarely exist for large mobile marine species, genetic tools have been critical in determining these separate stocks (for a review, see Heist, 2012), but other methods including morphological variation as well as ecological tracers, including stable isotopes (essentially carbon and nitrogen), fatty acids and contaminant loads also can provide important data (e.g. Borrell *et al.*, 2006; Quérouil *et al.*, 2013). Also, the composition of parasite loads can be informative because geographically separated populations may exhibit differences in their respective parasite faunas (Evans and Teilmann, 2009). Because different parasites are found in different locations and habitats around the world, comparing the types of parasites found in sharks may help to determine whether sharks found in different areas are part of a single population or separate.

In general, highly mobile coastal shark species tend to exhibit little population substructure along coasts where they exhibit a continuous distribution, but there can be considerable differentiation among populations of different ocean basins (Heist, 2012). Thus, effective management for these species often requires cooperative management among nations. For less mobile coastal species, however, population substructuring can occur even along a continuous coastal distribution (e.g. zebra sharks (*Stegostoma fasciatum*) (Dudgeon *et al.*, 2009) and leopard sharks (*Triakis semifasciata*) (Lewallen *et al.*, 2007)). In fragmented environments, such as around archipelagos, blacktip reef shark (*Carcharhinus melanopterus*) genetic population structure is mainly driven by geographic distance between islands (Vignaud *et al.*, 2013). This trait is also found in larger predatory coastal- and reef-associated species such as lemon sharks (*Negaprion*), for which significant isolation by distance has been found in *N. brevirostris* (primarily Atlantic species) with no evidence for contemporary transatlantic gene flow across an oceanic distance of ~2,400 km. In *N. acutidens* (Indo-Pacific species), the lowest control region diversity has been found. Therefore, restricted oceanic dispersal and high coastal connectivity highlights the need for both local and international management efforts for these coastal and vulnerable sharks (Schultz *et al.*, 2008; Vignaud *et al.*, 2013). However, situations are species-specific, depending on the ecological traits of the species considered and life history parameters, effective population size and time since divergence. Indeed, whitetip reef shark (*Triaenodon obesus*) genetic population structure does not indicate strong coastal connectivity observed in other reef sharks (such as blacktip reef sharks) and suggests oceanic dispersal behaviours (Whitney *et al.*, 2012). Therefore, for reef sharks dispersing in oceanic waters, island-associated management measures such as marine protected areas may not be effective.

Patterns of population structure vary among widely distributed pelagic species. However, relatively few studies have been produced from large-scale studies such as on whale sharks (Castro *et al.*, 2007) or scalloped hammerhead sharks (*S. lewini*) (Duncan *et al.*, 2006). In general, and not surprisingly, large and migratory sharks show limited population genetic structural diversity, even at large spatial scales, including at the global level. Based on global sampling of whale sharks, limited population division and no evidence for cryptic evolutionary partitions were found. However, significant mitochondrial DNA haplotype[2] frequency differences were found between the Atlantic and the Indo-Pacific regions. Overall, whale shark population genetic structure highlights the need for development of broad international approaches for management and conservation of this and related vulnerable species (Castro *et al.*, 2007). For other species with more disjunct distributions or reproductive philopatry, some levels of structure may be found, such as for the scalloped hammerhead shark. From a global sampling from 20 nursery areas around the world, population subdivisions in several species are strong (Duncan *et al.*, 2006). Genetic discontinuity is primarily associated with oceanic barriers. Overall, nursery populations linked by continuous coastlines have high connectivity, but oceanic dispersal by females is rare (Duncan *et al.*, 2006).

As highlighted for other large marine vertebrates such as cetaceans, the use of ecological tracers such as dietary indicators (e.g. stomach contents, stable isotopes, trace metal concentrations) might provide complementary insights on the definition of management units for sharks (e.g. Quérouil *et al.*, 2013). It is particularly true for species showing limited genetic population structure across large spatial scales, such as whale sharks and other oceanic epipelagic species. Genetic data alone may be insufficient to evaluate stock structure because low dispersal between demographically distinct populations may prevent genetic differentiation, especially in large populations (Wade and Angliss, 1997). Therefore, investigating population structure and defining ecological stocks (population segments) using dietary indicators (e.g. stable isotopes, trace metal concentration, etc.) on multiple tissues could provide important insights in light of contemporary threats, especially fisheries.

Habitat use and movements

Understanding patterns of habitat use and movement across numerous spatial and temporal scales up to and including migrations are critical for assessing vulnerability to fisheries and other anthropogenic factors (e.g. Queiroz *et al.*, 2005; Simpfendorfer *et al.*, 2011). Furthermore, gaining a functional understanding of these behaviours is necessary to predict how sharks might respond to the considerable changes occurring in marine environments (e.g. climate change, habitat modification, changes in prey availability and predation risk) (Heithaus *et al.*, 2010, 2012). For many years, habitat use and movements of sharks were inferred from catch data or tag–recapture programmes associated with commercial and recreational fisheries (e.g. Kohler *et al.*, 1998). New technologies from acoustic to satellite telemetry, however, have greatly expanded researchers' abilities to quantify the movements and habitat decisions of sharks (Sims, 2010; Simpfendorfer *et al.*, 2011; Simpfendorfer and Heupel, 2012). Many species of sharks make extensive movements that can vary from large-scale seasonal migrations undertaken consistently by large portions of populations to apparently less directed or individually varying movements (Simpfendorfer and Heupel, 2012). There is also a high variability in the spatial extent of movements of sharks that is likely the result of all or some combination of metabolic rates and energetic needs, locomotion capacities and reproductive cycles.

Some shark species make extensive movements, while others have a restricted home range throughout their life times. Blue, tiger and great white sharks can cross ocean basins (e.g. Bonfil *et al.*, 2005; Queiroz *et al.*, 2005; Heithaus *et al.*, 2007a). Shortfin mako sharks make extensive movements of up to 4,500 km (Casey and Kohler, 1992). These movements and ocean-basin scale migrations likely are related to the overall patchiness and scarcity of food resources, in conjunction with directed movements for social and reproductive purposes. For many oceanic shark species, movements appear relatively unpredictable. Conversely, a number of coastal shark species undertake annual migrations that are predictable in space and time, such as along the east coast of the United States for blacktip sharks (*Carcharhinus limbatus*) (Castro, 1996). Conversely, blacktip reef sharks at Palmyra atoll have small home ranges and show low levels of migration between lagoons over periods of several years (Papastamatiou *et al.*, 2010).

For other reef-associated sharks, such as grey reef sharks (*Carcharhinus amblyrhynchos*) from northern Australia, site fidelity is limited and large-scale movement occurs (Heupel *et al.*, 2010), while in fragmented insular environments movements between reefs are limited and site fidelity higher (Field *et al.*, 2010). For a vast diversity of shark species, there are significant horizontal, vertical and sex-mediated ontogenetic shifts of habitat use that have been documented. The use of nursery areas by sharks provides evolutionary benefits of size-based habitat use to minimize predation and intraspecific competition (for a review, see Grubbs, 2010).

Studies on habitat use of sharks highlight the context-dependence of shark movements and habitat use. However, the drivers of habitat use and movements are still poorly understood. In large predatory sharks, movements and habitat use patterns appear to be linked to prey availability (Heithaus *et al.*, 2002; Barnett *et al.*, 2010). Increasingly, biologists are recognizing that individuals can vary considerably in their behaviour even within age/sex classes and broadly similar habitats (Araùjo *et al.*, 2011). Although not generally considered for sharks, recent studies suggest that shark populations also may display individual specialists even within generalist populations. For example, adult tiger sharks captured in the same habitat can display very different patterns of habitat preference over short temporal scales (Heithaus *et al.*, 2002) and long ones (Meyer *et al.*, 2010). Within nursery areas, some individual bull sharks display consistent use of marine food webs, while others specialize on estuarine and freshwater prey, and still others are generalized in their foraging habitat use (Matich *et al.*, 2011).

Trophic ecology

Knowledge of feeding relationships is fundamental for understanding community structure, dynamics and ecosystem functioning and is important for predicting how particular species may respond to changes in the abundance of prey, predators and competitors. For example, endothermic sharks (including five lamnid sharks and the common thresher shark (*Alopias vulpinus*)) that have higher metabolic rates are likely to be more impacted by possible changes of prey availability and quality (i.e. energy content) due to climate change and habitat modification, and might be less resilient than ectothermic species. Shark trophic ecology has been investigated using a variety of approaches and methods, including the use of stomach content analyses (for reviews, see e.g. Cortés, 1999; McElroy *et al.*, 2006; Papastamatiou *et al.*, 2006) and chemical tracers of diets such as stable isotopes (Hussey *et al.*, 2011; Kinney *et al.*, 2011; Speed *et al.*, 2011; Heithaus *et al.*, 2013), fatty acids (e.g. Belicka *et al.*, 2012; McMeans *et al.*, 2012) and heavy metals (e.g. Domi *et al.*, 2005; McMeans *et al.*, 2010). In general, these different techniques bring complementary insights and must be employed with adequate understanding of the limitations of each technique (e.g. Domi *et al.*, 2005; McMeans *et al.*, 2010).

All sharks are carnivorous. The most common prey taxa are teleosts and cephalopods, although crustaceans are also common prey for some species (Cortés, 1999). For the largest predatory species (e.g. white sharks, tiger sharks, sevengill sharks, great hammerhead sharks), larger prey taxa including other elasmobranchs, marine reptiles and marine mammals may make up important components of their diets (e.g. Cortés, 1999). Often, sharks are referred to as 'top' or 'apex' predators regardless of the species in question. This designation, however, obscures considerable variation in shark trophic positions and functional roles. Large-bodied species do tend to occupy top trophic levels in food webs, while smaller size classes and species tend to forage at lower trophic levels (Cortés, 1999; Heithaus and Vaudo, 2012). The obvious exceptions to this trend are the large planktivorous species – whale, basking and megamouth sharks.

While a considerable amount of data on trophic interactions – especially stomach contents analysis – exist for numerous species (see Cortés, 1999), there remains a considerable need to gain further, and more detailed, data on diets of many populations. Such data, including an understanding of how diets might vary within and among individuals, populations and species, and across space and time, are critical for developing and modelling the role and importance of sharks in marine communities (see below).

Variation in foraging behaviour – including spatial and temporal variation in response to changes in prey availability or variation between sexes due to differing habitat use patterns – is common in sharks (see Heithaus and Vaudo, 2012). Diets of many species also change throughout their lives (ontogenetic variation) (e.g. Lowe *et al.*, 1996; Estrada *et al.*, 2006; Hussey *et al.*, 2011; Rabehagasoa *et al.*, 2012). Because of their large changes in body size and habitats, in many species sharks capture smaller prey early in life and gradually add larger prey individuals and taxa as they grow.

Diets may vary among individuals of the same age class found in the same basic habitats. Such individual variation could be very important in management plans if different foraging patterns lead to different vulnerabilities or roles in ecosystems (Bolnick *et al.*, 2003). Such variation can occur in even apparently 'generalist' species. Although at the population level many prey taxa might be consumed, particular individuals could specialize on a small number of these. Although not widely investigated in sharks, this pattern occurs in juvenile bull sharks in a Florida nursery, but not in a population of tiger sharks in Shark Bay, Western Australia (Matich *et al.*, 2011).

An area of considerable current research effort is the degree to which species found in the same basic habitats are 'functionally redundant'. The question of to what degree individual species fill similar ecological roles in ecosystems is important in light of declining populations. If species are functionally redundant, the loss of one or several may not result in large-scale community rearrangements because of compensation by other species (e.g. Kitchell *et al.*, 2002). In some cases, it has been suggested that large-bodied coastal species might be trophically redundant (Myers *et al.*, 2007). Recent studies, however, suggest that sympatric species likely do show considerable variation in trophic interactions (e.g. Kinney *et al.*, 2011; Heithaus *et al.*, 2013). While this may suggest that functional redundancy is low, these data cannot answer the question of whether there would be niche expansion if a species were to be removed from a community (i.e. character displacement might relax). Therefore, further studies should address this problem across different shark communities and should be extended to co-occurring top predators (see Heithaus *et al.*, 2013).

Ecological importance

Understanding the consequences of functionally removing sharks from marine ecosystems is critical for effective conservation planning in many locations. This topic is very difficult to investigate empirically because of declines in shark populations and the difficulty in conducting manipulative experiments or long-term observational studies. Despite this, a combination of modelling efforts, fisheries time-series data from numerous locations and directed empirical work have begun to provide important insights. Several recent reviews (e.g. Heithaus *et al.*, 2008, 2010; Feretti *et al.*, 2010) have addressed this topic, so we only provide a brief overview here.

It is now clear that not all sharks are keystone predators, but some species in some situations may be particularly important in maintaining ecosystem structure and function. In what habitats could such dynamics occur? What species are more or less important to ecosystem dynamics? Such questions are critical to predicting the consequences of overfishing of sharks and making a case for precautionary management of their populations. Yet these questions are among the most difficult to answer.

Studies addressing the ecological importance of elasmobranchs are relatively rare, and are difficult to compare (especially between species and ecosystems) because methods used to address this question are diverse, including time-series data, ecosystem models, exclosure experiments and field studies (Heithaus *et al.*, 2010). Top predators from diverse ecosystems have the potential to impact their communities through direct predation, risk effects and their interaction (Heithaus *et al.*, 2008). Estes *et al.* (2011) argued that strong top-down effects of predators are likely the rule rather than the exception, based on the broad-scale community rearrangements that accompany the loss or reintroduction of top predators. Sharks can play important roles in marine ecosystems through diverse mechanisms, but their relative importance may significantly vary among ecosystems, species and contexts (Heithaus *et al.*, 2010).

In Shark Bay, Western Australia, empirical data have revealed strong risk effects of tiger sharks on a diversity of mesoconsumers, including dolphins, seabirds and large herbivores like green turtles (*Chelonia mydas*) and dugongs (*Dugong dugon*) (Heithaus and Dill, 2002; Heithaus, 2005; Heithaus *et al.*, 2007b; Wirsing *et al.*, 2007). In other systems, such as the open ocean, large pelagic sharks may not affect the abundance of their prey and are therefore not considered as keystone top predators. Evidence from ecosystem models from the central Pacific Ocean suggest pelagic shark declines may be mitigated by compensatory increases in populations of large teleosts (Kitchell *et al.*, 2002). However, these models generally categorize pelagic sharks into a single homogenous trophic group when in fact there may be more intricate interspecies habitat and feeding preferences and, consequently, trophic roles in open ocean ecosystems. More empirical data is consequently needed to validate this potential scenario to refine existing ecosystem models.

Long-term observational and experimental studies in a pristine seagrass ecosystem in Shark Bay, Western Australia suggest that risk-effects induced by the top predator, tiger sharks, are pervasive (reviewed in Heithaus *et al.*, 2012), and cascade to seagrass communities (Burkholder *et al.*, 2013). It remains unclear, however, why results in Shark Bay differ markedly from recent studies in Yellowstone and whether they apply to other marine ecosystems, such as coral reefs. For example, the limited visibility in Shark Bay (usually <3 m) makes it impossible for shark prey to assess whether tiger sharks are present in the general vicinity in a manner analogous to elk that can adaptively respond to wolf presence or absence within a general area (Winnie, 2012). Thus, tiger shark prey must shift habitats based on long-term (e.g. seasonal) risk within a habitat rather than to acute risk. Also, could the diversity of trophic pathways and alternative prey items for predators attenuate risk effects? In coral reef ecosystems, Madin *et al.* (2010) found changes in predation risk elicit behavioural responses in foraging patterns across multiple prey fish species. Anti-predator behavioural responses may have greater effects by occurring over entire assemblages and operate over shorter temporal scales in transmitting top-down effects. These behavioural changes may, in turn, drive previously unsuspected alterations in reef food webs. However, no studies have focused on potential behavioural interactions among mesopredators and top predators on reef ecosystems that could have considerable consequences for the spatial and temporal pattern of risk effects at the lower trophic levels. Despite the importance of this question, there remains considerable work to be done.

Effect of disturbance and environmental change

Investigating how human activities interact with sharks, particularly fisheries, is relatively well documented (Simpfendorfer *et al.*, 2011); even if data are lacking for some regions – e.g. Indian Ocean (see Smale, 2008) – and little is known about the extent of mortality in small-scale fisheries of most developing countries where shark fisheries have important social and economic value (see e.g. McVean *et al.*, 2006). In contrast, little is known about the effect of other human impacts, disturbance and environmental changes on sharks. For example, over the last two decades, eco-tourism based on viewing and interacting with marine megafauna has become increasingly popular, including diving and snorkelling with sharks and rays (Vianna *et al.*, 2012). Shark tourism, including provisioning (commonly called shark feeding), may have significant effects on shark behaviour, ecology and population dynamics. Shark provisioning is a recent but common practice around the globe, consisting of provisioning sharks with food in order to concentrate them over a small area for viewing purposes. Indeed, this activity generally leads to increased shark population densities (Brunnschweiler and Baensch, 2011), induces behavioural modifications, e.g. increased aggressiveness, site fidelity (Clua *et al.*, 2010) and can lead to impoverished body condition (Semeniuk and Rothley, 2008).

Shark feeding also can affect trophic interactions (e.g. Caribbean reef sharks (*Carcharhinus perezii*) in the Bahamas) and, by extension, their ecological role in coral reef ecosystems (Maljkovitc and Coté, 2011). In Moorea (French Polynesia), reef shark provisioning enhances parasitic infestations in blacktip groupers (*Epinephelus fasciatus*) (Vignon *et al.*, 2010). However, little is known about broader effects of shark tourism (including provisioning). Impacts on the structure of the wider reef community could operate through both increased predation rates by dense aggregations of sharks or modifications to prey behaviour in response to increased encounter rates with sharks (see Heithaus *et al.*, 2008). Further assessment of the effect of shark tourism at both population and ecosystem levels will be critical to ensuring the sustainable use of sharks and their economic benefits through non-consumptive use.

Assessing the effect of ongoing global, regional and even local environmental changes on sharks and other elasmobranchs is also important. Using a framework from fisheries ecological risk assessments (see Hobday *et al.*, 2011), Chin *et al.* (2010) developed a risk assessment for the effect of climate change on elasmobranchs from the Great Barrier Reef region. Based on their biological and ecological attributes, it is hypothesized that changes in temperature, freshwater inputs and ocean circulation will have the most widespread effects on sharks and rays from this region, especially on most coastal and freshwater species (Chin *et al.*, 2010). Extension of this type of work will be important for conservation and management of sharks around the world.

Extreme environmental events are likely to occur in greater frequency and intensity due to climate change (Goswami *et al.*, 2006). Understanding the short- and long-term impacts of these extreme events on large-bodied predators such as sharks will provide insight into the spatial and temporal scales at which environmental disturbances in top-down processes may persist within and across ecosystems. During an extended period of extremely cold water temperatures in a bull shark nursery of southwest Florida, juvenile bull sharks either permanently left the system or died (Matich and Heithaus, 2012). Once sharks returned in the system, both the size structure and abundance of the individuals present in the nursery had changed significantly. The broader impacts of this change to the trophic dynamics of the estuary and the importance of episodic disturbances to bull shark population dynamics will require continued monitoring, but are of interest because of the ecological roles of bull sharks within coastal estuaries and oceans (Matich and Heithaus, 2012).

Conclusions

Despite a considerable increase in shark scientific research during the last decade, gaps still exist in many fields, including taxonomy, trophic ecology and ecological role (particularly in deep-sea, open ocean and coral reef ecosystems), population structure and connectivity, and the combination of evolutionary and contemporary ecological indicators of population subdivision. Recent activities such as shark tourism might also impact populations at different levels, which need to be further investigated, along with the effect of environmental change due to habitat modification and global changes. There is an increasing need for multi- and inter-disciplinary approaches to address research questions outlined in this chapter, and develop effective management measures for conservation of sharks.

Notes

1 Parthenogenesis is a form of asexual reproduction in which the egg develops without fertilization.
2 A *haplotype* is a group of genes, which is inherited together by an organism from a single parent. Mitochondrial DNA is inherited from an individual's mother.

References

Araùjo, M. S., Bolnick, D. I. and Layman, C. A. (2011) 'The ecological causes of individual specialization', *Ecology Letters*, vol. 14, pp. 948–958.

Barnett, A., Abrantes, K. G., Stevens, J. D., Bruce, B. D. and Semmens, J. M. (2010) 'Fine-scale movements of the broadnose sevengill shark and its main prey, the gummy shark', *PLoS One*, vol. 5, no. 12.

Belicka, L. L., Matich, P., Jaffé, R. and Heithaus, M. R. (2012) 'Fatty acids and stable isotopes as indicators of early-life feeding and potential maternal resource dependency in the bull shark *Carcharhinus leucas*', *Marine Ecology Progress Series*, vol. 455, pp. 245–256.

Bolnick, D. I., Svanback, R., Fordyce, J. A., Yang, L. H., Davis, J. M., Hulsey, C. D. and Forister, M. L. (2003) 'The ecology of individuals: incidence and implication for individual specialisations', *The American Naturalist*, vol. 161, pp. 1–28.

Bonfil, R., Meÿer, M., Scholl, M. C., Johnson, R., O'Brien, S., Oosthuizen, H., Swanson, S., Kotze, D. and Paterson, M. (2005) 'Transoceanic migrations, spatial dynamics, and population linkages of white sharks', *Science*, vol. 310, pp. 100–103.

Borrell, A., Aguilar, A., Tornero, V., Sequeira, M., Fernandez, G. and Alis, S. (2006) 'Organochlorine compounds and stable isotopes indicate bottlenose dolphin population subpopulation structure around the Iberian Peninsula', *Environment International*, vol. 32, no. 4, pp. 516–523.

Brunnschweiler, J. M. and Baensch, H. (2011) 'Seasonal and long-term changes in relative abundance of bull sharks from a tourist shark feeding site in Fiji', *PLoS One*, vol. 6, no. 1.

Burkholder, D. A., Heithaus, M. R., Fourqurean, J. W., Wirsing, A. and Dill, L. M. (2013) 'Patterns of top-down control in a seagrass ecosystem: could a roving apex predator induce a behaviour-mediated trophic cascade?' *Journal of Animal Ecology*, vol. 82, no. 6, pp. 1192–1202.

Bush, A. and Holland, K. (2002) 'Food limitation in a nursery area: estimates of daily ration in juvenile scalloped hammerheads, *Sphyrna lewini* (Griffitz and Smith, 1834) in Kane'ohe Bay, O'ahu, Hawai'i', *Journal of Experimental Marine Biology and Ecology*, vol. 278, pp. 157–178.

Camhi, M. D., Pikitch, E. K. and Babcock, E. A. (eds) (2008) *Sharks of the Open Ocean: Biology, Fisheries and Conservation*, Blackwell Publishing, Oxford.

Carrier, J. C., Musick, J. A. and Heithaus, M. R. (2004) *Biology of Sharks and Their Relatives*, CRC Press, Boca Raton, FL.

Carrier, J. C., Musick, J. A. and Heithaus, M. R. (2010) *Biology of Sharks and Their Relatives II: Biodiversity, Adaptive Physiology and Conservation*, CRC Press, Boca Raton, FL.

Carrier, J. C., Musick, J. A. and Heithaus, M. R. (2012) *Biology of Sharks and Their Relatives*, 2nd edn, CRC Press, Boca Raton, FL.

Casey, J. G. and Kohler, N. E. (1992) 'Tagging studies on the short-fin mako (*Isurus oxyrinchus*) in the western North Atlantic', *Australian Journal of Marine and Freshwater Research*, vol. 43, pp. 45–60.

Castro, A. L. F., Stewart, B. S., Wilson, S. G., Hueter, R. E., Meekan, M. G., Motta, P. J., Bowen, B. W. and Karl, S. A. (2007) 'Population genetic structure of Earth's largest fish, the whale shark (*Rhincodon typus*)', *Molecular Ecology*, vol. 16, pp. 5183–5192.

Castro, J. I. (1996) 'Biology of the blacktip shark, *Carcharhinus limbatus*, off southeastern United States', *Bulletin of Marine Science*, vol. 59, pp. 508–522.

Chapman, D. D., Shivji, M. S., Louis, E., Sommer, J. and Prodöhl, P. A. (2007) 'Virgin birth in a hammerhead shark', *Biology Letters*, vol. 3, pp. 425–427.

Chapman, D. D., Firchau, B. and Shivji, M. S. (2008) 'Parthenogenesis in a large requiem shark, the blacktip *Carcharhinus limbatus*', *Journal of Fish Biology*, vol. 73, pp. 1473–1477.

Chin, A., Kyne, P. M., Walker, T. I. and McCauley, R. B. (2010) 'An integrated risk assessment for climate change: analysing the vulnerability of sharks and rays on Australia's Great Barrier Reef', *Global Change Biology*, vol. 16, pp. 1936–1953.

Clua, E., Burray, N., Legendre, N., Mourier, J. and Planes, S. (2010) 'Behavioural response of sicklefin lemon sharks *Negaprion acutidens* to underwater feeding for ecotourism purposes', *Marine Ecology Progress Series*, vol. 414, pp. 257–266.

Compagno, L. J. V. (1990) 'Alternative life-history styles of cartilaginous fishes in time and space', *Environmental Biology of Fishes*, vol. 28, pp. 33–75.

Conrath, C. L. and Musick, J. A. (2012) 'Reproductive biology of elasmobranchs', in J. C. Carrier, J. A. Musick and M. R. Heithaus (eds), *Sharks and Their Relatives*, 2nd edn, CRC Press, Boca Raton, FL.

Cortés, E. (1999) 'Standardized diet compositions and trophic levels of sharks', *Journal of Marine Science*, vol. 56, pp. 107–117.

Cortés, E., Brooks, E. N. and Gedamke, T. (2012) 'Population dynamics, demography, and stock assessment', in J. C. Carrier, J. A. Musick and M. R. Heithaus (eds), *Sharks and Their Relatives*, 2nd edn, CRC Press, Boca Raton, FL.

Domi, N., Bouquegneau, J. M. and Das, K. (2005) 'Feeding ecology of five commercial shark species of the Celtic Sea through stable isotope and trace metal analysis', *Marine Environmental Research*, vol. 60, pp. 551–569.

Dudgeon, C. L., Broderick, D. and Ovenden, J. R. (2009) 'IUCN classification zones concord with, but underestimate, the population genetic structure of the zebra shark *Stegostoma fasciatum* in the Indo-West Pacific', *Molecular Ecology*, vol. 18, pp. 248–261.

Dulvy, N. K. and Reynolds, J. D. (2009) 'Skates on thin ice', *Nature*, vol. 462, p. 417.

Dulvy, N. K., Baum, J. K., Clarke, S., Compagno, L. J. V., Cortés, E., Domingo, A., Fordham, S., Fowler, S., Francis, M. P., Gibson, C., Martínez, J., Musick, J. A., Soldo, A., Stevens, J. D. and Valenti, S. (2008) 'You can swim but you can't hide: the global status of and conservation of pelagic sharks and rays', *Aquatic Conservation: Marine and Freshwater Ecosystems*, vol. 18, pp. 459–482.

Duncan, K. M., Martin, A. P., Bowen, B. W. and De Couet, H. G. (2006) 'Global phylogeography of the scalloped hammerhead shark (*Sphyrna lewini*)', *Molecular Ecology*, vol. 15, pp. 2239–2251.

Estes, J. A., Terborgh, T., Brashares, J. S., Power, M. E., Berger, J., Bond, W. J., Carpenter, S. R., Essington, T. E., Holt, R. D., Jackson, J. B. C., Marquis, R. J., Oksanen, L., Oksanen, T., Paine, R. T., Pikitch, E. K., Ripple, W. J., Sandin, S. A., Scheffer, M., Shurin, J. B., Sinclair, A. R. E., Soulé, M. E., Virtanen, R. and Wardle, D. A. (2011) 'Trophic downgrading of Planet Earth', *Science*, vol. 333, pp. 301–306.

Estrada, J. A., Rice, A. N., Natanson, N. J. and Skomal, G. B. (2006) 'Use of isotopic analysis from vertebrae in reconstructing ontogenetic feeding ecology in white sharks', *Ecology*, vol. 87, pp. 829–834.

Evans, P. G. H. and Teilmann, J. (2009) *Report of ASCOBANS/HELCOM Small Cetacean Population Structure Workshop*, 8–10 October 2007, Bonn, Germany.

Ferretti, F., Worm, B., Britten, G. L., Heithaus, M. R. and Lotze, H. K. (2010) 'Patterns and ecosystem consequences of shark declines in the ocean', *Ecology Letters*, vol. 13, pp. 1055–1071.

Field, I. C., Meekan, M. G., Speed, C. W., White, W. and Bradshaw, C. J. A. (2010) 'Quantifying movement patterns for shark conservation at remote coral atolls in the Indian Ocean', *Coral Reefs*, vol. 30, pp. 61–71.

Gilmore, R. G., Dodrill, J. W. and Linley, P. A. (1983) 'Reproduction and embryonic development of the sand tiger shark, *Odontaspis Taurus* (Rafinesque)', *Fishery Bulletin*, vol. 81, pp. 201–225.

Goldman, K. J., Cailliet, G. M., Andrews, A. H. and Natanson, L. J. (2012) 'Assessing the age and growth of Chondrichthyan fishes', in J. C. Carrier, J. A. Musick and M. R. Heithaus (eds), *Sharks and Their Relatives*, 2nd edn, CRC Press, Boca Raton, FL.

Goswami, B. M., Venugopal, V., Sengupta, D., Madhusoodanan, M. S. and Xavier, P. K. (2006) 'Increasing trend of extreme rain events over India in a warming environment', *Science*, vol. 314, pp. 1442–1445.

Grogan, E. D., Lund, R. and Greenfest-Allen, E. (2012) 'The origin and relationships of early chondrichthyans', in J. C. Carrier, J. A. Musick and M. R. Heithaus (eds), *Sharks and Their Relatives*, 2nd edn, CRC Press, Boca Raton, FL.

Grubbs, R. D. (2010) 'Ontogenetic shifts of movements and habitat use', in J. C. Carrier, J. A. Musick and M. R. Heithaus (eds), *Sharks and Their Relatives II: Biodiversity, Adaptative Physiology and Conservation*, CRC Press, Boca Raton, FL.

Gruber, S. H., de Marignac, J. R. C. and Hoenig, J. M. (2001) 'Survival of juvenile lemon sharks at Bimini, Bahamas, estimated by mark-depletion experiments', *Transactions of the American Fisheries Society*, vol. 130, pp. 376–384.

Heinicke, M. P., Naylor, G. J. P. and Hedges, S. B. (2009) 'Cartilaginous fishes (Chondrichthyes)', in S. B. Hedges and S. Kumar, *The Timetree of Life*, Oxford University Press, Oxford.

Heist, E. J. (2012) 'Genetics of sharks, skates and rays', in J. C. Carrier, J. A. Musick and M. R. Heithaus (eds), *Sharks and Their Relatives*, 2nd edn, CRC Press, Boca Raton, FL.

Heithaus, M. R. (2005) 'Habitat and group size of pied cormorants (*Phalacrocorax varius*) in a seagrass ecosystem: possible effects of food abundance and predation risk', *Marine Biology*, vol. 147, pp. 27–35.

Heithaus, M. R. and Dill, L. M. (2002) 'Food availability and tiger shark predation risk influence bottlenose dolphin habitat use', *Ecology*, vol. 83, pp. 480–491.

Heithaus, M. R. and Vaudo, J. J. (2012) 'Predator–prey interactions', in J. C. Carrier, J. A. Musick and M. R. Heithaus (eds), *Sharks and Their Relatives*, 2nd edn, CRC Press, Boca Raton, FL.

Heithaus, M. R., Dill, L. M., Marshall, G. J. and Buhleier, B. (2002) 'Habitat use and foraging behavior of tiger sharks (*Galeocerdo cuvier*) in a seagrass ecosystem', *Marine Biology*, vol. 140, pp. 237–248.

Heithaus, M. R., Wirsing, A. J., Dill, L. M. and Heithaus, L. (2007a) 'Long-term movements of tiger sharks satellite-tagged in Shark Bay, Western Australia', *Marine Biology*, vol. 151, pp. 1455–1461.

Heithaus, M. R., Frid, A., Wirsing, A. J., Dill, L. M., Fourqurean, J., Burkholder, D., Thomson, J. and Bejder, L. (2007b) 'State-dependant risk-taking by green turtles mediates top-down effects of tiger shark intimidation in a marine ecosystem', *Journal of Animal Ecology*, vol. 76, pp. 837–844.

Heithaus, M. R., Frid, A., Wirsing, A. J., Worm, B. (2008) 'Predicting ecological consequences of marine top predator declines', *Trends in Ecology and Evolution*, vol. 23, no. 4, pp. 202–210.

Heithaus, M. R., Frid, A., Vaudo, J. J., Worm, B. and Wirsing, A. J. (2010) 'Unravelling the ecological importance of elasmobranchs', in J. C. Carrier, J. A. Musick and M. R. Heithaus (eds), *Sharks and Their Relatives II: Biodiversity, Adaptative Physiology and Conservation*, CRC Press, Boca Raton, FL.

Heithaus, M. R., Wirsing, A. J. and Dill, L. M. (2012) 'The ecological importance of intact top-predator populations: a synthesis of 15 years of research in a seagrass ecosystem', *Marine and Freshwater Research*, vol. 63, pp. 1039–1050.

Heithaus, M. R., Vaudo, J., Kreicker, S., Layman, C. A., Krützen, M., Burkholder, D. A., Gastrich, K., Bessey, C., Sarabia, R., Cameron, K., Wirsing, A., Thomson, J. A. and Dunphy-Daly, M. M. (2013) 'Apparent resource partitioning and trophic structure of large-bodied predators in a relatively pristine seagrass ecosystem', *Marine Ecology Progress Series*, vol. 481, pp. 225–237.

Heupel, M. R., Simpfendorfer, C. A. and Fitzpatrick, R. (2010) 'Large-scale movements and reef fidelity of grey reef sharks', *PLoS ONE*, vol. 5, no. 3.

Hobday, A. J., Smith, A. D. M., Stobutzki, I. C., Bulman, C., Daley, R., Dambacher, J. M., Deng, R. A., Dowdney, J., Fuller, M., Furlani, D., Griffiths, S. P., Johnson, D., Kenyon, R., Knuckey, I. A., Ling, S. D., Pitcher, R., Sainsbury, K. J., Sporcic, M., Smith, T., Turnbull, C., Walker, T. I., Wayte, S. E., Webb, H., Williams, A., Wise, B. S. and Zhou, S. (2011) 'Ecological risk assessment for the effects of fishing', *Fisheries Research*, vol. 108, pp. 373–384.

Hussey, N. E., Dudley, S. F. J., McCarthy, I. D., Cliff, G. and Fisk, A. T. (2011) 'Stable isotope profiles of large marine predators: viable indicators of trophic position, diet and movement in sharks?', *Canadian Journal of Fisheries and Aquatic Sciences*, vol. 68, pp. 2029–2045.

Kinney, M. F. and Simpfendorfer, C. A. (2009) 'Reassessing the value of nursery areas to shark conservation and management', *Conservation Letters*, vol. 2, pp. 53–60.

Kinney, M. J., Hussey, N. E., Fisk, A. T., Tobin, A. J. and Simpfendorfer, C. A. (2011) 'Communal or competitive? Stable isotope analysis provides evidence of resource partitioning within a communal shark nursery', *Marine Ecology Progress Series*, vol. 439, pp. 263–276.

Kitchell, J. F., Essington, T. E., Boggs, C. H., Schindler, D. E. and Walters, C. J. (2002) 'The role of sharks and longline fisheries in a pelagic ecosystem of the central Pacific' *Ecosystems*, vol. 5, pp. 2002–2016.

Kohler, N. E., Casey, J. G. and Turner, P. A. (1998) 'NMFS Cooperative shark tagging program, 1962–93: an atlas of shark tag and recapture data', *Marine Fisheries Review*, vol. 60, no. 2, pp. 1–87.

Kyne, P. M. and Simpfendorfer, C. A. (2010) 'Deepwater chondrichthyans', in J. C. Carrier, J. A. Musick and M. R. Heithaus (eds), *Sharks and Their Relatives II: Biodiversity, Adaptative Physiology and Conservation*, CRC Press, Boca Raton, FL.

Last, P. R. and Stevens, J. D. (2009) *Sharks and Rays of Australia*, Havard University Press, London.

Lewallen, E. A., Anderson, T. W. and Bohonak, A. J. (2007) 'Genetic structure of leopard shark (*Triakis semifasciata*) populations in California waters', *Marine Biology*, vol. 152, pp. 599–609.

Lowe, C., Wetherbee, B. M., Crow, G. L. and Tester, A. L. (1996) 'Ontogenetic dietary shifts and feeding behavior of tiger sharks, *Galeocerdo cuvier*, in Hawaiian waters', *Environmental Biology of Fishes*, vol. 47, pp. 203–211.

McElroy, D. W., Wetherbee, B. M., Mostello, C. S., Lowe, C. G., Crow, G. L. and Wass, S. C. (2006) 'Food habits and ontogenetic changes in the diet of the sandbar shark, *Carcharhinus plumbeus*, in Hawaii', *Environmental Biology of Fishes*, vol. 76, pp. 81–92.

McMeans, B. C., Svavarsson, J., Dennard, S. and Fisk, A. (2010) 'Diet and resource use among Greenland sharks (*Somniosus microcephalus*) and teleosts sampled in Icelandic waters using δ13C, δ15N, and mercury', *Canadian Journal of Fisheries and Aquatic Sciences*, vol. 67, pp. 1428–1438.

McMeans, B. C., Arts, M. T. and Fisk, A. T. (2012) 'Similarity between predator and prey fatty acid profiles is tissue dependant in Greenland sharks (*Somniosus microcephalus*): implications for diet reconstruction', *Journal of Experimental Marine Biology and Ecology*, vol. 429, pp. 55–63.

McVean, A. R., Walker, S. C. J., Fanning, E. (2006) 'The traditional shark fisheries of southwest Madagascar: a study in the Toliara region', *Fisheries Research*, vol. 82, pp. 280–289.

Madin, E. M. P., Gaines, S. D. and Warner, R. R. (2010) 'Field evidence for pervasive indirect effects of fishing on prey foraging behavior', *Ecology*, vol. 91, no. 12, pp. 3563–3571.

Maljković, A. and Côté, I. M. (2011) 'Effects of tourism-related provisioning on the trophic signatures and movement patterns of an apex predator, the Caribbean reef shark', *Biological Conservation*, vol. 144, pp. 859–865.

Matich, P. and Heithaus, M. R. (2012) 'Effects of an extreme temperature event on the behaviour and age structure of an estuarine top predator, *Carcharhinus leucas*', *Marine Ecology Progress Series*, vol. 447, pp. 165–178.

Matich, P., Heithaus, M. R. and Layman, C. (2011) 'Contrasting patterns of individual specialization and trophic coupling in two marine apex predators', *Journal of Animal Ecology*, vol. 80, pp. 294–305.

Meyer, C. G., Papastamatiou, Y. P. and Holland, K. N. (2010) 'A multiple instrument approach to quantifying the movement patterns and habitat use of tiger (*Galeocerdo cuvier*) and Galapagos sharks (*Carcharhinus galapagensis*) at French Frigate Shoals, Hawaii', *Marine Biology*, vol. 157, pp. 1857–1868.

Musick, J. A. and Ellis, J. (2005) 'Reproductive evolution of chondrichthyans', in W. C. Hamlet (ed.), *Reproductive Biology and Phylogeny of Chondrichthyans*, Science Publishers, Enfield, NH.

Myers, R. A., Baum, J. K., Shepherd, T. D., Powers, S. P. and Peterson, P. H. (2007) 'Cascading effects of the loss of apex predatory sharks for a coastal ocean', *Science*, vol. 315, pp. 1846–1850.

Naylor, G. J. P., Caira, J. N., Jensen, K., Rosana, A. M., Straube, N. and Lakner, C. (2012a) 'Elasmobranch phylogeny: a mitochondrial estimate based on 595 species', in J. C. Carrier, J. A. Musick and M. R. Heithaus (eds), *Sharks and Their Relatives II: Biodiversity, Adaptative Physiology and Conservation*, CRC Press, Boca Raton, FL.

Naylor, G. J. P., Caira, J. N., Jensen, K., Rosana, A. M., White, W. T. and Last, P. R. (2012b) 'A DNA sequence-based approach to identification of shark and ray species and its implications for global elasmobranch diversity and parasitology', *Bulletin of the American Museum of Natural History*, vol. 367, pp. 1–262.

Papastamatiou, Y. P., Wetherbee, B. M., Lowe, C. G. and Crow, G. L. (2006) 'Distribution and diet of four species of carcharhinid shark in the Hawaiian Islands: evidence for resource partitioning and competitive exclusion', *Marine Ecology Progress Series*, vol. 320, pp. 239–251.

Papastamatiou, Y. P., Friedlander, A. M., Caselle, J. E. and Lowe, C. G. (2010) 'Long-term movement patterns and trophic ecology of blacktip sharks (*Carcharhinus melanopterus*) at Palmyra atoll', *Journal of Experimental Marine Biology and Ecology*, vol. 386, pp. 94–102.

Priede, I. G., Froese, R., Bailey, D. M., Bergstad, O. A., Collins, M. A., Dyb, J. A., Henriques, C., Jones E. G. and King, N. (2006) 'The absence of sharks from abyssal regions of the world's ocean', *Proceedings of the Royal Society B*, vol. 373, pp. 1435–1441.

Queiroz, N., Lima, F. P., Maia, A., Ribeiro, R. P., Correia, R. P. and Santos, A. M. (2005) 'Movement of blue shark, *Prionace glauca*, in the north-east Atlantic based on mark-recapture data', *Journal of the Marine Biological Association of the UK*, vol. 85, pp. 1107–1112.

Quérouil, S., Kiszka, J., Cordeiro, A. R., Cascao, I., Freitas, L., Dinis, A., Alves, F., Serrao Santos, R. and Bandarra, N. M. (2013) 'Investigating stock structure and trophic relationships among island-associated dolphins from the oceanic waters of the North Atlantic from fatty acid and stable isotope analyses', *Marine Biology*, vol. 160, no. 6, pp. 1325–1337.

Rabehagasoa, N., Lorrain, A., Bach, P., Potier, M., Jaquemet, S., Richard, P. and Ménard, F. (2012) 'Isotopic niches of the blue shark *Prionace glauca* and the silky shark *Carcharhinus falciformis* in the southwestern Indian Ocean', *Endangered Species Research*, vol. 17, pp. 83–92.

Schultz, J. K., Feldheim, K. A., Gruber, S. H., Ashley, M. V., McGovern, T. M. and

Bowen, B. W. (2008) 'Global phylogeography and seascape genetics of the lemon shark (genus *Negaprion*)', *Molecular Ecology*, vol. 17, pp. 5336–5348.

Semeniuk, C. A. D. and Rothley, K. D. (2008) 'Costs of group-living for a normally solitary forager: effects of provisioning tourism on southern stingrays *Dasyatis americana*', *Marine Ecology Progress Series*, vol. 357, pp. 271–282.

Shivji, M., Clarke, S., Pank, M., Natanson, L., Kohler, N. and Stanhope, M. (2002) 'Genetic identification of pelagic shark body parts for conservation and trade monitoring', *Conservation Biology*, vol. 16, pp. 1036–1047.

Simpfendorfer, C. A. and Heupel, M. R. (2012) 'Assessing habitat use and movements', in J. C. Carrier, J. A. Musick and M. R. Heithaus (eds), *Sharks and Their Relatives*, 2nd edn, CRC Press, Boca Raton, FL.

Simpfendorfer, C. A., Heupel, M. R., White W. T. and Dulvy, N. K. (2011) 'The importance of research and public opinion to conservation management of sharks and rays: a synthesis', *Marine and Freshwater Research*, vol. 62, pp. 518–527.

Sims, D. W. (2010) 'Tracking and analysis techniques for understanding free-ranging shark movements and behaviour', in J. C. Carrier, J. A. Musick and M. R. Heithaus (eds), *Sharks and Their Relatives II: Biodiversity, Adaptative Physiology and Conservation*, CRC Press, Boca Raton, FL.

Smale, M. J. (2008) 'Pelagic shark fisheries in the Indian Ocean', in M. D. Camhi, E. K. Pikitch and E. A. Babcock (eds), *Sharks of the Open Ocean: Biology, Fisheries and Conservation*, Blackwell Publishing, Oxford.

Speed, C. W., Meekan, M. G., Field, I. C., McMahon, C. R., Abrantes, K. and Bradshaw, C. J. A. (2011) 'Trophic ecology of reef sharks determined using stable isotopes and telemetry', *Coral Reefs*, vol. 31, pp. 357–367.

Stevens, J. D. (2010) 'Epipelagic oceanic elasmobranchs', in J. C. Carrier, J. A. Musick and M. R. Heithaus (eds), *Sharks and Their Relatives II: Biodiversity, Adaptative Physiology and Conservation*, CRC Press, Boca Raton, FL.

Vianna, G. M. S., Meekan, M. G., Pannell, D. G., Marsh, S. P. and Meeuvig, J. J. (2012) 'Socio-economic value and community benefits from shark-diving tourism in Palau: a sustainable use of reef shark populations', *Biological Conservation*, vol. 145, pp. 267–277.

Vignaud, T., Clua, E., Mourier, J., Maynard, J. and Planes, S. (2013) 'Microsatellite analyses of blacktip reef shark (*Carcharhinus melanopterus*) in a fragmented environment show structured clusters', *PLoS ONE*, vol. 8, no. 4.

Vignon, M., Sasal, P., Johnson, R. L. and Galzin, R. (2010) 'Impact of shark feeding tourism on surrounding fish populations off Moorea Island (French Polynesia)', *Marine and Freshwater Research*, vol. 61, pp. 163–169.

Wade, P. R. and Angliss, R. (1997) *Guidelines for Assessing Marine Mammal Stocks: Report of the* GAMMS *Workshop*, Seattle, Washington, 3–5 April 1996, Office of Protected Resources, National Marine Fisheries Service, Silver Spring, MD.

Walker, T. I. (1998) 'Can shark resources can be harvested sustainably? A question revisited with a review of shark fisheries', *Marine and Freshwater Research*, vol. 49, pp. 553–572.

Whitney, N. M., Robbins, W. D., Schultz, J. K., Bowen, B. W. and Holland, K. N. (2012) 'Oceanic dispersal in a sedentary reef shark (*Triaenodon obesus*): genetic evidence for extensive connectivity without a pelagic larval stage', *Journal of Biogeography*, vol. 39, pp. 1144–1156.

Winnie Jr, J. A. (2012) 'Predation risk, elk, and aspen: tests of a behaviorally mediated trophic cascade in the Greater Yellowstone Ecosystem', *Ecology*, vol. 93, pp. 2600–2614.

Wirsing, A. J., Heithaus, M. R. and Dill, L. M. (2007) 'Living on the edge: dugongs prefer to forage in microhabitats that allow escape from rather than avoidance of predators', *Animal Behaviour*, vol. 74, pp. 93–101.

Chapter 5

Shark conservation, governance and management

The science–law disconnect

Paolo Momigliano and Rob Harcourt

Introduction

Shark populations have experienced a dramatic global decline over the past few decades (Baum *et al.*, 2003; Ferretti *et al.*, 2008; Baum and Myers, 2004). The almost universal global collapse of shark populations is driven by two main factors. The first is the rise in demand for shark products (Lack *et al.*, 2006; Rose, 1996), which has led to a sharp increase in fishing effort and landings over the last 30 years. The second is the intrinsic vulnerability of sharks to fishing pressure, due to their conservative life history strategies (Field *et al.*, 2009). In general, sharks are K-selected, i.e. they are long-lived, slow-growing and take a long time to reach sexual maturity (Last and Stevens, 2009; also see Chapter 2). They invest considerable amounts of energy in the production of a few offspring that then have a high survival rate. These characteristics make them susceptible to even modest levels of fishing mortality. Unlike in many bony fishes (teleosts), recruitment is tightly linked to stock size, meaning that any level of mortality in adult stocks will have immediate consequences in terms of recruitment in the following years (Smith *et al.*, 1998). Recruitment overfishing, the level of harvesting at which the reproductive potential of a population is affected, starts early in the history of most shark fisheries. The rebound potential for shark populations is therefore lower than most other harvested marine resources. However, while this provides the rationale for sharks' intrinsically high risk of extinction, by the same reasoning lies therein a nugget of hope for successful management.

Conservative life history strategies lead to predictable demographies (Bradshaw *et al.*, 2013). Recruitment levels in shark populations are usually stable compared to many commercially important teleosts, because the investment of substantial resources into offspring production means that juveniles are less susceptible to short-term environmental fluctuations. Moreover, the rise in fishing effort has the potential to provide access to a large amount of shark life history information. In addition to this improved data, the long life expectancy of sharks makes them amenable to mark–recapture analysis, from which survival and dispersal capabilities may be estimated (Bradshaw *et al.*, 2013). These data can be used to produce viability analyses and predict future population trends, which can provide the scientific bases of future management policies aimed at the sustainable harvest of commercially important species and the recovery of threatened populations (Aires-da-Silva and Gallucci, 2007; Bradshaw *et al.*, 2007; Otway *et al.*, 2004).

The development of effective policies for shark conservation is a complicated process that relies on a series of sequential steps involving scientific communities, as well as the policy makers and other stakeholders (see below). Since sound scientific data are needed to inform decision makers, scientific effort needs to be directed towards areas relevant to the development of conservation policies. Knowledge gaps that prevent the development of efficient conservation strategies must be identified, and future research must be directed towards addressing scientific uncertainties. Conservation policies need to be evidence-based, and subject to continuous scientific evaluation and review. The effectiveness of management policies also needs to be scientifically assessed based on clear performance indicators, and revised management strategies need to be developed based on such assessment. This process involves continuous feedback between scientific enquiry and policy development (see below). The recommendations of the United Nations International Plan of Action for the Conservation and Management of Sharks (IPOA-Sharks) (FAO, 1998; see also Chapter 3) highlight the importance of evidence-based management and continuous feedback between the scientific community and policy makers.

Here we consider some of the main causes of potential mismatches in the science–policy feedback process. We review the last 20 years of scientific studies of shark conservation and management, and identify underlying issues that can lead to misplaced scientific effort. We also present examples where the scientific community and policy makers have worked together in an organic way to develop effective management strategies, and compare these with where the process has broken down or even failed to start. Finally, we suggest a possible way out of this morass through the effective adoption of the Adaptive Management Approach.

Is scientific effort misplaced?

A critical step in the development of effective management policies is scientific assessment. If science is to provide appropriate knowledge needed by policy makers, then scientific effort needs to be directly relevant to management. Globally, if scientific effort is directed towards the development of management policies, we could predict that it would be concentrated in geographic areas where sharks are under high levels of threat or endangerment, and targeted at species that are of major conservation concern.

We analysed the global scientific output in shark management and conservation over the past 20 years (1 January 1992 to 31 December 2011) in order to evaluate whether scientific effort has been most effectively utilized. We undertook a Web of Science search and identified peer-reviewed articles reporting original research containing the words 'shark' and 'conservation' or 'management' in their title, abstract or listed as keywords. For each paper, we recorded target species (up to five), and the location where the study was conducted. The final list included 479 publications.

A sharp increase in research effort has occurred in the last seven years (Figure 5.1). Empirical studies on shark conservation and management were very rare in the 1990s (in 1992 only two studies were published), but in the 2000s shark conservation and management studies became increasingly more common, and in 2011 80 studies on topics relevant to shark conservation were published worldwide. This trend suggests that considerable effort has been placed in research relevant to the conservation and management of shark species at the global scale. However, if we deconstruct the data and look at how scientific effort has been distributed across countries and across species, some clear trends arise.

Geographic bias in scientific and fishing effort

Since fishing mortality is the highest threat to shark populations (Field *et al.*, 2009), if scientific effort was directed towards areas of highest need we would expect scientific output to be correlated with fishing effort on a geographical basis. Nations responsible for the majority of shark landings should place considerably more effort into research relevant to fishery management. However, if we plot nation by nation scientific effort against shark landings, a very different picture emerges (Figure 5.2).

A handful of states are responsible for the vast majority of shark landings. Indonesia (>100,000 tonnes/year), India (>70,000 tonnes/year), Spain (>60,000 tonnes/year), Taiwan (>40,000 tonnes/year), Mexico, Argentina and the

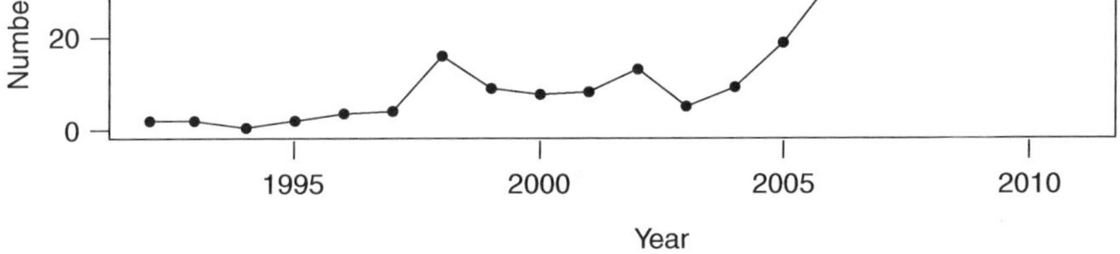

Figure 5.1 Global trend of scientific effort (number of publications) in the period 1992–2011 including in their title, abstract or keywords the words 'shark' and 'conservation' or 'management'.

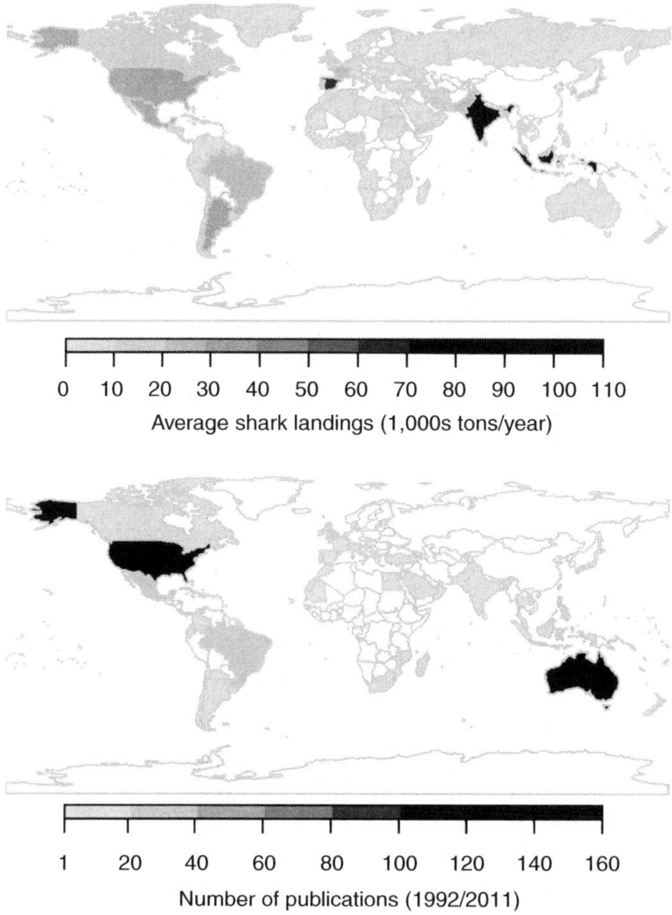

Figure 5.2 National contributions to shark landings (above) and scientific output (below) (source: shark landing data were obtained from the FAO).

United States (>30,000 tonnes/year) make up approximately half of the total landings. Nevertheless, with the exception of the United States and Mexico, these states have placed very little research effort in shark conservation and management (Figure 5.2). Indonesia and India are the leading harvesters of shark products in the world, but these countries rank very low in terms of scientific output. Only nine studies were conducted in Indonesia during the past 20 years, all of which were basic accounts of species composition and basic life history traits from major landing sites (White, 2007a, 2007b, 2010; White *et al.*, 2008; White and Kyne, 2010; Varkey *et al.*, 2010; Blaber *et al.*, 2009). While these studies may constitute a basis for future scientific assessment of national fisheries, they are inadequate with respect to providing necessary information for the development of evidence-based management policies. The situation is very similar in India, Spain, Taiwan and Argentina. More than half of the studies published in the past 20 years have been carried out in the United States and Australia (144 and 117, respectively). While the United States is an important player in shark fisheries at the global scale, Australia, with landings totalling fewer than 10,000 tonnes per year, contributes only 1 per cent towards total global catches. The fact that the United States and Australia are leading the way in shark research is not surprising. The United States leads scientific research globally, producing as many papers across science annually as the rest of the world combined, while Australia is one of the top ten states worldwide in terms of scientific impact (Benz *et al.*, 2004). Furthermore, the United States has economically important shark fisheries, and Australia harbours the highest diversity of shark fauna on Earth (White and Kyne, 2010).

The most likely reason for the disconnect between the production of quality, relevant science and catch size is that scientific effort is highly correlated with economic wealth (Benz *et al.*, 2004), and the countries that are responsible for most of the shark catches are comparatively poor. Research is expensive, and often funded directly by governments, particularly in areas relevant to natural resource management. Developing countries such as Indonesia, and even comparatively more wealthy countries such as India and Mexico, simply do not have the research capacity and the financial resources to carry out extensive research surveys relevant to natural resource management on the same scale as the United States or Australia.

This geographic bias has important consequences in terms of management, and had major repercussions for the implementation of Nation Plans of Action for the Conservation and Management of Sharks (NPOA-Sharks) following the IPOA-Sharks guidelines (see Chapter 3). The two countries that contributed the most to global scientific effort in shark management and conservation were among the first to implement NPOAs (in 2001 and 2004, respectively) (NPOA-Australia, 2004; NPOA-USA, 2001). Australia is the only country in which the NPOA strictly followed the IPOA-Sharks guidelines (Davis and Worm, 2012), and is the only nation that has carried out extensive reviews of the first NPOA, conducted a new shark assessment report and released a second NPOA in 2012 (NPOA-Australia, 2012). By comparison, countries that are major players in the shark fishing industry but did not invest in shark conservation research, such as India and Indonesia, have still failed to produce NPOAs following the IPOA-Sharks guidelines. While India has not implemented an NPOA, the Indonesian government has committed to manage its shark resources through the formulation of an NPOA. However, the Indonesian NPOA released in 2010 did not propose any specific management strategy; rather, it simply highlighted the need to obtain more scientific data to inform management without specifying a framework for increasing research effort. If advances are to be made through mechanisms such as the IPOA, then the most significant shark fishing nations must be encouraged and assisted to develop and implement effective NPOAs. Enhanced collaboration among institutions in developing countries and leading countries in conservation research are likely to be a key process for increasing local research capacity.

Shark conservation science and the issue of taxonomic chauvinism

The goal of conservation biology is to provide the scientific tools needed for the preservation of species that are, either directly or indirectly, threatened by anthropogenic processes (Soulé, 1985). If conservation research is to be informative in terms of management of threatened species, it must give preference to species that are subject to the highest risks and depend for their survival upon the prompt implementation of conservation policies. This leads to a quandary, as species that are threatened are usually less common and/or abundant than species facing little threat and are therefore often more difficult to study. Accordingly, we wondered whether research effort in shark conservation and management does in fact reflect conservation priority, or whether other factors, such as economic importance or the 'charisma' of the study organism are at play. We define economically important species as those species that are directly targeted by important fisheries (data from the IUCN), and charismatic species as sharks that are well-known by the general public and are often used either as flagships for environmental organizations or as eco-tourism attractions (primarily the great white shark, whale shark, basking shark, mako shark, tiger shark, oceanic whitetip shark, hammerhead sharks, grey reef shark and grey nurse/sand tiger/ragged tooth shark).

We found that while research effort is very high for Vulnerable and Near Threatened species, only a small fraction of the scientific output is directed towards species that are Endangered and Critically Endangered (Figure 5.3a). Furthermore, of the 20 most studied shark species, only one is Endangered, but most are either charismatic, of economic importance or both (Figure 5.3b). Species that received the most scientific interest are often not the ones facing the highest threats. Research effort is biased towards charismatic species and species of economic importance, while comparatively little research effort is placed on species that are facing immediate risk of extinction or on species for which insufficient data are available for assessment. This is despite the fact that this scientific effort is specifically linked to conservation and/or management.

Under-representation of endangered and critically endangered species

Scientific output (standardized by species diversity) is not homogeneous across species listed in different IUCN categories ($\chi^2 = 736.8$, df $= 5$, $p < 0.0001$). The

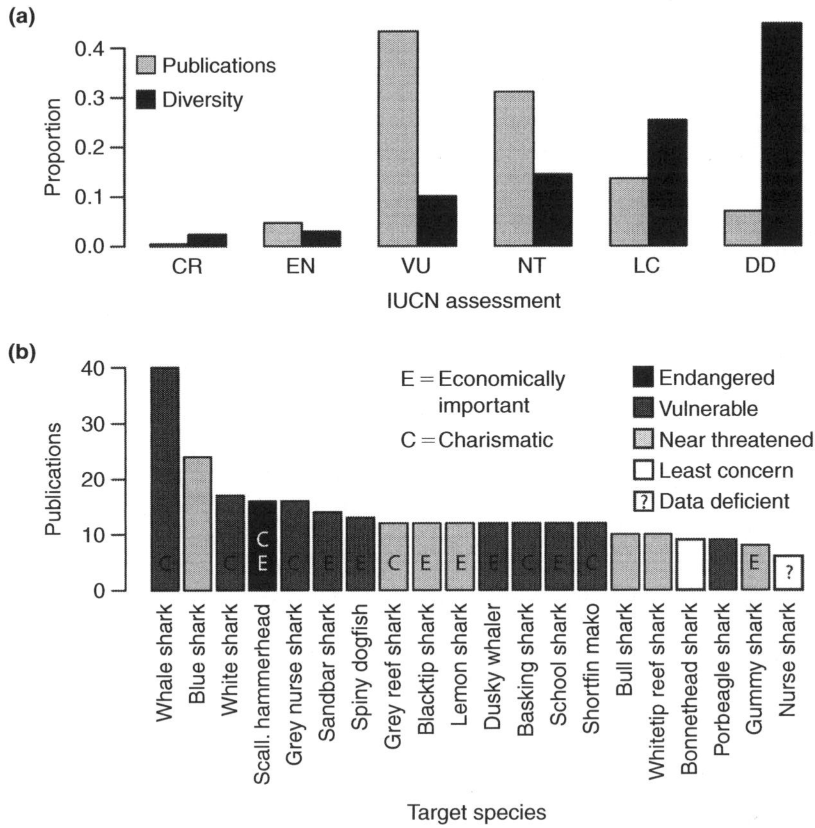

Figure 5.3 Proportion of the scientific output and taxonomic diversity for each IUCN assessment class (a), and number of publications for the most well-studied 20 species of sharks grouped by IUCN assessment (b).

proportion of the scientific output on Near Threatened, Vulnerable and Endangered species is higher than the proportion of taxonomic diversity that is accounted for by these categories, while for Least Concern species it is lower. This trend indicates that scientists are focusing more on species of conservation concern than on species facing no threat. However, while Near Threatened and Vulnerable species received much attention from the scientific community, of the 479 scientific articles reviewed, only 22 (<5 per cent) had Endangered and Critically Endangered species as their target. Of these, 16 (>70 per cent) were focused on a single species of economic importance: the scalloped hammerhead (*Sphyrna lewini*). Alarmingly, Data Deficient species comprise nearly 50 per cent of shark taxonomic diversity, and yet received virtually no attention by the scientific community. The lack of data for these taxa hampers any attempt at effective management.

There are objective difficulties in conducting informative research on Endangered and Critically Endangered species. Common, widespread and abundant species do not usually go extinct in the blink of an eye: they first become rare. Therefore, species that are facing immediate threats of extinction are often rare to begin with and/or have limited distribution ranges, making collecting data a challenging task. It must be stressed that species that are rare or have low densities at present are not necessarily ecologically unimportant, and may have been abundant and relatively common in the past (Pauly, 1995). For example, the angelshark (*Squatina squatina*) was once a common catch in the Mediterranean, but is now extremely rare and has been extirpated throughout most of its range (Cacchi and Notarbartolo di Sciara, 2000; Morey *et al.*, 2006). Similarly the Harrison's dogfish was a common catch in the southeastern Australia deep-water trawling industry, but became rare as a result of overfishing (Graham *et al.*, 2001). Adding to the difficulty of obtaining scientific data, Critically Endangered and Endangered species are often endemic to countries that have limited capacity to undertake research. Of the seven species of angelsharks listed as Critically Endangered and Endangered, five occur in countries with a poor record of research in shark management (Taiwan, Argentina, Ecuador) (data from IUCN). Another example is the Endangered whitefin topeshark (*Hemitriakis leucoperiptera*), endemic to degraded coastal waters of the Philippines, a country where only a single peer-reviewed study related to shark management and conservation has been conducted in the past two decades. The underrepresentation of Endangered and Critically Endangered species in the literature is, in part, related to the strong geographic bias in research effort, which we reported earlier.

Are shark researchers taxonomic chauvinists?

Sharks are an extremely diverse group, numbering in excess of 500 species. However, more than 60 per cent of the published literature has focused on a limited group of 20 species and the ten most studied species contribute >40 per cent to the scientific output over the last two decades.

Among the 20 most studied taxa, only one is listed globally by the IUCN as Endangered. All but five are either well-known charismatic species, or species that are directly targeted by economically important fisheries. There are, of course, obvious reasons for concentrating research effort towards species of economic importance. First, to ensure the economic and ecological sustainability of target fisheries. Furthermore, many fisheries are managed on a single species cost-recovery basis and therefore it is easier to obtain public funding for species of economic importance. This is combined with the management requirement to collect data on major target species, meaning that these data are often readily available in the form of fishers' logbooks and other records. On the other hand, species-level data for by-catch species of little economic importance are often scarce.

While directed fisheries have contributed to the collapse of many shark stocks around the globe, the highest threat to shark population is probably represented by mixed fisheries in which species with a low rebound potential are caught as by-catch in an otherwise sustainable industry (Musick *et al.*, 2000). Therefore, the lack of reliable data and the low level of scientific attention that by-catch species receive may have the effect of delaying management action. One example of the effect of fisheries on by-catch shark species is the collapse of deepwater dogfish (Squalidae) and angelshark (*Squatina* spp.) stocks in south-east Australia. These slow-growing deepwater sharks were caught as by-catch in the lucrative gemfish (*Rexea solandri*) fishery. Since no information on by-catch trends was available for the first three decades of the fishery, by the time the first scientific data on by-catch became available their populations had already declined by nearly 99 per cent (Graham *et al.*, 2001).

Our review also reveals that shark research specifically relating to conservation and management is skewed towards charismatic species. This bias towards charismatic species is not a prerogative of shark researchers. Taxonomic chauvinism is a well-known issue in ecology and conservation science (Bonnet *et al.*, 2002; Clark and May, 2002). Researchers may choose 'popular' organisms as their target species because of their personal preference, or because it is easier to leverage funding. Furthermore, publishing studies in high-impact scientific journals is often easier if a popular species is chosen, reflecting a taxonomic bias in the peer-review process (Bonnet *et al.*, 2002). For example, a reasonably trivial discovery, such as the occurrence of sex-bias dispersal, may earn the authors a *Nature* paper if the species involved is the great white shark (Pardini *et al.*, 2001). Focusing on charismatic species is not necessarily a bad strategy in aiming at conservation for the greater good of marine life in general, and flagship species have proven their worth in other fields of conservation. Charismatic sharks may act as 'flagships', creating public awareness and stimulating conservation action. However, due to their generally wide-ranging habits and given the absence of informative science for the majority of other taxa, creating public awareness by focusing on flagship species is unlikely to provide major benefits to the majority of shark species.

Is management evidence-based?

The implementation of management policies is a complex process. While scientific evidence may suggest which actions need to be undertaken to ensure the conservation of a species, other factors play a major role in policy development. Efficient evidence-based management strategies may seem unfeasible because of their economic cost, low chances of success or because they may not be welcomed by stake-holders and the wider community that perceive them as a limitation of their freedom to use natural resources for economic and leisure activities. Due to the complexity of marine ecosystems as a whole, science may point to management actions that are counter-intuitive and therefore unlikely to win stakeholder support. The result may be failure to initiate conservation action or, worse, implementation of management policies that may be achievable, but lack a biological basis and therefore are likely to be ineffective (Svancara *et al.*, 2005). Here we review a case in which scientific data informed a successful evidence-based management strategy, and two cases in which no management actions followed scientific assessment.

The management of sandbar sharks in the United States and the Mediterranean Sea

The sandbar shark (*Carcharhinus plumbeus*) is a coastal species that supports large commercial fisheries around the globe. Sandbar sharks are large and long-lived, reaching sexual maturity at 15–16 years, and have low reproductive output (Sminkey and Musick, 1995). Because of their life history strategies they are very susceptible to fishery overexploitation, and have been listed by the IUCN as Vulnerable (Musick *et al.*, 2009). While fishery stocks have been over-exploited in many different countries, management of sandbar sharks in the United States is an example of appropriate management based on sound scientific data. Here we review the fundamental steps in scientific assessment and policy development of sandbar shark fisheries in the United States, and contrast these with the situation in the Mediterranean Sea.

In the United States, sandbar shark landings started to increase dramatically in the 1980s, following a rise in demand of shark products. Landings peaked in 1989 and started to decline thereafter. By the early 2000s, spawning stocks had declined by approximately 70 per cent (SEDAR, 2011). In 1993, the Fishery Management Plan for Sharks of the Atlantic Ocean (1993 FMP) established a framework to determine fishery quotas and bag size limits based on maximum sustainable yield (MSY). In the 1990s and 2000s, significant effort had been made in identifying fishing stocks using genetic and mark–recapture data and collecting life history parameters to estimate demographic responses to fishery mortality and rebuilding strategies. Most of these efforts led to the publication of high-quality, peer-reviewed articles that were the basis of stock assessment reports (Heist and Gold, 1999; Heist *et al.*, 1995; Merson and Pratt Jr, 2001; Rechisky and Wetherbee, 2003; Grubbs *et al.*, 2007; McCandless and Frazier, 2010). The National Marine Fisheries Service (NMFS) of the National Oceanic and Atmospheric Administration (NOAA) convened fishery stock assessments for the sandbar sharks in 1996, 2002, 2005/2006 and again in 2011. Following each of the stock assessments, new management strategies were implemented (SEDAR, 2011). These included reduced fishery quotas and recreational bag limits (1999), the establishment of time/area fishery closures, prohibition of shark finning (2006), the establishment of a rebuilding strategy (2008) and of a research fishery for the collection of life history traits of sandbar sharks (2008). Since 2008, it has been illegal to land any sandbar sharks without a scientific permit. While stocks are still depleted and recovery may take decades, this is an example of how scientific effort can inform appropriate adaptive management.

Unlike the United States stocks, sandbar sharks are not subject to management in the Mediterranean Sea. Once commonly caught, and often seen at fish markets in the Levantine and Sicily, sandbar shark numbers have experienced a dramatic decline and virtually disappeared from landings in most of the Mediterranean (Ferretti *et al.*, 2005), with the exception of the Gulf of Gabès in southern Tunisia (Saïumldi *et al.*, 2005). They are still sporadically caught as by-catch in tuna and swordfish longline fisheries (Megalofonou, 2005). Following a local assessment, the IUCN listed sandbar shark in the Mediterranean as Endangered (Musick *et al.*, 2009). However, no rebuilding strategy has been implemented in the Mediterranean Sea and stocks remain unmanaged. Important nursery grounds have been identified off the coast of Tunisia and Turkey, but no spatial closures have been implemented to protect juveniles. In 2003 an Action Plan for the Conservation of Cartilaginous Fishes in the Mediterranean Sea was released (UNEP, 2003), and a new shark assessment report was presented in 2009. While in these documents the sandbar shark is listed as a commercial species, no stock assessment and no management actions are planned for the Mediterranean Sea.

The Shark Meshing (Bather Protection) Program in New South Wales

The Shark Meshing (Bather Protection) Program (SMP) was established in New South Wales (NSW) in 1937 and has operated continuously since. The SMP was introduced following a spate of shark attacks at Sydney beaches and it is designed to reduce shark attacks and interactions between sharks and swimmers. To achieve these goals, the NSW government established a system of large mesh gillnets deployed immediately proximate to 51 popular beaches along the coast of NSW. The SMP is not a physical barrier to prevent sharks from reaching popular beaches, but rather aims at reducing interactions with large sharks by culling local populations. The intent of the SMP is to reduce densities of large, dangerous sharks (e.g. white sharks, tiger sharks and bull sharks), but these species have always constituted a relatively small proportion of the catch.

In the first decades of the SMP, grey nurse sharks (*Carcharias taurus*) were caught in large numbers (Reid *et al.*, 2011), particularly in the Newcastle region circa 200km north of Sydney,[1] where the SMP appears to have been a contributing factor in the dramatic decline of this species (Green *et al.*, 2009). The eastern Australian grey nurse shark population is now listed as Critically Endangered under the *Environment Protection and Biodiversity Conservation Act* (1999)[2] and as an isolated population of <2,000 individuals (Ahonen *et al.*, 2009; Stow *et al.*, 2006) is facing extinction if threatening processes are not mitigated (Otway *et al.*, 2004). Few grey nurse sharks are now caught in beach nets in NSW, probably due to the reduction in their numbers, yet the SMP still accounts for approximately 5–10 per cent of anthropogenic mortality (Reid *et al.*, 2011). Accordingly, the SMP remains one of the key threatening factors for the eastern Australian population. Grey nurse sharks are not the only protected non-target species that is caught as by-catch in the SMP. Hammerheads have made up more than 50 per cent of the catch in the SMP over the past two decades (Green *et al.*, 2009). Three species of hammerheads are caught in the SMP: the smooth hammerhead (*Sphyrna zygaena*), which likely makes up the vast majority of the catch; the great hammerhead (*S. mokorran*); and the scalloped hammerhead (*S. lewini*). The smooth hammerhead is listed by the IUCN as Vulnerable and the great hammerhead and the scalloped hammerhead are fully protected species in NSW and listed respectively as Vulnerable and Endangered. In March 2009, a report to the NSW Department of Primary Industries reviewed the existing NSW SMP and, using all the available scientific evidence, made explicit recommendations about alternatives to shark nets in order to reduce by-catch in areas where grey nurse sharks are caught (Green *et al.*, 2009). While the SMP appears to have been effective in reducing shark fatalities since its establishment, alternative bather protection programmes exist that are more selective with respect to target species. One alternative strategy is to replace part of the nets with baited drumlines, which consists of baited hooks secured above the bottom (Dudley *et al.*, 1998; Sumpton *et al.*, 2011). A long-term study in Queensland showed that baited drumlines are efficient in catching dangerous sharks, while greatly reducing by-catch of endangered shark species, including hammerheads and grey nurse sharks, as well as increasing by-catch survival rates (Sumpton *et al.*, 2011). The partial replacement of mesh nets with baited drumlines has been shown to be effective in avoiding an increase in shark attacks in South Africa (Cliff and Dudley, 2011), where the replacement programme is now being expanded.

Despite evidence that the SMP is classified under legislation as a Key Threatening Process[3] to more than one protected, threatened species in NSW, that alternatives exists and that all the science points to the effectiveness of alternatives both to mitigate conservation issues and maintain protection, management decisions do not concur. The NSW government has continued the SMP in its current form despite recommendations solicited directly from its own Department of Primary Industries (Green *et al.*, 2009). In fact, the SMP has been championed by the NSW government for decades as an effective strategy for bather protection, and it is likely that an extensive review of the SMP will attract a heated public debate.

The adaptive management approach: resolving the science management disconnect?

In summary, we have seen that science can effectively inform appropriate management policy, but that critical to effective management is that the stakeholders, including science practitioners, are all brought on board in the process. How can this be done most effectively? We propose that one method that may help reduce the apparent disconnect is to adopt the adaptive management approach based on the Adaptive Environmental Assessment and Management (AEAM) process originally proposed by Holling (1978). Research suggests that this approach provides an effective tool in the long-term management of complex and uncertain environments (Walters, 1986; Walters and Green, 1997; though see Walters, 2007 for how successful it has proven in practice).

The adaptive management approach provides a useful framework because the objective is to formulate a workable management plan while also trying to gain a better understanding of the underlying ecology through experimentation. AEAM probes the dynamic responses of a system in order to improve management and is particularly important when counterintuitive responses arise. For example, scientists or managers may attempt to base predictions on simple, common sense arguments (e.g. 'reducing mortality rate of sharks should cause their abundance to increase'), when in fact the complexity of ecological systems means that responses may depend on indirect and multiple causal pathways whereby reduction in mortality in one life history phase may actually decrease production. Management problems typically differ from pure scientific problems in a number of ways:

- management questions commonly imply a much broader perspective on a system than technical experts adopt;
- management questions are about distinguishing between alternative policies, not about precision in prediction, as such; and
- the breadth of interests implied in management questions requires confronting ignorance and uncertainty.

The adaptive management approach confronts these issues explicitly. Its core methodologies include:

- bringing multiple perspectives into dialogue to develop a broad view of the problems;
- embracing uncertainty by focusing on exploring its shape, rather than by trying to eliminate it across the board.

We suggest that an appropriate approach to resolve the disconnect is for research to be driven by a focus on achieving workable management outcomes informed as much as possible by objective scientific investigation. A powerful method to enable this approach consists of conducting workshops involving key stakeholders (fisheries management agencies, scientists, shark fishing/tourism industry, etc.), the objectives of which are to:

- identify the various perspectives on the problem;
- seek to reach consensus on the nature and scope of the problem being addressed;

- achieve a better understanding of shark/fisheries interactions and to gain an understanding of all information currently available;
- identify gaps and shortfalls in existing information;
- prioritize data-gathering efforts to focus on that information required to direct management or to test specific hypotheses; and
- identify potential management objectives

Walters (2007) has outlined both the strength of this approach and also identified the risks of failure. He points out that while AEAM workshops frequently can provide consensus about the need for an experimental management programme, that without a champion (usually from within a regulatory agency, the '*compleat emmanuensis*' *sensu* Holling 1978), AEAM programmes fail to materialize.

Given the rate at which shark populations are declining, and the relatively limited scientific effort apportioned to understanding their demise, the time is ripe for a renewed attempt to enact management with a common purpose and with the highest chance of success. We have learnt only too well that management cannot succeed without stakeholder support. The most powerful management incorporates science as a means of informing best practice. AEAM has struggled not to gain consensus in terms of desired outcomes, which is relatively straightforward, but to follow through with effective experimental approaches due to the complexity of marine ecosystems combined with the expense of monitoring the process.

We suggest that with the new opportunities that arise from technological advances, we might be on the verge of a new and effective era in management. With new technology comes the ability to create novel and innovative monitoring systems that use the experience and expertise of the industry partners themselves (e.g. electronic tagging, geo-referenced GPS, electronic logbooks) to economically collect the data. This is what is required for large-scale AEAM experimentation and is now feasible even in relatively poor countries. This, combined with the ability to economically communicate widely and swiftly to all stakeholders and for real-time monitoring of catches, combined with the ability to model ecosystems with a much higher degree of finesse, bodes well for future success.

Notes

1 The Newcastle region is the area surrounding Newcastle, a coastal city located in the NSW Hunter Region, approximately 160km north of Sydney.

2 The *Environment Protection and Biodiversity Conservation Act* (1999) is the most significant federal environmental legislation in Australia, providing the main legislative framework for the protection of the Australian environment, including its biodiversity.

3 A Key Threatening Process is a process that threatens or may threaten the survival, abundance or evolutionary development of a native species or ecological community.

The SMP is listed as a Key Threatening Process under the *NSW Fisheries Management Act 1994* and the *Threatened Species Conservation Act 1995* because of its adverse effects on great white sharks (*Carcharodon carcharias*), the critically endangered grey nurse shark (*Carcharias taurus*), hammerheads (*Sphyrna* spp.) and other non-target sharks, as well as Vulnerable and Endangered marine mammals (dugongs, fur seals, etc.) and turtles.

References

Ahonen, H., Harcourt, R. and Stow, A. (2009) 'Nuclear and mitochondrial DNA reveals isolation of imperilled grey nurse shark populations (*Carcharias taurus*)', *Molecular Ecology*, vol. 18, pp. 4409–4421.

Aires-Da-Silva, A. M. and Gallucci, V. F. (2007) 'Demographic and risk analyses applied to management and conservation of the blue shark (*Prionace glauca*) in the North Atlantic Ocean', *Marine and Freshwater Research*, vol. 58, pp. 570–580.

Baum, J. K. and Myers, R. A. (2004) 'Shifting baselines and the decline of pelagic sharks in the Gulf of Mexico', *Ecology Letters*, vol. 7, pp. 135–145.

Baum, J. K., Myers, R. A., Kehler, D. G., Worm, B., Harley, S. J. and Doherty, P. A. (2003) 'Collapse and conservation of shark populations in the Northwest Atlantic', *Science*, vol. 299, pp. 389–392.

Benz, G. W., Hocking, R., Kowunna Sr, A., Bullard, S. A. and George, J. C. (2004) 'A second species of Arctic shark: Pacific sleeper shark *Somniosus pacificus* from Point Hope, Alaska', *Polar Biology*, vol. 27, pp. 250–252.

Blaber, S., Dichmont, C., White, W., Buckworth, R., Sadiyah, L., Iskandar, B., Nurhakim, S., Pillans, R. and Andamari, R. (2009) 'Elasmobranchs in southern Indonesian fisheries: the fisheries, the status of the stocks and management options', *Reviews in Fish Biology and Fisheries*, vol. 19, pp. 367–391.

Bonnet, X., Shine, R. and Lourdais, O. (2002) 'Taxonomic chauvinism', *Trends in Ecology and Evolution*, vol. 17, pp. 1–3.

Bradshaw, C. J., Mollet, H. F. and Meekan, M. G. (2007) 'Inferring population trends for the world's largest fish from mark–recapture estimates of survival', *Journal of Animal Ecology*, vol. 76, pp. 480–489.

Bradshaw, C. J., Mollet, H. F. and Meekan, M. G. (2013) 'More analytical bite in estimating targets for shark harvest', *Marine Ecology Progress Series*, vol. 488, pp. 221–232.

Cacchi, M. and Notarbartolo Di Sciara, G. (2000) 'The cartilaginous fishes in the Italian Seas, a resource that urges to be protected', *Biologia Marina Medditeranea*, vol. 7, pp. 296–311.

Clark, J. A. and May, R. M. (2002) 'Taxonomic bias in conservation research', *Science*, vol. 297, pp. 191–192.

Cliff, G. and Dudley, S. F. (2011) 'Reducing the environmental impact of shark-control programs: a case study from KwaZulu-Natal, South Africa', *Marine and Freshwater Research*, vol. 62, pp. 700–709.

Davis, B. and Worm, B. (2012) 'The International Plan of Action for Sharks: how does national implementation measure up?' *Marine Policy*, vol. 40, pp. 194–204.

Dudley, S., Haestier, R., Cox, K. and Murray, M. (1998) 'Shark control: experimental fishing with baited drumlines', *Marine and Freshwater Research*, vol. 49, pp. 653–661.

FAO (1998) *International Plan of Action for the Conservation and Management of Sharks*, FAO, Rome.

Ferretti, F., Myers, R. A., Sartor, P. and Serena, F. (2005) 'Long term dynamics of the chondrichthyan fish community in the upper Tyrrhenian Sea', ICES Doc CM 2005/N:25.

Ferretti, F., Myers, R. A., Serena, F. and Lotze, H. K. (2008) 'Loss of large predatory sharks from the Mediterranean Sea', *Conservation Biology*, vol. 22, pp. 952–964.

Field, I. C., Meekan, M. G., Buckworth, R. C. and Bradshaw, C. J. (2009) 'Susceptibility of sharks, rays and chimaeras to global extinction', *Advances in Marine Miology*, vol. 56, pp. 275–363.

Graham, K., Andrew, N. and Hodgson, K. (2001) 'Changes in relative abundance of sharks and rays on Australian South East Fishery trawl grounds after twenty years of fishing', *Marine and Freshwater Research*, vol. 52, pp. 549–561.

Green, M., Ganassin, C. and Reid, D. D. (2009) *Report into the NSW Shark Meshing (Bather Protection) Program*, NSW Department of Primary Industries, Orange, Australia.

Grubbs, R. D., Musick, J., Conrath, C. L. and Romine, J. G. (2007) 'Long-term movements, migration, and temporal delineation of a summer nursery for juvenile sandbar sharks in the Chesapeake Bay region', *American Fisheries Society Symposium*, vol. 50, pp. 63–85.

Heist, E. J. and Gold, J. R. (1999) 'Microsatellite DNA variation in sandbar sharks (*Carcharhinus plumbeus*) from the Gulf of Mexico and mid-Atlantic Bight', *Copeia*, vol. 1999, pp. 182–186.

Heist, E. J., Graves, J. E. and Musick, J. A. (1995) 'Population genetics of the sandbar shark (*Carcharhinus plumbeus*) in the Gulf of Mexico and Mid-Atlantic Bight', *Copeia*, vol. 1995, pp. 555–562.

Holling, C. S. (1978) *Adaptive Environmental Assessment and Management*, John Wiley and Sons, London.

Lack, M. and Sant, G. (2006) *World Shark Catch, Production and Trade 1990–2003*, Department of the Environment and Heritage, Canberra.

Last, P. R. and Stevens, J. D. (2009) *Sharks and Rays of Australia*, Havard University Press, London.

McCandless, C. and Frazier, B. (2010) *Standardized Catch Rates for Sandbar and Blacknose Sharks Caught During the South Carolina COASTSPAN and SCDNR Red Drum Surveys*, SEDAR 21, Data Workshop Document.

Megalofonou, P. (2005) 'Incidental catch and estimated discards of pelagic sharks from the swordfish and tuna fisheries in the Mediterranean Sea', *Fishery Bulletin*, vol. 103, pp. 620–634.

Merson, R. R. and Pratt Jr, H. L. (2001) 'Distribution, movements and growth of young sandbar sharks, *Carcharhinus plumbeus*, in the nursery grounds of Delaware Bay', *Environmental Biology of Fishes*, vol. 61, pp. 13–24.

Morey, G., Moranta, J., Riera, F., Grau, A. M. and Morales-Nin, B. (2006) 'Elasmobranchs in trammel net fishery associated to marine reserves in the Balearic Islands (NW Mediterranean)', *Cybium*, vol. 30, pp. 125–132.

Musick, J. A., Burgess, G., Cailliet, G., Camhi, M. and Fordham, S. (2000) 'Management of sharks and their relatives (Elasmobranchii)', *Fisheries*, vol. 25, pp. 9–13.

Musick, J. A., Stevens, J. D., Baum, J. K., Bradai, M., Clò, S., Fergusson, I., Grubbs, R. D., Soldo, A., Vaccho, M. and Vooren, C. M. (2009) '*Carcharhinus plumbeus*', *IUCN Red List of Threatened Species, Version 2012.2*, available at www.iucnredlist.org, accessed 31 September 2013.

NPOA-Australia (2004) *National Plan of Action for the Conservation and Management of Sharks (Shark-plan)*, Department of Agriculture, Fisheries and Forestry, Australian government, Canberra.

NPOA-Australia (2012) *National Plan of Action for the Conservation and Management of Sharks (Shark-plan 2)*, Department of Agriculture, Fisheries and Forestry, Australian government, Canberra.

NPOA-USA (2001) *United States National Plan of Action for the Conservaion and Management of Sharks*, Department of Commerce, National Oceanic and Atmospheric Administration, National Marine Fisheries Service, Silver Spring, MD.

Otway, N. M., Bradshaw, C. J. and Harcourt, R. G. (2004) 'Estimating the rate of quasi-extinction of the Australian grey nurse shark *Carcharias taurus* population using deterministic age- and stage-classified models', *Biological Conservation*, vol. 119, pp. 341–350.

Pardini, T., Jones, C. S., Noble, L. R., Kreiser, B., Malcom, H., Bruce, B. D., Stevens, J. D., Cliff, G., Scholl, M. C., Francis, M. P., Duffy, C. A. J. and Martin, A. P. (2001) 'Sex-biased dispersal of great white sharks', *Nature*, vol. 412, pp. 139–140.

Pauly, D. (1995) 'Anecdotes and the shifting baseline syndrome of fisheries', *Trends in Ecology and Evolution*, vol. 10, p. 430.

Rechisky, E. L. and Wetherbee, B. M. (2003) 'Short-term movements of juvenile and neonate sandbar sharks, *Carcharhinus plumbeus*, on their nursery grounds in Delaware Bay', *Environmental Biology of Fishes*, vol. 68, pp. 113–128.

Reid, D. D., Robbins, W. D. and Peddemors, V. M. (2011) 'Decadal trends in shark catches and effort from the New South Wales, Australia, Shark Meshing Program 1950–2010', *Marine and Freshwater Research*, vol. 62, pp. 676–693.

Rose, D. A. (1996) *An Overview of World Trade in Sharks and Other Cartilaginous Fishes*, TRAFFIC International, Cambridge.

Saïumldi, B., Bradaï, M. N., Bouaïumln, A. G., Guéacutelorget, O. and Capapé, C. (2005) 'The reproductive biology of the sandbar shark, *Carcharhinus plumbeus* (Chondrichthyes: Carcharhinidae), from the Gulf of Gabès (southern Tunisia, central Mediterranean)', *Acta adriatica*, vol. 46, pp. 47–62.

SEDAR (2011), *HMS Sandbar Shark*, SEDAR, North Charleston, SC.

Sminkey, T. R. and Musick, J. A. (1995) 'Age and growth of the sandbar shark, *Carcharhinus plumbeus*, before and after population depletion', *Copeia*, vol. 1995, pp. 871–883.

Smith, S. E., Au, D. W. and Show, C. (1998) 'Intrinsic rebound potentials of 26 species of Pacific sharks', *Marine and Freshwater Research*, vol. 49, pp. 663–678.

Soulé, M. E. (1985) 'What is conservation biology?', *BioScience*, vol. 35, pp. 727–734.

Stow, A., Zenger, K., Briscoe, D., Gillings, M., Peddemors, V., Otway, N. and Harcourt, R. (2006) 'Isolation and genetic diversity of endangered grey nurse shark (*Carcharias taurus*) populations', *Biology Letters*, vol. 2, pp. 308–311.

Sumpton, W. D., Taylor, S. M., Gribble, N. A., McPherson, G. and Ham, T. (2011) 'Gear selectivity of large-mesh nets and drumlines used to catch sharks in the Queensland Shark Control Program', *African Journal of Marine Science*, vol. 33, pp. 37–43.

Svancara, L. K., Brannon, J. R., Scott, M., Groves, C. R., Noss, R. F. and Pressey, R. L. (2005) 'Policy-driven versus evidence-based conservation: a review of political targets and biological needs', *BioScience*, vol. 55, pp. 989–995.

UNEP (2003) *Action Plan for the Conservation of Cartilaginous (Chondrichthyans) in the Mediterranean Sea*, Mediterranean Action Plan, RAC/SPA, MAP, Tunis.

Varkey, D. A., Ainsworth, C. H., Pitcher, T. J., Goram, Y. and Sumaila, R. (2010) 'Illegal, unreported and unregulated fisheries catch in Raja Ampat Regency, Eastern Indonesia', *Marine Policy*, vol. 34, pp. 228–236.

Walters, C. J. (1986) *Adaptative Management of Renewable Resource*, Macmillan Publishing, New York.

Walters, C. J. (2007) 'Is adaptive management helping to solve fisheries problems?', *AMBIO: A Journal of the Human Environment*, vol. 36, pp. 304–307.

Walters, C. J. and Green, R. (1997) 'Valuation of experimental management options for ecological systems', *Journal of Wildlife Management*, vol. 61, pp. 987–1006.

White, W. T. (2007a) 'Aspects of the biology of carcharhiniform sharks in Indonesian waters', *Journal of the Marine Biological Association of the UK*, vol. 87, pp. 1269–1276.

White, W. T. (2007b) 'Catch composition and reproductive biology of whaler sharks (Carcharhiniformes: Carcharhinidae) caught by fisheries in Indonesia', *Journal of Fish Biology*, vol. 71, pp. 1512–1540.

White, W. T. (2010) 'Aspects of maturation and reproduction in hexanchiform and squaliform sharks', *Journal of Fish Biology*, vol. 76, pp. 1362–1378.

White, W. T. and Kyne, P. (2010) 'The status of chondrichthyan conservation in the Indo-Australasian region', *Journal of Fish Biology*, vol. 76, pp. 2090–2117.

White, W. T., Barton, C. and Potter, I. (2008) 'Catch composition and reproductive biology of *Sphyrna lewini* (Griffith & Smith) (Carcharhiniformes, Sphyrnidae) in Indonesian waters', *Journal of Fish Biology*, vol. 72, pp. 1675–1689.

Chapter 6

Human perceptions and attitudes towards sharks

Examining the predator policy paradox

Christopher Neff

Introduction

The meaning given to the human–shark relationship has had a profound impact on shark management and governance for centuries. This connection has been one of great reverence as well as great fear. Local Indigenous fishing activities in the Pacific gave roles of leadership to fishers who swam with sharks (Beckwith, 1917). Rather than a one-way relationship, this worked in both directions, with sharks helping the community. The presence of sharks meant the presence of fish and the survival of the society. However, the more dominant public perception has been one of sharks as a threat to survival, with the rise of recreational water-use and shark bite incidents. The result has been a political tension between public perceptions of sharks, shark bite prevention policies and shark conservation that has implications for shark conservation governance.

Understanding the importance of shark bite prevention policies is critical to shark conservation governance for three reasons. First, these policies can indiscriminately kill endangered shark species. Second, these policies can challenge and undermine existing shark conservation laws. And third, policy responses that target sharks for culls send a message to the public that sharks should be feared and this weakens public support, damaging broader shark conservation efforts. Alternative approaches following shark bites that consider the role of humans and the value of sharks are therefore powerful instruments in advancing shark conservation.

This chapter addresses the way perceptions about sharks and shark bites can impact shark conservation and improve management. Simply put, the things the public cares about are more likely to be saved and protected by governments than those that are feared (Czech *et al.*, 1998). The framing of shark bites presents a challenge by asking for narratives and responses that appreciate and protect the threat. In this way, the stories presented around shark bites on humans are critically important to shark conservation. I argue that governments must address a 'predator policy paradox' (Neff, 2012) in which policy makers face decisions about protecting shark species that may harm the public. Addressing this paradox improves the governance of sharks by sustaining public support for the conservation of sharks both in-shore and off-shore. Here, the potential threats sharks pose are reconciled with the multiple causal factors involved and the value they provide to the oceans.

Background

The governance of sharks near coastlines is a complex public policy endeavour. Many governments address the predator policy paradox by instituting shark control methods that kill sharks in targeted or unselective ways. The history of shark nets in Australia over 80 years (Neff, 2012) tells that story. And the rise of shark hunts since 2010 (Neff and Yang, 2013; Neff and Hueter, 2013) has been clear in locations such as Egypt, Russia, Reunion Island, Mexico, the Seychelles and Western Australia. Less discussed, however, is the emergence of policy responses based on *human factors* that contribute to human–shark interactions and are more consistent with shark conservation. These policies focus on regulating different human behaviours that may lead to human–shark interactions.

One example of shark bite policy responses based on human factors are 2002 regulations aimed at restrictions on shark eco-tourism in Hawaii. The Act stated, 'The measure's purpose is to insure public safety in near shore waters by banning commercial shark feeding operations that may aggravate the problem of aggressive shark behavior towards swimmers and surfers' (DLNR, 2002). More recently, this continued in Hawaii following a fatal shark bite on Maui in August 2013. The Mayor noted the role of *human factors* leading to these incidents. He stated,

> I don't think we're going to have a huge escalation [in shark bite incidents] unless we keep acting silly and depleting all of the natural resources and dirtying up the resources, where it makes it more difficult for the sharks to determine we're there.
>
> (*Maui News*, 2013)

The impact of coastal development has also been linked to the rise of shark bite incidents. A study by Hazin *et al.* (2008, p. 199) reviewed the increase in shark bite incidents in Recife, Brazil. They found that a major construction project was linked to these incidents, stating 'the construction and growth of the Suape Port, located just to the south of Recife, has resulted in major environmental degradation and is likely to have played a role in the recent onset of shark attacks'. The response to this new data has been to ban surfing along certain beaches in Brazil (*Orlando Sentinel*, 1999). Consistent with this are recent bans on swimming near seals in Cape Cod (Omer, 2012).

In addition, proposals have been made to limit the number of licensed commercial cage diving operators around white sharks in South Australia and in Western Australia (Phillips, 2012). At issue was the way commercial chumming (also called berleying) around white shark populations can change shark behaviour. Huveneers *et al.* (2012, p. 12) note:

> Sites where white sharks aggregate are often targeted by wildlife tourism operators to run cage-diving tours. As a result, these sites are areas where white sharks can be exposed to frequent interactions and a high level of interference from human activities. For example, some sites in South Africa have up to seven different cage-diving operators working simultaneously, with some cage-diving operators hosting up to three expeditions per day.

In Western Australia, in 2012, the government banned cage dive operations off its coast. Fisheries Minister Norman Moore stated, 'While there was no determination from the study about the longer-term effects on shark behaviour or outside the study area, I would prefer to take no risks until more is known' (AAP, 2012).

In Cape Town, officials have also begun an enclosure net trial at Fish Hoek beach to create a barrier between sharks and people, with strict environmental standards being placed on the enclosure (including removing it each night). A Western Australia local council has also supported enclosure nets designed to sit fixed in the water (AAP, 2013).

The emphasis on *human factors* responses harken back to a previous period of the 1930s in Australia regarding the role of people's behaviour. In 1929, a 'shark bait' law (SMC, 1929) was passed by the New South Wales (NSW) government that placed a £10 fine on swimmers who went out too far (Neff, 2012). Sewage outfalls and abattoir run-off were also seen as attractants for sharks, with changes recommended to pipelines in Sydney (Neff, 2012).

More recent shifts are predicated on the consideration of a range of causal factors that lead to these incidents. These frames fall outside of the classic *Jaws* schema, where innocent swimmers are placed in one category while a rogue shark that is hunting them is placed in another. I suggest that the introduction of new images of shark bites that contrast with 'Jaws effect' (Neff and Hueter, 2013) framing is important in this process.

Scientific analyses that label shark bites as accidents (Maxwell, 1949), mistaken identity (Tricas and McCosker, 1984), the result of defensiveness (Gruber, 1988) or human activity (Hazin *et al.*, 2008) can paint vivid causal stories based on the familiarity that people see between people and sharks. A good example is the way in which the public perceives shark bites as cases of mistaken identity between humans and seals. Whether this is in fact true is less important than the impact that it had on changing the fundamental conception of sharks as intentionally biting humans. Here a different message was introduced that said that we are 'in the way, not on the menu' (Neff, 2012; Neff and Hueter, 2013).

Thus, a contemporary policy trend has emerged to remedy the conflicts between shark control and shark conservation through policies that place the onus on human factors and behaviour in the occurrence of shark bites and their future prevention. These human-based measures are founded in frames which value sharks rather than blaming them for bite incidents.

To examine the way public perceptions impact the direction of policies that favour shark control or human factors I review the way the media identified problems and solutions following shark bite events in South Africa, the United States and Australia. In the first two, local and state governments experienced positive feedback towards human factor policy solutions. However, in Australia, the shark bite incident reinforced negative feedback in favour of shark control policies due to the dominance of traditional policy making venues and the framing of public risk.

This chapter moves forward in three parts: first, I begin by noting the literature regarding public perceptions of sharks in surveys and media analyses. Second, I examine the media reporting following incidents in Western Australia in 2000, Florida in 2001 and Cape Town in 2004 to examine the connections between the portrayal of problems and solutions and the selection of policies that focus on killing sharks to address the issue or that prioritize human factors as a means of shark bite prevention. Lastly, a discussion and conclusion reviews the implications of the data and provides final comments.

Public perceptions of sharks

Over the past 30 years, a duality of frames and policies has emerged as images of sharks have led to competing policies for public safety or shark control and shark protection or conservation. Attention becomes crucial as new ideas and information about sharks' behaviour and their shrinking populations challenge the old myths, drama and imagery of human–shark interactions. At odds are the media and public, which commonly identify sharks as 'man-eaters', portraying beachgoers at constant risk of a bite, and those scientists and environmentalists who suggest that sharks are important and vulnerable creatures of nature, which do bite, but would prefer to avoid humans altogether.

Examining public perceptions and policy making during the periods following shark bites remains an understudied area within the literature. Politically, these choices rely largely on how risk is framed, the stability of decision-making institutions, and the strength of alternative frames and options. This chapter uses a problem definition analysis to look at the problem and solution of sharks and human–shark interactions by the public. The important role of problem definition in framing the issue can be seen in a number of public surveys that have been conducted regarding public feelings toward sharks. How a problem is framed informs the solution (Rochefort and Cobb, 1994). Deborah Stone (1989) defines problem definition identification as 'a process of image making, where the images have to do fundamentally with attributing cause, blame, and responsibility' (Stone, 1989). As a result, causal stories can facilitate or block policy change.

In addition, the selection of policy responses impacts public perceptions. Poumadere and Mays (2003) suggest that 'responses to risk event[s] actually define the risk itself: the construction of the event, psychologically and socially shared in interaction and in collective sense making, itself shapes the danger' (Poudamere and Mays, 2003, p. 209). Moreover, the identification of the problem and allocation of blame establishes the 'possibility of control' (Stone, 1989, p. 283). By assigning intent to sharks within this causal story they become a problem to be controlled and solved. However, the identification of the problem through harm and risk assumes a number of biases. Because policy outcomes following periods of instability can 'lead to lurches in policy making' and changes in 'issue definitions' (Jones, 1994, p. 24) one-sided framings can arise. Indeed, while causal stories are strongest when they are 'broadly acceptable, technically feasible and cost effective to merit consideration' (Kingdon cited in Wood, 2006, p. 424) they also remain open to false or emotive impacts.

A number of surveys begin to paint a picture of the separations between frames related to shark conservation and those based on shark bite prevention. In a survey conducted by Spruill (1997), she stated:

> only 30% thought that the killing of sharks was a serious problem; however, when asked their reaction to the statement that, in some places, fins are cut off living sharks that are then thrown back into the water to die, 42% responded that it made them 'extremely angry'. This may indicate that inhumane treatment of any animal transcends how we may view a particular species.

It is not clear that the public sees a connection between support for anti-finning efforts and support for local shark conservation of dangerous species. Following the United States' 'Summer of the Shark' in 2001, the Baltimore Aquarium released the results of a survey in 2003 which found that 'More than 80 per cent said shark populations are "just right" or "too high".' (National Aquarium of Baltimore, 2002). In addition, 'More than 70 per cent believe that sharks are dangerous.' And finally, 'nearly 60 per cent of respondents said they thought sharks need protection'. These competing frames highlight two different problem definitions that are based on the local nature of shark species. In all, we see low support for sharks following the Summer of the Shark 2001.

In South Australia, there were a number of fatal shark bite incidents in the early 2000s. Lamb *et al.* (2005) conducted a survey that included both surfers and non-surfers to examine perceptions of real risk versus perceived risk from shark bites. Respondents estimated that there had been more shark bite incidents over the past 50 years (up to 14 incidents), which was higher than the six incidents during that period. In addition, their survey found that non-surfers had a higher degree of fear of shark bites (4.6 out of 10) than surfers (1.9 out of 10) (Lamb *et al.*, 2005).

A survey conducted by the author in Cape Town, South Africa examined local perceptions of white sharks before and after a shark bite in 2010–2011. Respondents were asked to indicate their level of support or pride in local marine life, including sharks, seals and dolphins. This survey took place at Fish Hoek and Muizenberg beaches in June and October 2010 (Figure 6.1). Pride and support were measured on a Likert-type scale of 1–10, with 1 indicating little pride and 10 indicating a lot of pride.

There were three main points from this research. First, the level of reported pride in sharks was not correlated to the occurrence of the shark bite incident. Or, put another way, not only did the level of support for sharks not go down after the shark bite, the statistical analysis indicated that there was no relationship between the two. This suggests that the public is able to distinguish its feelings about local shark populations from the occurrence of a localized shark bite. Second, while there was also no statistical relationship between respondents' feelings towards seals and the shark bite, the empirical data saw a noticeable drop in seal pride following the incident. Since a seal was involved in the incident, this may have indicated that the public felt the seal was more responsible than the shark. However, the third point is less encouraging. The fact that pride and support for sharks remains so low, even in communities with longstanding public education campaigns, suggests a continuing problem in support for sharks.

Yet, support for white sharks following a shark bite incident is not unheard of. In the state of Massachusetts, the Cape Cod coastline appears to be very supportive despite a non-fatal shark bite in 2012. In this case, the different result from a stereotypical *Jaws* 'outcome' may have helped. In addition, the economic benefit of white sharks in the community that is felt by the public appears to be more effective than public fears.

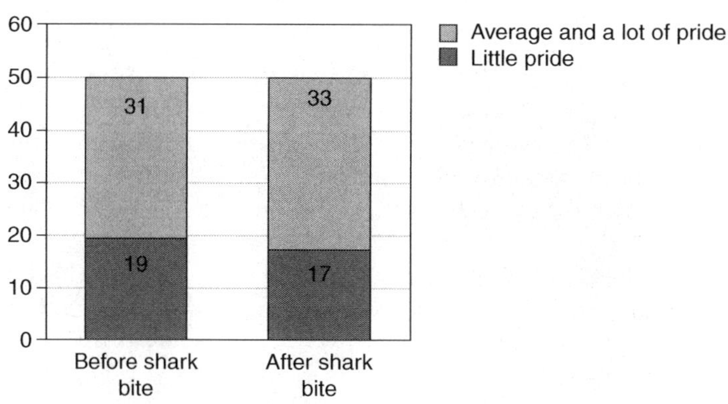

Figure 6.1 Survey responses to pride in local white shark populations in Cape Town, South Africa before and after a shark bite incident (source: Neff and Yang, 2013).

Media analyses

There have been a number of media analyses that look at newspaper reports regarding sharks. Boissonneault *et al.* (2005) examined reporting of grey nurse sharks in Australia between 1969 and 2003. They report an increase in news stories since 2001 largely based around attention to the declines in the local population; however, they note 'the majority of the news articles 53% (16) on the topic fell within a more neutral range' (Boissonneault, 2005, p. 16).

Muter *et al.* (2013) reviewed all media reports of sharks in newspapers in Australia and the United States over a ten-year period (2000–2010). Three important points emerge from this analysis. First, Muter *et al.* (2013) found that media reports in Australia were more negative, with 58 per cent of all articles looking at 'attacks on people' compared to 47 per cent of American reports. Second, scientists commented 15 per cent of the time in Australia, 10 per cent less than the 25 per cent in American reports. Lastly, politicians commented in 8 per cent of Australian reports, 7 per cent higher than the 1 per cent in shark stories in the United States.

In all, the addition of the shark finning campaign may be related to shark bite prevention responses because if sharks can be perceived as victims and as sympathetic animals then this provides an opening for a new look at the species. Indeed, both the accidental nature of shark bites and sharks having their fins cut off before being killed construct a new image that contradicts the 'man-eater' label and the 'movie-monster' image. The challenge to these perceptions provides valuable opportunities to educate the public so that if human–shark interactions occur, policy responses can incorporate shark conservation values into the decision. However, if these openings provided opportunities for new approaches we might expect policy responses that reflect these changes in appreciation and public attitudes. This is not the case following many shark bite incidents. For instance, in 2009 a series of shark bite incidents in NSW resulted in a review of the beach nets that use gillnets to cull sharks that swim in the in-shore area (NSW, 2009). Despite scientific recommendations dating back to 2006 (NSW, 2006) to remove the gillnets during the months of September and October because this period represents the most great white shark deaths and the fewest human–shark interactions (see Table 6.1), the 2009 policy document affirmed the use of nets during those months (NSW, 2009).

Shark bite case studies

A review of three cases helps to distinguish between shark bite periods that result in shark control and those that respond based on *human factors*. I begin by providing a context for each location based on their conservation and shark bite prevention institutions. I then examine the media reporting regarding three incidents.

South Africa was the first country to attempt beach-netting enclosures, doing so in Durban in 1907, but Cape Town beaches do not utilize these. Cape Town

Table 6.1 Comparing white sharks killed in NSW shark nets (1990–2008) and shark bites and fatalities in NSW (1900–2009)

Elasmobranchs	*January*	*February*	*March*	*April*	*September*	*October*	*November*	*December*	*Total*
Great whites caught in NSW nets, 1990–2008	9	6	3	6	36	21	9	10	*100*
Number of attacks in NSW, 1900–2009	55	29	23	24	5	12	11	29	*188*
Number of fatalities from shark bites in NSW, 1900–2009	18	9	8	4	0	0	1	12	52

beach safety is governed by the City of Cape Town's Environmental Management Department, which funds the shark spotter programme, as well as Lifesaving South Africa, which is 'the acknowledged national aquatic safety authority' (LSSA, 2007). Cape Town also provides a website for the public to gain additional information about the shark spotter programme, as well as posting flags on the beach in coordination with signs to alert beachgoers of shark activity.[1]

In 1991, South Africa was also the first country in the world to institute protective legislation for white sharks. Widespread concern among scientists regarding their falling numbers led the government to action, which 'prohibited the catching or killing of white sharks without a permit' (Wintner and Cliff, 1999, p. 153). Currently, sharks are protected federally in South Africa through the *Marine Living Resources Act of 1998* with 'the whale shark and the basking shark added to the prohibited species list' in 2005 (NSB, 2007).

In the United States, the most shark bite incidents occur along the state of Florida's coastline. Neither beach netting nor drum lines are used in the United States. Indeed, this minimal level of beach safety in Florida has been noted by researchers, who state that 'It is of particular interest that shark attacks have not led to the introduction of protective measures at mainland beaches, in contrast to what has happened in other parts of the world' (Dudley, 2006, p. 103). In Florida, beach safety is conducted through local county management. The Florida Department of Environmental Protection provides signage for local beaches to alert beachgoers, including notices of dangerous marine life (DEP, 2007). However, the governing authority of beaches is maintained county to county.

In 1990, the United States designated sharks as a 'highly migratory species' allowing them greater protection within economic exclusion zones (EEZs) (water 3–200 nautical miles offshore). In 1996, the law was further amended to reduce over-fishing and minimize the by-catch mortality of sharks. Marine conservation efforts in the United States are governed by the National Marine Fisheries Service, an agency within the National Oceanic and Atmospheric Administration (NOAA). In 2001 the United States released its National Plan of Action (NPOA) regarding shark management, in accordance with federal law (NMFS, 2001).

In Florida, sharks are protected within their coastal waters. While the coastline is managed by the Department of Environmental Protection's Florida Coastal Management Program (DEP, 2007), conservation of sharks and marine life is governed by the Florida Fish and Wildlife Conservation Commission (FFWC), which was formed in 1999 as part of a state Constitutional Amendment. The FFWC issues and enforces rules regarding fish and wildlife protection. Previous laws protecting sharks included Florida's 1992 'Shark Rule', which protected six species including the basking, whale, white, sand tiger, bigeye sand tiger and spiny dogfish sharks. Additional sharks were provided protection in 2006.

Australian shark control policies include the use of beach meshing or netting, particularly in NSW and Queensland, as well as aerial patrols and, under certain circumstances, the authority to seek out and kill sharks that pose a threat to beachgoers (EA, 2002). Most shark bite incidents in Australia have occurred in NSW, but there has not been a fatal bite incident since 1993, in Byron Bay (Taronga Zoo, 2007). By contrast, the states of Western Australia and South Australia, which do not use beach netting, have had a number of encounters resulting in fatalities in the past several years. In Western Australia, beach safety is managed by the Department of Fisheries and Surf Life Saving WA.

In Australia, white sharks were also the first to receive protection within federal waters in 1997. This attention towards white sharks coincided with greater national attention paid to biodiversity issues and the release of Australia's Oceans Policy. Then Environment Minister Robert Hill stated,

> Australians must cast aside their negative perceptions of sharks – shark attacks cause fewer fatalities in Australia than bee stings or lightning strikes. We must realise that these giants of our oceans, which play a vital role in our marine ecosystems, are in danger of disappearing forever.
>
> (Hill, 1997)

Sharks were initially protected under the *Endangered Species Act* (CSIRO, 1999), but current conservation efforts fall under the *Environment Protection and Biodiversity Conservation Act 1999* (DEH, 2007). Protected sharks include the 'Grey nurse and speartooth shark, as critically endangered, the northern river shark as endangered and the whale and white shark which are listed as vulnerable' (DEH, 2007). In 2001, Australia also launched the National Plan of Action for Sharks in concert with a Recovery Plan for the white shark population.

Local coastlines remain under state jurisdictions, up to three nautical miles from the shoreline. In Western Australia, conservation is governed through multiple jurisdictions, including the Department of Environment and Conservation and Department of Fisheries, with the Minister for the Environment holding chief responsibility. The state has fully protected white sharks in coastal waters from commercial and recreational fishing and in 2000 banned shark finning (Western Australia Department of Fisheries, 2005).

Analysing newspaper accounts

I provide a media analysis of newspaper coverage following the shark bite incidents, identifying and interpreting key variables addressed by reports. These illustrate and characterize the frames following the different shark bite incidents and establish their relationships to policy outcomes in the three countries. Newspapers were targeted based on their coverage of shark bite incidents and their high distributions. This analysis compared key variables such as risk factors discussed, problem and solution identifications and persons commenting, with policy outcomes in South Africa, the United States and Australia for a quantitative review of concepts. In addition, it conducted a qualitative comparison of issues advocated and policy outcomes adopted, connecting the impact of these framing variables to policy decisions.[2]

In Western Australia, the first focal incident involved a fatal shark bite to Ken Crew at Cottesloe beach in Perth in November 2000 and also includes reporting on two fatal incidents in South Australia in September 2000 to Cameron Bayes and Jevan Wright. The shark was identified as the problem in 56 per cent of the media reports. In addition, laws that protect sharks were identified as the problem in 8 per cent of newspapers stories. Other factors such as seal migrations, overfishing and weather, combined, totalled 24 per cent of the reported problems. Here, the overwhelming frame was the shark as the problem and *human factors* were framed in a more minor role (Figure 6.2).

Solutions to this event included punitive measures against the shark. The highest percentage of solutions, 41 per cent, called for killing the shark (Figure 6.3), while 22 per cent pointed to closing the beaches and 11 per cent suggested staying out of the water in response to the bites. While there was a mixture of solutions, those relating to human behaviour remained predicated on killing the shark. Stated differently, the public felt it important to stay out of the water until this shark was killed. One swimmer stated, ‘nothing will convince us that it is gone, even if this shark goes away, it can happen again at any time’ (Hickman, 2000a). Thus, these were not two competing causal stories, one based on the need to kill the shark and the other noting the role of human activity in the water. Both stories pointed to one causal narrative where the presence of one particularly intently driven or ‘rogue’ shark was the threat to be solved (Coppleson, 1958).

Other information was reported following the killing, challenging the rogue shark causal story. Greenpeace Australia stated that ‘it's disappointing that the reaction is to kill a shark simply for doing what it does in its own environment’

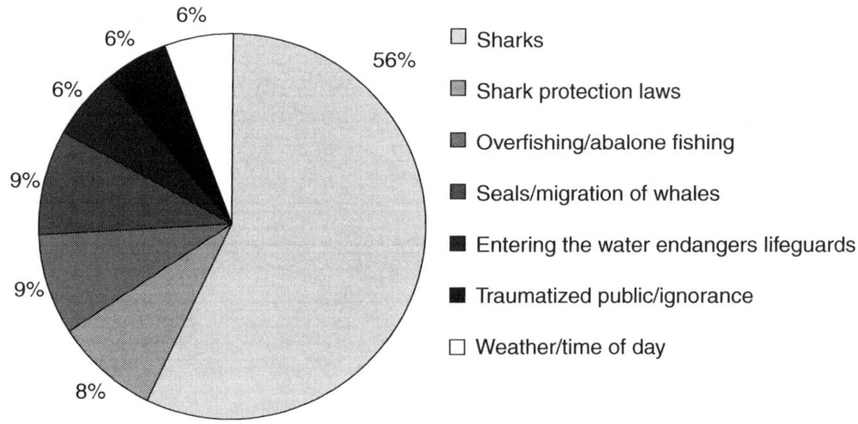

Figure 6.2 Australia: problem identification.

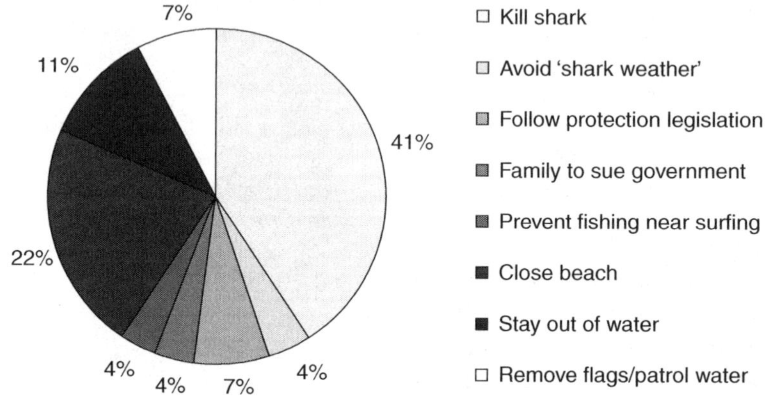

Figure 6.3 Australia: solution identification.

(Kennan, 2000a) and the same article concluded by noting that 'officials said a baby seal spotted near the scene of the attack may have lured the white pointer into the shallows where Mr Crew died' (Keenan, 2000a). In addition, public reaction to the week-long hunt for the shark was not unanimous in support of killing the shark. Newspaper reports from *The Australian* stated that 'the death of Mr Crew and the shark hunt has sparked "almost unprecedented reaction on local talkback radio, with two-thirds of callers against destroying the white pointer"' (Keenan, 2000b). CSIRO shark biologist John Stevens even noted that humans do not fall within a shark's diet, stating, 'if they did, I can assure you we would be having rather more attacks than we do' (Brook, 2000). These messages, however, did not resonate with policy makers and were not able to shift attention away from the entrenched rogue shark frame.

Of those commenting following the bite incidents, 46 per cent were witnesses or passers-by who saw the bite incident and 16 per cent were representatives of the state government, including the Fisheries Minister and Premier (Figure 6.4). As a result, I suggest that the large percentage of emotional responses from the witnesses and institutional reinforcement by the government, totalling 62 per cent of commentators, limited alternative policy options following this incident. Indeed, while experts accounted for 10 per cent of commentators, their contributions represented a minority voice. Rather, the identified solutions reflected an emotional causal story cemented by the strength of government institutions.

In the second case, I reviewed 15 US newspaper articles from the *Associated Press* that addressed shark bite incidents in the state of Florida, beginning with the bite on Jessie Arbogast in July. This analysis reveals public identification of hazards and risks as well as indicating potential solutions to address the perceived problems. In all, the media coverage and the public responses are shown to be consistent with the state government's responses and policy outputs.

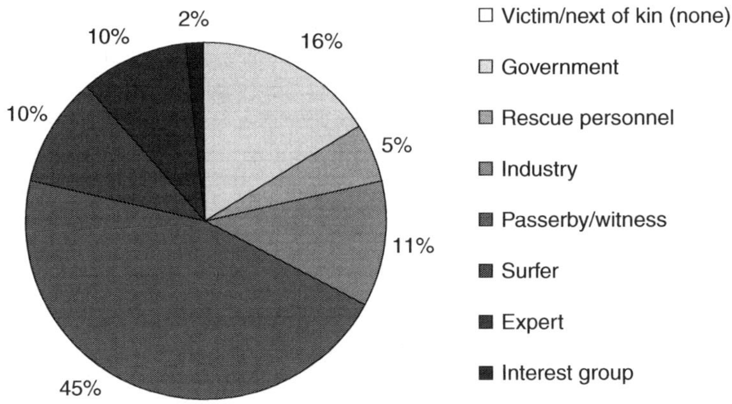

Figure 6.4 Australia: persons commenting.

The local, public response to shark bites in Florida acknowledged that shark bites on the public were a problem. Of the problem variables in newspaper reports, 40 per cent identified sharks (Figure 6.5). Yet contextual factors that contributed to the bites, such as baitfish in the water, local fisherman cleaning their catches and high turbidity, were identified in nearly every article. Indeed, 22 per cent of identified problems were noted as contributing factors to the shark bites, with an additional 14 per cent suggesting mistaken identity by the shark. Taken together, 36 per cent of comments identified conditions in the water as the problem.

The contextual perspective of the Florida shark bite reports was consistent, despite the rise in the number of bites over a short period. Following six shark bites over one weekend, at New Smyrna Beach, the paper reported, 'A combination of murky water, caused by recent heavy rains pouring or stirring up silt

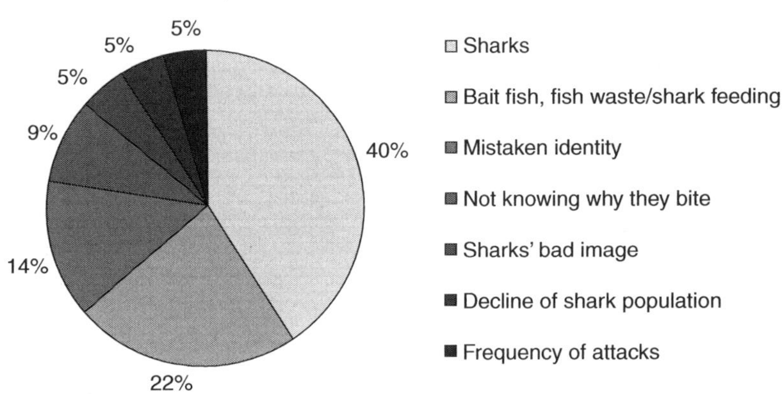

Figure 6.5 USA: problem identification.

into the water and an unusually crowded beach due to a surfing contest, may have caused the sharks to mistake humans for fish' (Schneider, 2001). Moreover, following the tenth bite in ten days, the reports stated, 'the water contains small fish, which draw the sharks closer to shore to feed' (AP, 2001).

Overall, there appears to be a public recognition of the level of risk involved with swimming in this region. One local resident commented, 'When you step into the water, you step into the food chain' (Branom, 2001). Another report noted that 'surfers, lifeguards and shark experts were quick to point out that the shark encounters are nothing new' (Schneider, 2001). Thus, while sharks were identified as a problem, the causal story is more complex, with an appreciation and understanding that human behaviour and ecosystem conditions play roles in shark bites. In this way, we see how contextual information and framing of the events can impact responses, lessening unrealistic myths.

The public discourse on solutions to the leading problems of sharks and water conditions was to bring people out of the water. Clearing beaches accounted for 58 per cent of solutions discussed, noted in Figure 6.6. The clearing of beaches includes evacuating patches of shoreline for shorter periods of time, rather than closing an entire beach for one or several days. Chief of Marine Rescue Jay Moyles stated, 'We pulled the swimmers out when the shark was making its runs through and we're monitoring the situation. This is standard operating procedure' (Branom, 2001). Closing beaches accounted for an additional 11 per cent, combining for 69 per cent of solutions.

In addition, the regulation and banning of shark feeding and shark fishing were proposed as solutions to the perceived increase in risk of bites due to human behaviour. These solutions accounted for 10 per cent of comments. One report on this issue stated that 'Fishermen attract sharks by putting blood and chopped fish in the water, a process known as chumming' (Kaczor, 2001). The presence of pier fishing and fish cleaning, near beaches in particular, were identified as problems in the bite on Jessie Arbogast.

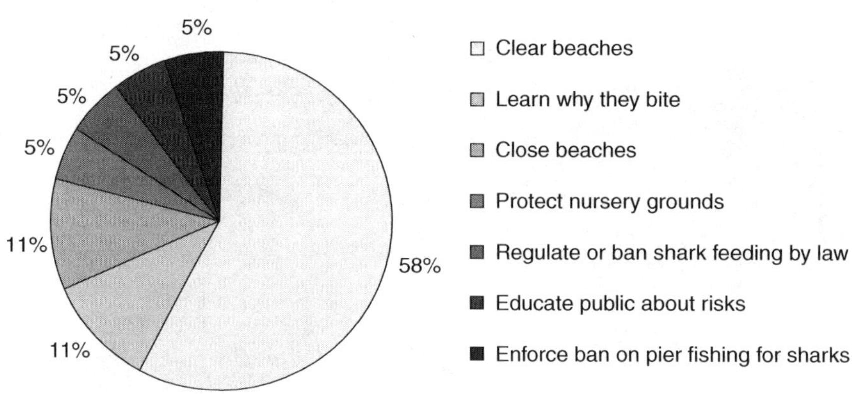

Figure 6.6 USA: solution identification.

Other suggestions looked to the reasons for shark bites, with one report addressing the theory of probabilities and suggesting that the spate of bites was consistent with statistically random patterns that happen in nature. An expert stated, 'if such attacks were purely "random" and independent of each other, it is not surprising that they seem to occur in "clumps"' (Penn State, Smeal College of Business Administration, 2001).

All of the solutions addressed pointed towards management of human behaviour following shark bites. Removing people from beaches, banning feeding of sharks, banning fishing for sharks, greater education and research as well as protecting shark nurseries, suggest a human-centred model for limiting the risks faced by sharks.

The list of persons commenting in Florida newspaper reports, illustrated in Figure 6.7, allows for an analysis of framing influences and stakeholder involvement. Of those commenting, 36 per cent were rescue personnel, including police, lifeguards and medical staff, 20 per cent were experts, making them the second highest percentage of commentators, including the International Shark Attack File, based in Florida. In addition, victims accounted for 12 per cent of commentators. Perhaps the most significant data, however, is that government representatives made up only 8 per cent of commentators. This suggests that the identification of problems and solutions was not restricted by institutional forces. Thus, the frame following shark bites was focused on victims and reducing their levels of risk rather than sharks themselves.

The third case review is in Cape Town, following the fatal shark bite to Tyna Webb in 2004. A review of newspaper coverage following the incident looked at statements that identified the problem; of these 47 per cent (Figure 6.8) indicated the shark was the problem, with reports stating that 'an exceptionally large shark, believed to be a six-metre-long Great White, seized the elderly resident of Sunny Cove, Fish Hoek, in its jaws' (du Plessis, 2004a). The *Cape*

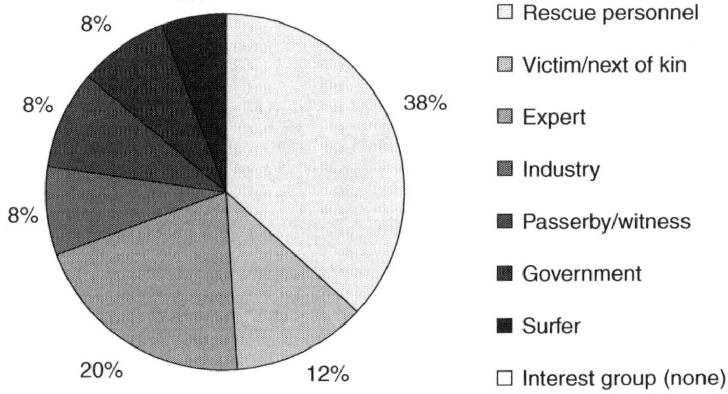

Figure 6.7 USA: persons commenting.

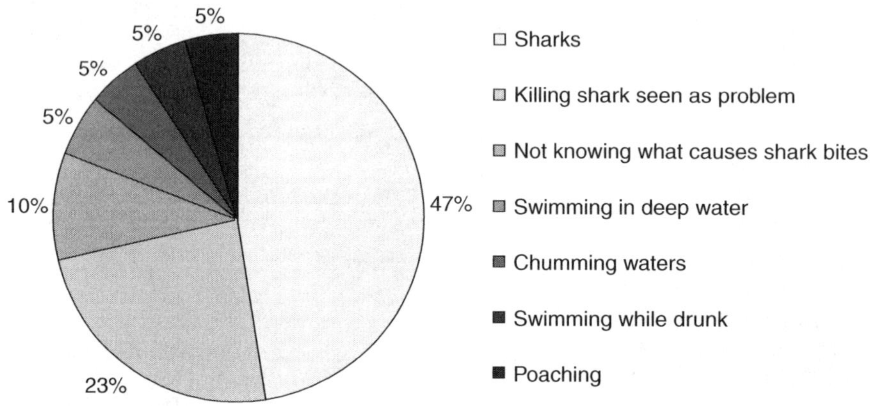

Figure 6.8 South Africa: problem identification.

Times reported that 'many people have phoned radio show hosts and written letters to MCM saying the shark should be killed' (Smetherham, 2004). Yet when the issue of killing the shark was raised, it was seen as the second biggest problem, with 23 per cent responding. One of Tyna's daughters stated that the last thing her mother would want was a 'revenge attack' and that her mother 'respected the shark's domain, that when she went swimming she knew she was entering their domain' (Smetherham, 2004). In addition, the Shark Concern Group shifted the focus by calling on the Environment Minister to ban chumming from cage diving boats (Gosling, 2004a).

Moreover, other issues including contextual factors were identified as the problem and included human behaviours that may contribute to bites, such as swimming in deep water, chumming the waters, and poaching, which account for a collective 15 per cent of comments. Thus, the causal story in South Africa provided a mixed frame based to a large degree on incident conditions outside of the shark. Reports noted that the time of Tyna Webb's swim put her in the path of sharks during feeding periods. 'Conditions at the time were high sea temperatures, accompanied by an influx of fish into the bay, and trek fishermen had just caught and released a large number of fish in a part of the bay' (du Plessis, 2004b). In addition, Webb herself was warned previously about the dangers of swimming so far out – 120 metres from shore. A fellow resident stated, 'I told Tyna not to swim out so deep', adding, 'I spoke to Tyna often, but she had a fatalistic view of it' (du Plessis, 2004a).

While the solutions noted in newspaper reports included the killing of sharks, they overwhelmingly addressed the role of human behaviour. Of the 18 per cent of solutions which called for killing the sharks, this included vigilante groups that threatened to fill chickens with glass and throw them into the ocean (Figure 6.9). MCM expert Hermann Oosthuizen received such a call from the group and stated: 'I told him it was illegal to kill Great Whites in South Africa

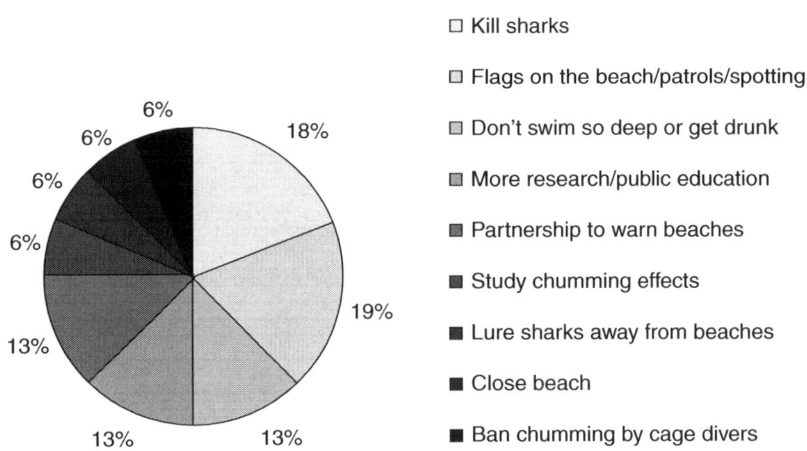

Figure 6.9 South Africa: solution identification.

and that he would be prosecuted. I asked him if he also wanted to kill all humans since he has a far greater chance of being killed by a human than a shark' (Gosling, 2004b).

Indeed, more attention was focused on efforts to regulate human activities and inform beachgoers. Kalk Bay Harbour Master Pat Stacey stated, 'I can't help but think that the real solution would have been to warn the public in a very clear way' (du Plessis, 2004b). The data show that 19 per cent of comments looked at the placement of flags on beaches as well as patrols and spotters to get swimmers out of the water more quickly following a shark sighting. Another 13 per cent addressed a partnership with fishermen and lifeguards to alert the public more quickly, while concern was also raised about the effect of chumming from fishermen and cage divers. A spokesman for the Environment Minister stated, 'Marine Coastal Management has for some time been undertaking scientific investigations into the effect, if any, on shark behaviour of shark cage-diving and the associated practice of chumming' (Gosling, 2004a).

In all, the solutions mentioned focused on the problems of human activity, rather than shark activity in Cape Town waters. This information suggests a causal story where proper management of *human factors* will reduce risk factors and where punitive action towards sharks is unwelcome. It also illustrates the heated and mobilized efforts of conservation forces in response to solutions which would conflict with shark conservation.

An analysis of persons commenting in *Cape Times/Cape Argus* newspapers, illustrated in Figure 6.10, shows that rescue personnel were the largest group, with 25 per cent of commentators. Witnesses and passers-by provided 21 per cent of comments and government representatives were third with 15 per cent. Interest groups and experts accounted for a combined 16 per cent of comments,

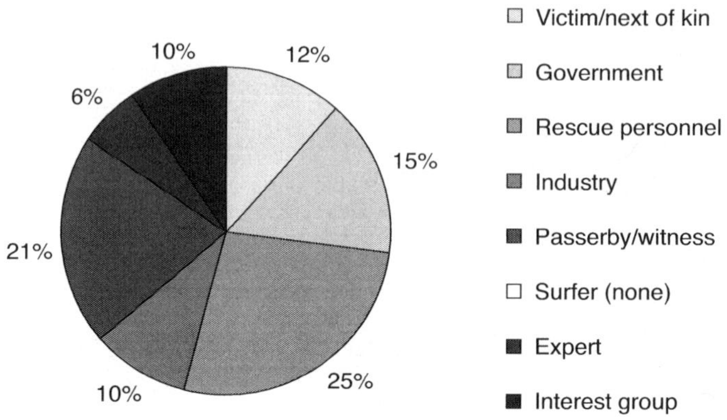

Figure 6.10 South Africa: persons commenting.

just above that of the government, suggesting diverse inputs from actors. I argue that the emphasis on comments from multiple actors and the smaller role of the government allowed for more alternative solutions to be framed and policies addressed following the shark bite incident.

While not all interest groups and experts were advocates for greater protection of sharks, most were outspoken against killing sharks through vigilante justice or netting. Nan Rice of the Dolphin Action and Protection Group spoke against imposing nets, stating 'They would upset the whole ecosystem of False Bay' (Smetherham, 2004). The result was creative ideas for managing sharks, including drawing them away from shore with chumming, providing walkie-talkies to fishermen in case they see sharks and studying the impact of the cage diving industry. In all, these solutions represent human-centred management from fishermen, lifeguards, residents, scientists and policy makers to lower the risks of human–shark interactions.

Discussion and conclusion

A test of how much animals matter to humans is how we treat them following human–wildlife conflicts. How are conservation values located in the political dialogue regarding dangerous, threatening and predatory animals? Predator–prey fundamentals include aggressive behavioural instincts designed to maximize survival and protection by eliminating other predators as a threat. This formula contrasts the nature of humans as apex predators of our environment, while clearly acknowledging our vulnerabilities to the actions of sharks. This susceptibility means that understanding that human survival depends on the continued existence of predators that can harm us is an example of a civilization's step forward.

This chapter reviewed the way in which the framing of problems and solutions influenced the direction of policy responses following shark bites. At issue was the tension involved in shark bite policy making and represented in the predator policy paradox. A review of three cases illustrates how the inclusion of certain actors in media reporting creates perceptions that emphasize human factors or shark control as the central argument in shark bite prevention. In South Africa and the United States, the inclusion of multiple actors in media reporting helped include marine conservation messaging that destabilized image monopolies of sharks and provided an opening for considerations of human behaviour in the selection of policy tools. In Australia, the dominance of entrenched mythologies about sharks combined with government control provided less room for policy alternatives. Thus, the ideas put forward by stakeholders challenge or endorse the causal stories that frame the risks, allocate blame and identify problems and solutions following shark bites. This has real implications for shark conservation governance because the contestation of fear-based frames with considerations of human factors can help reconcile shark bites and shark conservation.

These case studies affirm the impact of public policies dedicated to shark bite prevention on shark conservation. If sharks are framed in policy terms as an enemy that needs to be killed, this undermines shark conservation by reducing public support for sharks and weakening the political capital of organizations that advocate on their behalf. Alternatively, shark bite policy responses that treat sharks as a critical part of the ecosystem and mirror conservation values engage long-term public support and assist in shark conservation governance.

This analysis represents a beginning in addressing an emerging trend in the way *human factors* are used to address the predator policy paradox. It also offers a comparative analysis of the experiences in South Africa, the United States and Australia between shark policies and the framing of shark bites and when conservation values may rise above shark control. In many cases, the history of dramatic and fearsome shark bites on humans has not stopped the conservation of endangered shark species. The first shark species to be protected by any jurisdiction in the world was the grey nurse shark (*Carcharias Taurus*) in 1984 by NSW (Otway *et al.*, 2004). Previously believed to be a 'man-eater', the species was now understood to be docile.

Calls for retribution, such as cullings and shark hunts, are responses consistent with a predator–prey reaction. Challenges have also been presented to the conservation status of sharks to weaken their legal protections from fishing. A cluster of shark bites in Western Australia led the state government to challenge federal shark conservation laws. The moral implication of such treatment has been raised by Carson and Darling (1962), who wrote 'By acquiescing in an act that causes such suffering to a living creature, who among us is not diminished as a human being?'

I conclude by noting that the governance of sharks matters not simply because reconciling beach safety and species conservation are public policy goals, but because the fullness of humanity and democracy cannot be found in primal politics that support predator–prey existence. The survival of humankind depends on the survival of other predators. While it may be easier to ask what sharks can do for humans, the protection and conservation of sharks in face of the threats they pose illustrate a core facet of our societal and political evolution.

Appendix: content analysis – newspaper articles

I South Africa/Cape Town

Bamford, H. (2004) 'Monster shark rips teen to death', *Cape Argus*, 12 September.
Cape Times, (2004) 'Inquest after suspected poacher's body found', *Cape Times*, 8 June.
du Plessis, H. (2004a) 'Swimmers plunge in despite shark attack', *Cape Argus*, 16 November.
du, Plessis, H. (2004b) 'Sea conditions may have drawn shark to shore', *Cape Argus*, 18 November.
Fortein, T. and Fortein, T. (2004) 'My warning could not save Tyna', *Cape Argus*, 16 November.
Gophe, M. (2004) 'Fish Hoek lifeguards launch shark watch', *Cape Argus*, 21 November.
Gosling, M. (2004a) 'Vigilantes threaten to take aim at sharks', *Cape Times*, 18 November.
Gosling, M. (2004b) 'Killer shark may have been aroused – expert', *Cape Times*, 16 November.
Peters, A. (2004) 'Beaches closed after shark sightings', *Cape Argus*, 22 November.
Smetherham, J. (2004a) 'Witnesses tell of shark victim's last seconds', *Cape Times*, 16 November.
Smetherham, J. (2004b) 'Marine experts reject calls for shark nets', *Cape Times*, 17 November.
Smetherham, J. (2004c) 'If you hear a siren, get out of the water', *Cape Times*, 22 November.
Smetherham, J. and Ndenze, B. 'Poacher killed as nature bites back', *Cape Times*, 7 June.
Smetherham, J. (2004) 'Did shark feed on poacher?', *Cape Times*, 11 June.
Smetherham, J. (2004) 'Humans are not on sharks' menu, says expert', *Cape Times*, 25 November.

II USA/Florida

AP (2001a) 'Beach Patrol keeps shark-infested surf beach closed', *Associated Press*, 28 August.
AP (2001b) 'Shark bites Panhandle surfer near site of boy's attack', *Associated Press*, 16 July.
AP (2001c) 'Georgia scientists fighting sharks' bad press', *Associated Press*, 18 July.
AP (2001d) 'Sharks attack six surfers in two days off Daytona area beaches', *Associated Press*, 20 August.
AP (2001e) 'Ninth person in a week bitten by shark off Florida's New Smyrna Beach', *Associated Press*, 26 August.
AP (2001f) 'Beach patrol keeps shark-infested surf beach closed', *Associated Press*, 28 August.

AP (2001g) 'National seashore adds shark warning to literature', *Associated Press*, 29 August.
Branom, M. (2001a) 'Seventh surfer in four days bit by shark', *Associated Press*, 21 August.
Branom, M. (2001b) 'Shark bites woman off Gulf Coast; New Smyrna Beach re-opened', *Associated Press*, 31 August.
Kaczor, B. (2001a) 'Surgeons reattach 8-year-old boy's arm, bitten off by shark at Florida beach', *Associated Press*, 7 July.
Kaczor, B. (2001b) 'Shark fishing banned at pier near area where boy was attacked', *Associated Press*, 18 July.
Kaczor, B. (2001c) 'Report provides details about rescue of 8-year-old boy who was victim of shark attack', *Associated Press*, 20 July.
Kallestad, B. (2001) 'Shark researcher trying to nail down cause of attack on 8-year-old Jessie', *Associated Press*, 15 July.
Penn State, Smeal College of Business Administration (2001) 'Shark attacks may be a "poisson burst"'. *ScienceDaily*. 23 August. Available at: www.sciencedaily.com/releases/2001/08/010823084028.htm.
Schneider, M. (2001) 'Shark attacks bring jitters to surfer-popular beach', *Associated Press*, 21 August.
Word, R. (2001) 'Florida commission votes to ban dives where tourists swim with sharks; food used as lure', *Associated Press*, 7 September.

III Australia/Western Australia

Australian, The (2000) 'Shark hunters licensed to kill', *The Australian*, 7 November.
Brook, S. (2000) 'In the way of a killing machine', *The Australian*, 11 November.
Daly, B. (unknown) 'Swimmers defy shark ban to beat heat', *The Australian*, 13 November.
Hickman, B. (2000a) 'Sharks sightings keep The Pod out of water', *The Australian*, 10 November.
Hickman, B. (2000b) 'Councils urged to close beaches', *The Australian*, 10 November.
Hickman, B. (2000c) 'White water wader throws caution to wind', *The Australian*, 9 November.
Keenan, A. (2000a) 'Prayer for a mate on beach he loved – aftermath of attack', *The Australian*, 8 November.
Keenan, A. (2000b) 'City divided over the fate of man-eating shark – aftermath of attack', *The Australian*, 8 November.
Macfarlane, D. (2000) 'We should track down and kill man-eaters – shark hunter – tragedies on our coast', *The Australian*, 27 September.
Macfarlane, D. (2000) 'Hunting ban carries fine, two-year jail sentence', *The Australian*, 26 September.
Martin, R. and Brook, S. (2000) 'Air, sea hunt for man-eater', *The Australian*, 7 November.
Martin, R. and Keenan, A. (2000) 'A scream, and blood in the sea', *The Australian*, 7 November.
Plane, T. and Altmann, C. (2000) 'Second fatal shark attack', *The Australian*, 26 September.
Price, M. (2000a) 'Seaside culture shattered in fatal seconds', *The Australian*, 7 November.

Price, M. (2000b) 'Where terror's wave broke the dawn', *The Australian*, 11 November.
Price, M. (2000c) 'Survivors relive the horror', *The Australian*, 7 November.
Spencer, M. (2000a) 'Great white kills honeymoon surfer', *The Australian*, 25 September.
Spencer, M. (2000b) 'Shark weather preceded fatal attack', *The Australian*, 26 September.
Spencer, M. (2000c) 'When grief swam into Anxious Bay', *The Australian*, 27 September.
Spencer, M. (2000d) 'Signs point to shark horror', *The Australian*, 30 September.

Notes

1 The website can be accessed at http://sharkspotters.org.za.
2 The articles themselves were selected using Factiva and were analysed in date order, targeting reports within ten days of bite incidents where possible. In South Africa, the *Cape Times/Cape Argus* media group is among the biggest of the English-based newspapers delivering in morning/afternoon intervals. Fifteen articles were reviewed within periods not exceeding ten days of the bite incident. In Florida, coverage was a significant issue given that the bite incidents occurred across the state and as a series, over a longer period of time. The *Associated Press (AP)* was selected to provide more consistent coverage of the events, with 15 articles reviewed beginning on 6 July and ending on 7 September. Lastly, *The Australian* was selected given its high circulation and coverage of the bite incident in WA as well as SA. Twenty articles were analysed for this account within ten days of the event. To standardize the data, given the different numbers of articles, percentages were used to reflect values in variable categories.

References

AAP (2012) 'WA govt bans shark-cage tourism', *Australian Associated Press*, 23 July, available at www.news.com.au/breaking-news/national/wa-govt-bans-shark-cage-tourism/story-e6frfku9-1226420438484, accessed 10 March 2014.
AAP (2013) 'WA's first shark net to be installed at Coogee Beach', *Australian Associated Press*, 12 July, available at www.perthnow.com.au/news/western-australia/was-first-shark-net-to-be-installed-at-coogee-beach/story-fnhocxo3-1226678585449, accessed 10 March 2014.
AP (2001) 'Beach Patrol keeps shark-infested surf beach closed', *Associated Press*, 28 August.
Beckwith, M. W. (1917) 'Hawaiian shark aumakua', *American Anthropologist*, vol. 19, no. 4, pp. 503–517.
Boissonneault, M. F., Gladstone, W., Scott, P. and Cushing, N. (2005) 'Grey nurse shark human interactions and portrayals: a study of newspaper portrayals of the grey nurse shark from 1969–2003', *Electronic Green Journal*, vol. 22, no. 1, pp. 1–15.
Branom, M. (2001) 'Seventh surfer in four days bit by shark', *Associated Press*, 21 August.
Brook, S. (2000) 'In the way of a killing machine', *The Australian*, 11 November.
Carson, R. and Darling, L. (1962) *Silent spring*, Houghton Mifflin, Boston, MA.
Coppleson, V. (1958) *Shark Attack*, Angus and Robertson, Sydney.
CSIRO (1999) 'White sharks: filling the gaps in our knowledge', Information Sheet no. 35, May, available at www.marine.csiro.au/LeafletsFolder/35shark.html, accessed 1 December 2013.

Czech, B., Krausman, P. R. and Borkhataria, R. (1998) 'Social construction, political power, and the allocation of benefits to endangered species', *Conservation Biology*, vol. 12, no. 5, pp. 1103–1112.

DEH (2007) *Marine species conservation*, available at www.environment.gov.au/coasts/species/index.html, accessed 10 March 2014.

DEP (2007) *Florida Coastal Management Program: Beach Access and Safety Program*, available at www.dep.state.fl.us/mainpage/programs/cmp.htm, accessed 10 March 2014.

DLNR (2002) 'Hawaii Department of Land and Natural Resources: Customer Help Website', http://hawaiideptland.custhelp.com, accessed 10 March 2014.

du Plessis, H. (2004a) 'Swimmers plunge in despite shark attack', *Cape Argus*, 16 November.

du, Plessis, H. (2004b) 'Sea conditions may have drawn shark to shore', *Cape Argus*, 18 November.

Dudley, S. (2006) 'International review of responses to shark attack', in D. C. Nel and T. P. Peschak (eds), *Finding a Balance: White Shark Conservation and Recreational Safety in the Inshore Waters of Cape Town, South Africa*, WWF South Africa Report Series 2006/Marine/001.

EA (Environment Australia) (2002) 'White Shark Recovery Plan', www.environment.gov.au/system/files/resources/a0dfdef5-a1ba-41a6-bd3f-8a6a0a4bdd5a/files/greatwhite-shark.pdf, accessed 10 March 2014.

Gosling, M. (2004a) 'Killer shark may have been aroused – expert', *Cape Times*, 16 November.

Gosling, M. (2004b) 'Vigilantes threaten to take aim at sharks', *Cape Times*, 18 November.

Gruber, S. (1988) 'Why do sharks attack people?', *Naval Research Review*, vol. 40, no. 1, pp. 2–19.

Hazin, F. H., Burgess, G. H. and Carvalho, F. C. (2008) 'A shark attack outbreak off Recife, Pernambuco, Brazil: 1992–2006', *Bulletin of Marine Science*, vol. 82, no. 2, pp. 199–212.

Hickman, B. (2000a) 'Sharks sightings keep The Pod out of water', *The Australian*, 10 November.

Hill, R. (1997) 'Australia Sounds Shark Alert', Minister for the Environment, Australian Government, Press Release, 17 December 1997, available at www.environment.gov.au/minister/env/97/mr17dec97.html, accessed 10 March 2014.

Huveneers, C., Rogers, P. J., Beckmann, C. L., Semmens, J., Bruce, B. and Seuront, L. (2012) *Effects of a Cage-diving Operation on the Fine-scale Movement of White Sharks* (Carcharodon carcharias), Final Report to the Department of Environment, Water and Natural Resources Wildlife Conservation Fund and the Nature Foundation of South Australia, South Australian Research and Development Institute (Aquatic Sciences), Adelaide, SARDI Research Report Series No. 657, SARDI Publication No. F2012/000417-1.

Jones, B. (1994) *Reconceiving Decision-Making in Democratic Politics: Attention, Choice and Public Policy*, University of Chicago Press, Chicago, IL.

Kaczor, B. (2001) 'Shark fishing banned at pier near area where boy was attacked', *Associated Press*, 18 July.

Keenan, A. (2000a) 'Prayer for a mate on beach he loved – aftermath of attack', *The Australian*, 8 November.

Keenan, A. (2000b) 'City divided over the fate of man-eating shark – aftermath of attack', *The Australian*, 8 November.

Lamb, B., Baughman, S., Keynes, S., Moylan, S. and Tomlinson, D. (2005) *Shark Attacks: Myth vs. Reality: Comparing the Perceived Versus Actual Risk of Shark Attack in the Fleurileu Peninsula*, available at http://furcs.flinders.edu.au/education/med_stud/y2/posters/2005%20HMF%20sharks.pdf, accessed 10 March 2014.

LSSA (2007) 'Mission statement of Lifesaving SA', available at www.lifesaving.co.za/about.php, accessed 25 September 2007.

Maui News (2013) 'Maui mayor says shark nets, hunting not ideal', *Maui News*, 27 August.

Maxwell, C. B. (1949) *Surf: Australians Against the Sea*, Angus and Robertson, Sydney.

Muter, B. A., Gore, M. L., Gledhill, K. S., Lamont, C. and Huveneers, C. (2013) 'Australian and US news media portrayal of sharks and their conservation', *Conservation Biology*, vol. 27, no. 1, pp. 187–196.

National Aquarium of Baltimore, 'Americans hooked on shark myths: national survey shows people know little about sharks', Press release, 14 May, Baltimore, MD.

Neff, C. (2012) 'Australian beach safety and the politics of shark attacks', *Coastal Management*, vol. 40, no. 1, pp. 88–106.

Neff, C. and Hueter, R. (2013) 'Science, policy, and the public discourse of shark "attack": a proposal for reclassifying human–shark interactions', *Journal of Environmental Studies and Sciences*, vol. 3, no. 1, pp. 65–73.

Neff, C. L. and Yang, J. Y. H. (2013) 'Shark bites and public attitudes: policy implications from the first before and after shark bite survey', *Marine Policy*, vol. 38, pp. 545–547.

NMFS (2001) *Final United States National Plan of Action for the Conservation and Management of Sharks*, February, National Marine Fisheries Service, available at www.nmfs.noaa.gov/sfa/Final%20NPOA.February.2001.htm, accessed 10 March 2014.

NSB (2007) 'Shark attack in South Africa today', *Natal Sharks Board*, available at www.shark.co.za/SASharkAttacksMore, accessed 10 March 2013.

NSW (2006) *Scientific Shark Protection Summit Report*, NSW Department of Primary Industries, available at www.dpi.nsw.gov.au/__data/assets/pdf_file/0008/137294/Report-from-theScientific-Shark-Protection-Summit.pdf, accessed 10 March 2014.

NSW (2009) *Report into the NSW Shark Meshing (Bather Protection) Program*, NSW Department of Primary Industries, available at www.dpi.nsw.gov.au/__data/assets/pdf_file/0008/137294/Report-from-the-Scientific-Shark-Protection-Summit.pdf, accessed 10 March 2014.

Omer, S. (2012) 'Great white shark sightings prompt swimming ban off Cape Cod', *MSNBC.com*, available at http://usnews.nbcnews.com/_news/2012/07/02/12527733-great-white-shark-sightings-prompt-swimming-ban-off-cape-cod?lite, accessed 10 March 2014.

Orlando Sentinel (1999) 'Brazilians keep surfing despite ban and sharks', *Orlando Sentinel*, available at http://articles.orlandosentinel.com/1999-05-13/news/9905130257_1_state-of-pernambuco-recife-brazil, accessed 10 March 2014.

Otway, N. M., Bradshaw, C. J. and Harcourt, R. G. (2004) 'Estimating the rate of quasi-extinction of the Australian grey nurse shark (*Carcharias taurus*) population using deterministic age- and stage-classified models', *Biological Conservation*, vol. 119, no. 3, pp. 341–350.

Penn State, Smeal College of Business Administration (2001) 'Shark attacks may be a "poisson burst"'. *ScienceDaily*. 23 August. Available at: www.sciencedaily.com/releases/2001/08/010823084028.htm.

Phillips, Y. (2012) 'WA says no to shark loving thrillseekers', *Perth Now*, 7 July, available atwww.perthnow.com.au/news/wa-ban-on-shark-cages/story-e6frg12c-1226419829214, accessed 10 March 2014.

Poumadere, M. and Mays, C. (2003) 'The dynamics of risk amplification and attenuation in context: a French case study', in N. Pidgeon, R. E. Kasperson and P. Slovic (eds), *The Social Amplification of Risk*, Cambridge University Press, Cambridge.

Rochefort, D. A. and Cobb, R. W. (1994) *The Politics of Problem Definition: Shaping the Policy Agenda*, University of Kansas, Kansas.

Schneider, M. (2001) 'Shark attacks bring jitters to surfer-popular beach', *Associated Press*, 21 August.

SMC (1929) *General Report of Sub-Committee for Presentation to the Meeting of General Committee*, Shark Menace Committee, New South Wales.

Smetherham, J. (2004) 'Marine experts reject calls for shark nets', *Cape Times*, 17 November.

Spruill, V. N. (1997) 'US public attitudes toward marine environmental issues', *Oceanography*, vol. 10, pp. 149–152.

Stone, D. (1989) 'Causal stories and the formation of policy agendas', *Political Science Quarterly*, vol. 104, no. 2, pp. 281–300.

Taronga Zoo (2007) 'Australian shark attack file', www.zoo.nsw.gov.au/content/view.asp?id=235, accessed 10 March 2014.

Tricas, T. C. and McCosker, J. E. (1984) 'Predatory behavior of the white shark (*Carcharodon carcharias*), with notes on its biology', *California Academy of Sciences*, vol. 43, no. 14, pp. 221–238.

Western Australia Department of Fisheries (2005) *WA Sharks, Shark Fisheries and Safety Tips*, Department of Fisheries, Western Australia, available at www.fish.wa.gov.au/docs/pub/SharkSafetyTips/index.php?0000, accessed 1 December 2013.

Wintner, S. and Cliff, G. (1999) 'Age and growth determination of the white shark, *Carcharodon carcharias*, from the east coast of South Africa', *NOAA Fishery Bulletin*, vol. 97, no. 1, pp. 153–169, available at http://fishbull.noaa.gov/15winter.pdf, accessed 10 March 2014.

Wood, R. (2006) 'Tobacco's tipping point: the master settlement agreement as a focusing event', *The Policy Studies Journal*, vol. 34, no. 3, pp. 419–435.

Part III

Actors and stakeholders

Chapter 7

Collaborations for conservation

Anissa Lawrence

Introduction

For more than 20 years, conservationists have been trying to reduce the decline in global shark populations, and while there have been some successes, the global increase in fishing pressure and trade has continued. Furthermore, up to 75 per cent of global catch of sharks is now estimated to be illegal and therefore unreported (Clarke *et al.*, 2006).

The challenge is how to reduce overfishing of sharks globally and encourage governments to make and enforce the policy and regulatory changes needed for this to happen. A new paradigm is required through which to drive change and transform the operating environment in which sharks are caught, traded and consumed. An integrated suite of tools and approaches is essential to address the global shark industry and tackle the challenges it provides if we are to have any success in reducing the pressure globally on sharks.

What has generally been missing from traditional approaches has been a focus on collaboration with the fishing industry and markets – working directly with shark supply chains and using them to drive change towards conservation and sustainable utilization. Supplementing traditional approaches with this alternate one is generally proving effective in transforming other commodities towards responsible management, trade and consumption globally.

This chapter explores the opportunities new market-based collaborative approaches offer towards tackling the global shark crisis. Several case studies are provided where innovative and effective market-based collaborations between the fishing industry, seafood sector, government and conservation non-governmental organizations (NGOs) are improving shark conservation and management. While many initiatives are in their infancy, they nevertheless provide good examples of the new theory of change emerging around integrated shark conservation and management, using market-based approaches.

Background

Until recently it was (and still is in many quarters) the popular belief that our oceans could provide us with a never-ending supply of fish, including sharks.[1] Science, however, has demonstrated that globally, many shark populations are in decline; some by more than 90 per cent (Hisano *et al.*, 2011; Camhi *et al.*, 2009; Dulvy *et al.*, 2008; Baum and Myers, 2004; Stevens *et al.*, 2000). While there may be differing rates and reasons for these declines (Yates *et al.*, 2012; Chin *et al.*, 2012; Hisano *et al.*, 2011; Dulvy *et al.*, 2008), without exception, overfishing is the predominant reason. The biological characteristics of most shark species – maturing late, having few young and being long-lived – makes them particularly vulnerable to overexploitation, with less potential to sustain intensive fishing pressure (Dulvy *et al.*, 2008; Simpfendorfer, 2000; Musick *et al.*, 2000). There are now 182 shark species (or 17 per cent) listed as Critically Endangered, Endangered or Vulnerable on the IUCN *Red List* and 504 shark species (or 46 per cent) on which there is insufficient data to make an assessment. This growing body of evidence of the threatened state and continuing declines of many shark species is prompting increasing international concern for shark stocks and a heightened awareness of the need for improved conservation and management.

Historically, shark conservation action has focused on creating and improving fishery management frameworks (e.g. Musick *et al.*, 2000; Barker and Schluessel, 2005). Often, these actions have come about as a result of advocacy from conservation NGOs. Such efforts have been critical in establishing a framework for the conservation and management of sharks globally and are aimed at taking steps to curb unregulated fishing effort and trade for some species (see Chapters 2 and 3). Despite this, the reality has been that the decline in many shark populations has continued due to the increasing demand for shark fin from Asia, ongoing unregulated shark fisheries in many countries and the slow pace at which international regulatory instruments are being implemented. In addition, the broad geographic distribution and migratory nature of sharks has often made it difficult to define and implement effective conservation and management strategies (Knip *et al.*, 2012).

In the last 10–15 years, approaches taken by conservation NGOs have changed. This has resulted in an increasing focus on more holistic approaches to addressing the decline of shark populations globally through building responsible consumption, trade and management. While campaigning has continued for the adoption of shark fishing and finning bans, and the establishment of marine protected areas focused on sharks ('shark parks'), more innovative conservation approaches have centred around reducing demand for shark fins, increasing the supply and sourcing of more sustainable options, as well as improving the management of shark fishing. Therefore, the focus of some NGOs has become working with the fishing industry, the seafood supply chain, consumers and governments through market-based partnership approaches, including promoting certification and responsible sourcing policies (see Chapter 9). In addition, the recognition by retail and processing corporations and fishing industries of their social responsibility to meet the growing expectations of their consumers has provided opportunities for the conservation sector to engage collaboratively with the private sector in a way that has never been seen before. This market-based approach for conservation has in general been well-received by the fishing industry, seafood supply chains and by the public across many western countries, with the results providing surprisingly good outcomes for sharks and the marine environment. The challenge is how to achieve similar results across other regions, such as Asia, where demand for sharks is greatest.

China is the world's largest seafood consumer (FAO, 2012). Driven by growing domestic income and an increase in the diversity of fish available, per capita fish consumption in China in 2009 was 31.9 kg, more than double the global average (15.1 kg in 2009). By 2020, China may be consuming 35.9 kg of food fish per person annually (Delgado *et al.*, 2003), mostly because of growth in the Chinese middle-class population, many of which believe seafood is healthier than other animal protein (Xu *et al.*, 2012). The middle-class population is expected to reach 0.4 billion by 2020 (Atsmon *et al.*, 2012). While there is doubt about China's seafood consumption data (FAO, 2012), it provides an indication of the likely scale of Chinese seafood consumption and with its expected population growth, the significant ramifications for world fisheries, in particular luxury seafood such as shark fins (Fabinyi, 2011; FAO, 2012).

Shark fin is one of the world's most valuable food commodities, with its main consumers being people in Hong Kong, China, Singapore and other countries with ethnic Chinese populations. Collectively, Hong Kong, China and Singapore imported around 92 per cent of recorded global shark fin imports between 2000 and 2009 (FAO Fishstat, undated). A single bowl of shark fin soup can cost upwards of US$80 for a cup-sized bowl, or more than US$500 per kilogram for the cheapest shark fin (Consumer Council of Hong Kong, 2011). It is a part of traditional Chinese culture, dating back thousands of years and known as 'yú chì', translated literally as 'fish wing'. While shark fins were traditionally consumed at dinner banquets, predominantly as a symbol of status, wealth, power, prestige and honour in Chinese society and often reserved for special occasions like weddings, the growing economic prosperity and increased spending power of the Asian middle class, coupled with a rising Chinese population, has caused a significant increase in its demand (Mejuto *et al.*, 2004; Fong and Anderson, 2002; Rose, 1996; Fabinyi, 2011).

Shark fin is often referred to as a 'conspicuous consumption' product, meaning it is served to display social status publicly, for example, by posting the price of the fin outside the banquet hall. With the increase in economic prosperity, coupled with a rising population in mainland China, increased consumption is also moving beyond traditional special occasions (Clarke *et al.*, 2007; Clarke, 2004), for example, to other occasions such as birthday celebrations, family gatherings and important business deals. Other traditional beliefs around health and vitality also play a role in driving demand for shark fin. Clarke *et al.* (2007) noted that products from 'strong' or 'fierce' animals like sharks are believed to impart strength to those who eat them and thus were considered suitable for the imperial family. Shark fin is also considered to be a strengthening food or 'Pu', and to have medicinal qualities like a tonic, particularly for the older Chinese generation, in the same way the western cultures use chicken soup as a remedy.

Globally it is estimated that on average around 38 million – but as high as 73 million – sharks are traded annually, with around 30–52 million of those sharks used in the fin trade (Clarke *et al.*, 2006). Clarke *et al.* (2006) calculated that this equates to an average estimate for the global shark fin trade which is 3–5 times higher than FAO-based figures – the difference explained perhaps through illegal and unreported catch, along with missing data. Hong Kong is the world's largest shark fin trading centre, handling at least half of the global trade (Clarke, 2004), even though during the last few years many fins have been sent for processing directly in China. In 2008, using Hong Kong Census Trade Statistics, Oceana reported that 10,000 metric tonnes of shark fin were imported to Hong Kong from 87 countries, with the top five countries (Spain, Singapore, Taiwan, Indonesia and the United Arab Emirates) accounting for more than 60 per cent (Oceana, 2010).

What these analyses show is that the problem of declining shark populations is a global one that provides opportunity to develop a holistic solution-driven response to reducing the decline, drawing on the basic economics of demand and supply. Addressing the increasing demand for shark fin in Asia, particularly China, involves reducing markets in Asia and encouraging responsible supply globally, as well as ensuring effective management within shark catching and export countries. In fact, there is growing evidence to suggest that a more holistic conservation approach targeted at the supply chain is providing effective solutions to improving the management of fisheries in general (CEA, 2012), and as such may be useful for improving the management of global shark populations. With China being the world's largest consumer and importer of shark products, and experiencing a dramatic growth in per capita consumption of shark fin, it has a significant, important and growing role in finding solutions.

The role of the consumer

Over the last few decades, many conservation NGOs have focused on educating consumers to become non-consumers of, or modify their consumption patterns for, many products deemed to be having significant negative impacts on the environment or endangered species. In particular, many conservation NGOs have made significant investments in market-based consumer awareness campaigns for seafood as a way to reduce overfishing and encourage the fishing industry to improve their practices, with the idea that the consumer effectively becomes the regulator. The underlying premise is that if you educate consumers, they will be concerned about the effects that a purchasing choice has not only on themselves, but also on the marine environment (Harrison *et al.*, 2005; Sandikci and Ekici, 2009). Conservation NGOs attribute the problems of 'wrong' seafood decisions to a lack of information. The solution, as they see it, is to inform consumers about the seafood species they want to eat, sending the right signals to producers (Iles, 2007). These market-driven campaigns enable consumers to 'express their values, ideas, beliefs and overall identities' in relation to their social, environmental, historical and political contexts (Cherrier and Murray, 2007).

Several approaches for seafood social, market-based campaigns are utilized by conservation NGOs (with differing success rates), including boycotts, eco-labels and seafood guides (Roheim and Sutinen, 2006a). The mid 1990s marked the beginning of the sustainable seafood movement (McGovern, 2005), with one of the first large efforts to mobilize consumers in support of stronger fish conservation in 1998: the 'Give Swordfish a Break' campaign run by SeaWeb and the Natural Resources Defence Council. The campaign successfully advocated for recovery measures to restore North Atlantic swordfish, which had been severely depleted after decades of overfishing and mismanagement. Key to its success was the commitment by 700 chefs, hotel chains, cruise lines, retailers and airlines to sign a pledge, committing to remove North Atlantic swordfish from their menus and dining choices. The campaign officially ended in August 2000 following the adoption of international quota restrictions and the closure of nursery areas in US waters. In 2009, the Scientific Committee for the International Commission for the Conservation of Atlantic Tunas reported that the species had shown a consistent increase in recovery since 2000 and that the biomass was estimated to be just above maximum sustainable yield (SeaWeb, 2002; Anon, 2010).

In recent years, numerous campaigns have emerged across countries such as the United States, Europe and Canada to boycott seafood products, particularly shark fins (see Chapter 9). The details of these bans differ between jurisdictions, but generally contain a prohibition on possession, landing or sale of shark fins. While these efforts are commendable and reflect a shift in attitudes by consumers and are gaining the attention of government regulators, the sheer scale of consumption in Hong Kong and across Asia means these actions alone are unlikely to have any significant impact on curbing declining shark populations globally. Likewise, while western jurisdictional boycott campaigns may be successful in banning shark fins into a jurisdiction, they usually do not create incentives for producers to adopt sustainable practices because the boycott treats all producers as the same in the marketplace (Iles, 2007) and many larger alternate markets have remained open. Iles (2007) noted that the only way to change the underlying production system is through changes in sourcing, practices and extraction.

A multitude of sustainable seafood guides or advisory lists have emerged in many countries as centrepieces of consumer awareness campaigns. There are now over 200 guides available (Seaman, 2009) that come in all forms from wallet cards to smartphone apps and span many countries, including within Asia (Hong Kong, Malaysia, Singapore and Indonesia). These guides, such as the Monterey Bay Aquarium Seafood Watch programme, Australian Marine Conservation Sustainable Seafood Guide and World Wide Fund for Nature (WWF) country-based seafood guides use a ranking process, based on methodology and criteria that evaluate environmental and biological criteria of species, fisheries or aquaculture practices. Simple traffic-light style approaches are used to guide consumers away from those species considered overfished, towards those that are more sustainably fished. They generally provide information on which seafood items are 'Green – Best Choices', 'Orange – Good Alternatives' and 'Red – Avoid'. Sharks feature prominently across all guides as species to avoid.

However, whether these actions are directly leading to overall changes in reducing pressure on overfished sharks or consumption of shark fin is uncertain. An example of this lack of translation into shifts in consumption patterns is clearly seen in the dramatic increase in consumption of farmed shrimp and salmon between 1995 and 2010, even though many of these products are on the Seafood Watch red list (MBA, 2011). What is more likely is that they increase consumer awareness, where some consumers are willing to pay a premium for seafood that is healthy and sustainable (Boyle and Mott, 2009; Manget *et al.*, 2009; Seafood Choice Alliance, 2009; Xu *et al.*, 2012). Progressive retailers then respond with responsible sourcing policies geared around using eco-labels or boycotts.

It is important to note that consumer campaigns such as boycotts or seafood guides, while important in mobilizing consumers, have significant limitations. These types of market-based mechanisms are unable to discriminate between responsible and irresponsible fishing operations, and therefore impose a cost on responsible fishing operators (Roheim and Sutinen, 2006b). Furthermore, the multitude of guides can create consumer confusion (Jacquet and Pauly, 2007; Gerlach and Schudak, 2010) as many provide a national focus when the majority of seafood available for purchase is imported. They also tend to offer conflicting advice regarding the sustainability of a species due to the use of differing assessment criteria of varying degrees of scientific rigour for determining what species are caught from 'sustainable' fisheries (Jacquet *et al.*, 2009).

A lack of traceability of where seafood products are sourced and inconsistency and errors in product labelling mean that consumers often are unable to tell if the fish species they want to purchase at a local supermarket is from the unsustainable fishery referred to in a guide as one to avoid or whether it in fact is actually what the label claims it to be. Without strict fish name standards and labelling laws, the absence of traceability provides opportunities for suppliers to undermine environmental regulations, and therefore consumer campaigns, and label their fish as a more sustainable alternative or to deliberately deceive a consumer by calling it something else to maximize their profits; for example, sharks are often filleted, re-labelled and sold as flake, weakfishes or tuna (Jacquet and Pauly, 2008; Bostock and Herdson, 1985). This is assuming the consumer recognizes an eco-label in the first place as a way to identify sustainable products and guide purchaser decisions (Gallastegui, 2002).

One eco-label that is building brand recognition, and that is also based on sound science, is from the Marine Stewardship Council (MSC). The MSC standard measures a fishery's performance against internationally agreed, science-based global criteria and principles for sustainable fisheries, which require healthy target fish stocks, minimal ecosystem impacts and an effective and precautionary fisheries-management system. An independent team of expert scientists and a certifier undertakes the assessment against the MSC standard, which allows for external stakeholders with an interest in the fishery to feed into the assessment at various stages of the process. A survey commissioned by MSC in 2012–2013 found that 30 per cent – or more than one in four – of seafood buyers are aware of the MSC eco-label in the United States, Canada, United Kingdom, Germany, France and Japan. This is up from 23 per cent in 2010 (MSC, 2013).

Nevertheless, many consumer campaigns also lack the sophistication to monitor and undertake rigorous evaluations to measure whether their efforts are actually improving the conservation status of species such as sharks by reducing fishing pressure (Bates, 2010; Bridgespan Group, 2005). Certainly the little anecdotal evidence available from Hong Kong as to the success of shark fin boycott campaigns to date is showing mixed results (Qin, 2013; Strother and Kollemberg, 2013), and it is clear that for the seafood supply chain to engage in market-based approaches, particularly in Asia, it will take more than just consumer sentiment to cause a shift towards addressing global sustainability issues around sharks.

Corporate social responsibility, seafood production and eco-labelling

There is little doubt that some companies choose to be more responsible in the absence of a legal requirement to do so. The reasons are varied, but generally it is because being socially responsible is seen as good for business and will create a competitive advantage (Kotler and Lee, 2005; Porter and Kramer, 2006; Fombrun and Shanley, 1990; Brammer *et al.*, 2007; Maignan *et al.*, 1999; Rupp *et al.*, 2006; Valentine and Fleischman, 2008). Many companies have been rewarded by the market for improving their corporate social responsibility practice (Pohle and Hittner, 2008; Konar and Cohen, 2001; Cheung *et al.*, 2010; Arafat *et al.*, 2012).

The Asian Development Bank has identified five key drivers shifting the mindsets of business leaders globally that together are providing a strong argument for business success through the adoption of improved environmental performance (ADB, 2005). These drivers hold strong relevance for the transformation occurring with seafood businesses globally, but particularly in the Asia Pacific region and with respect to shark products (FAO, 2008; Nias and Lawrence, 2010):

1 entry into the global market – regional and global seafood markets are shifting;
2 emergence of an affluent middle class with market power;
3 the information revolution – the push for transparency;
4 urbanization – a growing demand for good corporate citizenship;
5 industrialization – aligning to global business processes and standards.

It is clear that the world's attitudes to seafood are shifting. Conservation NGOs are mobilizing consumer and business-to-business attitudes to build the case for both voluntary market-oriented product stewardship schemes and greater environmental regulation of business performance. These changes are leading to an emerging and relatively comprehensive intergovernmental policy framework, many national-level policy approaches, consumer outreach campaigns and strong engagement with the entire seafood supply chain. When the cumulative effects of these changes on the business climate are considered, a picture is emerging of how globalization and social change will fundamentally alter the 'rules of the game' for seafood businesses, including those that produce or source shark products (Nias and Lawrence, 2010). These pressures all point to the same conclusion – the old ways of doing business are over.

Globally, many seafood producers, suppliers and retailers are shifting their mindset and therefore behaviour to embrace corporate social responsibility. With this emergence of corporate social responsibility has come the necessity to understand what it means to really 'engage' stakeholders (Johnson-Cramer *et al.*, 2003) and how to move beyond control or interaction, towards fostering collaborative relationships and gaining a social licence to operate. For some of these organizations it has been a fundamental journey of forced self-discovery, towards understanding who their stakeholders are and what expectations they bring and how their actions impact on these stakeholders. Many in the seafood industry, particularly producers and those in the supply chain, are only now realizing that their stakeholders go beyond their direct suppliers or customers, to extend to the end consumer, investors and society in general.

Leaders in the seafood industry recognize that engagement of stakeholders, and sustainability and moral behaviour generally, are integral to their reputation and long-term business strategy if they are to remain relevant, capture market share and continue to operate cost effectively in a changing world. Many of these leaders are not waiting for regulators or even consumers to reshape their businesses, but rather are embracing the concept of sustainability head-on. For many seafood retailers, such as Tesco, Sainsbury's, Marks & Spencer, Aldi, Whole Foods, Walmart, Coles and Woolworths, it seems their approach has been to collaborate with environmental NGOs such as the WWF and Sustainable Fisheries Partnership to understand where the seafood they are selling comes from and then work with and invest in their supply chains to ensure that the seafood they sell is sourced responsibly. For most, this would mean a commitment to having all products responsibly sourced, preferably carrying a recognized eco-label by a certain date. It also means dropping certain seafood lines that they have identified as sourced from unsustainable fisheries, including shark products. The global impact of these commitments by the big retailers contributed to a large number of fisheries now seeking to have their product certified as sustainable through an eco-label.

Over the last ten years, advancing market incentives for sustainable seafood have been seen as an effective method for improving the sustainability of global fisheries. Market-oriented certification or eco-label schemes have proved effective. More than 30 schemes are now available, including the MSC, Friends of the Sea, Agreement on the International Dolphin Conservation Program and Fishwise (Parkes *et al.*, 2010; Roheim, 2009). The MSC has emerged as the leading or gold star standard for seafood eco-labels (WWF, 2009; Bush *et al.*, 2013; Gutiérrez *et al.*, 2012) and now dominates the global market with more than 19,500 products available and around ten million metric tonnes of wild-caught seafood (or over 11 per cent of the annual global harvest) from fisheries certified or in full assessment (MSC, 2013). This includes seafood provided from two MSC-certified shark fisheries, the British Columbia Spiny Dogfish Fishery and the US Atlantic Spiny Dogfish Fishery.

The question such certification programmes ultimately raise is whether they can reverse market forces that are currently driving unsustainable shark fishing and generate the demand and incentives that support sustainable fisheries. While there is little evidence in the literature to date to show whether even the most respected scheme is leading to a measurable reduction of fish stock declines (Bush *et al.*, 2013), there is some evidence emerging that the MSC is driving market forces towards sustainable fisheries for developed fishing states. Where the challenges lie for the MSC is with concerns that the scheme provides little incentive for continual improvement for fisheries once certified (Bush *et al.*, 2013), the lack of availability of the scheme to small-scale and developing-world fisheries, such as in Asia, and whether economic benefits from certification will reach small fisheries communities (Gulbrandsen, 2009; Perez-Ramirez *et al.*, 2012; Jacquet and Pauly, 2007). Despite small-scale fishers from developing countries harvesting most of the world's fish catch (FAO, 2012), there are only a few fisheries in developing countries that have been certified (e.g. Viet Nam Ben Tre clam, PNA Western and Central Pacific skipjack tuna). In addition, there are few MSC eco-labelled products available in supermarkets across Asia, although efforts are underway by the MSC to address this.

As noted earlier, there are now two MSC-certified shark fisheries, the British Columbia Spiny Dogfish Fishery and the US Atlantic Spiny Dogfish Fishery. However, given the biological challenges with respect to the majority of sharks, the shortcomings of even the most respected eco-label, particularly in many developing countries that are shark-fishing states and the significant consumption of shark products within Asia, the question remains as to whether eco-labels alone can slow the decline in global shark populations. For market-based approaches to be effective, an integrated suite of tools needs to be applied across the supply chain.

A new style of conservation and management for sharks

While conservation NGOs have played a major role in shaping public expectations of the seafood industry and in influencing both corporate and government engagement as discussed above, it is clear that more needs to be done to curb the global overfishing of sharks that goes beyond a reliance on the community or consumers to drive industry, political and policy change.

Past experience has proven that focusing solely on trying to improve management of sharks by working country by country, with often under-resourced and under-skilled governments or regulators with little incentive to improve industry practices, is a long, slow and costly process for NGOs that depends on strong political will at best and even then may not be effective. One thing is clear, given the scale, complexity and globalization of shark fisheries and markets, effective transformational approaches for improved shark conservation require integrated involvement and cooperation among all stakeholders that span countries and markets to develop long-term, holistic solutions that are acceptable and beneficial to all. Far-sighted conservation NGOs support innovative transformational approaches that promote a cross-cutting approach leading to (see Figure 7.1):

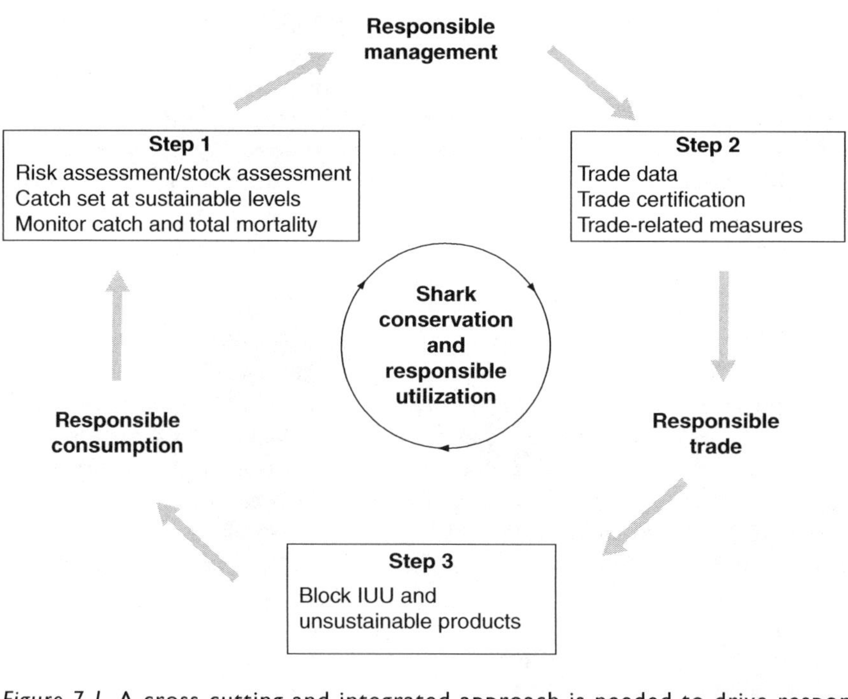

Figure 7.1 A cross-cutting and integrated approach is needed to drive responsible shark use (used with permission and adapted from Lack and Sant, 2009)

- responsible trade – providing sustainable sourcing options or alternative products;
- responsible consumption – reducing demand for shark products and promoting sustainable practices; and
- responsible management – enabling effective science-based fisheries management and regulatory frameworks that reduce overfishing of sharks and shark by-catch and promote sustainable practices at national, regional and international levels.

Just focusing on one aspect will not provide the scale of change needed to improve shark conservation. All dimensions need to be tackled, creating major challenges for NGOs – they do not have the resources, capacity or global coverage to be able to effectively approach shark conservation in this way. Some conservation NGOs are now collaborating with each other through alliances or through joint programmes to pool resources and capacity and complement expertise and reach in the name of improved shark conservation (see Chapter 9).

There are only a handful of conservation NGOs, such as WWF, who have the reach and resources to do so. Likewise, using traditional stakeholders such as the community and consumers to stimulate change is no longer enough. NGOs, governments and seafood sector leaders are beginning to see that the only way to address these daunting issues around sharks is to constructively work together, in partnership, to mainstream sustainability.

For most conservation NGOs and many of their donors, this approach is a major shift in the theory of change under which they operate – working *with* industry, seafood companies and governments, rather than working *against* them. Likewise for industry and the corporate sector, who for many years have fought against the 'green movement', shifting their approach towards working with NGOs is a significant risk that warrants careful risk management.

Effective business–conservation–government collaboration requires a number of critical elements:

- Establishing and maintaining trust to build true partnership approaches that foster collaboration to improve the performance of the fishing industry and seafood markets and explore shared and innovative solutions to complex ecological, social and economic challenges.
- Establishing a sound foundation of commonality from which to build and then being truly committed towards building solutions.
- Mobilizing joint resources to solve sustainability challenges.
- Working together to strengthen public-sector governance, capacity and institutions.

If effective, the result will be strengthened governance and performance in the seafood sector with respect to sharks and a clear social licence to operate.

Case studies

In order to illustrate the opportunities and effectiveness of multi-stakeholder collaborations, several case studies are explored below. These examples are important advances in their own right, but they also offer lessons that may be learned and applied in other contexts.

Reducing shark by-catch in Australian gillnet and trawl fisheries

SeaNet is an Australian government-funded environmental extension service to the fishing industry. It is managed by an industry-supported conservation NGO, OceanWatch Australia. It has laid the foundation for collaborative effort within the seafood sector in Australia and provides an excellent model for effective collaboration in other countries. Now in its fourteenth year, SeaNet aims to improve the industry's responsible fishing credentials and advance on-ground marine conservation of biodiversity and best-practice outcomes, while ensuring the industry remains internationally competitive. Eight extension officers work in partnership with commercial fishers to adopt environmentally sustainable practices. They do this through facilitating effective collaboration and dialogue between commercial fishers, researchers, government and the broader community, including consumers. Extension officers bridge the gap between industry, research and other relevant stakeholders, with proven success in promoting change in fishing practices.

SeaNet has fostered a number of collaborative projects focused on reducing the by-catch of sharks in Australian prawn trawl and gillnet fisheries.

Kimberley Gillnet and Barramundi Fishery (KGBF)

This fishery is located in the remote northwest of Australia. This commercial net and trawl fishery interacts with a Critically Endangered shark species, dwarf sawfish (*Pristis clavata*), which has been identified as one of the least sustainable species in this fishery (DFWA, 2011; Salini *et al.*, 2007). SeaNet works with the fishers, fisheries managers and researchers to develop innovative solutions to reduce interactions, including a trial to investigate the effectiveness of using electromagnetic devices to reduce by-catch and deter sawfish from gillnets in the KGBF. SeaNet is also utilizing a sawfish handling guide and video on handling and release techniques developed by fisheries managers. It is envisaged that industry will then implement a code of practice outlining best fishing practices for reducing interactions. The type of deterrent used has proven to be effective in the Western Australia abalone fishery, when attached to tuna sea-cages in South Australia and in the Queensland Northern Prawn Fishery. While this technology has yet to be trialled in a gillnet fishery, the potential benefits are positive given previous successes.

The Northern Prawn Fishery

This is Australia's most valuable federal fishery, supplying mainly banana and tiger prawns to overseas and domestic markets. In 2013 it was the first tropical shrimp trawl to receive MSC accreditation. For the Northern Prawn Fishery, the use of turtle exclusion devices (TEDs) and by-catch reduction devices (BRDs) is mandatory. While TEDs are effective at ensuring large sharks and rays are not caught in nets, smaller sharks and rays often pass through the TED (Brewer *et al.*, 2006). SeaNet worked with a net maker, Australian Fisheries Management Authority and industry to design and test a new BRD called the 'popeye fishbox'. It consists of a rigid frame that creates a turbulent back-current of water flow that allows fish to escape. Under certain conditions, and in conjunction with the use of a TED, the fishbox resulted in a 35 per cent reduction in the capture of small sharks and rays, a 48 per cent reduction in the amount of small fish and an 85 per cent reduction in sea snakes, with no significant change in prawn catch (Raudzens, 2007; Brewer *et al.*, 2006). Following these trials, this BRD was endorsed for use in the fishery, but concerns regarding crew safety have limited its adoption by fishers and further work is underway. For the moment, TEDs remain the primary mechanism for reduction in shark catch in the Northern Prawn Fishery.

Industry driving improved shark conservation through collaborative market-based solutions

The Southern Shark Industry Alliance (SSIA) is a peak industry body for the Australian shark sector of the Southern Shark and Scalefish Fishery, which predominantly uses demersal gillnets to catch gummy sharks (*Mustelus antarcticus*). The SSIA is utilizing a market-based approach underpinned by well-structured and strong collaboration between fishers, conservation NGOs, researchers and government to transform this fishery. The goal is MSC certification and improved product quality that will lead to less wastage and greater shelf life for retailers. Certification will also provide a fin by-product that gives confidence to Asian markets that it has been responsibly sourced and labelled, with minimal impact on non-target species.

This fishery has strong science underpinning a harvest strategy that applies a quota system to limit catch to sustainable levels. This method of fishing, while highly selective for ensuring that gummy shark populations have remained healthy for more than 20 years, has been under intense scrutiny for its impact on a listed shark species, school shark (*Galeorhinus galeus*), and marine mammals. As a result of its impact on these protected species, a number of significant closures were introduced at great economic cost to industry.

The SSIA, with support from the government, Woolworths (Australia's largest supermarket chain) and various conservation NGOs, is pursuing extensive trials of an old method (hook fishing) utilizing new technology. To date, results show this method is a viable sustainable alternative for targeting gummy shark. A concurrent MSC pre-assessment process and guidance suggests that the fishery will be able to attain MSC certification. Trials are now underway to determine the economic viability of this method, though indications to date are positive.

Reducing demand for shark products and providing responsible sourcing options or alternative products

WWF-Hong Kong commenced an integrated market-based Shark Fin Initiative in 2007 to reduce demand for shark fin and provide responsible sourcing options. The theory is that current and future levels of demand for shark fins are likely to be far higher than can be met from sustainably managed fisheries, and therefore it is critical that the consumption of shark fins in key markets such as Hong Kong is greatly reduced. In turn, this will minimize economic incentives for fishers to target sharks. WWF is working in collaboration with four stakeholder groups to deliver a market-based programme:

- *Consumers (public and corporate)* – encouraging consumers to boycott shark fin, supporting caterers offering shark fin-free banquets and working with corporates to pledge not to eat or serve shark fin at corporate functions.
- *Catering and restaurants* – encouraging their participation in the alternative shark-free menu programme.
- *Fisheries and government* – maintaining close dialogue with the Hong Kong government towards regulating the shark fin trade and improving traceability.

These initiatives led by WWF-Hong Kong are being complemented in other parts of the world, including Africa, America, Asia and Europe, where WWF is working with fishers, governments, seafood importers and distributors to promote MSC and chain of custody certification as credible systems to help maintain healthy shark populations, provide for reliable tracking of products from certified shark fisheries and formulate management plans aimed at building sustainable shark fisheries to assist in providing alternate responsibly sourced shark fin options in Hong Kong.[2]

The world's first 'sustainable' shark fishery

In 2011 the hook and line British Columbia North Pacific Spiny Dogfish Fishery became the first shark fishery to receive the MSC certification. North Pacific spiny dogfish (*Squalus suckleyi*) are a type of small coastal shark found from Baja, California to the Aleutian Islands, but are most common from the central Gulf of Alaska to central California. These sharks have a gestation period lasting almost two years, with litter sizes ranging from two to 16 pups (Bonham *et al.*,

1949; Ketchen, 1986; King and McFarlane, 2009). Just over 1,800 metric tonnes were caught in 2010 (DFO, undated), primarily for their meat, which is sold in the United Kingdom. Their fins are sent to Asia and their belly flaps to Germany. The fishery started in the 1870s, primarily for liver oil for lighting and later industrial lubrication, peaking in the 1930s and 1940s, when the livers were targeted for vitamin A (Ketchen, 1986; Bonfil, 1999) before stocks declined – and synthetic vitamin A was introduced, reducing its market demand (Bonfil, 1999). In the 1990s, with the collapse of the European and US spiny dogfish stocks, the fishery re-opened.

The North Pacific Spiny Dogfish Fishery is managed as part of the multi-species groundfish fishery of approximately 61 species and seven key sectors under an Integrated Fishery Management Plan for Groundfish. First introduced in 1998, and revised annually since that time, it requires that all groundfish must be accounted for, catches are managed on a stock-specific basis and fishers are individually accountable for their catch. To meet these objectives, the fishery uses 100 per cent on-board tamper-free camera-based electronic monitoring, in addition to dockside monitoring at designated landing sites. The hook and line method is highly selective and by-catch as a result is minimized. It has limited benthic habitat impacts and conservation strategies and closures are used to protect sensitive habitats such as corals and sponges. Ongoing engagement and dialogue occurs with conservation NGOs and other stakeholders in the management of the fishery. Industry and conservation NGOs developed an arrangement in the trawl fishery (which is not a part of the MSC certification but does have an allocation for spiny dogfish), including cold water coral by-catch quotas and an encounter protocol.

While the fishery has a long stock assessment history going back to 1979 (Wood *et al.*, 1979), a precautionary approach is taken for setting total allowable catch (TAC) limits for this fishery as there remains uncertainty over the size of stock biomass. A harvest strategy applies limited entry to this small-scale fishery, with individual transferable vessel quotas used regardless of whether a fish is retained or not. Fishers are required to land all dogfish whole, with fins attached. Current assessments (King and McFarlane, 2009; Wallace *et al.*, 2009) suggest that spiny dogfish stocks have somewhat recovered since the 1940s and have been stable for more than a decade and there are no conservation concerns. Canada Fisheries and Oceans (DFO) reviews the TAC limits annually, revising them if required in response to apparent changes in stock abundance (Mawani, 2009). Catch levels have been well below the TAC limits for the past 20 years (DFO, personal communication, 2012).

While the fishery has a number of conditions, to deepen knowledge and reduce uncertainty as a part of its MSC certification, it demonstrates that it is possible to have a sustainable shark fishery. While minimal in terms of market impact given the small size of the fishery, it provides an opportunity for the market to source responsible shark products, particularly shark fin.

Implementing trade controls through CITES regulations

The *Convention on International Trade in Endangered Species of Wild Fauna and Flora* (CITES) is an international agreement between 178 governments to control international wildlife trade. It works by subjecting international trade to certain controls (see Chapter 3). Concern for the conservation of sharks was first acknowledged internationally through the adoption of a CITES Resolution in 1994 on the Status of International Trade in Shark Species. Since then, there have been listings of a number of species (see Chapter 3). A CITES listing does not mean that the trade in these products is automatically controlled, nor does it reduce the need for comprehensive fisheries management. To establish effective monitoring and control systems, shark trading governments face many challenges, particularly with respect to poor data on catch and populations, inadequate domestic regulatory frameworks and poor traceability (Mundy-Taylor and Crook, 2013). In addition, understanding national, regional and global shark supply chains is a fundamental prerequisite for implementing traceability mechanisms. Addressing these challenges requires the many countries and stakeholders involved in global shark trade to work together to develop solutions that ensure the proper implementation of the CITES shark listings.

The European Union has granted €1.2 million to the CITES Secretariat to carry out a capacity-building programme specifically targeted at countries involved in the harvest of and trade in CITES-listed sharks and rays.

TRAFFIC, an international wildlife trade monitoring network, notes that collaborative market-based approaches could contribute to improving the traceability of shark products and assist in verification along the supply chain (Mundy-Taylor and Crook, 2013). Examples include eco-labelling schemes (such as that provided by the MSC), chain of custody measures (which verify a product at each point in the supply chain) and technological initiatives that can improve traceability (for example, by assigning unique identifiers to an individual fish to allow it to be traced back to the fisher that landed it using smartphone technology through Thisfish (www.thisfish.info)).[3] A collaborative project is currently underway to design and test a shark product labelling and tracking system (SharkTrack) and determine whether any existing fisheries product-labelling and tracking systems can be applied to the shark trade (TRAFFIC, personal communication, 2013).

Future opportunities for collaborative shark conservation

The above discussion illustrates the powerful role that collaborative initiatives can play in advancing shark conservation and management. The future of shark conservation will be dependent on the success of collaboration between industry, conservation NGOs, consumers, the seafood supply chain and governments to deliver market-based solutions that provide transformational change to halt and even reverse the rapid decline of global shark populations through building responsible consumption, trade and management. The challenge will be whether differences and politics can be put aside to find common ground from which to build trust and respect to provide a platform from which to develop, test and implement innovative market-based solutions. While other conservation measures such as advocating for improved enabling frameworks, establishing marine protected areas and ongoing fisheries improvement will remain relevant, positive outcomes will depend upon whether the demand for shark fins can be reduced, the supply and sourcing of more sustainable options increased and whether this translates into improved management of shark fishing at national, regional and international scales.

Certainly there are examples emerging of market-based approaches being applied to sharks, with the support of the fishing industry, the seafood supply chain and consumers and governments. The case studies have provided a snapshot of some of these initiatives and the challenges they face. Although the global momentum for sustainable seafood is likely to continue to support market-based solutions for sharks, the adoption of eco-labels such as the MSC is unlikely to be a silver bullet. Shark biological attributes are likely to reduce the opportunity of certification for providing responsibly sourced shark fin options at a scale needed to meet existing demand, so a combination of conservation measures will need to be applied.

The growing recognition by retailers, processing corporations and fishing industries of their social responsibility to meet the expectations of their consumers has provided the opportunity for the conservation sector to engage collaboratively with the private sector in a way that has never been seen before for shark conservation and, as the case studies have shown, this is translating into improved fishing practices, regulation and management.

Acknowledgements

The author would like to acknowledge the support and assistance kindly given by a number of individuals who provided invaluable insights and learning into the development of this chapter, including: Professor Michael Harte, National Marine Manager WWF-Australia; Tracy Tsang, Senior Programme Officer, Shark WWF-Hong Kong; Anthony Ciconte from Southern Shark Industry Alliance; Glenn Sant and Joyce Wu from TRAFFIC; and the SeaNet officers who have laid the foundation for collaborative efforts towards improving the sustainability of Australian fisheries.

Notes

1 The term 'shark' refers to all species of sharks, skates, rays and chimaeras (Class Chondrichthyes).
2 For more information, refer to the WWF-Hong Kong website: www.wwf.org.hk/en/whatwedo/footprint/seafood/sharkfin_initiative.

References

ADB (2005) *Asian Environment Outlook 2005: Making Profits, Protecting Our Planet – Corporate Responsibility for Environmental Performance in Asia and the Pacific*, Asian Development Bank, Manila.

Anon. (2010) 'Report of the 2009 Atlantic swordfish stock assessment', *Collective Volume of Science Papers ICCAT*, vol. 65, no. 1, pp. 1–123.

Arafat, Y. M., Warokka, A., Abdullah, H. H. and Septian, R. R. (2012) 'The triple bottom line effect on emerging market companies: a test of corporate social responsibility and firm value relationship', *Journal of Southeast Asian Research*, vol. 2012, pp. 1–66.

Atsmon, Y. Magni, M., Li, L. and Liao, W. (2012) *Meet the 2020 Chinese Consumer*, McKinsey and Company, Hong Kong.

Barker, M. J. and Schluessel, V. (2005) 'Managing global shark fisheries: suggestions for prioritizing management strategies', *Aquatic Conservation: Marine and Freshwater Ecosystems*, vol. 15, pp. 325–347.

Bates, C. H. (2010) 'Use of Social Marketing Concepts to Evaluate Ocean Sustainability Campaigns', *Social Marketing Quarterly*, vol. 16, pp. 71–96.

Baum, J. K. and Myers, R. A. (2004) 'Shifting baselines and the decline of pelagic sharks in the Gulf of Mexico', *Ecology Letters*, vol. 7, pp. 135–145.

Bonfil, R. (1999) 'The dogfish (*Squalus acanthias*) fishery off British Columbia, Canada and its management', in R. Shotton (ed.), *Case Studies of the Management of Elasmobranch Fisheries*, FAO, Rome.

Bonham, K., Sanford, F. B., Clegg, W. and Bucher, G. C. (1949) 'Biological and vitamin A studies of spiny dog fish landed in the State of Washington (*Squalus suckleyi*)', *Washington Department Fisheries Biology Bulletin*, vol. 49A, pp. 83–113.

Bostock, T. and Herdson, D. (1985) 'La pesca y utilizacion del tiburon en el Ecuador', *Guayaquil: Instituto Nacional de Pesca. Boletin Cientifico y Tecnico*, vol. 8, no. 10, pp. 21–28.

Boyle, P. and Mott, B. (2009) *America, the Ocean, and Climate Change: New Research Insights for Conservation, Awareness, and Action*, The Ocean Project, Providence, RI.

Brammer, S., Millington, A. and Rayton, B. (2007) 'The contribution of corporate social responsibility to organizational commitment', *International Journal of Human Resource Management*, vol. 18, pp. 1701–1719.

Brewer, D., Heales, D., Milton, D., Dell, Q., Fry, G., Venables, B. and Jones, P. (2006) 'The impact of turtle excluder devices and bycatch reduction devices on diverse tropical marine communities in Australia's northern prawn trawl fishery', *Fisheries Research*, vol. 81, pp. 176–188.

Bridgespan Group (2005) *Seafood Choices Evaluation, Prepared for the David & Lucile Packard Foundation*, Bridgespan Group, Boston, MA.

Bush, S. R., Toonen, H., Oosterveer, P. and Mol, A. P. J. (2013) 'The "devils triangle" of MSC certification: balancing credibility, accessibility and continuous improvement', *Marine Policy*, vol. 37, pp. 288–293.

Camhi, M. D., Valenti, S. V., Fordham, S. V., Fowler, S. L. and Gibson, C. (2009) *The Conservation Status of Pelagic Sharks and Rays: Report of the IUCN Shark Specialist Group Pelagic Shark Red List Workshop*, IUCN Species Survival Commission Shark Specialist Group, Newbury, UK.

CEA (California Environmental Associates) (2012) 'Charting a course to sustainable fisheries', 18 July.

Cherrier, H. and Murray, J. B. (2007) 'Reflexive dispossession and the self: constructing a processual theory of identity', *Consumption, Markets and Culture*, vol. 10, no. 1, pp. 1–29.

Cheung, Y. L., Tan, W., Ahn, H. J. and Zhang, Z. (2010) 'Does corporate social responsibility matter in Asian emerging markets?' *Journal of Business Ethics*, vol. 92, no. 3, pp. 401–413.

Chin, A., Tobin, A., Simpfendorfer, C. and Heupel, M. (2012) 'Reef sharks and inshore habitats: patterns of occurrence and implications for vulnerability', *Marine Ecology Progress Series*, vol. 460, pp. 115–125.

Clarke, S. C. (2004) 'Understanding Pressures on Fishery Resources through Trade Statistics: A Pilot Study of Four Products in the Chinese Dried Seafood Market', *Fish and Fisheries*, vol. 5, pp. 53–74.

Clarke, S. C., McAllister, M. K., Milner-Gulland, E. J., Kirkwood, G. P., Michielsens, C. G., Agnew, D. J., Pikitch, E. K., Nakano, H. and Shivji, M. S. (2006) 'Global estimates of shark catches using trade records from commercial markets', *Ecology Letters*, vol. 9, no. 10, pp. 1115–1126.

Clarke, S., Milner-Gulland, E. J. and Bjorndal, T. (2007) 'Social, economic, and regulatory drivers of the shark fin trade', *Marine Resource Economics*, vol. 22, pp. 305–327.

Consumer Council in Hong Kong (2011) 'Shop smart shark fin', http://shopsmart.consumer.org.hk/shopsmart/tr/hi_dr_sharksfin_hint.html, accessed 30 June 2013.

Delgado, C. L., Wada, N., Rosegrant, M. W., Meijer, S. and Ahmed, M. (2003) *Fish to 2020: Supply and Demand in Changing Global Markets*, Worldfish Center Technical Report 62, International Food Policy Research Institute and Worldfish Center, available at www.ifpri.org/sites/default/files/pubs/pubs/books/fish2020/oc44front.pdf, accessed 4 August 2013.

DFO (undated) 'Commercial fisheries', available at www.dfo-mpo.gc.ca/stats/commercial/land-debarq/sea-maritimes/s2010pq-eng.htm, accessed 4 August 2013.

DFWA (Department of Fisheries, Western Australia) (2011) *The State of the Fisheries and Aquatic Resources Report, North Coast Bioregion*, Department of Fisheries, Western Australia.

Dulvy, N. K., Baum, J. K., Clarke, S., Compagno, L. J. V., Cortes, E., Domingo, A., Fordham, S., Fowler, S., Francis, M. P., Gibson, C., Martnez, J., Musick, J. A., Soldo, A., Stevens, J. D. and Valenti, S. (2008) 'You can swim but you can't hide: the global status and conservation of oceanic pelagic sharks and rays', *Aquatic Conservation: Marine and Freshwater Ecosystems*, vol. 18, pp. 459–482.

Fabinyi, M. (2011) 'Historical, cultural and social perspectives on luxury seafood consumption in China', *Environmental Conservation*, vol. 39, no. 1, pp. 83–92.

FAO (2008) *The State of World Fisheries and Aquaculture*, FAO, Rome.

FAO (2012) *The State of World Fisheries and Aquaculture*, FAO, Rome.

FAO Fishstat (undated) FAOSTAT, available at http://faostat.fao.org/site/291/default.aspx, accessed 4 August 2013.

Fombrun, C. and Shanley, M. (1990) 'What's in a name? Reputation building and corporate strategy', *Academy of Management Journal*, vol. 33, pp. 233–258.

Fong, Q. S. W. and Anderson, J. L. (2002) 'International shark fin markets and shark management: an integrated market preference-cohort analysis of the blacktip shark (*Carcharhinus limbatus*)', *Ecological Economics*, vol. 40, pp. 117–130.

Gallastegui, I. G. (2002) 'The use of eco-labels: a review of the literature', *European Environment*, vol. 12, pp. 316–331.

Gerlach, A. and Schudak, A. (2010) 'Bewertung ökologischer und sozialer Label zur Förderung eines nachhaltigen Konsums', *Umweltpsychologie*, vol. 14, no. 2, pp. 30–44.

Gulbrandsen, L. H. (2009) 'The emergence and effectiveness of the Marine Stewardship Council', *Marine Policy*, vol. 33, pp. 654–660.

Gutiérrez, N. L., Valencia, S. R., Branch, T. A., Agnew, D. J., Baum, J. K., Bianchi, P. L., Cornejo-Donoso, J., Costello, C., Defeo, O., Essington, T. E., Hilborn, R., Hoggarth, D. D., Larsen, A. E., Ninnes, C., Sainsbury, K., Selden, R. L., Sistla, S., Smith, A. D. M., Stern-Pirlot, A., Teck, S. J., Thorson, J. T. and Williams, N. E. (2012) 'Eco-label conveys reliable information on fish stock health to seafood consumers', *PLoS ONE*, vol. 7, no. 8.

Harrison, R., Newholm, T. and Shaw, D. (2005) 'Pressure groups, campaigns and consumers', in R. Harrison, T. Newholm and D. Shaw (eds), *The Ethical Consumer*, Sage, London.

Hisano, M., Connolly, S. R. and Robbins, W. D. (2011) 'Population growth rates of reef sharks with and without fishing on the Great Barrier Reef: robust estimation with multiple models', *PLoS ONE*, vol. 6, no. 9.

Iles, A. (2007) 'Making the seafood industry more sustainable: creating production chain transparency and accountability', *Journal of Cleaner Production*, vol. 15, pp. 577–589.

Jacquet, J. L. and Pauly, D. (2007) 'The rise of seafood awareness campaigns in an era of collapsing fisheries', *Marine Policy*, vol. 31, pp. 308–313.

Jacquet, J. and Pauly, D. (2008) 'Trade secrets: renaming and mislabeling of seafood', *Marine Policy*, vol. 32, pp. 309–318.

Jacquet, J., Hocevar, J., Lai, S., Majluf, P., Pelletier, N., Pitcher, T., Sala, E., Sumaila, R. and Pauly, D. (2009) 'Conserving wild fish in a sea of market-based efforts', *Oryx*, vol. 44, pp. 45–56.

Johnson-Cramer, M. S., Berman, S. L. and Post, J. E. (2003) 'Reexamining the concept of "stakeholder management"', in J. Andriof, S. Waddock, S. Rahman and B. Husted (eds), *Unfolding Stakeholder Thinking*, vol. 2, Greenleaf Publishing, London.

Ketchen, K. S. (1986) *The Spiny Dogfish (*Squalus acanthias*) in the Northeast Pacific and a History of its Utilization*, Canadian Special Publication of Fisheries and Aquatic Sciences, Ottawa.

King, J. R. and McFarlane, G. A. (2009) 'Trends in abundance of spiny dogfish in the Strait of Georgia, 1980–2005', in V. F. Galluci, G. A. McFarlane and G. G. Bargmann (eds), *Biology and Management of Spiny Dogfish Sharks*, American Fisheries Society, Bethesda, MD.

Knip, M. D., Heupel, M. R. and Simpfendorfer, C. A. (2012) 'Evaluating marine protected areas for the conservation of tropical coastal sharks', *Biological Conservation*, vol. 148, pp. 200–209.

Konar, S. and Cohen, M. (2001) 'Does the market value environmental performance?', *Review of Economics and Statistics*, vol. 83, no. 2, pp. 281–309.

Kotler, P. and Lee, N. (2005) *Corporate Social Responsibility: Doing the Most Good for Your Company and Your Cause*, Wiley, Hoboken, NJ.

Lack, M. and Sant, G. (2009) *Trends in Global Shark Catch and Recent Developments in Management*, TRAFFIC International, Cambridge.

McGovern, D. (2005) *The Sustainable Seafood Movement: Transforming the Global Seafood Industry*, October, IntraFish Industry Report.

Maignan, I., Ferrell, O. C. and Hult, T. (1999) 'Corporate citizenship: cultural antecedents and business benefits', *Journal of the Academy of Marketing Science*, vol. 27, pp. 455–469.

Manget, J., Roche, C. and Munnich, F. (2009) *Capturing the Green Advantage for Consumer Companies*, Boston Consulting Group, Boston, MA.

Mawani, T. (2009) 'New monitoring and management regime: groundfish fisheries in British Columbia', in V. F. Galluci, G. A. McFarlane and G. G. Bargmann (eds), *Biology and Management of Spiny Dogfish Sharks*, American Fisheries Society, Bethesda, MD.

Mejuto, J., Garcia-Cortes, B. and de la Serna, J. M. (2004) *Preliminary Scientific Estimations of By-catches Landed by the Spanish Surface Longline Fleet in 1999 in the Atlantic Ocean and Mediterranean Sea*, ICCAT Collective Volume of Scientific Papers, No. 54.

MSC (Marine Stewardship Council) (2013) *Marine Stewardship Council Annual Report 2012/2013*, available at: www.msc.org/documents/msc-brochures/annual-report-archive/annual-report-2012-13-english, accessed 5 March 2014.

Mundy-Taylor, V. and Crook, V. (2013) *Into the Deep: Implementing CITES Measures for Commercially-Valuable Sharks and Manta Rays – Report Prepared for the European Commission*, TRAFFIC International, Cambridge.

Musick, J. A., Burgess, G., Cailliet, G., Camhi, M. and Fordham, S. (2000) 'Management of sharks and their relatives (Elasmobranchii)', *Fisheries*, vol. 25, pp. 9–13.

Nias, R. and Lawrence, A. J. (2010) *Doing 'Green' Business in the Coral Triangle: The Case for Sustainable Seafood*, WWF Indonesia, Sundaland, Indonesia.

Oceana (2010) 'The international trade of shark fins: endangering shark populations worldwide', available at www.oceana.org.cites, accessed 4 August 2013.

Parkes, G., Young, J. A., Walmsley, S. F., Abel, R., Harman, J., Horvat, P., Lem, A., MacFarlane, A., Mens, M. and Nolan, C. (2010) 'Behind the signs: a global review of fish sustainability information schemes', *Reviews in Fisheries Science*, vol. 18, pp. 344–356.

Perez-Ramirez, M., Phillips, B., Lluch-Belda, D. and Lluch-Cota, S. (2012) 'Perspectives for implementing fisheries certification in developing countries', *Marine Policy*, vol. 36, pp. 297–302.

Pohle, G. and Hittner, J. (2008) *Attaining Sustainable Growth through Corporate Social Responsibility*, IBM Institute for Business Value, IBM Global Business Services, New York.

Porter, M. E. and Kramer, M. R. (2006) 'Strategy and society: the link between competitive advantage and corporate social responsibility', *Harvard Business Review*, vol. 84, pp. 78–92.

Qin, A. (2013) 'Taste for shark fin fades slightly in China', *New York Times*, 28 January, available at www.nytimes.com/2013/01/29/world/asia/taste-for-shark-fin-fades-slightly-in-china.html, accessed 4 August 2013.

Raudzens, E. E. (2007) *At Sea Testing of the Popeye Fishbox Bycatch Reduction Device Onboard the FV Adelaide Pearl for Approval in Australia's Northern Prawn Fishery*, Australian Fisheries Management Authority, Canberra.

Roheim, C. A. (2009) 'An evaluation of sustainable seafood guides: implications for environmental groups and the seafood industry', *Marine Resource Economics*, vol. 24, pp. 301–310.

Roheim, C. A. and Sutinen, J. G. (2006a) *Trade and Market-Related Instruments to Reinforce Fisheries Management Measures to Promote Sustainable Fishing Practices*, report prepared for the ICTSD, Geneva and the OECD High Seas Task Force, Paris.

Roheim, C. A. and Sutinen, J. (2006b) *Trade and Marketplace Measures to Promote Sustainable Fishing Practices*, ICTSD, Paris.

Rose, D. A. (1996) *An Overview of World Trade in Sharks and Other Cartilaginous Fishes*, TRAFFIC International, Cambridge.

Rupp, D. E., Ganapathi, J., Aguilera, R. V. and Williams, C. A. (2006) 'Employee reactions to corporate social responsibility: an organizational justice framework', *Journal of Organizational Behavior*, vol. 27, pp. 537–543.

Salini, J., McAuley, R., Blaber, S., Buckworth, R., Chidlow, J., Gribble, N., Ovenden, J., Peverell, S., Pillans, R., Stevens, J., Stobutzki, I., Tarca, C. and Walker, T. (2007) *Northern Australian Sharks and Rays: The Sustainability of Target and Bycatch Species, Phase 2*, Fisheries Research and Development Corporation Report 2002/064, CSIRO, Melbourne.

Sandıkcı, O. and Ekici, A. (2009) 'Politically motivated brand rejection', *Journal of Business Research*, vol. 62, no. 2, pp. 208–217.

Seafood Choices Alliance (2009) *The European Marketplace for Sustainable Seafood 2007*, available at www.seafoodchoices.org/resources/documents/SCAEuroMPReport.pdf, accessed 4 August 2013.

Seaman, T. (2009) 'Are sustainable seafood lists supposed to confuse?', *IntraFish Media*, 25 February.

SeaWeb (2002) 'North Atlantic swordfish show dramatic recovery', Press Release, 3 October, available at www.seaweb.org/initiatives/swordfish/10.3.02.release.html, accessed 4 August 2013.

Simpfendorfer, C. A. (2000) 'Predicting population recovery rates for endangered western Atlantic sawfishes using demographic analysis', *Environmental Biology of Fishes*, vol. 58, pp. 371–377.

Stevens, J. D., Bonfil, R., Dulvy, N. K. and Walker, P. A. (2000) 'The effects of fishing on sharks, rays, and chimaeras (chondrichthyans), and the implications for marine ecosystems', *ICES Journal of Marine Science*, vol. 57, pp. 476–494.

Strother, J. and Kollenberg, M. (2013) 'Shark fin consumption declines in Hong Kong', *Voice of America*, 20 June, available at www.voanews.com/content/shark-fin-consumption-declines-in-hong-kong/1685768.html, accessed 4 August 2013.

Valentine, S. and Fleischman, G. (2008) 'Ethics programs, perceived corporate social responsibility and job satisfaction', *Journal of Business Ethics*, vol. 77, pp. 159–172.

Wallace, S., McFarlane, G., Campana, S. and King, J. R. (2009) 'Status of spiny dogfish in Atlantic and Pacific Canada', in V. F. Gallucci, G. A. McFarlane and G. G. Bargmann (eds), *Biology and Management of Spiny Dogfish Sharks*, American Fisheries Society, Bethesda, MD.

Wood, C. C., Ketchen, K. S. and Beamish, R. J. (1979) 'Population dynamics of spiny dogfish (*Squalus acanthias*) in British Columbia waters', *Journal of the Fisheries Research Board of Canada*, vol. 36, pp. 647–656.

WWF (2009) *Assessment Study of On-Pack, Wild-Capture Seafood Sustainability Certification Programmes and Seafood Eco-labels: An Independent Assessment by Accenture Development Partners*, WWF International, Gland, Switzerland.

Xu, P., Zeng, Y., Fong, Q., Lone, T. and Liu, Y. (2012) 'Chinese consumers' willingness to pay for green- and eco-labeled seafood', *Food Control*, vol. 28, pp. 74–82.

Yates, P. M., Heupel, M. R., Tobin, A. J. and Simpfendorfer, C. A. (2012) 'Diversity in young shark habitats provides the potential for portfolio effects', *Marine Ecology Progress Series*, vol. 458, pp. 269–281.

Chapter 8

The role of the tourism industry

Christine A. Ward-Paige

Introduction

A thriving and sustainable marine tourism industry balances human use with the requirements of the natural environment (Wilson and Tisdell, 2003). However, there are many examples where human use has been prioritized at the expense of the surrounding environment, resulting in degraded coastal habitats (Lotze *et al.*, 2006) and depleted wildlife populations (Jackson *et al.*, 2001; Lotze and Worm, 2008). The marine tourism industry consists of a variety of stakeholders that depend on abundant and diverse natural resources (Orams, 1999). Therefore, there is momentum to reduce anthropogenic impacts, mitigate past degradations, recover populations and monitor environmental conditions to ensure long-term sustainable use. This trend towards improved monitoring, conservation and management is particularly evident in the industry of shark and ray tourism (Simpfendorfer *et al.*, 2011; Ward-Paige *et al.*, 2012), which is demonstrated by a growing number of research projects that are facilitated by the tourism industry (Couturier *et al.*, 2011; Ward-Paige and Lotze, 2011; Whitney *et al.*, 2012; see Box 8.1 for a case study on the Great Fiji Shark Count), and associated operational and policy changes advocated for by the tourism industry (Brunnschweiler, 2010; Pew Environment Group, 2011).

This chapter outlines the role of the tourism industry in shark conservation, governance and management. Although many aspects of the tourism industry may have a role to play in shark conservation (e.g. restaurants providing local, sustainably caught fish, communities modifying or removing shark exclusion devices to not endanger wildlife, or hotel developments that protect and maintain shark nursery areas), here I focus on the sector of the marine tourism industry that interacts directly with sharks and rays in the wild. This includes recreational fishers (both catch-and-keep and catch-and-release), divers, snorkelers and vessel-based operations. The role of this sector in shark conservation and management includes: (1) increasing the value of individual sharks and rays beyond the one-off value that may be acquired by commercial fishing; (2) facilitating research by directing research questions, supporting research programmes and supplying data to research programmes that solicit the help of resource users; and (3) using the scientific literature to develop best practices for shark and ray encounters, and to advocate for management strategies that promote long-term sustainability. Finally, I explore possible avenues for future collaborations between researchers and the tourism industry, and highlight the need for effective alliances and communication to ensure the necessary data are collected to improve our understanding of sharks and rays, and their conservation and management needs.

Box 8.1 Great Fiji Shark Count: tourism industry generated data used for establishing contemporary baselines and monitoring

The Great Fiji Shark Count (GFSC) is a tourism industry coordinated, researcher facilitated, citizen contributed project that collects data on shark, ray and turtle populations in Fiji. The project recruits all fishers, divers and snorkelers, regardless of experience level, to participate in April and November each year. During these months, using the Current Sighting Survey (CSS; eShark) for divers and an adapted version for fishers, the GFSC collects spatially and temporally explicit information on effort (e.g. dive duration, fishing hook soak times) and encounters with shark, ray and turtle species. The goal is to establish contemporary baselines of abundance, and then to monitor these populations in the future to determine the success of management strategies and identify conservation needs as they arise. As well, because these data are synonymous with those collected in the global eShark survey, Fiji shark and ray populations can also be monitored in a global context.

In summary, in 2012, the GFSC collected a total of 5,343 dives from 1,234 groups (1–18 dives per group) from 349 sites across Fiji. The average diver experience was high, with an average of 1,018 dives in their life and 506 dives in Fiji. Sharks and rays were observed on 3,189 (60 per cent) and 580 (11 per cent) of dives, respectively. A total of ten shark and five ray species were encountered. When present, divers encountered an average of 28 scalloped hammerhead sharks, 11 bull sharks, six blacktip reef sharks, six grey reef sharks, five tawny nurse sharks, four sicklefin lemon sharks, three whitetip reef sharks, three silvertip sharks, two tiger sharks, one zebra shark, one guitarfish species, three blue spotted stingray, two manta ray species, two round ribbontail rays, one bluespotted ribbontail ray and one spotted eagle ray. Although many were commonly encountered (e.g. 1,999 dives with whitetip reef sharks), some were only rarely encountered. For example, tiger sharks and guitarfish were only observed on two dives. Hawksbill or green turtles were observed in 1,169 records. Shark nurseries were reported for blacktip reef sharks and bull sharks (one site each) and shark mating was not observed. Recreational fishers reported two bull sharks and one spotted eagle ray on one of eight fishing trips, with feeding/baiting fish in all instances. These results, and especially the encounters with rare species, demonstrate the value of high-frequency censuses for monitoring shark and ray communities, and further underline the value of data generated by the marine tourism industry.

Increased economic value

There is a long history of shark- and ray-related tourism, with recreational shark fisheries dating back to at least the early 1900s (Viele, 1996; Ferretti *et al.*, 2008; McClenachan, 2008). Since the early 1990s, however, improved understanding of shark behaviour (Bres, 1993), reports of declining populations (Dulvy *et al.*, 2008) and shifts in the public's perception of sharks (Whatmough *et al.*, 2011) have prompted growth and diversification of shark and ray tourism (Gallagher and Hammerschlag, 2011), with a shift towards non-consumptive (no kill) encounters. Today, although recreational fishing for sharks occurs, non-consumptive shark targeted tourism activities are widespread and include recreational catch-and-release fishing, scuba diving, snorkelling, and vessel-based observations. As such, tourists visit various locations specifically to interact with a variety of sharks and ray species, thereby providing economic incentives for maintaining healthy shark and ray populations.

With more than 376 shark eco-tourism (non-consumptive) operators around the world (Gallagher and Hammerschlag, 2011), shark tourism presents a potentially important economic return for many coastal nations. An estimated 500,000 divers per year target encounters with sharks (Topelko and Dearden, 2005), visiting more than 300 dive sites in 40 countries (Carwardine and Watterson, 2002). Single-day dive, snorkel or recreational catch-and-release fishing adventures that target sharks or rays can cost more than US$100–200 (Gallagher and Hammerschlag, 2011; www.bluesharkcharters.com). Studies on divers' 'willingness to pay' suggest that sharks and rays are a top attraction (White, 2008), which has increased the economic value of individual animals targeted for tourism well beyond the one-off value of a commercially caught individual. Even 20 years ago, in the Maldives, a single grey reef shark was valued at US$3,300 per year if used for tourism purposes, compared to the US$32 if caught and sold by a fisherman (Anderson and Ahmed, 1993). Today, the value is considerably more. In Palau, for example, an individual reef shark is estimated to have an annual value of US$179,000 or a lifetime value of US$1.9 million to the tourism industry, compared to a maximum of US$108 in a fishery (Vianna *et al.*, 2010).

Although the value of a shark or ray in the tourism industry can exceed that gained by a fisher in the commercial trade, their worth in the tourism industry varies by species and location. The most sought-after species for shark encounters is the whale shark, attracting snorkelers and divers to the Maldives, Honduras, Mexico, Belize, Ecuador, Philippines, Thailand, South Africa, Tanzania, Mozambique, Australia and the Seychelles (Gallagher and Hammerschlag, 2011). In Western Australia alone, 8,000–10,000 tourists visit Ningaloo Reef in the two-month season that whale sharks are present and generate US$7.8 million (Catlin and Jones, 2010). Similarly, manta rays are widely targeted for tourism encounters, including off Hawaii, Australia, Mozambique (Ward-Paige *et al.*, 2013) and in the Maldives, where they are valued at more than

US$8.1 million (Anderson *et al.*, 2011). As such, shark and ray encounter tourism is valued at US$78 million in the Bahamas (Cline, 2008), US$4.9 million in the Seychelles (Rowat and Engerlhardt, 2007) and US$32 million (289 million rand) for shark cage diving in Gansbaai, South Africa (Hara *et al.*, 2003). In Palau, shark encounter tourism generates US$18 million per year, or 8 per cent of the GDP – roughly 24 times the tax revenue generated by the fishing industry (Vianna *et al.*, 2010).

Facilitate research

Through the observations of naturalists, stakeholders and citizen scientists, there is a long history of collaboration between the tourism industry and scientists that crosses many disciplines (Silvertown, 2009). For example, since the early 1900s, several bird research organizations have developed methodologies to harness citizen participation, which have produced data that have enabled spatial and temporal descriptions of bird population abundance, distribution and movement (Sullivan *et al.*, 2009). Today, with open access scientific journals and mass media outlets, these collaborations have surged as parties have come to realize the other's value – researchers for describing the environment that supports the tourism industry and the tourism industry for facilitating scientific research by generating questions, supporting data collection and generating data. Again, using birds as an example, eBird has been developed as an online citizen-based observation network where bird watchers collect, manage and store their observations in a unified database (Sullivan *et al.*, 2009). The ease of reporting online has allowed members of the public to regularly provide data, thus gathering millions of observations per year and providing comprehensive datasets that allow for important population descriptions and near real-time monitoring.

The tourism industry also has an important role to play in scientific research on sharks and rays. Together, these parties are moving marine ecology towards more detailed, real-time inventories and descriptions of marine animal populations, including that of sharks and rays (Arzoumanian *et al.*, 2005; Ward-Paige *et al.*, 2011). These improved descriptions serve to enhance our understanding of marine animals, including their behaviour (e.g. movement; Couturier *et al.*, 2012; Whitney *et al.*, 2012), population trends (Theberge and Dearden, 2006; Ward-Paige *et al.*, 2010, 2011, 2013; Ward-Paige and Lotze, 2011) and ecological needs such as feeding, cleaning or mating areas (Oliver *et al.*, 2011), and help to inform on conservation and management requirements (Bansemer and Bennett, 2010; Ward-Paige *et al.*, 2013). In turn, this knowledge can be used to enhance encounters and contribute to the long-term sustainability of the resources that support the tourism industry. Figure 8.1 offers a visualization of the role of the tourism industry in research.

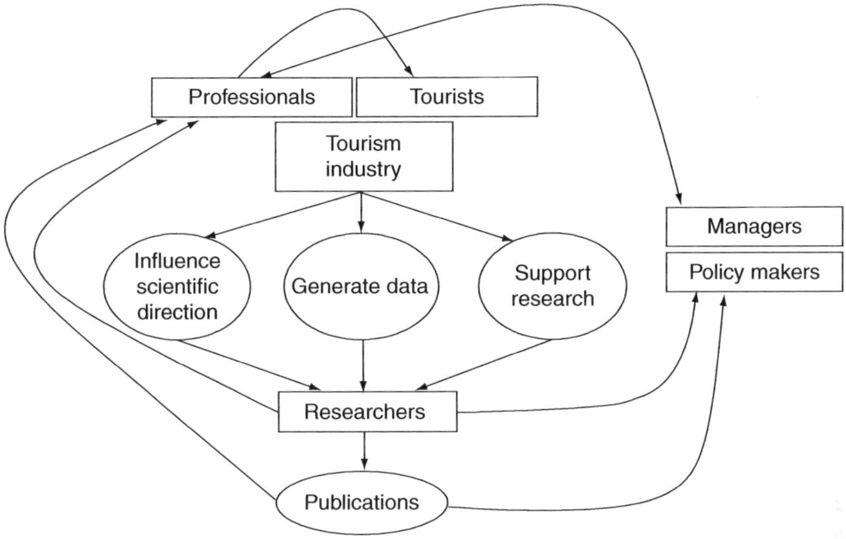

Figure 8.1 Flow chart depicting the role of the tourism industry.

Support research

Ecological studies of relatively rare and mobile marine species, such as sharks and rays, often require months to years of monitoring, are expensive and fraught with logistical and technical difficulties. For example, to understand the movement patterns and migratory behaviour of sharks or rays, animals need to be tagged and monitored for extended periods of time. This type of research often requires various types of support (e.g. boats, fuel, docks, accommodations), and local expert knowledge to direct scientific questions, locate animals and describe best practices for catching and releasing animals targeted in studies. A review of the 'acknowledgements' section of many ecological papers on sharks and rays illustrates this important collaboration and the valuable contributions that members of the tourism industry have made to research. For example, dive shops, resorts, tour guides and other individuals from the dive tourism industry have been acknowledged for 'logistical support', 'field and technical support', 'contributed photographs' and 'supporting tagging efforts in the field' (Riley *et al.*, 2009; Brunnschweiler and Baensch, 2011; Couturier *et al.*, 2011; Graham *et al.*, 2012).

Generate data

Data generated by the tourism industry have made numerous studies possible, especially those showing widespread patterns or long-term trends in shark or ray distribution and abundance. Because members of the tourism industry regularly explore the marine environment, making thousands of trips per year, they have the potential to provide a lot of data. For example, divers have submitted over 170,000 dives to the Reef Environmental Education database, 1.8 million dives to eShark (with ~620,014 dives to the eManta project within eShark; Ward-Paige *et al.*, 2013) and 22,762 records of whale sharks to ECOCEAN. When collated, these observations can greatly increase the quantity of data available for scientific investigations, thus extending datasets beyond the spatial and temporal limits that can be obtained by scientific observation alone. These data have originated from archived records, personal logbooks and photographs that document existing conditions, and through direct solicitation by scientists to members of the tourism industry to act as expert witnesses by providing their own observations and experiences.

Archive and distribute observations

Carefully recorded and archived observations and experiences have the potential to shed light on a broad spectrum of topics. Historical accounts and records can be invaluable for putting contemporary trends in perspective. For these reasons, it is valuable for members of the tourism industry to keep carefully detailed records using photographs, logbooks and memoires, even if their use for scientific investigation is not immediately apparent.

Archived photographs, memoires and logbooks made by members of the tourism industry and general public can contain vast amounts of invaluable data, even if only qualitative. Scientists have used personal accounts made by resource users decades or centuries after being recorded. For example, historical accounts from the northern Line Islands were used to illustrate that past abundances of sharks seem 'incredible' when put in the context of contemporary conditions (Sandin *et al.*, 2008). Also, in the greater Caribbean, pre-twentieth-century reports stating that sharks are 'plentiful' and 'one of the most common types of fishes' were used to demonstrate that the current absence of sharks on reefs is not the natural condition (Ward-Paige *et al.*, 2010). When combined with other accounts and data sources, qualitative reports can even be quantified to describe detailed trends. For example, sighting observations and logbooks of recreational fishers were combined with commercial fishery landings and scientific surveys to recreate past abundances of sharks in the Mediterranean Sea, which were used to reveal that populations have been depleted to <1–4 per cent of their former abundance (Ferretti *et al.*, 2008). Even isolated reports can provide important and novel information that would otherwise not be possible without the observations made by the tourism industry. In the Maldives, for example, photographs of injured whale sharks were used to illustrate that hunting continues despite legal protection, document the speed and degree to which these sharks healed from amputations or deep wounds and to show the degree of site fidelity (Riley *et al.*, 2009).

The value of accounts that record effort (e.g. length of time spent fishing or diving) and number and size of each species can be particularly valuable. Archived photographs from trophy fishing tournaments, for example, have been used to document trends in fish size, community structure, migratory routes and spatial and temporal stock trends. In the Florida Keys, historical photographs of the trophy fishery were used to document changes in fish size and composition, showing 50 per cent declines in shark sizes and shifts from large predatory sharks (white, hammerhead, silky and reef sharks) to immature sharpnose, reef and bonnethead sharks over a 50-year period (McClenachan, 2008). Similarly, in KwaZulu-Natal, South Africa, trophy-fishing records documenting fishing effort and catch information were used to describe elasmobranch communities and long-term trends in population size (Pradervand *et al.*, 2007). Records of effort and shark counts by species in cage diving expeditions in Hawaii have been used to describe seasonal and long-term changes in Galapagos, sandbar and tiger sharks (Meyer *et al.*, 2009). Public sightings data have been used to describe spatial and temporal distribution patterns of basking sharks on the European shelf (Southall *et al.*, 2005; Witt *et al.*, 2012). Divers' logbooks documenting general encounters of marine fauna in the Andaman Sea, that included number, sex, total estimated length and physical descriptions of whale sharks, were used to document declines in whale shark sightings (Theberge and Dearden, 2006). Inevitably, these data can be used to inform management plans, implement sanctuaries or protected areas and closed seasons.

Participate

Data generated by the general public are not standardized, such that site selection is not random, effort is not consistent, participants have very different levels of experience and pursue diverse interests. However, surveys that accommodate these biases have the potential to be informative and may be used to monitor patterns in populations. As such, members of the tourism industry are increasingly being viewed as a group of expert witnesses of the marine environment. Based on this understanding, the tourism industry can now participate in a variety of projects that aim to improve our knowledge of sharks and rays (see Table 8.1 for a summary of publications that used tourism industry contributed data on sharks or rays).

Participating in scientific surveys that summarize past observations through interviews (either in person, online, by phone, etc.) can be a valuable way for the tourism industry to contribute data relatively quickly. These types of data collection initiatives are often made as preliminary investigations, or as a last resort in the case of data-poor situations. For example, recreational sports fishers interviewed by Everglades National Park personnel, in Florida, United States, regarding their catches of smalltooth sawfish were used to monitor and document temporal population trends of this endangered species (Carlson *et al.*, 2007). Also, the Historical Sighting Survey (HSS, eShark), where scuba divers

Table 8.1 Examples of publications resulting from data generated by the members of the tourism industry

Industry	*Method*	*Findings*	*Location*	*Species*	*Collection organization*	*Reference*
Fishing	Catch	Temporal trends in relative abundance, species composition, length	Florida, US	Hammerhead, white, Caribbean reef, silky, sharpnose, bonnethead	N/A	McClenachan, 2008
		Relative abundance	Florida, US	Smalltooth sawfish	N/A	Carlson *et al.*, 2007
Diving	Photographs	Movement, reproductive seasonality, fisheries interactions, habitat use	Hawaii, US	Whitetip reef	Whitetip Research Project	Whitney *et al.*, 2012
		Threat of fishing injury	East coast, Australia	Grey nurse	N/A	Bansemer and Bennett, 2010
		Temporal trends in relative abundance, sex ratio, reproductive status	Fiji	Bull	N/A	Brunnschweiler and Baensch, 2011
		Absolute abundance, distribution, movement patterns	Global	Whale	ECOCEAN	Arzoumanian *et al.*, 2005
		Distribution, behaviour (site fidelity and movement)	Eastern Australia	Manta ray	Project Manta	Couturier *et al.*, 2011
		Absolute abundance, behaviour, seasonality, sex ratio	Maldives	Manta ray	N/A	Kitchen-Wheeler *et al.*, 2011
		Relative abundance, temporal trends, size, behaviour	Thailand	Whale	N/A	Theberge and Dearden, 2006

	Reports	Spatial patterns	Greater Caribbean	Requiem	REEF	Stallings, 2009
		Spatial and temporal patterns in relative abundance, seasonality, habitat use	Greater Caribbean	Yellow stingray	REEF	Ward-Paige *et al.*, 2011
		Spatial trends and temporal patterns in relative abundance	Greater Caribbean	Bonnethead, blacknose, Atlantic sharpnose, sandtiger, blacktip, tiger, silky, spinner, lemon, bull, whale, Caribbean reef, hammerhead	REEF	Ward-Paige *et al.*, 2010
	Recollections	Spatial and temporal patterns in relative abundance, species diversity	Thailand	Leopard, whale, blacktip reef, whitetip reef, blacktip, nurse, bamboo, oceanic whitetip, grey reef, bull	eShark	Ward-Paige and Lotze, 2011
		Spatial and temporal patterns in relative abundance, diversity, exploitation	Global	Manta ray, devil ray	eShark (eManta)	Ward-Paige *et al.*, 2013
Boat watching	Photographs	Absolute abundance, seasonal trends, habitat use	UK	Basking	Basking Shark Watch	Witt *et al.*, 2012
		Spatial distribution patterns in relative abundance	European shelf	Basking	Basking Shark Watch	Southall *et al.*, 2005
	Reports	Temporal trends in relative abundance, species composition	Hawaii, US	Galapagos, sandbar, tiger	N/A	Meyer *et al.*, 2009

summarize their diving and encounter history, was used to document spatial patterns and temporal trends in shark and ray populations in the Andaman Sea and Gulf of Thailand (Ward-Paige and Lotze, 2011). An adaptation of this HSS survey, to include questions regarding human use, was used to describe spatial and temporal trends of global manta and mobulid populations, eco-tourism, conservation strategies, fishing and markets (Ward-Paige *et al.*, 2013).

Members of the tourism industry can also contribute everyday observations to a variety of science-based research programmes that target the observations of resource users. The Reef Environmental Education Foundation (REEF; reef.org), for example, recruits divers to record abundance indices of all fish on every dive, including sharks and rays. Tabulated across all habitat types, depths and sites, and across broad regions (e.g. Hawaii, greater Caribbean, etc.), these data are useful for describing distributions, habitat preferences and spatial and temporal trends in abundance and community structure. This dataset has been used to describe spatial and temporal patterns in yellow stingrays (Ward-Paige *et al.*, 2011) and mobulid rays (Ward-Paige *et al.*, 2013), and to reveal large-scale absences of sharks on reefs in the greater Caribbean (Ward-Paige *et al.*, 2010). Similarly, the CSS solicits all divers to contribute a record of every dive, whether or not sharks were observed. This survey is being used around the world to establish baseline abundances of sharks and rays. In this case, the zeros (where sharks or rays are not observed) can be particularly important when monitoring for the success of management and conservation strategies (see Box 8.1 for a case study on the GFSC). As well, the Range Extension Database and Mapping project (REDMAP), based out of the University of Tasmania, Australia, has developed an online site that asks all marine resource users, including divers and fishers, to report their encounters with a suite of target species that will be used to monitor changes in the distribution of marine animals through time (e.g. moving pole-ward) as a way to examine the impacts of climate change.

A few species-specific projects have also solicited the assistance of the tourism industry. By submitting photographs with encounter details (e.g. location, date, etc.) of sharks or rays, researchers are able to identify individual animals from unique markings to inform on movement patterns, site fidelity and to estimate absolute abundance. ECOCEAN and Manta Trust, for example, collect photographs of whale sharks and manta rays from the general public – more than 4,400 whale sharks and 3,000 manta rays have been identified so far (whaleshark.org, G. Stevens, personal communication, 2013). The Whitetip Reef Shark project of Hawaii used divers' photographs of 178 individual whitetip reef sharks to document movement patterns, reproduction, seasonality and fishing pressure (Whitney *et al.*, 2012). As well, in the Red Sea, scientists solicited recreational divers in the tourism industry to record the number, size and sex composition of grey reef sharks to establish baseline population abundances (Hussey *et al.*, 2013).

Promote best practices for shark encounters and management

Members of the marine tourism industry are likely to benefit from policies that protect sharks and rays, in economic gains, satisfaction of encounters and to maintain their intrinsic worth. Consequently, it is in the best interest of the leaders of the tourism industry to raise awareness and foster positive attitudes towards sharks within the community and to visitors (Topelko and Dearden, 2005), thereby sustaining a high economic value of live sharks (Dobson, 2006; Topelko and Dearden, 2005). It should, therefore, also be important to maximize encounter experiences by ensuring that individual animals are not negatively affected by encounters (e.g. fleeing) and that populations are healthy to improve the chance of encounter. With these realizations, members of the tourism industry have initiated platforms for scientific research to help understand what is needed to protect sharks, developed best-practice guidelines for encounters with sharks and rays and have advocated for precautionary or science-based management strategies.

Best practices for encounters

Encounters with sharks and rays can negatively impact their behaviour, physiology and survivorship; however, the degree of impact depends on the species and encounter type (e.g. fishing vs. diving). Recreational fishing, for example, is well documented to have negative effects on fish populations (Coleman *et al.*, 2004), including for sharks (Bansemer and Bennett, 2010; Whitney *et al.*, 2012). There is no doubt that catch-and-keep activities that kill sharks have detrimental effects on individual animals. However, the effect of catch-and-release fishing is unclear. Some studies show that the detrimental effects are limited. For example, Atlantic sharpnose sharks caught on hook-and-line show high survival rates, at least in the short-term (Gurshin and Szedlmayer, 2004). Similarly, sandbar sharks exposed to high anaerobic exercise, such as that following hook-and-line capture, were found not to have been physiologically compromised, suggesting that there may be little effect on mortality rates (Brill *et al.*, 2008). Conversely, other studies suggest that caution is needed when using catch-and-release as a conservation tool since mortality and sublethal physiological and behavioural consequences can be high (Hueter, 1994). For example, sharks often suffer major traumas to internal organs, gills and mouths after being hooked (Borucinska *et al.*, 2002; Bansemer and Bennett, 2010; Whitney *et al.*, 2012). They also show signs of abnormal behaviour, including disorientation, loss of equilibrium and changes in movement after being released (Gurshin and Szedlmayer, 2004; Skomal *et al.*, 2010), which could leave them vulnerable to predation while attempting to recover. Importantly, sand tiger sharks, a critically endangered species in the Southwest Atlantic that swallows their prey whole, has been shown to swallow hooks, rather than snagging in the mouth, which can severely damage internal organs (Lucifora *et al.*, 2009).

Encounters by scuba divers and snorkelers can also affect sharks and rays. The presence of divers can cause aberrant behaviours that include changed migratory pathways and displacement from breeding and feeding grounds (Orams, 2002). These changes are best documented for whale sharks (Davis *et al.*, 1997; Quiros, 2007), with reports of individuals diving away, porpoising (up and down), eye rolling, banking and shuddering in the presence of divers (Norman, 1999; Quiros, 2007). Coincidently, growth in tourism popularity has coincided with decreased whale shark sightings (Quiros, 2007). As well, sharks and rays are often baited to increase reliability and duration of encounters. Although long-term feeding of sharks has been shown not to change behaviour in some populations (Maljković and Cote, 2011), it is controversial because of the possibility of habituation to humans for food, or shifts in their ecology from occurring in unnaturally high densities (Bruce and Bradford, 2011; Shackley, 1998; Orams, 2002; Newsome *et al.*, 2004; Corcoran *et al.*, 2013).

Even with this limited scientific evidence, many proactive members of the marine tourism industry, and associated organizations and communities, have developed guidelines for best practices when encountering sharks and rays. For example, trophy-fishing tournaments are increasingly moving towards catch-and-release fishing, with stringent procedures governing the fishing process to maximize survival rates. For example, the Guy Harvey Institute's Ultimate Shark Challenge in Florida, United States, requires that vessels have on-board observers, that sharks be brought to the boat as quickly as possible to minimize stress, minimum qualifying sizes depending on species to discourage catching small individuals, securing the sharks head and tail, properly tag the shark so that future data may also be collected, cutting the leader as close to the hook as possible, prohibiting spinning reels and non-stainless steel hooks so that the hooks can rust out if not removed, using inline circle hooks only (no treble- or J-hooks), among other regulations.[1] As well, as a precautionary measure, baiting sharks for diving encounters is now prohibited in some areas, such as in Florida, Hawaii, the Cayman Islands and South Africa (Carwardine and Watterson, 2002).

Similarly, on Australia's Ningaloo Reef, where thousands of tourists regularly encounter whale sharks, efforts are in place to ensure that sharks using the reserves are not disturbed by boating and interaction activities (CALM, 2005, p. 51; Catlin and Jones, 2010). As such, a whale shark Code of Conduct was developed in 1995, with input from the marine tourism industry, to mitigate negative impacts (Davis *et al.*, 1997). This code prohibits attempting to touch or ride a whale shark, restricting whale shark movement, approaching closer than 3 m from the head or 4 m from tail, flash photography, use of motorized propulsion aids or scuba diving equipment, and limits the number of people in the water at a time to fewer than ten. A similar code of practice has also been developed for diving with critically endangered grey nurse sharks in Australia

(NSWF, 2002), endangered basking sharks on the European shelf, manta rays, and Greenland sharks.[2]

Best practices for management

Many shark and ray populations have declined (Stevens *et al.*, 2000; Dulvy *et al.*, 2008), but there is a possibility for slowing and reversing these negative trends using precautionary and science-based conservation and management strategies (Ward-Paige *et al.*, 2012). Armed with the best available science and reports showing the economic value of healthy shark and ray populations, members of the tourism industry have collaborated with outside organizations (e.g. non-governmental agencies) and scientists to develop optimal management and conservation strategies for sharks and rays. Example strategies include implementing shark and ray sanctuaries or no-take/no-entry zones, regulating international trade (e.g. through the *Convention on International Trade in Endangered Species* (CITES)) and other fisheries management regulations (e.g. size limits, bag limits, species prohibitions, etc.; see Chapter 15). Then, with the support of the broader community, governments have been lobbied to implement these plans.

As such, many laws protecting sharks and rays have been, at least in part, the result of a vocal marine tourism industry. Shark sanctuaries, which are commonly in the form of bans on commercial fishing and on the exportation of shark products, have been implemented in Palau (2009), Maldives (2010), Honduras (2010), the Bahamas (2011), the Republic of the Marshall Islands (2011), French Polynesia, the Cook Islands and New Caledonia (2013), all of which have important marine tourism industries (see Chapter 9). In March 2013, five shark species (oceanic whitetip, scalloped hammerhead, great hammerhead shark, smooth hammerhead shark and porbeagle shark) and two manta ray species (oceanic and reef manta) were added to Appendix II of CITES, joining the basking shark, whale shark, white shark and sawfish (see Chapter 3) – all of which are large charismatic fish, and with the exception of porbeagle sharks, have established shark eco-tourism operations (Gallagher and Hammerschlag, 2011).

Regulating fishing and trade of species, through shark sanctuaries, finning regulations, CITES listings and science- or precautionary-based fisheries management strategies are necessary to improve the possibility of recovery of shark and ray populations (Ward-Paige *et al.*, 2011; Chapman *et al.*, 2013). However, successful monitoring and enforcement of best practices can be equally important, especially where illegal fishing and high levels of tourism are a problem. Enforcement can be directed towards detecting illicit trade (Chapman *et al.*, 2013) and by directly monitoring fishing and encounter activities. In some regions, the tourism industry has played a vital role in creating effective enforcement strategies. For example, the no-take zone and shark sanctuary in Raja Ampat, a remote area of Indonesia, is leased from local villages by a resort

(Misool Eco Resort). In this area, enforcement patrol boats and teams are funded by outside donors. Offenders are escorted to the local village, boats impounded, catch confiscated and a fine is levied by community leaders in a traditional court, with monies going to the community. This has apparently reduced the incidence of infraction to a very low level.

Future role of the marine tourism industry

There is scientific consensus that properly managed and enforced protected areas generally increase species richness, density and average size of fish (Worm *et al.*, 2009), which are the same attributes preferred by recreational fishers and divers (Lynch *et al.*, 2004). Therefore, there is incentive for leaders of the tourism industry, and the general public, to ensure that the best science is available to properly manage sharks and rays. Knowledge of the status of many sharks and rays has improved recently; however, much of the information that is fundamental to informing conservation strategies (e.g. nursery areas, mating areas, abundance and migratory routes) remains unknown (see Chapters 2 and 4).

Assembling all the daily observations of the thousands of members of the tourism industry, including fishers, divers, snorkelers, vessel operators and even surfers, kayakers and stand-up paddle-boarders, could improve these data gaps. However, it is important that the surveys gathering these data be carefully designed to ensure that all observations, whether by fishers, divers or vessel operators, are collected in a standardized and efficient way that will allow for robust statistical analysis to make science-based conclusions. Surveys that collect data without attention to these details, such as those that prioritize outreach, could divert the participating public from expertly designed projects and therefore be detrimental to the integrity of the science that aims to understand these systems. Therefore, if the tourism industry adopts or engages in this role, it would be most efficient to support scientific surveys and research that are designed to better understand and explain the marine ecosystem. With full support from the marine tourism industry, and careful scientific considerations to the data being collected, it may be possible to move towards real-time monitoring, similar to what is now the case for birds and flowers on land.[3] Armed with an enhanced understanding of what conservation and management strategies are needed for shark and ray populations, with accurate communication of results, there may be hope for attaining a thriving marine tourism industry that balances human use and the requirements of sharks and rays.

Notes

1 See www.ultimatesharkchallenge.squarespace.com/tournament-rules.

2 See the following websites: www.sharktrust.org (shelf); www.mantawatch.com (manta rays); and www.geerg.ca (Greenland sharks).

3 See the following websites for data: www.eBird.org (birds); and www.journeynorth.org (flowers).

References

Anderson, R. C. and Ahmed, H. (1993) *The Shark Fisheries of the Maldives: A Review*, Ministry of Fisheries and Agriculture, Republic of Maldives and FAO, Rome.

Anderson, R. C., Adam, M. S. and Goes, J. I. (2011) 'From monsoons to mantas: seasonal distribution of *Manta alfredi* in the Maldives', *Fisheries Oceanography*, vol. 20, pp. 104–113.

Arzoumanian, Z., Holmberg, J. and Norman, B. (2005) 'An astronomical pattern-matching algorithm for computer-aided identification of whale sharks *Rhincodon typus*', *Journal of Applied Ecology*, vol. 42, pp. 999–1011.

Bansemer, C. S. and Bennett, M. B. (2010) 'Retained fishing gear and associated injuries in the east Australian grey nurse sharks (*Carcharias taurus*): implications for populations recovery', *Marine and Freshwater Research*, vol. 61, pp. 97–103.

Borucinska, J., Kohler, N., Natanson, L. and Skomal, G. (2002) 'Pathology associated with retained fishing hooks in blue sharks, *Prionace glauca* (L.), with implications for their conservation', *Journal of Fish Diseases*, vol. 25, pp. 515–521.

Bres, M. (1993) 'The behaviour of sharks', *Reviews in Fish Biology and Fisheries*, vol. 3, pp. 133–159.

Brill, R., Bushnell, P., Schroff, S., Seifert, R. and Galvin, M. (2008) 'Effects of anaerobic exercise accompanying catch-and-release fishing on blood-oxygen affinity of the sandbar shark (*Carcharhinus plumbeus*, Nardo)', *Journal of Experimental Marine Biology and Ecology*, vol. 354, pp. 132–143.

Bruce, B. and Bradford, R. W. (2011) *The Effects of Berleying on the Distribution and Behaviour of White Sharks,* Carcharodon carcharias, *at the Neptune Islands, South Australia*, Department of Environment and Natural Resources, South Australia.

Brunnschweiler, J. M. (2010) 'The Shark Reef Marine Reserve: a marine tourism project in Fiji involving local communities', *Journal of Sustainable Tourism*, vol. 18, no. 1, pp. 29–42.

Brunnschweiler, J. M. and Baensch, H. (2011) 'Seasonal and long-term changes in relative abundance of bull sharks from a tourist shark feeding site in Fiji', *PLoS ONE*, vol. 6, no. 1.

CALM (2005) *Management Plan for the Ningaloo Marine Park and Muiron Islands Marine Management Area: 2005–2015*, Department of Conservation and Land Management, Western Australia.

Carlson, J. K., Osborne, J. and Schmidt, T. W. (2007) 'Monitoring the recovery of smalltooth sawfish, *Pristis pectinata*, using standardized relative indices of abundance', *Biological Conservation*, vol. 136, pp. 195–202.

Carwardine, M. and Watterson, K. (2002) *The Shark Watcher's Handbook*, BBC Worldwide Ltd, London.

Catlin, J. and Jones, R. (2010) 'Whale shark tourism at Ningaloo Marine Park: a longitudinal study of wildlife tourism', *Tourism Management*, vol. 31, pp. 386–394.

Chapman, D. D., Frisk, M. J., Abercrombie, D. L., Safina, C., Gruber, S. H., Babcock, E. A., Feldheim, K. A., Pikitch, E. K., Ward-Paige, C., Davis, B., Kessel, S., Heithaus, M. and Worm, B. (2013) 'Give shark sanctuaries a chance', *Science*, vol. 339, p. 757.

Cline, W. (2008) *Shark Diving Overview for the Islands of the Bahamas*, Report of the Bahamas Ministry of Tourism, Cline Marketing Group, Nassau.

Coleman, F. C., Figueira, W. F., Ueland, J. S. and Crowder, L. B. (2004) 'The impact of United States recreational fisheries on marine fish populations', *Science*, vol. 305, pp. 1958–1960.

Corcoran, M. J., Wetherbee, B. M., Shivji, M. S., Potenski, M. D., Chapman, D. D. and Harvey, G. M. (2013) 'Supplemental feeding for ecotourism reverses diel activity and alters movement patterns and spatial distribution of the Southern Stingray, *Dasyatis americana*',' *PLoS ONE*, vol. 8.

Couturier, L. I. E., Jaine, F. R. A., Townsend, K. A., Weeks, S. J., Richardson, A. J. and Bennett, M. B. (2011) 'Distribution, site affinity and regional movements of the manta ray, *Manta alfredi* (Krefft, 1868), along the east coast of Australia', *Marine and Freshwater Research*, vol. 62, pp. 628–637.

Couturier, L. I. E., Marshall, A. D., Jaine, F. R. A., Kashiwagi, T., Pierce, S. J., Townsend, K. A., Weeks, S. J., Bennett, M. B. and Richardson, A. J. (2012) 'Biology, ecology and conservation of the Mobulidae', *Journal of Fish Biology*, vol. 80, pp. 1075–1119.

Davis, D., Banks, S., Birtles, A., Valentine, P. and Cuthill, M. (1997) 'Whale sharks in Ningaloo Marine Park: managing tourism in an Australian marine protected area', *Tourism Management*, vol. 18, pp. 259–271.

Dobson, J. (2006) 'Sharks, wildlife tourism, and state regulation', *Tourism in Marine Environments*, vol. 3, pp. 15–23.

Dulvy, N. K., Baum, J. K., Clarke, S., Compagno, L. J. V., Cortes, E., Domingo, A., Fordham, S., Fowler, S., Francis, M. P., Gibson, C., Martinez, J., Musick, J. A., Soldo, A., Stevens, J. D. and Valenti, S. (2008) 'You can swim but you can't hide: the global status and conservation of oceanic pelagic sharks and rays', *Aquatic Conservation: Marine and Freshwater Ecosystems*, vol. 18, pp. 459–482.

Ferretti, F., Myers, R. A., Serena, F. and Lotze, H. K. (2008) 'Loss of large predatory sharks from the Mediterranean Sea', *Conservation Biology*, vol. 22, pp. 952–964.

Gallagher, A. J. and Hammerschlag, N. (2011) 'Global shark currency: the distribution, frequency, and economic value of shark ecotourism', *Current Issues in Tourism*, vol. 14, no. 8, pp. 1–16.

Graham, R. T., Witt, M. J., Castellanos, D. W., Remolina, F., Maxwell, S., Godley, B. J. and Hawkes, L. A. (2012) 'Satellite tracking of manta rays highlights challenges to their conservation', *PLoS ONE*, vol. 7.

Gurshin, C. W. D. and Szedlmayer, S. T. (2004) 'Short-term survival and movements of Atlantic sharpnose sharks captured by hook-and-line in the north-east Gulf of Mexico', *Journal of Fish Biology*, vol. 65, pp. 973–986.

Hara, M., Maharaj, I. and Pithers, L. (2003) *Marine-based Tourism in Gansbaai: A Socio-economic Study*, Final report for the Department of Environmental Affairs and Tourism, South Africa.

Hueter, R. E. and Manire, C. A. (1994) 'Bycatch and catch–release mortality of small sharks in the Gulf coast nursery grounds of Tampa Bay and Charlotte Harbor', *Mote Marine Laboratory Technical Report*, vol. 368, pp. 1–183.

Hussey, N. E., Stroh, N., Klaus, R., Chekchak, T. and Kessel, S. T. (2013) 'Scuba diver observations and placard tags to monitor grey reef sharks, *Carcharhinus amblyrhynchos*, at Sha'ab Rumi, The Sudan: assessment and future directions', *Journal of the Marine Biological Association of the United Kingdom*, vol. 93, pp. 299–308.

Jackson, J. B. C., Kirby, M. X., Berger, W. H., Bjorndal, K. A., Botsford, L. W., Bourque, B. J., Bradbury, R. H., Cooke, R., Erlandson, J., Estes, J. A., Hughes, T. P., Kidwell, S., Lange, C. B., Lenihan, H. S., Pandolfi, J. M., Peterson, C. H., Steneck, R. S., Tegner, M. J. and Warner, R. R. (2001) 'Historical overfishing and the recent collapse of coastal ecosystems', *Science*, vol. 293, pp. 629–638.

Kitchen-Wheeler, A.-M. Ari, C. and Edwards, A. J. (2011) 'Population estimates of Alfred mantas (*Manta alfredi*) in central Maldives atolls: North Male, Ari and Baa', *Environmental Biology of Fishes*, vol. 93, pp. 557–575.

Lotze, H. K. and Worm, B. (2009) 'Historical baselines for large marine animals', *Trends in Ecology and Evolution*, vol. 24, pp. 254–262.

Lotze, H. K., Lenihan, H. S., Bourque, B. J., Bradbury, R. H., Cooke, R. G., Kay, M. C., Kidwell, S. M., Kirby, M. X., Peterson, C. H. and Jackson, J. B. C. (2006) 'Depletion, degradation, and recovery potential of estuaries and coastal seas', *Science*, vol. 312, pp. 1806–1809.

Lucifora, L. O., Garcia, V. B. and Escalante, A. H. (2009) 'How can the feeding habits of the sand tiger shark influence the success of conservation programs?', *Animal Conservation*, vol. 12, pp. 291–301.

Lynch, T. P., Wilkinson, E., Melling, L., Hamilton, R., Macready, A. and Feary, S. (2004) 'Conflict and impacts of divers and anglers in a marine park', *Environmental Management*, vol. 33, no. 2, pp. 196–211.

McClenachan, L. (2008) 'Documenting loss of large trophy fish from the Florida Keys with historical photographs', *Conservation Biology*, vol. 23, pp. 636–643.

Maljković, A. and Côte, I. M. (2011) 'Effects of tourism-related provisioning on the trophic signatures and movement patterns of an apex predator, the Caribbean reef shark', *Biological Conservation*, vol. 144, no. 2, pp. 859–865.

Meyer, C. G., Dale, J. J., Papastamatiou, Y. P., Whitney, N. M. and Holland, K. N. (2009) 'Seasonal cycles and long-term trends in abundance and species composition of sharks associated with cage diving ecotourism activities in Hawaii', *Environmental Conservation*, vol. 36, pp. 104–111.

Newsome, D., Lewis, A. and Moncrieff, D. (2004) 'Impacts and risks associated with developing, but unsupervised, stingray tourism at Hamelin Bay, Western Australia', *International Journal of Tourism Research*, vol. 6, pp. 305–323.

Norman, B. M. (1999) 'Aspects of the biology and ecotourism industry of the whale shark *Rhincodon typus* in northwestern Australia', MPhil Thesis, Murdoch University at Murdoch, WA, Australia.

NSWF (2002) *Protecting the Grey Nurse Shark, a Guide for Fishers and Divers*, New South Wales Fisheries, Sydney.

Oliver, S. P., Hussey, N. E., Turner, J. T. and Beckett, A. J. (2011) 'Oceanic sharks clean at coastal seamount', *PLoS ONE*, vol. 6.

Orams, M. (1999) *Marine Tourism: Development, Impacts and Management*, Routledge, New York.

Orams, M. (2002) 'Feeding wildlife as a tourism attraction: a review of issues and impacts', *Tourism Management*, vol. 23, pp. 281–293.

Pew Environment Group (2011) 'Global shark conservation', www.pewenvironment.org/campaigns/global-shark-conservation/id/8589941059, accessed 22 September 2013.

Pradervand, P., Mann, B. Q. and Bellis, M. F. (2007) 'Long-term trends in the competitive shore fishery along the KwaZulu-Natal coast, South Africa', *African Zoology*, vol. 42, pp. 216–236.

Quiros, A. L. (2007) 'Tourist compliance to a Code of Conduct and the resulting effects on whale shark (*Rhincodon typus*) behavior in Donsol, Philippines', *Fisheries Research*, vol. 84, pp. 102–108.

Riley, M. J., Harman, A. and Rees, R. G. (2009) 'Evidence of continued hunting of whale sharks *Rhincodon typus* in the Maldives', *Environmental Biology of Fishes*, vol. 86, pp. 371–374.

Rowat, D. and Engelhardt, U. (2007) 'Seychelles: a case study of community involvement in the development of whale shark ecotourism and its socio-economic impact', *Fisheries Research*, vol. 84, pp. 109–113.

Sandin, S. A., Smith, J. E., DeMartini, E. E., Dinsdale, E. A., Donner, S. D., Friedlander, A. M., Konotchick, T., Malay, M., Maragos, J. E., Obura, D., Pantos, O., Paulay, G., Richie, M., Rohwer, F., Schroeder, R. E., Walsh, S., Jackson, J. B. C., Knowlton, N. and Sala, E. (2008) 'Baselines and degradation of coral reefs in the Northern Line Islands', *PLoS ONE*, vol. 3.

Shackley, M. (1998) '"Stingray City": managing the impact of underwater tourism in the Cayman Islands', *Journal of Sustainable Tourism*, vol. 6, pp. 328–338.

Silvertown, J. (2009) 'A new dawn for citizen science', *Trends in Ecology and Evolution*, vol. 24, pp. 467–471.

Simpfendorfer, C. A., Heupel, M. R., White, W. T. and Dulvy, N. K. (2011) 'The importance of research and public opinion to conservation management of sharks and rays: a synthesis', *Marine and Freshwater Research*, vol. 62, pp. 518–527.

Skomal, G. and Bernal, D. (2010) 'Physiological responses to stress in sharks', in J. C. Carrier, J. A. Musick, and M. R. Heithaus (eds), *Sharks and Their Relatives II*, CRC Press, Boca Raton, FL.

Southall, E. J., Sims, D. W., Metcalfe, J. D., Doyle, J. I., Fanshawe, S., Lacey, C., Shrimpton, J., Solandt, J.-L. and Speedie, C. D. (2005) 'Spatial distribution patterns of basking sharks on the European shelf: preliminary comparison of satellite-tag geolocation, survey and public sightings data', *Journal of the Marine Biological Association of the UK*, vol. 85, pp. 1083–1088.

Stallings, C. D. (2009) 'Fishery-independent data reveal negative effect of human population density on Caribbean predatory fish communities', *PLoS ONE*, vol. 4.

Stevens, J. D., Bonfil, R., Dulvy, N. K. and Walker, P. A. (2000) 'The effects of fishing on sharks, rays, and chimaeras (chondrichthyans), and the implications for marine ecosystems', *ICES Journal of Marine Science*, vol. 57, pp. 476–494.

Sullivan, B. L, Wood, C. L., Iliff, M. J., Bonney, R. E., Fink, D. and Kelling, S. (2009) 'eBird: a citizen-based bird observation network in the biological sciences', *Biological Conservation*, vol. 142, pp. 2282–2292.

Theberge, M. M. and Dearden, P. (2006) 'Detecting a decline in whale shark *Rhincodon typus* sightings in the Andaman Sea, Thailand, using ecotourist operator-collected data', *Oryx*, vol. 40, pp. 337–342.

Topelko, K. N. and Dearden, P. (2005) 'The shark watching industry and its potential contribution to shark conservation', *Journal of Ecotourism*, vol. 4, pp. 108–128.

Vianna, G. M. S, Meekan, M. G., Pannell, D., Marsh, S. and Meeuwig, J. J. (2010) *Wanted Dead or Alive? The Relative Value of Reef Sharks as a Fishery and an Ecotourism Asset in Palau*, Australian Institute of Marine Science and University of Western Australia, Perth.

Viele, J. (1996) *The Florida Keys: A History of the Pioneers*, Pineapple Press, Sarasota, FL.

Ward-Paige, C. A. and Lotze, H. K. (2011) 'Assessing the value of recreational divers for censusing elasmobranchs', *PLoS ONE*, vol. 6, no. 10.

Ward-Paige, C. A., Mora, C., Lotze, H. K., Pattengill-Semmens, C., McClenachan, L., Arias-Castro, E. and Myers, R. A. (2010) 'Large-scale absence of sharks on reefs in the greater-Caribbean: a footprint of human pressures', *PLoS ONE*, vol. 5.

Ward-Paige, C. A., Pattengill-Semmens, C., Myers, R. A. and Lotze, H. K. (2011) 'Spatial and temporal trends in yellow stingray abundance: evidence from diver surveys', *Environmental Biology of Fishes*, vol. 90, pp. 263–276.

Ward-Paige, C. A., Keith, D. M., Worm, B. and Lotze, H. K. (2012) 'Recovery potential and conservation options for elasmobranchs', *Journal of Fish Biology*, vol. 80, pp. 1844–1869.

Ward-Paige, C. A., Davis, B. and Worm, B. (2013) 'Global population trends and human use patterns of Manta and Mobula Rays', *PLoS ONE*, vol. 8.

Whatmough, S., Van Putten, I. and Chin, A. (2011) 'From hunters to nature observers: a record of 53 years of diver attitudes towards sharks and rays and marine protected areas', *Marine and Freshwater Research*, vol. 62, pp. 755–763.

White, L. (2008) 'Sea the value: quantifying the value of marine life to divers', MSc Thesis, Duke University at Durnham, NC.

Whitney, N. M., Pyle, R. L., Holland, K. N. and Barcz, J. T. (2012) 'Movements, reproductive seasonality, and fisheries interactions in the whitetip reef shark (*Triaenodon obesus*) from community-contributed photographs', *Environmental Biology of Fishes*, vol. 93, pp. 121–136.

Wilson, C. and Tisdell, C. (2003) 'Conservation and economic benefits of wildlife-based marine tourism: sea turtles and whales as case studies', *Human Dimensions of Wildlife: An International Journal*, vol. 8, pp. 49–58.

Witt, M. J., Hardy, T., Johnson, L., McClellan, C. M., Pikesley, S. K., Ranger, S., Richardson, P. B., Solandt, J., Speedie, C., Williams, R. and Godley, B. J. (2012) 'Basking sharks in the northeast Atlantic: spatio-temporal trends from sightings in UK waters', *Marine Ecology Progress Series*, vol. 459, pp. 121–134.

Worm, B., Hilborn, R., Baum, J. K., Branch, T. A., Collie, J. S., Costello, C., Fogarty, M. J., Fulton, E. A., Hutchings, J. A., Jennings, S., Jensen, O. P., Lotze, H. K., Mace, P. M., McClanahan, T. R., Minto, C., Palumbi, S. R., Parma, A. M., Ricard, D., Rosenberg, A. A., Watson, R. and Zeller, D. (2009) 'Rebuilding global fisheries', *Science*, vol. 325, pp. 578–585.

Chapter 9

Shark conservation efforts

As diverse as sharks themselves

Jill Hepp and Elizabeth Griffin Wilson[1]

> Sharks have everything a scientist dreams of. They're beautiful – God, how beautiful they are! They're like an impossibly perfect piece of machinery. They're as graceful as any bird. They're as mysterious as any animal on earth. No one knows for sure how long they live or what impulses – except for hunger – they respond to. There are more than two hundred and fifty species of shark, and every one is different from every other one.
>
> Peter Benchley, *Jaws*

The predator becomes the prey

Catapulted into the public limelight in the mid 1970s by Peter Benchley's book *Jaws* and the Steven Spielberg movie based on it, sharks have been considered fearsome creatures at the top of the ocean's food chain. Sharks have been around for millions of years, but in the last few decades it has become clear that it is necessary to protect these animals. As their numbers plummet because of intense fishing pressure, as scientists uncover move about the important role they play in marine ecosystems, as divers seek out opportunities to spend time underwater with them, a plethora of shark-focused conservation efforts are being carried out around the world.

As Peter Benchley notes in *Jaws*, shark species come in many shapes and sizes. The same can be said of the conservation efforts that have been carried out to reverse the decline in shark populations over the last two decades. The shark conservation landscape is diverse and includes a range of different organizations and individuals with a variety of goals and ways of working. Some are local or international non-governmental organizations (NGOs), some are quasi-governmental and some are simply passionate and focused individuals who care deeply about sharks. Some efforts focus primarily on increasing the amount of scientific information known about shark populations. There are campaigning-oriented groups that work to advance shark policies and laws and still others that focus primarily on public awareness and education. This landscape also includes organizations working only on sharks, as well as groups whose purview includes many other species.

Making the case for saving sharks is not always an easy task. Sharks are scary to a lot of people. Sharks do not generate the same deeply rooted public concern like more 'cuddly' and charismatic marine wildlife such as whales, sea turtles or dolphins. Additionally, there is the stark economic reality. Shark fins can be an especially lucrative seafood product that, in some fisheries, make up a sort of 'bonus' wage for fishermen. It can be hard to convince people to change their ways, especially when money is involved. Further complicating matters, shark fishing often goes unregulated or unmonitored as fisheries managers are generally busy with a lot of responsibilities for other, more commercially important species like tuna and swordfish.

However, in the last several years there has been a growing recognition by scientists, fishery managers, policy makers, media and the general public that sharks are in trouble and action is needed. This can be attributed to the cumulative, dedicated efforts of many individuals and groups. This chapter will attempt to profile several of these conservation efforts and a number of resulting scientific and policy outcomes. Given the sheer number of organizations working on shark conservation and how much they vary in size, focus and reach, it would be difficult to cover in detail all the past and current shark conservation efforts in this chapter. A list of organizations is provided (Box 9.1) as an overview of the breadth and diversity of shark conservation efforts; however, we recognize that there are many other groups, local, national and international in scope, that we have undoubtedly missed from this list.

Just as elephants have become endangered due to the trade in ivory, sharks have become imperilled because of the trade in their fins. Easily dried and traded, shark fins are transported from the far reaches of the globe to trade centres such as Hong Kong or Singapore for use in the Asian delicacy shark fin soup. With commercial fishing vessels able to reach waters that previously were not fished decades ago and current sophisticated systems for international transport, the shark fin trade sources from a huge number of countries and nearly all parts of the world's oceans. Hong Kong, the world's largest shark fin market, received shark fins from 83 different countries in 2011 (Census and Statistics Department, 2012). With so many fishing countries from around the world supplying shark fins to the international market, depletion of shark populations has become a widespread issue as very few countries have shark conservation or management measures in place to ensure the level of fishing is sustainable. The work and results of the conservation groups discussed in this chapter highlight one important facet of the collective effort needed to improve the status of sharks.

The scientific basis for conservation

For decades, two questions have reoccurred in respect to the sustainability of the shark fin trade. How many sharks are being killed each year? And how many is too many? Various studies have been conducted over the years providing some

Box 9.1 Organizations with significant shark-related awareness or policy advocacy programmes

The ADM Capital Foundation (ADMCF)
The Bahamas National Trust (BNT)
Bloom Association Hong Kong
The Coral Reef Alliance (CORAL)
Conservation International
Environment & Animal Society of Taiwan (EAST)
Greenpeace
Hong Kong Shark Foundation (HKSF)
Humane Society International (HSI)
Humane Society of the United States (HSUS)
International Fund for Animal Welfare (IFAW)
IUCN Shark Specialist Group (IUCN SSG)
The Jane Goodall Institute (China)
National Aquarium
Manta Trust
Micronesia Conservation Trust (MCT)
Monterey Bay Aquarium
MarViva
Natural Resources Defense Council (NRDC)
Nature University (formerly Green Beagle)
The Pew Charitable Trusts (Pew)
Oceana
PRETOMA
Project Aware
Sea Shepherd Conservation Society
Shark Advocates International
Shark Allies
Shark Angels
Shark Savers
Shark Research Institute (SRI)
Shark Trust
The Nature Conservancy
TRAFFIC
WildAid
Wildlife Conservation Society (WCS)
World Wildlife Fund

of the answers. Dr Shelley Clarke, one of the world's leading experts on the shark fin trade, showed that as of 2000, between 26 and 73 million sharks per year were caught globally to supply the fin trade (Clarke *et al.*, 2006). The same study also showed that this estimate of global shark catch may be three to four times higher than the official statistics reported by the United Nation's Food and Agriculture Organization (FAO) (Clarke *et al.*, 2006). Other studies revealed significant declines of specific species in particular areas, thus making the case that whatever the number being removed was, it was too high (Baum *et al.*, 2003; Baum and Myers, 2004; Dulvy *et al.*, 2008; Ferretti *et al.*, 2008). In 2013, an updated assessment of the number of sharks killed on an annual basis was released. Dr Boris Worm led a team of scientists in authoring a scientific paper showing that the number of sharks killed each year in commercial fisheries is estimated at approximately 100 million, with a range between 63 million and 273 million. The study also showed that the rate of fishing for shark species, many of which grow slowly and reproduce late in life, exceeds their ability to recover (Worm *et al.*, 2013).

Understanding the extent of impact has been important in terms of establishing how significantly the global shark fin trade has depleted shark populations around the world. The International Union for the Conservation of Nature (IUCN), the world's largest professional network of conservationists, established the IUCN SSG in 1991. The SSG was instrumental in raising the first warnings that sharks were in trouble.[2]

According to Dr Samuel Gruber, aka 'Doc Gruber', one of the founders and the first chair of the SSG, he was at the 1991 American Elasmobranch Society meeting in New York, sitting in the audience minding his own business, when the then chair of the IUCN Species Survival Commission, George Rabb asked him to establish the SSG right there and then, on the spot. According to Doc,

> Tell you the truth I was dumbfounded. I can remember taking the podium and asking George if he had somehow made a typo. Yes, I was interested in conservation but had no formal training in the field and further I was a research scientist without any real understanding of the vicious politics involved. Still I bit the bullet and agreed to give it a try. This was the year that I recovered from 'terminal' cancer so I thought I could take on most anything!
>
> (Gruber, personal communication, 2013)

The SSG was designed to have global representation and Vice Chairs from around the world were selected including, among others, Alberto Amorim (Brazil), George Burgess (United States), Sarah Fowler (United Kingdom), Supap Monokolprasit (Thailand), Professor Roberto Menni (Argentina) and Carl Safina (United States). Over 20 years later, the IUCN SSG now comprises approximately 170 experts from 55 different countries. They are experts in the fields of shark biology, conservation, management, fisheries and taxonomy. According to the IUCN website 'they are connected by their joint goal to promote the sustainable use, wise management and conservation of all sharks, rays and chimaeras' (IUCN SSG, 2013). The mission of the SSG is to promote the long-term conservation of the world's sharks and related species (the skates, rays and chimaeras), effective management of their fisheries and habitats and, where necessary, the recovery of their populations. The members of the SSG work together to assess the threat status of sharks, rays and chimaeras, collate knowledge into scientific publications and reports and to give independent science-based advice to decision makers and management authorities.

The well-known and respected IUCN *Red List of Threatened Species* (commonly referred to as just the *Red List*) now includes assessments for all 476 identified species of sharks (200 or so more species than originally identified when *Jaws* was published). The situation is not positive, with assessments showing that 11 are Critically Endangered, 15 Endangered, 48 Vulnerable and 69 Near Threatened with extinction. Currently, 212 shark species are considered Data Deficient, so their conservation status is unknown (IUCN, 2012). These scientific assessments are crucial for determining which shark species need immediate protection and are therefore vital for helping to guide conservation efforts. The IUCN assessments are commonly used by governments around the world to help prioritize conservation efforts.

According to Doc Gruber, the efforts by the SSG to have the Animals Committee of the *Convention on International Trade in Endangered Species of Wild Fauna and Flora* (CITES) address elasmobranchs at its 1995 meeting in Fort Lauderdale, Florida was a seminal moment (Gruber, personal communication, 2013). The committee requested that FAO do a study and eventually a strong effort was initiated to get the sawfish listed in CITES. This meeting arguably laid the groundwork for all the other CITES shark and ray listings that have occurred during the last two decades (see Chapter 3).

Focused on finning

In the mid 1990s, protection for sharks by national governments or regional fishery management organizations (RFMOs) was almost nonexistent, but the scale of the shark fin trade was immense. By 1995, nearly 800,000 tons of sharks were reported caught by countries providing data to the FAO and reported landings were continuing to rise (FAO, 2013). In addition to the scientific assessments of shark populations and advocating for having CITES address sharks, other major early shark conservation efforts were primarily focused on stopping the practice of finning. Shark finning is known widely in the conservation and fisheries communities as the practice of cutting off the shark fins and discarding the rest of the shark at sea. This practice allowed fishermen to keep the fins, the most lucrative part of the shark, on board the vessel without taking up space with the rest of the shark body. Sharks were often referred to by those in the fishing sector as 'trash fish' as their meat was generally worth much less per pound than other commercially exploited fish species such as swordfish or tuna. However, shark fins command high prices, which often led to the practice of shark finning.

The first wave of shark conservation efforts in the late 1990s and early 2000s focused on getting laws and measures enacted to make the practice of finning illegal. These efforts often characterized finning as brutal or wasteful. For example, in the United States, the *Shark Finning Prohibition Act* was signed into law in 2000 and amended the *Magnuson-Stevens Fishery and Conservation and Management Act* 'to eliminate the wasteful and unsportsmanlike practice of shark finning'. The new regulations required that all shark carcasses be retained on board the fishing vessel, rather than being discarded at sea. These types of regulations were generally designed to implement a fin-to-body weight ratio system. This ratio system aimed to prevent shark finning by requiring fishermen to bring fins and carcasses to shore in a specified weight ratio. While this system was an enormous step forward in ending shark finning, it was not perfect because the regulation did not accommodate the fact that different species of sharks have different fin-to-carcass ratios, mixing and matching of fins and carcasses could occur to maximize profit, and species identification was difficult.

Other countries that put in place measures to end shark finning during the late 1990s and early 2000s include Brazil, Canada, Costa Rica, Ecuador, South Africa and others. The conservation battles were often hard fought as the fisheries interests were reluctant to change their business practices, and in many places were well organized and politically influential. In many cases, these anti-finning rules were the first laws or regulations the country had taken up specifically concerning sharks. And in some cases, even after laws or regulations were put in place, additional and consistent NGO pressure was required to bring public attention to the conservation plight of sharks and to ensure the effective enforcement of these policies.

A particularly hard fought campaign took place in Costa Rica. According to Randall Arauz, President of the Costa Rican NGO PRETOMA,

> Costa Rica was formerly the hub of the Taiwanese shark fin industry in Central America. The main obstacle in the battle against the shark fin industry was the firm political support it enjoyed by the Costa Rican Fisheries Institute. It took quite an amount of public exposure, such as secretly shot videos of up to 30 tons of fins landed in a single night, as well as solid and credible science, to shame the country into abiding by its own laws.
>
> (Randall, personal communication, 2013)

But the effort was well worth it, as Costa Rica is now a leader against shark finning. Costa Rica was one of the first countries to put in place a shark finning ban that required sharks to be landed with their fins still naturally attached. Currently, the fins naturally attached method is considered the gold standard for how to enforce bans on shark finning. A shark finning ban implemented through a requirement that fins remain naturally attached to the body of the shark until the shark is brought back to port prevents the mixing and matching of high-value shark fins and meat, aids in species identification and data collection and facilitates monitoring and enforcement (Fowler and Séret, 2010).

Many other countries have followed Costa Rica's example by instituting fins naturally attached measures, including Chile, Colombia, El Salvador and

Venezuela. In some cases these countries were putting finning measures in place for the first time; in other places, such as the United States and European Union (EU), they moved from the ratio method and it involved years of advocacy work.

The EU first made finning an illegal practice in 2003, but many organizations felt there was a need to strengthen this measure and close loopholes that could potentially allow finning to occur undetected. The Shark Alliance, formed to address this need, is a coalition of shark conservation groups focused on strengthening the EU finning regulations by advocating for a fins naturally attached policy instead of a fin-to-body weight ratio system. The Shark Alliance also advocates for setting science-based, precautionary catch limits for sharks, providing special protections for endangered sharks and urging complementary measures at international fora. The European Elasmobranch Association, Shark Trust, Project Aware Foundation and the Pew Charitable Trusts are all steering group members of the Shark Alliance. Since 2008, the Shark Alliance has coordinated 'European Shark Week' on an annual basis to raise awareness and advance the efforts to strengthen the EU finning ban. After several years of campaigning and advocacy efforts by the Shark Alliance, the EU put in place the European Community Action Plan for the Conservation and Management of Sharks in 2009 (CPOA, 2009). In June 2013, the efforts of the Shark Alliance came to fruition when the EU Council of Ministers adopted a much strengthened EU ban on shark finning that requires all sharks to be landed with their fins still attached (Shark Alliance, 2013).

In the United States it also took considerable efforts to shift from a fin-to-body weight ratio to a fins naturally attached measure. While many organizations, including Oceana, the Pew Charitable Trusts, Shark Advocates International, IFAW and the Humane Society, were involved in the multi-year effort to pass the US *Shark Conservation Act* of 2010 (the law that required sharks be landed in the United States with their fins naturally attached), one of the most interesting efforts involved a coalition of shark attack survivors from around the globe that came together to advocate for shark conservation. The group of more than a dozen individuals was organized by Pew's Debbie Salamone, herself a survivor of a shark attack, and includes a school principal, a Wall Street banker, an Australian Navy diver, a Paralympic swimmer and a professional photographer.[3] Despite terrifying attacks and grave injuries, these survivors recognize the need for shark conservation and speak out on behalf of the sharks, captivating audiences and policy makers with their unique perspective on the need for shark conservation. In addition to successfully advocating for the passage of the US *Shark Conservation Act* of 2010, the group has helped raise awareness about sharks at the United Nations, spoken out in support of shark sanctuaries and have even starred in a 2012 Discovery Channel Shark Week episode called 'Shark Fight' that highlighted their conservation efforts (Discovery Communications, 2012). The efforts of this group of shark attack survivors are not only helping change policy, they are helping to reform the *Jaws* image of sharks and changing public perception of the ocean's top predators.

The current landscape of national, state and local shark conservation efforts

National efforts

While shark finning bans provide a much needed legal framework for prohibiting the practice of shark finning, alone they do not adequately protect sharks. According to a recent scientific study, the number of sharks killed in fisheries has not declined, nor has the number of fins being traded through Hong Kong (Worm *et al.*, 2013). This is likely because finning bans do not specifically reduce overall mortality of sharks; they only regulate how the shark is brought back to dock. Finning bans also do not ensure that the sharks that are fished or the fins in trade are harvested in a sustainable manner. In light of this, many organizations have expanded the focus of their work to include other, more comprehensive policies that have the potential to provide greater conservation outcomes. These policies have included state- or city-level bans on the sale of shark fins, the creation of country-wide 'shark sanctuaries' by prohibiting commercial shark fishing within a country's exclusive economic zone (EEZ), the adoption of conservation and management measures by RFMOs and trade control measures through additional species listings in CITES.

In 2009 Palau's president announced the creation of the Palau Shark Sanctuary during an address at the United Nations (United Nations, 2009). This announcement that shark fishing would be prohibited in all 600,000+ square kilometres of the country's EEZ was met with applause by the UN General Assembly. Since 2009, other governments around the world have stepped forward to fully protect sharks by creating shark sanctuaries (Table 9.1).

Table 9.1 Countries that have created shark sanctuaries by prohibiting commercial fishing for sharks in their entire EEZ since the inception of Pew's global shark conservation campaign

Sanctuary	*EEZ km²*	*EEZ mi²*	*Established*
Palau	604,289	233,317.287	2009
Maldives	916,189	353,742.551	2010
Honduras	240,240	92,757.183	2011
The Bahamas	629,293	242,971.386	2011
Tokelau	319,031	123,178.558	2011
Republic of the Marshall Islands	1,992,232	769,205.076	2011
French Polynesia	4,767,242	1,840,642.426	2012
Cook Islands	1,960,135	756,812.355	2012
New Caledonia	1,245,000	480,697.1874	2013
Total	12,673,651	4,893,324.01	

Note
EEZs are sourced from the Sea Around Us project webpage at the University of British Columbia (www.seaaroundus.org).

To date, this amounts to an impressive 12.6 million square kilometres of ocean where sharks are now legally protected from commercial fishing pressure (see Chapter 14). Because of the leadership of these governments, for the first time ever, sharks are afforded the same level of legal protection as other marine wildlife such as whales. This has been a game-changer for conservation efforts. Creating sanctuaries and banning the commercial harvest of these species has begun to slowly shift the public perception from creatures that should only be feared or fished to wildlife deserving of strong protections.

The Pew Charitable Trusts has advocated for the creation of these sanctuaries by providing scientific expertise, policy advice and training for enforcement agents. In most cases, these sanctuaries are not formally designated marine protected areas, but rather the sanctuaries have been created by passing laws or amending fishing regulations to make it illegal to directly target sharks while fishing commercially. In most cases, prohibitions are also in place concerning the retention of shark by-catch and, in some countries, trade in shark fins or other products is not allowed. Shark sanctuaries provide a precautionary, overarching framework to protect sharks, especially in places where stock assessments, data collection and enforcement efforts are simply too expensive or time-consuming given the available resources. Because shark sanctuaries cover huge swaths of ocean, they help provide the scale of protection needed for the wide-ranging and highly migratory species.

In some places, the creation of a shark sanctuary was a response to scientific information detailing that declines of local shark populations because of ongoing directed shark fishing. For example, in the Maldives, the ban on directed shark fishing was put in place after dramatic shark population declines were observed (IOTC, 2011). The decline in sharks in the Maldives was viewed as problematic because the country generated a large percentage of its foreign revenue from tourism and diving. The closing of the directed shark fishery and the prohibition on trade in shark products was designed to allow for the rebuilding of the depleted shark populations.

In other places, the creation of a shark sanctuary was more precautionary in nature. For example, in September 2010, the *Tribune*, a local newspaper in the Bahamas, began reporting about a seafood trader who had expressed interest in initiating shark fin exports from the Bahamas (Reynolds, 2010). In the Bahamas, shark populations are relatively robust and healthy because of limitations on the use of long-lining gear that the country implemented in the 1990s. Shark diving is big business in the Bahamas, with shark-related tourism contributing more than US$800 million dollars to the Bahamian economy over the past 20 years (Bahamas Dive Association, 2008). Before a directed shark fishery or fin trade had a chance to develop, an outreach effort was spearheaded by the Bahamas National Trust and the Pew Environment Group, as well as many local individuals and businesses. Subsequently, the fisheries regulations were amended to include provisions specifically prohibiting commercial shark fishing or shark fin trade.

The presence of healthy shark populations can be more lucrative for a country than a directed shark fishery. Several other studies have been conducted in recent years that estimate the economic value of shark dive tourism in comparison to shark fishing. These studies have helped make a persuasive case for shark conservation and the creation of sanctuaries. An economic valuation for Palau estimated the annual value to the tourism industry of an individual reef shark at a dive site in Palau was US$179,000 or US$1.9 million over its lifetime. In contrast, a single reef shark would only bring an estimated US$108 if fished (Vianna *et al.*, 2010). A similar study, also supported as part of Pew's global shark conservation campaign, estimated shark tourism generated over US$42.2 million per year in revenue and taxes in Fiji in 2010 (Vianna *et al.*, 2011).

Efforts at the state and local levels

In some locations where national-level bans on directed shark fishing or sale of shark fins are not currently possible, NGOs have worked to secure bans on the state, territory or city level. This movement started in the US state of Hawaii, where the effort was led by state Senator Clayton Hee, and shark advocate Stefanie Brendl. On 29 May 2010, Hawaii became the first state to ban the possession, sale and distribution of shark fins when Hawaii Senate Bill 2169 was signed by Governor Linda Lingle.[4] This was an especially important step forward in shark conservation because Hawaii was a hub for the shark fin trade and restaurants in Hawaii served a significant amount of shark fin soup.

Bolstered by the Hawaii legislation and the passage of the US *Shark Conservation Act* of 2010, NGOs turned their focus to California, another of the top US markets for shark fin soup consumption. The California effort involved numerous NGOs such as the Humane Society, WildAid, Oceana, the Monterey Bay Aquarium, Asian-American organizations, chefs and even celebrities January Jones and Leonardo DiCaprio. The bill, authored by Assembly members Paul Fong, a Democrat born in China, and Jared Huffman, was signed into law by Governor Jerry Brown on 7 October 2011.[5]

In addition to California, similar legislation was signed into place in Oregon, Washington, Guam and the Commonwealth of the Northern Mariana Islands (CNMI) in 2011. In November 2012, American Samoa extended their existing measures by banning the catching and possession of sharks within waters under their jurisdiction (within three nautical miles of the shoreline) (Pew Environmental Group, 2012). Illinois banned the sale of shark fins in 2012, followed by Delaware, Maryland and New York in 2013.[6]

In 2007 Canadian filmmaker Rob Stewart released *Sharkwater*, an above- and below-water documentary that debunks the myth of sharks as man-eaters via up-close encounters and exposes the dirty underbelly of the shark fin trade (Sharkwater Productions Inc., 2006). The film is the anti-*Jaws* and made a significant contribution to raising awareness about shark conservation, both in Canada and abroad. In 2011 and 2012, bolstered by the new level of awareness in Canada and with the support of the Humane Society International Canada, WildAid and local organizations, the Canadian cities of Abbotsford, Brantford, Duncan, Langley (both the city and township), London, Maple Ridge, Mississauga, New Westminster, Newmarket, North Vancouver, Oakville, Ontario, Pickering and Port Moody all passed bans on the sale of shark fins (Humane Society International, 2013).

Efforts to conserve sharks on the high seas

NGO efforts to protect sharks on the high seas, where no single country has the ability to make laws and international cooperation is key, have been attempted through effective advocacy at the RFMO level. RFMOs have been established to meet a variety of management objectives and have varying jurisdictions and geographical reach. Often they have been established to manage the most commercially important fish species such as tuna and swordfish. In some cases, sharks fall under the RFMO's jurisdiction as managed species, and in other cases RFMOs can manage sharks because they are caught as by-catch in fisheries managed by the RFMOs. The countries who are members of some RFMOs such as the International Commission for the Conservation of Atlantic Tunas (ICCAT), Inter-American Tropical Tuna Commission (IATTC), Indian Ocean Tuna Commission (IOTC) and the Western and Central Pacific Fisheries Commission (WCPFC) all agreed to measures prohibiting shark finning in 2004, 2005, 2005 and 2006, respectively (ICCAT, 2004; IATTC, 2005; IOTC, 2005; WCPFC 2006). In addition, over the past five years and at the urging of groups like Pew, Oceana and the HSI, these RFMOs have also agreed to several measures related to species of concern (Table 9.2).

For example, ICCAT, IATTC, IOTC and WCPFC have all now prohibited the retention of any oceanic whitetip sharks caught by fisheries under their

Table 9.2 RFMO shark measures prohibiting retention

Regional Fisheries Management Organization	*Prohibition on retention*
International Commission for the Conservation of Atlantic Tunas (ICCAT)	Bigeye thresher (2009) Oceanic whitetip (2010) Hammerhead sharks (Family Sphyrnidae) (2010) Silky sharks (2011)
Inter-American Tropical Tuna Commission (IATTC)	Oceanic whitetip (2011)
Western and Central Pacific Fisheries Commission (WCPFC)	Oceanic whitetip (2012)
Indian Ocean Tuna Commission (IOTC)	Thresher sharks (Family Alopiidae) (2010) Oceanic whitetip (2013)

jurisdiction. ICCAT has by far been the most proactive of these RFMOs in terms of agreeing measures for sharks and now has measures in place prohibiting the retention of bigeye thresher sharks, hammerhead sharks and silky sharks, as well as oceanic whitetip sharks. While ICCAT has done more for sharks than most other RFMOs, nonetheless, it still only has conservation and management measures in place for just a handful of the dozens of shark species caught in its fisheries. In addition, none of these RFMOs has taken the step of putting in place a catch limit for a shark species.

Other fora have also provided opportunities for shark advocates to advance shark conservation across national jurisdictions and on the high seas. The *Convention on the Conservation of Migratory Species of Wild Animals* (CMS) is an intergovernmental treaty that aims to conserve migratory species, and has been used to promote cooperation between countries to advance conservation. Much of the momentum for initiating negotiations on sharks at CMS was the result of efforts by Sarah Fowler and the IUCN SSG, with two reports authored by the SSG providing scientific support for the negotiations (IUCN SSG, 2007; IUCN *et al.*, 2007). HSI, World Wildlife Fund (WWF) and others also played significant roles. The roles of NGOs and other advocates have been important in terms of pushing the Convention signatories to take action.

In addition to protection via listing of some species of sharks on the Appendices of the CMS, a Memorandum of Understanding (MoU) on the Conservation of Migratory Sharks was adopted under the CMS in 2010, with the objective to 'achieve and maintain a favorable conservation status for migratory sharks'. The MoU, which has 26 signatories as of February 2013, is focused on increasing international cooperation to ensure action is taken to protect sharks and applies to the shark species listed in the CMS Appendices.

Conservation efforts to regulate the international shark fin trade

Due to its global nature, a global solution to control the fin trade, especially trade in endangered species, is important if healthy shark populations are to be possible in the future. CITES is the only treaty that regulates the international wildlife trade at a global level. The protections that these listings have secured are credited with bringing some species back to healthier population levels and preventing others from declining further and therefore many NGOs and shark conservationists have viewed it as a particularly important tool to protect shark populations. At the beginning of 2013 only three shark species were listed on CITES Appendix II, despite the major role that international trade has played in driving the declines. Basking and whale sharks were protected by CITES in 2002, followed by great white sharks in 2004.

In 2010 every proposal to list commercially valuable marine species, including eight species of sharks, was defeated at the 15th meeting of the Conference of the Parties (CoP15) to CITES, in Doha, Qatar. At the time, it was a crushing blow for shark conservation advocates who strongly believed the proposals had merit and that the convention would have strong conservation implications for the proposed species. Efforts were redoubled by proponent countries and organizations and, after a three-year initiative, a groundbreaking victory occurred in March 2013 at the 16th Conference of the Parties (CoP16) to CITES in Bangkok, Thailand (see Chapter 2).

This outcome was not a matter of chance, Pew, WWF, IFAW, HSI, Wildlife Conservation Society, WildAid, Shark Savers and many others worked around the world in the lead-up to the March 2013 decision. The overarching goal was straightforward: have enough governments vote yes to regulating international trade in some of the most economically valuable, yet ecologically vulnerable and threatened, shark and manta ray species. Like most truly groundbreaking changes in the environmental field, this achievement was the result of efforts by numerous organizations, countries and scientists from around the world working collectively to achieve a common goal.

Well before government delegates voted 'yes' or 'no' on proposals in Bangkok, NGOs and governments worked together to identify the species of sharks to be proposed for listing and compiled updated scientific information to prepare the justification for protection. In addition, dedicated efforts were made to overcome some of the arguments that had been raised in previous listing attempts. Advocates for the proposals worked with scientists such as Dr Demian Chapman and Debra Abercrombie on techniques to identify products in trade from the proposed species[4] and Manta Trust, Shark Savers and WildAid provided access to the most up-to-date manta ray research. Advocates travelled to key countries and held regional meetings around the world to build support for the proposals. For example, IFAW organized workshops in the Middle East, WWF conducted focused outreach efforts in Africa and HSI worked in Asia. These are just some examples of the widespread advocacy efforts which, together, attempted to reach almost all of the 178 governments that are parties to CITES.

By the 4 October 2012 deadline to submit proposals to the Secretariat, 37 countries (including the 27 member states of the EU) had co-sponsored, in various combinations, four proposals to protect oceanic whitetip, hammerhead and porbeagle sharks, as well as all species of manta rays.

Just prior to the start of the meeting in Bangkok, a team of marine scientists published a scholarly paper, estimating that the current global annual shark mortality is close to a staggering 100 million sharks per year, a mortality rate that is too high to maintain healthy shark populations (Worm *et al.*, 2013). The paper created significant media attention and helped position the shark proposals among the most high-profile at the Bangkok meeting. At the CoP, the government proposal sponsors, Pew and others coordinated events, held press briefings with shark and manta ray scientists, organized meetings and receptions, conducted shark fin identification demonstrations, conducted outreach to undecided governments, participated in the formal debate and much more to make the case for accepting the listing proposals.

The end result of CITES CoP16 was groundbreaking in that all four proposals received enough votes to pass. Because of those 'yes' votes, seven species of sharks and rays will now receive unprecedented global protection as the international trade in their products will be strictly regulated. Since most of these new shark species protected by CITES are primarily targeted for their fins, their listings will cause a fundamental shift in the global shark fin trade because monitoring and reporting will now be required. Countries that do not currently regulate shark fishing will now need to devise fisheries management measures or prohibit the export of these species. The development of fisheries management capabilities in these countries will have spillover benefits for other shark species as well.

It became clear during the CITES meeting in Bangkok that momentum is growing for shark conservation, particularly in regions such as Latin America and Africa. This momentum is likely to help enhance other conservation and management efforts, including measures at RFMOs, national shark fishing regulations and the establishment of new shark sanctuaries.

Shark conservation and management – and CITES – will never be the same. The outcomes of March 2013 did not occur by chance. It took years of strategic planning and hard, dedicated teamwork. Without the leadership and interest of key governments combined with the networks of large NGOs with the capabilities, campaign focus and global reach of organizations like Pew, as well as other groups with strong relationships in particular regions, and the cooperation of scientists, this sort of change in international policy forums would be nearly impossible.

Efforts to drive down shark fin demand

In addition to efforts to reduce fishing mortality and control trade, there is another significant piece of the shark conservation landscape – the efforts that focus on reducing demand in Hong Kong and mainland China, the region of the world where the vast majority of shark fin soup is consumed. In an unprecedented move, in July 2012, China's State Council announced that it would instruct all levels of government agencies to stop serving shark fins at official receptions within one to three years (Wassener, 2012). This has the potential to be an immensely positive step forward.

Conservation efforts have primarily been concentrated on educating consumers and encouraging them to abstain from eating shark fin soup. Some of the organizations provide consumers with information related to the conservation status of sharks and others have focused more on the inhumane aspects of shark finning. Bloom Association, Hong Kong Shark Foundation, Shark Savers, WWF, and WildAid have all carried out shark conservation awareness or research efforts in this region.[7]

In addition to government banquets, shark fin soup is often served as part of wedding celebrations in East Asia. Some of these groups have undertaken campaigns focused on gaining commitments from couples who are getting married to remove shark fin soup from their wedding banquet menu. For example, the Hong Kong Shark Foundation held a contest in 2012 named 'Happy Hearts Love Sharks'. By their estimates, this campaign resulted in wedding banquets where over 16,000 bowls of shark fin soup were not served (Hong Kong Shark Foundation, 2013).

Similarly, shark fin soup is often offered as part of a set menu at banquets hosted to solidify business relationships. Some of these groups, like the WWF in Hong Kong, have successfully organized campaigns with the goal of gaining commitments from businesses in the financial sector to remove shark fin soup from banquet menus (WWF, 2013).

In recent years, WildAid has carried out highly visible marketing campaigns in mainland China. Yao Ming, a retired professional basketball player, who is originally from Shanghai, China, has worked closely with WildAid to support their wildlife trade awareness campaign with the message '*When the buying stops, the killing can too*'. In 2006, Yao Ming pledged not to consume shark fin soup after learning how it is produced and has appeared in a number of advertisements and public service announcements produced by WildAid (WildAid, 2013).

Other efforts have focused on understanding the drivers behind the demand for shark fin soup through polling and public opinion research. Bloom Association Hong Kong commissioned some of the first public opinion polling on this conservation issue in Hong Kong in 2009 and 2010. This survey found that 9 per cent of respondents believed that a shark's fin would grow back after being sliced off. Interestingly, while 73 per cent of people had consumed shark fin soup at least once in the year before the survey, 78 per cent of respondents thought it acceptable to not include shark fin soup in a wedding banquet menu. An even larger percentage of respondents (88 per cent) believed that the Hong Kong government should prohibit the sale of products that involve killing endangered species (Bloom Association, 2011).

The next generation of shark conservation efforts

Before his death, Peter Benchley became a proponent of protecting sharks. 'In the 25 years since "Jaws" was first released, sharks have experienced an unprecedented and uncontrolled attack.' He went on to say 'Sharks are much more the victims than the villains' (Reuters, 2010). While Benchley changed his opinion of sharks, many others have not and the shark conservation community must continue to work to raise awareness and convince both the public and policy makers that healthy oceans need sharks. Similarly, while progress has been made in shark conservation and management in recent decades, there is much work to do to ensure that shark populations do not decline any further and are eventually able to recover. Shark finning is still legal in some places, no shark catch limits exist in any of the major tuna RFMOs, many countries have largely unregulated shark fisheries, the only shark species regulated at the international level are those with already severely depleted populations and shark sanctuaries only cover 3.5 per cent of the world's oceans.

Large or small, domestic or international, consumer or policy focused, science or advocacy oriented, there is a role for many in shark conservation. Together they complement each other and contribute to significant change in shark conservation and management. These advancements potentially would not have happened without the increased public awareness and enhancement of baseline knowledge through research and political pressure that these organizations generate. With many countries considering how to manage sharks post-CITES 2013, other governments on the verge of declaring shark sanctuaries and RFMOs poised to start actively managing shark fisheries for the first time, there is unprecedented hope for the oceans' top predators.

Notes

1 A senior officer with The Pew Charitable Trusts, Jill Hepp directed the organization's global shark conservation campaign. Elizabeth Griffin Wilson is Director of International Ocean Policy for The Pew Charitable Trusts.
2 The SSG website can be accessed at www.iucnssg.org.
3 For a compilation on shark attack survivors, see www.pewenvironment.org/news-room/compilations/attack-survivors-unite-to-save-sharks-85899401011.
4 The legislation can be accessed at www.capitol.hawaii.gov/Archives/measure_indiv_Archives.aspx?billtype=SB&billnumber=2169&year=2010.
5 The bill can be accessed at www.leginfo.ca.gov/pub/11-12/bill/asm/ab_0351-0400/ab_376_bill_20111007_chaptered.html.
6 See the following links for access to the legislation: Illinois: www.ilga.gov/legislation/BillStatus.asp?DocNum=4119&GAID=11&DocTypeID=HB&SessionID=84&GA=97; Delaware: http://openstates.org/de/bills/147/HB41/documents/DED00003772/; Maryland: http://mgaleg.maryland.gov/webmga/frmMain.aspx?pid=flrvotepage&tab=subject3&id=hb1148,s-1081&stab=02&ys=2013RS; New York: http://assembly.state.ny.us/leg/?default_fld=&bn=A01769&term=2013&Summary=Y&Actions=Y&Text=Y&Votes=Y.
7 See the following links for further information: http://hksharkfoundation.org/campaigns/shark-free-weddings/; www.wwf.org.hk/en/whatwedo/footprint/seafood/sharkfin_initiative/companies_say_no_to_shark_fin/; www.wildaid.org/sharks.

References

Bahamas Diving Association (2008) *Shark Diving Overview for the Islands of the Bahamas*, Bahamas Diving Association, Nassau.

Baum, J. K., and Myers, R. A. (2004) 'Shifting baselines and the decline of pelagic sharks in the Gulf of Mexico', *Ecology Letters*, vol. 7, pp. 135–145.

Baum, J. K., Myers, R. A., Kehler, D. G., Worm, B., Harley, S. J. and Doherty, P. A. (2003) 'Collapse and conservation of shark populations in the Northwest Atlantic', *Science*, vol. 199, pp. 389–392.

Bloom Association (2011), 'Bloom's shark research', available at www.bloomassociation.org/hk/blooms-shark-research, accessed 8 August 2013.

Census and Statistics Department (2012) *Aquaculture Fisheries Statistics*, Government of the Hong Kong Special Administrative Region, Hong Kong.

Clarke, S. C., McAllister, M. K., Milner-Gulland, E. J., Kirkwood, G. P., Michielsens, C. G. J., Agnew, D. J., Pikitch, E. K., Nakano, H. and Shivji, M. S. (2006) 'Global estimates of shark catches using trade records from commercial markets', *Ecology Letters*, vol. 9, pp. 1115–1126.

CPOA (2009) *Communication from the Commission to the European Parliament and the Council on a European Community Action Plan for the Conservation and Management of Sharks*, 5 February, COM 40, European Commission, Brussels.

Discovery Communications (2012) *Shark Fight*, Discovery Communications, Silver Spring, MD.

Dulvy, N. K., Baum., J. A., Clarke, S., Compagno, L. J. V., Cortés, E., Domingo, A., Fordham, S., Fowler, S., Francis, M. P., Gibson, C., Martínez, J., Musick, J. A., Soldo, A., Stevens, J. D. and Valenti, S. (2008) 'You can swim but you can't hide: the global status and conservation of oceanic pelagic sharks and rays', *Aquatic Conservation: Marine and Freshwater Ecosystems*, vol. 18, pp. 459–482.

FAO (2013) 'Global capture production data', Fisheries and Aquaculture Department, available at www.fao.org/fishery/statistics/global-captureproduction/query/en, accessed 7 August 2013.

Ferretti, F., Myers, R. A., Serena, F. and Lotze, H. K. (2008) 'Loss of large predatory sharks from the Mediterranean Sea', *Conservation Biology*, vol. 22, pp. 952–964.

Fowler, S. and Séret, B. (2010) *Shark Fins in Europe: Implications for Reforming the EU Finning Ban*, European Elasmobranch Association and IUCN Shark Specialist Group, Vancouver.

Hong Kong Shark Foundation (2013), 'Happy hearts love sharks', http://happyheartslovesharks.org/hk, accessed 16 October 2013.

HSI (2013) 'National laws, multi-lateral agreements, regional and global regulations on shark protection and shark finning', www.hsi.org/assets/pdfs/shark_finning_regs_2013.pdf, accessed 8 August 2013.

IATTC (2005) *Resolution on the Conservation of Sharks Caught in Association with Fisheries in the Eastern Pacific Ocean*, Resolution C-05-03, available at www.iattc.org/PDFFiles2/Resolutions/C-05-03-Sharks.pdf, accessed 16 October 2013.

ICCAT (2004) *Recommendation by ICCAT Concerning the Conservation of Sharks Caught in Association with Fisheries Managed by ICCAT*, Resolution 2004-10, available at www.iccat.int/Documents/Recs/compendiopdf-e/2004-10-e.pdf, accessed 16 October 2013.

IOTC (2005) *05/05 Concerning the Conservation of Sharks caught in Association with Fisheries Managed by IOTC*, Resolution 05/05, available at www.iotc.org/files/CMM/IOTC%20-%20Compendium%20of%20ACTIVE%20CMMs%2015%20September%202013.pdf, accessed 6 October 2013.

IOTC (2011) *Status of Shark Fisheries in the Maldives*, IOTC-2011-WPEB07-56, available at www.iotc.org/files/proceedings/2011/wpeb/IOTC-2011-WPEB07-56.pdf, accessed 8 August 2013.

IUCN (2012) *The IUCN Red List of Threatened Species. Version 2012.2*, available at www.iucnredlist.org, accessed 6 November 2012.

IUCN SSG (2007) *Background Paper on the Conservation Status of Migratory Sharks and Possible Options for International Cooperation under the Convention on Migratory Species*, Bonn, Germany.

IUCN SSG (2013) 'Shark special group', available at www.iucnssg.org, accessed August 2013.

IUCN, UNEP and CMS (2007) *Review of Chondrichthyan Fishes, 2007*, prepared by the

Shark Specialist Group of the IUCN Species Survival Commission on behalf of the CMS Secretariat, IUCN and UNEP/CMS Secretariat, Bonn, Germany.

Pew Environmental Group (2012) *How World Leaders Are Protecting Sharks*, available at www.pewenvironment.org/uploadedFiles/PEG/Publications/Other_Resource/HowWorldLeadersAreProtectingSharksFinal%20(1).pdf, accessed 16 October 2012.

Reuters (2000) '"Jaws" author says sharks victims, not villains', *CNN*, 19 July, available at http://archives.cnn.com/2000/NATURE/07/19/jaws.image.reut, accessed 7 August 2013.

Reynolds, M. (2010) 'Seafood firm may move into shark fin, sea urchins', *The Tribune*, 6 September.

Shark Alliance (2013) 'European Union closes loopholes in shark finning ban', www.sharkalliance.org/content.asp?did=38294, accessed 25 September 2013.

Sharkwater Productions Inc. (2006) *Sharkwater*, Sharkwater Productions Inc., Canada.

United Nations (2009) 'Palau unveils plan at UN for shark sanctuary in its territorial waters', available at www.un.org/apps/news/story.asp?Cr=general+assembly&Cr1=&NewsID=32253, accessed 16 October 2013.

Vianna, G. M. S., Meekan, M. G., Pannell, D., Marsh, S. and Meeuwig, J. J. (2010) *Wanted Dead or Alive? The Relative Value of Reef Sharks as a Fishery and an Ecotourism Asset in Palau*, Australian Institute of Marine Science and University of Western Australia, Perth.

Vianna, G. M. S., Meeuwig, J. J., Pannell, D., Sykes, H. and Meekan, M. G. (2011) *The Socio-economic Value of the Shark-diving Industry in Fiji*, Austalian Institute of Marine Science, University of Western Australia, Perth.

Wassener, B. (2012) 'China says no more shark fin soup at state banquets', *New York Times*, 3 July, available at www.nytimes.com/2012/07/04/world/asia/china-says-no-more-shark-fin-soup-at-state-banquets.html?_r=0, accessed 16 October 2013.

WCPFC (2006) 'Conservation and management measure 2006–05', available at www.wcpfc.int/system/files/Conservation%20and%20Management%20Measure-2006-05%20%5BSharks%5D.pdf, accessed 16 October 2013.

WildAid (2013) 'Sharks', available at www.wildaid.org/sharks, accessed 16 October 2013.

Worm, B., Davis, B., Kettemer, L., Ward-Paige, C. A., Chapman, D., Heithaus, M. R., Kessel, S. T. and Gruber, S. H. (2013) 'Global catches, exploitation rates and rebuilding options for sharks', *Marine Policy*, vol. 40, pp. 194–204.

WWF (2013) 'Companies say no to shark fin', available at www.wwf.org.hk/en/whatwedo/footprint/seafood/sharkfin_initiative/companies_say_no_to_shark_fin, accessed 16 October 2013.

Part IV

Risks and rewards

Chapter 10

Economic rationale for shark conservation

Andrés M. Cisneros-Montemayor and U. Rashid Sumaila[1]

Introduction

It is now clear that shark[2] populations worldwide have experienced large-scale declines (Bonfil *et al.*, 2005; Dulvy *et al.*, 2008). The main cause is the continued and rapid expansion of global fishing fleets, coupled with the naturally low population growth rates of most sharks (Smith *et al.*, 1998). Though there are several charismatic shark species, such as whale sharks (*Rhyncodon typus*), elasmobranchs as a group have historically been overlooked in conservation efforts, largely due to a lack of fisheries data and perhaps also to a generally negative public image (Topelko and Dearden, 2005). For example, almost half of all elasmobranchs listed under the IUCN as threatened or endangered were added since 2009 (Biery *et al.*, 2011). While this is startlingly recent, it is also an encouraging action on the part of managers, conservation groups, the public and academics concerned with shark conservation.

Although both local and large-scale effects have been extensively documented, data on the scale of ongoing shark fishing mortality are often uncertain. According to FAO fisheries statistics (collected and submitted by each member state), 720,000 tonnes of sharks were landed in 2009; the most recent independent research estimates total landings at 1.4 million tonnes, or 100 million sharks (Worm *et al.*, 2013). It is troubling to recognize that many shark catches are processed at sea and thus never reported (Chen and Phipps, 2002), in addition to the many caught and landed by illegal, unregulated and unreported fisheries (Pramod *et al.*, 2008).

An often-overlooked aspect of shark overexploitation, at least by modern fisheries, is the overwhelming significance of demand from Asian markets for global fishing effort (Clarke *et al.*, 2006). This includes demand for shark fins and other products, generally valued as luxury goods in Asian cuisine and traditional medicine. Although there are many efforts currently underway to stem trade of shark products in Europe, the Americas and some parts of Asia, very large centres of demand remain, for example in mainland China and Taiwan.

There is a growing interest in the economic benefits of sharks for eco-tourism at both local and global scales (Gallagher and Hammerschlag, 2011; Clua *et al.*,

2011; Topelko and Dearden, 2005). Economic benefits from shark watching are particularly evident at the local level, where operations are often run by local ex-fishers, and most profits remain in the community (Gallagher and Hammerschlag, 2011). In the better-established sites around the world, these benefits can be quite substantial. For example, individual sharks in French Polynesia were estimated to have an eco-tourism value of around US$1,250 per kilogram (based on data in Clua *et al.*, 2011 and species length–weight relationships), compared with a landed value to local fishers of US$1.6 per kilogram for shark meat (Sumaila *et al.*, 2007; see Chapters 8 and 12). Some prominent shark watching sites are Ningaloo Reef (Australia), Donsol (Philippines), Gansbaai (South Africa), Holbox Island (Mexico) and Gladden Spit (Belize) (Irvine and Keesing, 2007). As these varied international locations suggest, the global distribution of sharks raises an interesting question regarding the potential for shark watching at other sites.

Shark conservation has achieved a great deal from an ethical and ecological perspective, and is increasingly gaining traction at the highest levels of international governance (Vincent *et al.*, 2013). For example, after many years of contentious debates, in 2013 a landmark agreement was reached to add five commercially valuable shark and ray species to Appendix II of the *Convention on International Trade in Endangered Species* (CITES) listings (CITES, 2013). Here we analyse the issue from a resource management viewpoint using economic and social performance metrics. We thus provide the first global estimate of current and potential contributions of shark eco-tourism in terms of tourist participation, expenditures and employment, and contrast and discuss these findings with shark fishing landed values. These indicators were selected as they are the benefits captured by tourism operators or fishers, who, unlike final consumers, have the most to gain or lose from practices that trade-off ecological degradation for economic benefits (Ransom and Mangi, 2010).

Methods

'Shark watching' can mean very different things, but we define the activity here as any form of observing sharks in their natural habitat, without any intention to harm the animals. This includes watching them from boats, underwater with snorkel or scuba gear (with or without luring them with bait), during day trips or longer live-aboard tours. This means that we do not include other activities, such as aquaria and recreational fishing, which provide economic benefits and, if carried out in specific ways, may not cause undue harm to populations. The performance indicators that we focus on for this study are as follows:

- *participation:* the number of people who participate in shark watching (as defined above) at a given site;
- *employment*: the number of jobs (full-time equivalents) directly supported by shark watching tourism at a given site;

- *expenditures*: money spent by tourists that is wholly or partially attributable to watching sharks in a given location. All values presented are in 2013 USD.

We frame our global analysis in terms of UN-defined regions and subregions,[3] which make it easier to search for, visualize, compute and compare estimates over the wide range of ecosystems and socio-economic conditions of the shark watching sites identified.

Shark fisheries

It is important to place the contribution of shark watching tourism in context at a global scale, so central data on global shark fisheries, including landings, trade and landed value, were compiled using FAO statistics (FAO, 2011) and species and country-specific ex-vessel fish prices (the price paid to fishers for their catch; Sumaila *et al.*, 2007).

Results and discussion

Shark watching as an economic activity has expanded and is now carried out throughout the world (Figure 10.1). As some sites earn more economic benefits from shark watching, it is unsurprising that other localities with similar ecological opportunities are made aware and establish their own operations. The scale of current economic benefits was nonetheless surprising; the sum of expenditures solely at sites with available information is about US$223 million per year,

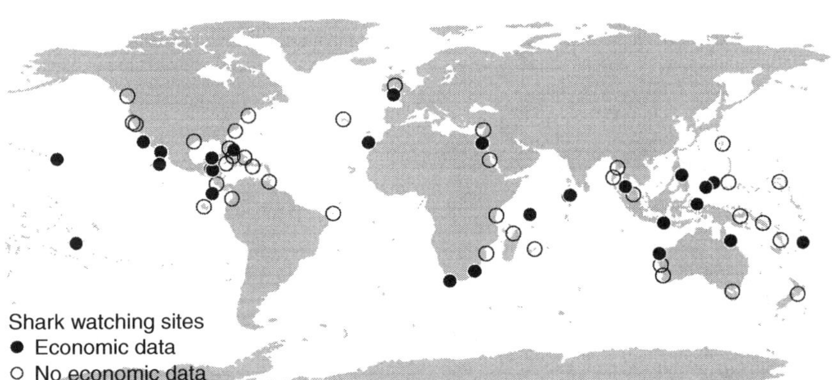

Figure 10.1 Shark watching sites included in this study (filled circles denote sites with available economic data, open circles are sites with no available data).

more than the total landed value of sharks in the corresponding countries (Table 10.1). Our estimates including sites without available economic data suggest that, globally, shark watching generates almost US$327 million, already almost half the value of global shark fisheries, and supports over 10,000 jobs (Table 10.2).

Benefits from shark watching are growing quickly, with an average yearly increase in visitors at shark watching sites of almost 30 per cent during the last 20 years, which can be expected to increase further as new sites become better established. It is already evident that benefits are not only significant, but are being captured in every region of the world (Table 10.2). Tourism growth

Table 10.1 Locations (by country) with available data on yearly shark watching expenditure (for countries with more than one site, only available data are included here, i.e. no estimates are included)

Site	*Shark watching expenditures, US$ thousands*	*Shark landed value, US$ thousands*
Australia[1,2,3]	24,246	11,143
Bahamas[4,5]	85,558	–
Belize[6]	375	25
Costa Rica[7]	6,188	3,041
Egypt[5]	145	381
Fiji[8]	232	–
French Polynesia[9]	5,620	229
Honduras[5]	150	–
Indonesia[3,5]	4,220	70,751
Maldives[10,11]	11,787	546
Micronesia[3]	4,160	–
Mexico[5,12,13]	12,908	22,384
Palau[3,14]	21,160	–
Philippines[15]	235	5,874
Seychelles[15]	3,609	15
South Africa[16,17]	6,317	497
Spain[18]	25,526	46,214
Thailand[19]	4,368	12,856
United Kingdom[5]	33	15,115
United States[5,20]	6,609	18,368
Total	223,446	207,448

Data sources: [1] Stoeckl *et al.*, 2010; [2] Catlin *et al.*, 2010; [3] Heinrichs *et al.*, 2011; [4] Cline, 2008; [5] Cisneros-Montemayor *et al.*, 2013; [6] Carne, 2008; [7] Enric Sala, pers. comm.; [8] Brunnschweiler, 2010; [9] Clua *et al.*, 2011; [10] Anderson *et al.*, 2010; [11] IUCN, www.iucn.org; [12] Iñiguez-Hernandez, 2008; [13] De la Parra-Venegas, 2008; [14] Vianna *et al.*, 2010; [15] Norman and Catlin, 2007; [16] Dicken and Hosking, 2009; [17] Hara *et al.*, 2003; [18] De la Cruz-Modino *et al.*, 2010; [19] Ziegler *et al.*, 2008; [20] Manta Pacific Research Foundation 2007 (in Heinrichs *et al.*, 2011).

Note
Shark landed values are total for the country using taxon-specific landings and price (based on data from Sumaila et *al.*, 2007; unavailable data marked with '–'). All values are per year, in 2013 US$.

Table 10.2 Estimated yearly economic benefits of shark watching by world region.

Region	*Expenditure, US$ millions*	*Shark watchers, thousands*	*Employment*
Africa	15	34	567
Eastern Africa	7.8	3	331
Northern Africa	0.87	0.4	38
Southern Africa	6.3	31	198
Americas	178	198	6,819
Caribbean	128	107	5,303
Central America	19.8	37	1,001
North America	16	43	138
South America	13.6	11	377
Asia	31.7	261	1,132
Eastern Asia	3.3	2	79
Southeastern Asia	10.4	20	215
Southern Asia	6.3	237	717
Western Asia	3.3	2	121
Europe	29.4	39	528
Western Europe	29.4	39	528
Oceania	72.5	58	1,625
Australia and New Zealand	41.5	29	267
Melanesia, Micronesia, Polynesia	31	29	1,358
Total	326.9	590	10,671

Note
Expenditures are in 2013 US$, employment is in full-time equivalents.

generally follows a well-documented logistic pattern (Cole, 2009; Butler, 1980). Industry growth is slow in the establishment phase as operations are streamlined and tourists become aware of the new offers. If successful in attracting tourists, this is followed by a boom in growth (the current status of shark watching); outfits get bigger and more emerge, offering similar services, until there is a saturation of the tourist market and the industry stabilizes. Based on observed growth trends and this known pattern of development, shark watching may eventually attract 2.5 times as many visitors as today, which would generate between US$327 million and US$816 million in visitor expenditures. These projections assume constant expenditure per capita, but real (inflation-adjusted) ticket prices at some sites have increased by 25 per cent during the last decade, another signal of increased demand from tourists (Gallagher and Hammerschlag, 2011).

Meanwhile, global shark landings and landed value have continued to steadily decline, mainly as a consequence of overfishing (Figure 10.2). According to official fishery data trends, over 720,000 tonnes of sharks were landed in 2009, a 20 per cent decline from the historic maximum in 2003 and representing around

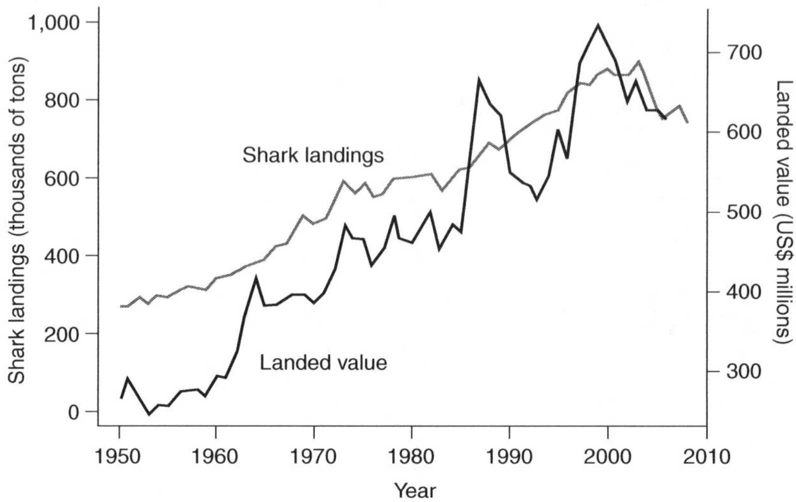

Figure 10.2 Global shark landings and landed value (source: based on data from FAO, 2011 and Sumaila *et al.*, 2007)

US$655 million in landed value (based on data from FAO, 2011 and Sumaila *et al.*, 2007). Over half of all shark catches were reported by the ten countries with the highest average shark catches during the decade: Indonesia, India, Spain, Taiwan, Mexico, Pakistan, Argentina, the United States, Japan and Malaysia (Lack and Sant, 2009). As we consider these declines in catch, it is important to keep in mind that global shark fishing capacity has both increased and expanded spatially (Myers and Worm, 2003; Swartz *et al.*, 2010), meaning that we are encountering fewer sharks even as we search harder. This makes catch declines during the past decade all the more worrisome, but is only one half of the economic picture.

Currently, nearly all value from shark products is created in Asian markets, either within or outside of Asia itself. While catches and landed value are declining (Figure 10.2), net imports and value of shark products continue to grow along with emerging Asian economies that value shark products, particularly shark fin soup, as a luxury good (Figure 10.3). It is important to recognize that the most important shark fishing nations (listed above; Table 10.1) can be quite distinct from the key consumer countries (Figure 10.3). This points to a need for more comprehensive and diverse sets of shark conservation policies that recognize the nature of the modern fishing industry and involve the various sets of stakeholders that comprise it.

For example, one bowl of shark fin soup may sell for over US$100 in Hong Kong; the average price paid to a fisherman for a shark is about 75 cents per kilogram (based on data from Sumaila *et al.*, 2007). The benefits accrued through the difference in the prices which are paid for shark products and what

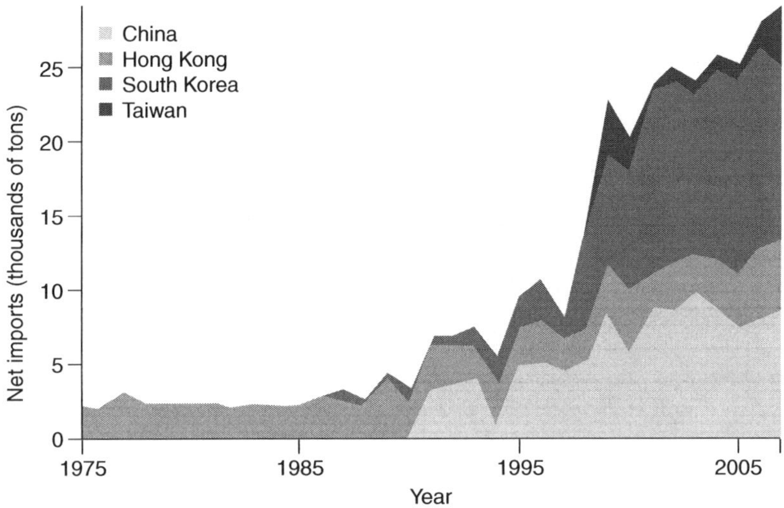

Figure 10.3 Net imports of shark products in main Asian markets (source: based on data from FAO, 2011)

they are sold for by middlemen has resulted in a thriving international trade, where middlemen can seek out new supply sources as local shark populations decline. This sequential depletion of small, localized shark populations is a key threat to global conservation efforts, but the nature of this industry also lends itself to potential controls through regulations on trade itself. Much of the global decline in shark populations can be viewed as an externality of luxury market demands, so conservation policies must also target this source in addition to traditional fishery restrictions.

In performing an accurate economic comparison of shark watching and shark fishing, one must be careful to account for the industry structure of each activity. As discussed earlier, most shark fisheries are driven by luxury markets, where consumer demand and prices are high, whereas fishermen normally see low prices for their catch, indicating that most profits are accrued by the transport, processing and retail sectors. Nevertheless, fishermen can supplement their incomes through the sale of other shark products, such as teeth, jaws and vertebrae for curios or traditional medicine, or simply target other species when sharks are not abundant. These alternate sources of income are an often overlooked benefit that fishermen enjoy, one that is for the most part foregone by tourist operators. Along the same lines, most eco-tourism operators (boat drivers, deckhands, guides, etc.) in developing countries are employees with fixed wages and largely depend on foreign tips that fluctuate seasonally. The role of side payments, a form of benefit sharing where tourism operators pay a fee to adjacent fishing communities not to fish at specific reefs, has emerged as an interesting option in this context. One example is Shark Reef Marine Reserve in Fiji, a marine protected area where dive tourism operators pay an annual fee to adjacent fishing communities not to fish at specific reefs (Brunnschweiler, 2010). This type of strategy should be further explored in sites that have localized aggregations of sharks that could benefit both fishermen and tourism.

The number of tourists that currently participate in shark watching around the world, about 590,000 (Table 10.2), is an important figure to consider. As a form of eco-tourism, participation in shark watching is important in and of itself because it can lead to increased awareness and support for conservation (Barnes, 2010; Garrod and Wilson, 2003), though this depends on how eco-tourism operations are managed and carried out in practice (Topelko and Dearden, 2005). There are concerns regarding potential ecological impacts of eco-tourism due to direct and indirect disturbance to organisms and habitat, including noise pollution (Williams *et al.*, 2002) and damage to coral reefs (Davis and Tisdell, 1995). While well-managed eco-tourism sites have generally resulted in improved ecosystem health and structure, these potential negative effects must be considered to ensure that sites provide sustained benefits.

In the case of shark watching in particular, the practice of provisioning (feeding or chumming the water to attract sharks) has been questioned due to possible effects on shark behaviour that may eventually lead to an undesirable increased attraction to human swimmers and boaters. This normally involves attracting sharks to tourism boats by trolling bait, throwing buckets of fish blood and parts overboard or by providing divers with dead fish so they may manually feed sharks. It seems logical that these practices would affect shark behaviour in the medium or long term, and many report observing these effects; for example, sharks following moving boats or aggregating at common chumming sites (M. Colleter, personal communication, 2013). However, to our knowledge, no scientific studies have yet found conclusive evidence of provisioning affecting long-term shark behaviour (e.g. Maljković and Côté, 2010; Brunnschweiler and McKenzie, 2010; Huveneers *et al.*, 2013), though this is a very interesting topic for ongoing research, particularly as shark eco-tourism grows and develops. In any case, this is only one of many topics that will undoubtedly eventually need to be addressed through a set of agreed-upon guidelines for shark eco-tourism operators.

Though there is an increasing number of documented shark watching operations, their economic contribution remains unknown at many sites (Figure 10.1), making estimations necessary for a global analysis (Table 10.2). Aside from possible errors in source data, the main potential error in our results is the selection of sites to include in our estimation. In a review of global shark watching, Gallagher and Hammerschlag (2011) identified 86 sites where shark watching occurs. We identified and focused upon data collection on 70 dedicated sites, representing 45 countries, all five FAO regions and 14 subregions (Figure 10.1). While sharks can be seen in many other places, these sites were identified as overwhelmingly dedicated to shark watching for at least part of the year. This makes our results conservative because at least some values would be estimated for any included site, although it does avoid potential issues with sites where sharks are often seen but are not the central attraction for tourists.

Data were found for 31 of our initial sites, which provided the basis for subsequent estimations; in addition to original research, data were gathered from peer-reviewed literature ($n = 6$), reports and conference proceedings ($n = 5$), government and NGO reports ($n = 7$) and personal communication ($n = 1$). Sites with large shark watching operations tend to be over-represented in the available literature, so our methods stressed conservative estimation. Using world subregions and relative tourist arrivals helped mitigate potential upward bias in estimates for sites without data, with revisions to site class providing an additional check when necessary. Overall, there were four main groups of sites with respect to expenditure: less than US$1 million per year ($n = 25$), US$1–5 million ($n = 30$), US$5–10 million ($n = 9$) and over US$10 million ($n = 6$). After completing data collection and analysis, sites with available economic information had an average expenditure of US$6.8 million per year, while sites with estimated data averaged US$2.4 million per year.

Elasmobranchs are widely distributed over all of the world's oceans, so sharks can technically be sighted anywhere and at any time; shark watching indeed takes place in sites all over the world (Figure 10.1). However, dedicated sites currently target a core group of species that are relatively accessible to humans (e.g. Gallagher and Hammerschlag, 2011). This usually means that the species aggregate in relatively specific temporal and spatial patterns and occur close to the surface. During this study, the main species identified as targets for shark watching were the whale (*Rhincodon typus*), great white (*Carcharodon carcharias*), tiger (*Galeocerco cuvier*), angel (*Squatina* spp.), hammerhead (*Shpyrna* spp.), galapagos (*C. galapagensis*), thresher (*Alopias* spp.), sandbar (*Carcharhinus plumbeus*), basking (*Cetorhinus maximus*) and reef (*Carcarhinus* spp., *Triaenodon* spp.) sharks, and the manta (*Manta birostris*, *M. alfredi*) and sting (Dasyatidae) rays.

One positive note is that the same traits that make some shark species amenable to tourism can also benefit conservation efforts. Charismatic appeal aside, species that aggregate in known temporal and spatial patterns, literally within sight of humans, can be easier to monitor and protect. This is especially true of species that remain around reefs or other fixed locations that can be protected by Marine Protection Agreements (MPAs), providing a safe haven for local populations (Sala *et al.*, 2002). However, many other species or populations of sharks can be much more widely distributed, or inhabit open oceans that make it much more difficult to enforce conservation or sustainable fishery policies. This requires international agreements and high-level diplomatic efforts, usually at the UN level or within regional fishery management organizations (RFMOs) comprising very large tracts of the open ocean. Fortunately, such efforts are slowly providing positive outcomes for shark populations. In addition to the CITES agreement that recently (2013) added key commercially valuable shark species to Appendix II of the listings (CITES, 2013), two of the largest global

RFMOs, the International Commission for the Conservation of Atlantic Tunas (ICCAT) and the Inter-American Tropical Tuna Commission (IATCC) have now established mandatory shark protection measures for specific species in their jurisdictional waters, covering 158 million km^2 within the Pacific and Atlantic Oceans.

As the ecological and economic value of sharks is increasingly recognized, more (and often even more comprehensive) protected areas are being established around the world and now cover almost 200 million km^2 to 2013, or around 50 per cent of global oceans. Perhaps mirroring the realization that shark conservation can generate good publicity and eco-tourism benefits, the number of countries establishing protection areas has rapidly increased, from 1 to 40 (including all EU parties) over 2009–2013 (Figure 10.4), with some major players in global shark fisheries planning similar measures (i.e. Mexico and Taiwan: Ho, 2011; Pew Environment Group, 2013). In the case of Mexico, where shark fisheries continue to be important for artisanal and industrial fisheries, progress has been gradual, but currently includes a yearly three-month moratorium on directed shark fisheries. In global terms, even relatively poor fishing communities, or those with important shark fisheries, can be amenable to shark conservation given proper economic incentives. This obviously includes establishing streams of sustainable income through the growth of shark watching eco-tourism.

Regarding the contribution of shark watching to overall shark conservation, whale watching is perhaps the most similar case study. The demise of the

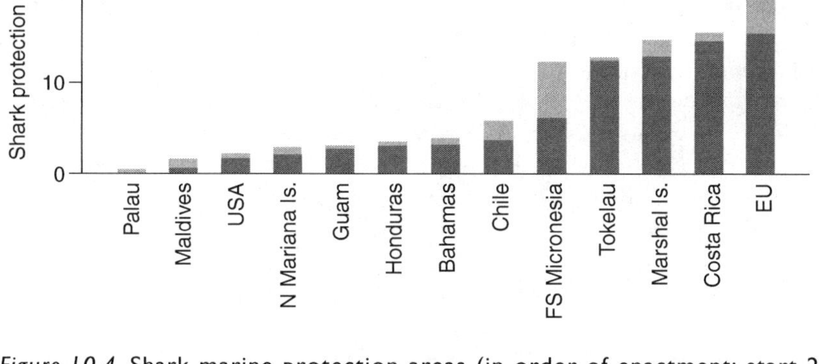

Figure 10.4 Shark marine protection areas (in order of enactment; start 2009), including sanctuaries and EEZ-wide finning bans (sources: Pew Environment Group, 2013; EU, 2003; La Nación, 2012)

whaling industry, which has led to marked improvements in many whale populations, was largely a result of decreased demand for whale products due to new substitutes (Davis *et al.*, 1988). However, the emergence of the global whale watching industry, currently generating over US$2 billion per year (O'Connor *et al.*, 2009) and with much potential for further growth (Cisneros-Montemayor *et al.*, 2010), has added a new dimension to arguments in support of conservation and responsible resource use. Working to promote consumer awareness and support for sustainability is therefore vital (Jacquet and Pauly, 2007), as it helps create new customers for eco-tourism while directly contributing to conservation. These types of clear win–win situations are essential for holistic conservation efforts rooted in the idea of sustainable development, and are, in a sense, the low-hanging fruits.

Fishermen can also transition into tourism themselves, as is occurring in several sites around the world (e.g. Irving and Keesing, 2007; Rossing, 2006). Though there are significant challenges to this transition, the common theme in stories of success is international interest and aid in the form of capacity building, including marketing strategies, customer service improvement and strong animal welfare guidelines, usually in the form of a code of conduct for tourism operators. A growing number of environmentally conscious tourists willing to pay to enjoy healthy ecosystems and shark populations will bring new economic options to coastal communities and both local and national governments, which can then decide for themselves how best to manage their resources and could even rely partially on tourists to help monitor their ecosystem status (Ward-Paige and Lotze, 2011). It is imperative that these efforts to transition into tourism define the responsibilities and rights of the many stakeholder groups in these areas in order to avoid issues of unrestricted competition that will, as with fisheries, inevitably lead to conflicts and decreased overall benefits (Wood *et al.*, 2013). Within developing-country sites, this *must* be developed in parallel with co-management involving local fishers and communities, as these settings can often result in marginalization of those most in need of alternative income sources (Hill, 2005; Cabral and Aliño, 2011).

Achieving both sustainable eco-tourism and fisheries centred on sharks is feasible. However, current fishing practices continue to pose a grave threat to shark populations worldwide. We have tried here to expand on the traditional picture of economic benefits from sharks, yet it is equally important to recognize that overfishing sharks is not only detrimental to potential sustainable shark fisheries, but can have drastic impacts on ecosystem-wide structure and benefits. The type and magnitude of these impacts are very difficult to anticipate and can include counter-intuitive changes in abundance of particular species or species groups, or larger and long-lasting shifts in ecosystem structure (Parsons, 1992; Heithaus *et al.*, 2008; Shackell *et al.*, 2009). Ultimately, managing our resources with a view towards ecosystem health will help ensure that we continue to obtain the economic benefits that sustain both coastal and global communities.

Acknowledgements

We thank the co-authors of the study this chapter was based on, Michele Barnes-Mauthe, Dalal Al-Abdulrazzak and Estrella Navarro-Holm, as well as all those who provided data for that study.

Notes

1 This chapter is based on the published article: Cisneros-Montemayor, A. M., Barnes-Mauthe, M., Al-Abdulrazzak, D., Navarro-Holm, E., Sumaila, U. R. (2013). 'Global economic value of shark ecotourism: implications for conservation', *Oryx* vol. 47, no. 3, pp. 381–388.
2 Unless otherwise specified, we use 'sharks' to refer to sharks (Selachimorpha), rays (Batoidea) and chimaeras (Chimaeriformes).
3 See www.unstats.un.org.

References

Anderson, R. C., Shiham Adam, M., Kitchen-Wheeler, A. M. and Stevens, G. (2010) 'Extent and economic value of manta ray watching in Maldives', *Tourism in Marine Environment*, vol. 7, no. 1, pp. 15–27.

Barnes, M. (2010) 'Shark ecotourism's possible contribution to shark conservation: increasing public awareness and addressing sharks' image problem', unpublished manuscript, University of Hawaii at Manoa, Honolulu, HI.

Biery, L., Palomares, M. L. D., Morisette, L., Cheung, W. W. L., Harper, S., Jacquet, J., Zeller, D. and Pauly, D. (2011) *Sharks in the Seas Around Us: How the Sea Around Us Project is Working to Shape Our Collective Understanding of Global Shark Fisheries*, a report prepared for the Pew Environment Group by the Sea Around Us Project, Fisheries Centre, the University of British Columbia, Vancouver.

Bonfil, R., Meÿer, M., Scholl, M. C., Johnson, R., O'Brien, S., Oosthuizen, H., Swanson, S., Kotze, D. and Paterson, M. (2005) 'Transoceanic migration, spatial dynamics and population linkages of White Sharks', *Science*, vol. 310, pp. 100–103.

Brunnschweiler, J. M. (2010) 'The Shark Reef Marine Reserve: a marine tourism project in Fiji involving local communities', *Journal of Sustainable Tourism*, vol. 18, no. 1, pp. 29–42.

Brunnschweiler, J. M. and McKenzie, J. (2010) 'Baiting sharks for marine tourism: comment on Clua *et al.* (2010)', *Marine Ecology Progress Series*, vol. 420, pp. 283–284.

Butler, R. (1980) 'The concept of a Tourism Area Life Cycle of Evolution: implications for management of resources', *Canadian Geographer*, vol. 24, no. 1, pp. 5–12.

Cabral, R. B. and Aliño, P. M. (2011) 'Transition from common to private costs: consequences of privatization of the coastal commons', *Ocean and Coastal Management*, vol. 54, pp. 66–74.

Carne, L. (2008) *Monitoring and Management of Whale Shark Tourism at Gladden Spit and the Silk Cayes Marine Reserve, Belize, 2003–2007*, 2nd International Whale Shark Conference, Holbox, Mexico, July.

Catlin, J., Jones, T., Norman, B. and Wood, D. (2010) 'Consolidation in a wildlife tourism industry: the changing impact of whale shark tourist expenditure in the Ningaloo coastal region', *International Journal of Tourism Research*, vol. 12, pp. 134–148.

Chen, V. Y. and Phipps, M. J. (2002) *Management and Trade of Whale Sharks in Taiwan*, a TRAFFIC East Asia Report, available at www.traffic.org/species-reports/traffic_species_fish9.pdf, accessed 3 March 2014.

Cisneros-Montemayor, A. M. and Sumaila, U. R. (2010a) 'A global estimate of benefits from ecosystem-based marine recreation: potential impacts and implications for management', *Journal of Bioeconomics*, vol. 12, pp. 245–268.

Cisneros-Montemayor, A. M., Sumaila, U. R., Kaschner, K. and Pauly, D. (2010b) 'The global potential for whale watching', *Marine Policy*, vol. 34, pp. 1273–1278.

Cisneros-Montemayor, A. M., Barnes-Mauthe, M., Al-Abdulrazzak, D., Navarro-Holm, E. and Sumaila, U. R. (2013) 'Global economic value of shark ecotourism: implications for conservation', *Oryx*, vol. 47, no. 3, pp. 381–388.

CITES (2013) 'CITES conference takes decisive action to halt decline of tropical timber, sharks, manta rays and a wide range of other plants and animals', available at www.cites.org/eng/news/pr/2013/20130314_cop16.php, accessed 3 March 2014.

Clarke, S. C., McAllister, M. K., Milner-Gulland, E. J., Kirkwood, G. P., Michielsens, C. G. J., Agnew, D. J., Pikitch, E. K., Nakano, H. and Shivj, M. S. (2006) 'Global estimates of shark catches using trade records from commercial markets', *Ecology Letters*, vol. 9, pp. 1115–1126.

Cline, W. (2008) *Shark Diving Overview for the Islands of the Bahamas*, Report of the Bahamas Ministry of Tourism, Cline Marketing Group, Nassau.

Clua, E., Burray, N., Legendre, P., Mourier, J. and Planes, S. (2011) 'Business partner or simple catch? The economic value of the sicklefin lemon shark in French Polynesia', *Marine and Freshwater Research*, vol. 62, pp. 764–770.

Cole, S. (2009) 'A logistic tourism model: resort cycles, globalization and chaos', *Annals of Tourism Research*, vol. 36, no. 4, pp. 669–714.

Davis, D. and Tisdell, C. (1995) 'Recreational scuba-diving and carrying capacity in marine protected areas', *Ocean and Coastal Management*, vol. 26, no. 1, pp. 19–40.

Davis, L. E., Gallman, R. E. and Hutchins, T. D. (1988) 'The decline of U. S. whaling: was the stock of whales running out?', *The Business History Review*, vol. 62, pp. 569–595.

De La Cruz-Modino, R., Esteban, R., Crilly, R. and Pascual-Fernández, J. (2010) *Bucear con tiburones y rayas en España. Análisis de su potencial en España y de los beneficios económicos de la actividad en las Islas Canarias*, Instituto Universitario de Ciencias Políticas y Sociales de la Universidad de La laguna y Nef, Tenerife, Canary Islands.

De La Parra-Venegas, R. (2008) *Proyecto Dominó: Informe Técnico General, 2003–2008*, available at www.domino.conanp.gob.mx, accessed 3 March 2014.

Dicken, M. L. and Hosking, S. G. (2009) 'Socio-economic aspects for the tiger shark diving industry within the Aliwal Shoal Marine Protected Area, South Africa', *African Journal of Marine Science*, vol. 31, no. 2, pp. 227–232.

Dulvy, N. K., Baum, J. K., Clarke, S., Compagno, L. J. V., Cortés, E., Domingo, A., Fordham, S., Fowler, S., Francis, M. P., Gibson, C., Martínez, J., Musick, J. A., Soldo, A., Stevens, J. D. and Valenti, S. (2008) 'You can swim but you can't hide: the global status and conservation of oceanic pelagic sharks and rays', *Aquatic Conservation: Marine and Freshwater Ecosystems*, vol. 18, pp. 459–482.

FAO (2011) *Fisheries Statistics and Information*, Fisheries and Aquaculture Department, available at www.fao.org/fishery, accessed 3 March 2014.

Gallagher, A. and Hammerschlag, N. (2011) 'Global shark currency: the distribution, frequency and economic value of shark ecotourism', *Current Issues in Tourism*, vol. 1, pp. 1–6.

Garrod, B. and Wilson, J. (2003) *Aspects of Tourism: Marine Ecotourism, Issues and Experiences*, Channel View Publications, Clevedon.

Hara, M., Maharaj, I. and Pithers, L. (2003) *Marine-based Tourism in Gansbaai: A Socio-economic Study*, prepared for the Department of Environmental Affairs by Programme for Land and Agrarian Studies, University of the Western Cape, available at http://sharkxplorers.com/pdf/gansbaai.pdf, accessed 21 November 2011.

Heinrichs, S., O'Malley, M., Medd, H. and Hilton, P. (2011) *The Global State of Manta and Mobula Rays: Manta Ray of Hope*, 2011 Report, available at www.sharksavers.org/images/stories/documents/The%20Global%20Threat%20to%20Manta%20and%20Mobula%20Rays.pdf, accessed 2 February 2012.

Heithaus, M. R., Frid, A., Wirsing, A. J. and Worm, B. (2008) 'Predicting ecological consequences of marine top predator declines', *Trends in Ecology and Evolution*, vol. 23, no. 4, pp. 202–210.

Hill, N. A. O. (2005) 'Livelihoods in an artisanal fishing community and the effect of ecotourism', Dissertation, Imperial College London.

Ho, E. (2011) 'Taiwan to become first Asian nation to ban shark finning', *Time*, 1 December, available at http://newsfeed.time.com/2011/12/01/taiwan-to-become-first-asian-nation-to-ban-shark-finning, accessed 3 March 2014.

Huveneers, C., Rogers, P. J., Beckmann, C., Semmens, J. M., Bruce, B. D. and Seuront, L. (2013) 'The effects of cage-diving activities on the fine-scale swimming behaviour and space use of white sharks', *Marine Biology*, vol. 160, no. 11, pp. 2863–2875.

Iñiguez-Hernández, L. (2008) 'Diagnóstico de la actividad turística desarrollada con tiburón blanco *Carcharodon carcharias* en Isla Guadalupe, Baja California', MSc Dissertation, Universidad Autónoma de Baja California, Mexico.

Irvine, T. R. and Keesing, J. K. (eds) (2007) *The First International Whale Shark Conference: Promoting International Collaboration in Whale Shark Conservation, Science and Management. Conference Overview, Abstracts and Supplementary Proceedings*, CSIRO Marine and Atmospheric Research, Western Australia.

IUCN (2001) *IUCN Shark Specialist Newsletter*, www.iucnssg.org/tl_files/Assets/pdf/SN/SN13%20LOW%20RES.pdf, accessed 3 March 2014.

Jacquet, J. L. and Pauly, D. (2007) 'The rise of seafood awareness campaigns in an era of collapsing fisheries', *Marine Policy*, vol. 31, no. 3, pp. 308–313.

Lack, M. and Sant, G. (2009) *Trends in Global Shark Catch and Recent Developments in Management*, TRAFFIC International, available at www.traffic.org/species-reports/traffic_species_fish34.pdf, accessed 3 March 2014.

La Nación (2012) 'Costa Rica prohíbe importar y exportar aletas de tiburón', www.nacion.com/archivo/Costa-Rica-prohibe-importar-exportar_0_1298270256.html, accessed 3 March 2014.

Maljković, A. and Côté, I. M. (2010) 'Effects of tourism-related provisioning on the trophic signatures and movement patterns of an apex predator, the Caribbean reef shark', *Biological Conservation*, vol. 144, no. 2, pp. 859–865.

Myers, R. A. and Worm, B. (2003) 'Rapid worldwide depletion of predatory fish communities', *Nature*, vol. 423, pp. 280–283.

Norman, B. and Catlin, J. (2007) *Economic Importance of Conserving Whale Sharks*, Report for the International Fund for Animal Welfare, Australia, available at www.whalesharkfest.com/pdf/economicimportance.pdf, accessed 2 February 2012.

O'Connor, S., Campbell, R., Cortez, H. and Knowles, T. (2009) 'Whale watching worldwide: tourism numbers, expenditures and expanding economic benefits, a special report from the International Fund for Animal Welfare', report prepared by Economists at Large.

Parsons, T. R. (1992) 'The removal of marine predators by fisheries and the impact of trophic structure', *Marine Pollution Bulletin*, vol. 25, pp. 51–53.

Pew Environment Group (2013) 'The truth about sharks', available at www.pewenvironment.org/news-room/other-resources/the-truth-about-sharks-85899362412, accessed 3 March 2014.

Pramod, G., Pitcher, T. J., Pearce, J. and Agnew, D. (2008) *Sources of Information Supporting Estimates of Unreported Fishery Catches (IUU) for 59 Countries and the High Seas*, Fisheries Centre Research Report 16, No. 4.

Ransom, K. P. and Mangi, S. C. (2010) 'Valuing recreational benefits of coral reefs: the case of Mombasa Marine National Park and Reserve, Kenya', *Environment Management*, vol. 45, pp. 145–154.

Rossing, P. A. (2006) 'Evaluating ecotourism in Mexico's biosphere reserves: whale watching activities in the world heritage site of Laguna San Ignacio, Baja California Sur, Mexico 1994–2002', MSc Thesis, University of British Columbia, Canada.

Sala, E., Aburto-Oropeza, O., Paredes, G., Parra, I., Barrera, J. C. and Dayton, P. K. (2002) 'A general model for designing networks of marine reserves', *Science*, vol. 298, pp. 1991–1993.

Shackell, N. L., Frank, K. T., Fisher, J. A. D., Petrie, B. and Leggett, W. C. (2009) 'Decline in top predator body size and changing climate alter trophic structure in an oceanic system', *Proceedings of the Royal Society B*, vol. 277, pp. 1353–1360.

Smith, S. E., Au, D. W. and Show, C. (1998) 'Intrinsic rebound potentials of 26 species of Pacific sharks', *Marine and Freshwater Research*, vol. 49, pp. 663–678.

Stoeckl, N., Birtles, A., Farr, M., Mangott, A., Curnock, M. and Valentine, P. (2010) 'Live-aboard dive boats in the Great Barrier Reef: regional economic impact and the relative values of their target marine species', *Tourism Economics*, vol. 16, no. 4, pp. 995–1018.

Sumaila, U. R., Marsden, A. D., Watson, R. and Pauly, D. (2007) 'A global ex-vessel price database: construction and applications', *Journal of Bioeconomics*, vol. 9, pp. 39–51.

Swartz, W., Sala, E., Tracey, S., Watson, R. and Pauly, D. (2010) 'The spatial expansion and ecological footprint of fisheries (1950 to present)', *PLoS ONE*, vol. 5, no. 12.

Topelko, K. N. and Dearden, P. (2005) 'The shark watching industry and its potential contribution to conservation', *Journal of Ecotourism*, vol. 4, no. 2, pp. 108–128.

Vianna, G. M. S., Meekan, M. G., Pannell, D., Marsh, S. and Meeuwig, J. J. (2010) *Wanted Dead or Alive? The Relative Value of Reef Sharks as a Fishery and an Ecotourism Asset in Palau*, Australian Institute of Marine Science and University of Western Australia, Perth.

Vincent, A. C. J., Sadovy, Y. J., Fowler, S. L. and Lieberman, S. (2013) 'The role of CITES in the conservation of marine fishes subject to international trade', *Fish and Fisheries*, available at http://onlinelibrary.wiley.com/journal/10.1111/%28ISSN%2914 67–2979/earlyview, accessed 3 March 2014.

Ward-Paige, C. A. and Lotze, H. K. (2011) 'Assessing the value of recreational divers for censusing elasmobranchs', *PLoS ONE*, vol. 6, no. 10.

Williams, R., Trites, A. W. and Bain, D. E. (2002) 'Behavioural responses of killer whales (*Orcinus orca*) to whale-watching boats: opportunistic observations and experimental approaches', *Journal of Zoology*, vol. 256, pp. 255–270.

Wood, A. L., Butler, J. R. A., Sheaves, M. and Wani, J. (2013) 'Sport fisheries: opportunities and challenges for diversifying coastal livelihoods in the Pacific', *Marine Policy*, vol. 42, pp. 305–314.

Worm, B., Davis, B., Kettemer, L., Ward-Paige, C. A., Chapman, D., Heithaus, M. R., Kessel, S. T. and Gruber, S. H. (2013) 'Global catches, exploitation rates, and rebuilding options for sharks', *Marine Policy*, vol. 40, pp. 194–204.

Ziegler, J., Dearden, P., Catlin, J. and Norman, B. (2008) *Assessing the Sustainability of Global Shark Tourism: Global Perspective*, 2nd International Whale Shark Conference, Holbox, Mexico, July 2008.

Chapter 11

Iconic species

Great white sharks, basking sharks and whale sharks

Ryan M. Kempster and Shaun P. Collin

Introduction

Sharks are a group of fishes that have captivated human attention throughout history. They comprise more than 400 species that have evolved for over 400 million years, making them one of the oldest living vertebrate groups (Compagno *et al.*, 2004). Over their long evolutionary history, sharks have diversified to become essential components of almost all marine environments. From the polar seas to tropical oceans, sharks range in size from just a few inches to over 15 metres in length. They can be found in shallow, freshwater rivers, and down to the ocean floor thousands of metres below the surface. Unfortunately, due to a general lack of understanding, sharks are often viewed by the public with fear and their sheer presence considered a threat, so their true value to ocean ecosystems is often overlooked. As a result, unlike other marine species (e.g. whales and dolphins), which have received, often overwhelming, public support, sharks have not benefited from the same attention and public pressure to lobby for their conservation. In contrast, public perception of sharks may have actually hindered their conservation (Simpfendorfer *et al.*, 2011; Neff and Yang, 2013).

Major threats to sharks

Due to overexploitation and the paucity of effective management strategies, many shark species are under significant risk of unrecoverable decline, with some species having declined to near extinction in recent years (Baum *et al.*, 2003; Baum and Myers, 2004; Verlecar *et al.*, 2007). Consequently, the impact of fishing on shark stocks around the world is now the focus of substantial international concern (Baum *et al.*, 2003; Clarke *et al.*, 2006; Robbins *et al.*, 2006; Hisano *et al.*, 2011; Lam and Sadovy de Mitcheson, 2011). Unprecedented declines in shark populations have revealed an inability to predict both the susceptibility of populations to collapse and their capacity for subsequent recovery.

The relatively slow growth and reproductive rates of sharks have resulted in the systematic depletion of many populations worldwide, largely due to an increasing demand for their fins in Asian markets (Dulvy *et al.*, 2008; Ferretti *et al.*, 2010). As a result, comparisons have been made between the plight of sharks today and the over-fishing of whales in the 1980s (Herndon *et al.*, 2010), which resulted in a global moratorium on whaling. Like whales, many shark species exhibit late maturity, slow growth and low reproductive rates, making them extremely vulnerable to collapse with relatively little fishing pressure, compared to other fishes (teleosts). Calculating the full extent of the decline in shark populations, their risk of extinction and the resulting cost to marine ecosystems has been challenging and controversial, mostly due to data limitations (Stevens *et al.*, 2000b; Carlson *et al.*, 2012; Worm *et al.*, 2013).

The practice of live shark finning, where the animal's fins are removed prior to the body being discarded at sea, makes it very difficult to calculate the true number of sharks caught each year (Clarke *et al.*, 2006; Worm *et al.*, 2013) as such discards are not usually reported to the relevant management agencies (Stevens *et al.*, 2000a; Worm *et al.*, 2013). This practice is globally widespread due to the high value of the fins in Asian markets. Anti-finning legislation has been gradually introduced in a number of countries, including the United States, Canada, the United Kingdom and Australia over the last ten years (Techera, 2012), yet the practice continues in other parts of the world (Worm *et al.*, 2013).

Global mortality of sharks was estimated at 1.41 million metric tonnes in 2010, which translates into an annual global mortality estimate of approximately 97 million sharks, with a total range between 63 and 273 million sharks (Worm *et al.*, 2013). Furthermore, Worm *et al.* (2013) estimated that the average exploitation rate of shark species ranged from 6.4 per cent to 7.9 per cent annually, which exceeds the average rebound rate of 4.9 per cent per year for many shark populations. Global shark mortality therefore needs to be reduced significantly in order to rebuild depleted populations and restore marine ecosystems with the important apex predators (Lack and Sant, 2011; Worm *et al.*, 2013).

In 1999, the International Plan of Action for Sharks (IPOA-Sharks, which also includes skates, rays and chimaeras) was launched by the Food and Agriculture Organisation (FAO), and a number of other management bodies (Davis and Worm, 2013). IPOA-Sharks aims to enhance their conservation and management, while also improving worldwide data collection. The plan recommended that all countries contributing to shark fishing mortality should participate in their management, and the development of a National Shark Plan by 2001. However, progress remains slow thus far, with limited adoption and implementation of IPOA goals at the national level (Lack and Sant, 2011; Davis and Worm, 2013; Worm *et al.*, 2013).

Growing support to protect sharks

A shift in public perception, from sharks being a danger to humans to humans being a danger to sharks, has captivated the attention of a new generation of ocean conservationists seeking to abolish the wasteful practice of shark finning. Where international agencies have failed to protect sharks in the past, conservationists are now picking up the baton to take on the challenge, and their voice is growing ever louder as the public begin to realize the true value of sharks in our oceans (Vianna *et al.*, 2012; Cisneros-Montemayor *et al.*, 2013). As a result of public pressure, many states and territories around the world have now banned the possession and trade of shark fins (Techera, 2012), and some island nations have even declared their territorial waters as shark sanctuaries, effectively no-take zones for sharks; however, the impact of such actions on a global scale have yet to be determined.

Internationally, inclusion of species in the *Convention on Migratory Species* (CMS) and the *Convention on International Trade in Endangered Species* (CITES) is the goal for most groups working for the conservation of shark species, but strong opposition, typically from Japan and China, has previously hampered most efforts for their inclusion. CITES acts to restrict international trade in a listed species, whereas CMS aims to prohibit the taking of listed migratory species. While offering protection, these treaties have been of limited utility for shark conservation given the very few shark species listed. Nevertheless, after years of lobbying for their protection, three iconic shark species, the white (*Carcharodon carcharias*; Figure 11.1), whale (*Rhincodon typus*; Figure 11.2) and

Figure 11.1 Photograph of a white shark (*Carcharodon carcharias*) (photo credit: Laura Ortega).

Figure 11.2 Photograph of two whale sharks (*Rhincodon typus*) (photo credit: Ryan Kempster).

basking (*Cetorhinus maximus*; Figure 11.3) sharks were the first species to receive international protection globally under both CITES and CMS. The apparent shared aspects of their biology and ecology, and the similar threats facing these three species were the driving force behind their listing in the Appendices of CMS and CITES, with the aim of developing a global approach for the conservation of migratory sharks.

The whale shark was the first shark species to be adopted by either CMS or CITES, with its listing in Appendix II of CMS in 1999, followed by a CITES Appendix II listing in 2003. The white shark followed in 2002, with its listing on Appendix I and II of CMS and subsequent CITES Appendix II listing in 2005. Finally, the basking shark was adopted by CITES and listed in Appendix II in 2003 prior to its inclusion by CMS and subsequent listing in Appendix I and II in 2005 (see Chapter 3 for more recently listed species).

The white, whale and basking sharks represent three iconic species that have now benefited from at least ten years of internationally regulated protection under either CMS, CITES or both. These species now represent the best examples of how well international agreements work to protect shark populations from decline. Determining the effectiveness of internationally regulated protection measures for sharks is of paramount importance to inform the development of future management plans. In this chapter we discuss the current state of biological knowledge of these three iconic species, how and why they were given

Figure 11.3 Photograph of a basking shark (*Cetorhinus maximus*) (photo credit: Greg Skomal).

such unprecedented measures of international and local protection, whether or not that protection is effective and our recommendations for the future management of shark species.

Current biological knowledge of iconic species

Understanding a species' population connectivity, their role in an ecosystem and trends in their abundance over time is crucial to the development of an effective management plan for potentially vulnerable species. Since their adoption by CITES and CMS, we now have a better understanding of these factors for the white, whale and basking sharks. The following section discusses the current biological knowledge of these three iconic species, with particular focus on what has been learnt since their protection.

Geographic range

White sharks have a global distribution with high concentrations in temperate coastal waters, but are known to inhabit open ocean waters far from land

(Compagno *et al.*, 2004). They range from the surface down to depths of over 1,000m, although they are typically found at depths of less than 250m (Last and Stevens, 2009). They are most commonly recorded in the waters of South Africa; eastern, western and particularly southern Australia; New Zealand; Japan; the Atlantic and Pacific coasts of North America; Central Chile; and the Mediterranean Sea (Compagno *et al.*, 2004; Last and Stevens, 2009).

Satellite tags have revealed that white sharks may undertake long-distance trans-oceanic migrations between South Africa and Australia (Pardini *et al.*, 2001; Bonfil *et al.*, 2005) and between California and Hawaii (Boustany *et al.*, 2002). However, more recent population genetics of white sharks has provided evidence of reproductive philopatry, whereby sharks return to the same location for breeding and parturition over many generations, resulting in distinct, isolated populations (Jorgensen *et al.*, 2010; Blower *et al.*, 2012). Therefore, despite white sharks being able to travel trans-oceanic distances, these migrations are likely to be somewhat rare, resulting in long-term genetic isolation. It then follows that regional white shark populations may be considered as demographically independent management units, which offer clear population assessment, monitoring and management options (Jorgensen *et al.*, 2010; Blower *et al.*, 2012).

Whale sharks are found throughout the world's tropical and warm temperate seas except the Mediterranean, typically between latitudes 30°N and 35°S (Compagno *et al.*, 2004; Stevens, 2007). Occasionally, individuals have been sighted at latitudes outside of their typical range, up to 44°N in Canada (Turnbull and Randell, 2006) and >35°S in New Zealand (Duffy, 2002). Whale sharks are mostly found in shallow coastal waters within a temperature range of approximately 21–25°C, although they are known to dive to depths of over 1,000m, where the temperature may be as low as 3.4°C (Graham *et al.*, 2006; Brunnschweiler *et al.*, 2009). They are most commonly recorded, year round, off the east coast of Taiwan, Honduras and the Seychelles, with seasonal aggregations common off the coasts of India, South Africa, Mexico and Western Australia (Compagno *et al.*, 2004; Last and Stevens, 2009).

Similar to white sharks, satellite tagging of whale sharks has demonstrated their ability to migrate trans-oceanic distances, i.e. from Mexico to the south Pacific island of Tonga (13,000km). In contrast to white sharks, genetic studies have not found significantly distinct populations of whale sharks, suggesting a globally panmictic[1] population (Rowat and Brooks, 2012). However, photo-identification studies of whale sharks suggest that they form seasonal size- and sex-segregated feeding aggregations and that a large proportion of individuals in these aggregations are philopatric[2] (Graham and Roberts, 2007). Significant gaps remain in our understanding of the distribution of this species, particularly with respect to the adults who are not found in the feeding aggregations (Rowat and Brooks, 2012).

Basking sharks occur throughout the world's temperate and boreal oceans, typically within a temperature range of 8–14°C, but they have been found in temperatures up to 24°C (Compagno *et al.*, 2004). Most sightings are from close to the surface (Sims *et al.*, 2003), but basking sharks are also known to dive to a depth of greater than 1,200 m in the winter months (Francis and Duffy, 2002; Gore *et al.*, 2008). In the northern hemisphere these sharks are commonly recorded in both the North Atlantic (between Atlantic and Arctic waters) and the North Pacific (from Japan to British Columbia) (Compagno *et al.*, 2004). In the southern hemisphere, records reveal their distribution spanning from South America to New Zealand (Last and Stevens, 2009).

Basking sharks are thought to undertake sex-segregated seasonal migrations from deep to shallow water in the summer months (Sims *et al.*, 2003). Given the difficulty of locating individuals when they typically migrate into deeper waters, the winter distribution of most populations, particularly pregnant females, are mostly unknown (Francis and Duffy, 2002; Sims *et al.*, 2003; Gore *et al.*, 2008). Although basking shark populations seem to be geographically isolated, Hoelzel *et al.* (2006) found low genetic diversity between those in the Atlantic and those in the Pacific Oceans, suggesting that female-mediated gene flow may occur across ocean basins. Therefore, the population of basking sharks in the northeast Atlantic, which have experienced immense exploitation, may show only limited recovery if mature adults are exposed to exploitation in other regions.

Reproduction

White sharks reproduce through a process known as aplacental viviparity, whereby embryos develop inside their mother, but are primarily nourished by feeding on unfertilized eggs in the womb (oophagy) (Dulvy and Reynolds, 1997). There is no evidence that white shark embryos cannibalize their siblings (embryophagy), as in sand tiger sharks (*Carcharias taurus*), where only one embryo survives in each uterus (Gilmore, 1993). The maximum litter size in white sharks is at least ten, which makes this form of embryophagy unlikely (Last and Stevens, 2009). Size at birth ranges from 110 cm to 160 cm (total length, TL) and gestation is thought to last approximately 12 months. Pregnant females are thought to give birth every 2–3 years, resulting in a very low yearly recruitment (Compagno *et al.*, 2004), and parturition occurs between spring and summer in warm-temperate neritic waters (Bruce, 1992).

Whale sharks reproduce through a process known as leicithotrophic viviparity, whereby embryos develop inside their mother, similar to white sharks, but do not gain any nourishment from their mother, instead feeding solely on a single yolk sac (Dulvy and Reynolds, 1997). As the mother is not providing additional nourishment to embryos – i.e. by producing unfertilized eggs as a food source – whale sharks are able to simultaneously incubate at least 300 viable embryos at one time (Joung *et al.*, 1996). Size at birth is thought to range from 55 cm to 64 cm TL, with an unknown length of gestation and reproductive frequency (Last and Stevens, 2009).

Basking sharks are thought to exhibit a similar reproductive strategy to that of other Lamnid sharks, such as the white shark. Embryos develop inside their mother, but are primarily nourished by feeding on unfertilized eggs in the womb (oophagy) (Dulvy and Reynolds, 1997). A single functional ovary contains a litter of six embryos, each encased in egg cases that hatch within the uterus (aplacental viviparity). Size at birth ranges from 150 cm to 170 cm TL, with a gestation period lasting between one and three years (Compagno *et al.*, 2004). It is thought that there is likely to be a resting period of at least one year between pregnancies, and therefore, taking into account the gestation period, a 2–4-year interval between litters (Pauly, 2002; Compagno *et al.*, 2004). Wounds caused by copulation have been recorded on basking sharks in British waters in May (Matthews and Parker, 1950), suggesting that mating may take place in early summer.

Growth

The maximum size attained by white sharks is estimated to be around 6 m TL (Compagno *et al.*, 2004). The majority of females mature between 450<cm> and 500 cm TL (Francis, 1996), and males mature between 350 and 410 cm TL (Pratt, 1996). Age at maturity is estimated at 12–17 years for females and 7–9 years for males. Life span is expected to be approximately 50+ years (Cailliet *et al.*, 2001).

The maximum size attained by whale sharks is a heavily debated topic, with the largest female so far estimated to be 20 m TL (Chen *et al.*, 1997), although other sources suggest a maximum length of up to 16–18 m TL (Colman, 1997; Sequeira *et al.*, 2013). Females are thought to reach sexual maturity by at least 7.7 m TL (Fowler, 2000). The presence of scars and abrasions on the claspers of whale sharks over 9 m TL at Ningaloo Marine Park (Norman, 1999) suggest that sexual activity, at least in males, is not common before attaining this length. No one has yet provided valid growth rates (in the wild), age at maturity or maximum age for whale sharks, although Pauly (2002) suggested a slow growth rate and estimated a life span of up to 100 years.

The maximum size attained by a basking shark is almost 14 m TL, with females maturing at 8–10 m TL and males at 5–7 m TL (Compagno *et al.*, 2004). Age at maturity is estimated at 16–20 years for females and 12–16 years for males (Compagno, 1984). The smallest free-swimming individuals recorded are about 1.7 m TL (Parker and Stott, 1965). However, the young are very rarely encountered until they reach more than 3 m TL (Compagno, 1984). Growth is estimated at 40 cm per year and life expectancy is thought to be similar to the white shark, i.e. approximately 50+ years (Pauly, 2002).

Diet

The global importance of pinnipeds (seals and sealions) as prey for white sharks is a popular view that is likely overstated, due to the regional bias in field observations towards areas where sharks and pinnipeds are sympatric. As a result, the role of white sharks as primary predators of pinnipeds has dominated much research due to the focus on seal predation being related to attacks on humans. In fact, before reaching sexual maturity white sharks have a predominantly piscivorous diet made up of a range of bony fishes, from sedentary demersal and benthic species to fast pelagic species, and ranging in size from small demersal and schooling fishes to large swordfishes and bluefin tuna. Adult white sharks are also active hunters of small cetaceans (whales, dolphins and porpoises), particularly in regions where pinnipeds are scarce or absent (Compagno *et al.*, 2004). Dead baleen whales and other large cetaceans may also contribute a significant amount to their diet in some areas (Fallows *et al.*, 2013). Isotopic analysis of vertebrae has revealed two distinct ontogenetic trophic shifts for white sharks: one following parturition (birth), marking a dietary switch from the absorption of yolk to predating on fishes; and one at a total length of >341 cm, representing a diet shift from larger fishes to marine mammals (Estrada *et al.*, 2006).

Whale sharks are one of only three species of filter feeding sharks, the other two being the megamouth (*Megachasma pelagios*) and basking (*Cetorhinus maximus*) sharks. Unlike the other two species, whale sharks do not rely on forward motion for filtration, but are able to hang vertically in the water column and suction feed by closing their gill slits and opening their mouths. It is thought that they are capable of detecting the tiny bioelectric fields of zooplankton as small as 1 mm in diameter (Kempster and Collin, 2011a, 2011b) and sieve them through the fine mesh of their gill-rakers (Taylor, 1994). They typically feed upon a variety of planktonic prey, small crustaceans and schooling fishes (Norman, 1999; Last and Stevens, 2009).

Basking sharks are typically associated with large surface aggregations of zooplankton, particularly along tidal and shelf-break fronts (Sims and Merrett, 1997; Sims *et al.*, 2003). In addition to zooplankton, they also feed on fish eggs and small fishes (Compagno *et al.*, 2004). By swimming open-mouthed with their gill-rakers erect and extended between the gill arches, they form a sieve to collect their prey (Matthews and Parker, 1950). Although they are regularly sighted at the surface, their large liver and high squalene levels are characteristic of deepwater sharks. In fact, during winter months, when zooplankton abundance is low, basking sharks shed their gill-rakers and spend their time in deeper water (Parker and Boeseman, 1954). As a result, it was previously thought that the basking sharks rests in deep water over winter, utilizing food reserves in its large liver (Parker and Boeseman, 1954). However, more recent energetics and tagging studies indicate that feeding still takes place at this time and that extensive horizontal and vertical migrations are undertaken throughout the winter months (Sims and Quayle, 1998; Sims *et al.*, 2003).

Developments in our understanding of sharks continually shape the way we view different species in the context of their conservation. For example, what once was a species thought to be in need of protection may now be one considered abundant, not necessarily through the implementation of protection measures, but through a better understanding of this species' life history. Therefore, to adequately protect a species we must first ensure that we understand their basic biology to know how, if at all, we can help them. Given the biological diversity among shark species, particularly the three iconic species in question, it is likely that their protection will require a multi-level approach, from international to local management.

Protection of iconic species

Population trend and current status

Many shark species are susceptible to rapid population decline, as they are slow to mature and have relatively low fecundity (Dulvy *et al.*, 2008; Stevens *et al.*, 2000a). In addition, localized population decline may be increased by fidelity to favoured sites (Hueter *et al.*, 2005). White sharks exemplify these traits (Smith *et al.*, 1998; Bruce *et al.*, 2006; Dulvy *et al.*, 2008) and, as a result, several abundance estimates suggest that their populations have declined significantly during the twentieth century, in parallel with the rise of industrialized fishing and marine recreation (Pepperell, 1992; Krogh, 1994; Baum *et al.*, 2003; Towner *et al.*, 2013) (Table 11.1). Threats to this species include targeted commercial and sports fisheries (Dulvy *et al.*, 2008), protective beach meshing programmes (Krogh, 1994), media-fuelled campaigns to kill white sharks in response to attacks on humans and degradation of inshore habitats used as nursery grounds. Nowhere in the world are white shark populations abundant and productive enough to sustain long-term directed fisheries. Notably, they are rarely represented in the elasmobranch by-catch of offshore oceanic pelagic fisheries (unlike shortfin mako (*Isurus oxyrinchus*) and porbeagle (*Lamna nasus*) sharks) (Dulvy *et al.*, 2008). Recent abundance estimates of white sharks in South Africa suggest that their numbers may be 50 per cent lower than previously thought (Towner *et al.*, 2013). Baum *et al.* (2003) estimated that white shark populations had declined by as much as 79 per cent between 1979 and 2003 (Table 11.1). The Vulnerable to Extinction status declared for white sharks by the International Union for the Conservation of Nature (IUCN) *Red List of Threatened Species* has remained unchanged since 1996, with its most recent assessment in 2009 (Fergusson *et al.*, 2009). In the Mediterranean, the species is listed as endangered (Cavanagh and Gibson, 2007). Where white shark populations are unprotected, their iconic status and the high value of their jaws and fins mean that they are subject to exploitation (Dulvy *et al.*, 2008). The removal of even a few individuals may have significant effects at discrete locations, such as the Farallon Islands in California, where, based upon observations following the cull of four local sharks in 1984, a significant drop in the predation of elephant seals was recorded (Pyle *et al.*, 1996).

Fisheries targeting whale sharks were prevalent in Southeast Asia and India prior to the turn of the last century (Joung *et al.*, 1996; Cavanagh *et al.*, 2003;

Table 11.1 Summary of population trend data for the white shark (*Carcharias carcharodon*).

Year	*Location*	*Data used*	*Trend*	*Source*
1986–2000	Northwest Atlantic	US pelagic long-line fleet catch data (CPUE)	79 per cent decline	Baum *et al.*, 2003
1978–1999	KwaZulu Natal, South Africa	Annual CPUE in beach protection nets	>60 per cent decline	Dudley, 2002
1950–1999	New South Wales, Australia	Annual CPUE in beach protection nets	>70 per cent decline	Reid and Krogh 1992; Malcolm *et al.*, 2001
1962–1998	Queensland Australia	Annual CPUE in beach protection nets and drum lines	60–75 per cent decline	Malcolm *et al.*, 2001
1966–1993	KwaZulu Natal, South Africa	Annual CPUE in beach protection nets	>66 per cent decline	Cliff *et al.*, 1996
1860–1990s	Adriatic Sea	All known records	>80 per cent decline	Soldo and Jardas, 2002
1980–1990	South Australia	Annual game fishing catch	94 per cent decline	Presser and Allen, 1995
1961–1990	Southeastern Australia	Capture in sports fishery relative to other large sharks	95 per cent decline	Pepperell, 1992
1950–1970	New South Wales, Australia	Average length of sharks caught in nets	Decline from 2.5 m to 1.7 m	NSW Fisheries, 1997

Source: CITES, 2004

Note
CPUE: catch per unit effort.

Stevens, 2007). Over this time, whale shark fisheries around the world were experiencing huge declines in catches (Joung *et al.*, 1996; Fowler, 2000; Chen *et al.*, 2002). Alava *et al.* (2002) describes a Taiwanese fishery from 1990 to 1997, during which time up to 799 whale sharks were taken. The fishery peaked in 1993 when approximately 180 sharks were landed, then steadily declined at an average rate of 27 per cent per year. Whale sharks were primarily taken for their meat, liver oil and fins (Compagno, 1984; Ramachandran and Sankar, 1990; Trono, 1996; Hanfee, 2001; Alava *et al.*, 2002). Liver oil was traditionally used for water-proofing boat hulls, and the huge fins, which were previously regarded as poor quality and thus not highly sought after (Chen *et al.*, 2002), are now demanding much higher prices, resulting in fisherman targeting larger specimens (Li *et al.*, 2012). Considering the highly lucrative shark fin industry and the emergence of a good market for fins and other body parts, whale sharks are increasingly likely to become the target of fisheries in China (Li *et al.*, 2012). As a consequence of declining landings, whale sharks were classified as vulnerable in 2000 by the IUCN *Red List* and worldwide fisheries were eventually banned (Li *et al.*, 2012). Although most of the bans happened more than a decade ago, a review of their IUCN *Red List* classification resulted in no change of status (Norman, 2005). The continuation of the Vulnerable status of whale sharks may be due to the low scrutiny of the implementation of regional bans, the Taiwanese commercial fisheries continuing to target whale sharks until 2007 and continued illegal fishing (Stewart and Wilson, 2005).

Fisheries targeting basking sharks have been characterized by distinct, long-term declines in landings following the removal of hundreds to thousands of individuals (CITES, 2002; Fowler, 2005b; Dulvy *et al.*, 2008). A few well-documented declines in catches by fisheries targeting basking sharks showed reduction in catches between 50 per cent and over 90 per cent (CITES, 2002; Fowler, 2005a). The large fins of basking sharks are among the most valuable on the international trade market (Fleming and Papageorgiou, 1997; Fowler, 2005b). Compagno (1984) considered the species to be extremely vulnerable to overfishing due to its slow growth, long-time maturity, long gestation period and low fecundity. Similar to white sharks and whale sharks, the vulnerable status declared for basking sharks by the IUCN has remained unchanged since 1996, with its most recent assessment being in 2005 (Fowler, 2005b). However, the North Pacific and Northeast Atlantic basking shark populations, which have been subject to target fisheries, are currently assessed as endangered (Fowler, 2005b). These assessments are based primarily on past records of rapidly declining local populations of basking sharks as a result of short-term fisheries exploitation and very slow population recovery rates. The basking shark has been exploited for several centuries for its liver oil (which can constitute up to 25 per cent of its body mass and is commonly used for lighting and other industrial applications), skin (which is often used as an alternative to leather) and flesh (which is used for food or fishmeal) (Rose, 1996; Fowler, 2005b).

Current level of protection

In addition to CITES and CMS, some states have taken extra steps to protect vulnerable (and iconic) species of sharks such as the white, whale and basking sharks, in their national waters: white sharks are currently protected at a national level in Australia, South Africa, Namibia, Israel, Malta and the United States (Fergusson *et al.*, 2009); whale sharks are protected in Australia, the Maldives, Philippines, India, Thailand, Malaysia, Honduras, Mexico, US Atlantic waters and a small area off Belize (Fowler, 2000; Chen *et al.*, 2002; Norman, 2005); basking sharks, which are strictly protected in the United Kingdom, Malta, New Zealand (but by-catch may be utilized) and US federal waters (Fowler, 2005b), are also listed in Annex II (Endangered or Threatened Species) of the *Barcelona Convention for the Protection of the Mediterranean Sea* (1976) Protocol Concerning Specially Protected Areas and Biological Diversity in the Mediterranean. The Mediterranean population of basking sharks is also listed in Appendix I of the *Bern Convention for the Conservation of European Wildlife and Habitats*.

In recent years, a number of countries have adopted policies that completely prohibit the possession and sale of shark products, irrespective of the species, which may afford additional protection to white, whale and basking sharks. Although these laws are strict and meant to act as a serious deterrent, loopholes and inadequate enforcement continue to undermine them. The legal trade in shark fins and the difficulty in identifying a species once fins are removed from the body continue to fuel the illegal trade of high-value fins from protected species (Marshall, 2011). Australia, for example, has developed a comprehensive and multi-disciplinary recovery plan for white sharks in its waters, but even Australia is not without an illegal trade in shark fins (Anderson and McCusker, 2005; Griffiths *et al.*, 2008; Marshall, 2011). CITES and CMS listings may have helped to slow down international trade in products from these vulnerable shark species, but they have not, and will not, completely eliminate the illegal trade, particularly while there is still a legal trade in place for the detached body parts (fins, teeth, cartilage, etc.) of other shark species.

Economic value of iconic species

Eco-tourism is becoming increasingly popular around the world. Such tourism can be a conservation tool by enabling wildlife to generate income, which subsequently benefits its own survival, purely by its existence as a viewing spectacle. The shark eco-tourism industry is a growing source of employment and tourism expenditures for many locations worldwide. The protection of live sharks, especially through dedicated protected areas, can directly benefit this industry. Cisneros-Montemayor *et al.* (2013) assessed the economic value of shark ecotourism worldwide and compared it to the value of sharks landed in shark fisheries (directed and by-catch) as reported to the FAO. They found that shark eco-tourism generates over US$314 million per year, a figure that could double in the next 20 years if current tourism trends continue. By comparison, the reported landed value of shark fisheries has been in decline despite an increase in fishing effort and extent (Cisneros-Montemayor *et al.*, 2013). Their results suggest that if trends continue, the protection of shark species could have important economic benefits.

White shark tourism has become very popular around the world, particularly in South Australia and South Africa, where these sharks are protected from all commercial fishing operations. Ironically, it is the perceived danger associated with these sharks that make them especially appealing to the growing eco-adventure market (Dobson *et al.*, 2005; Dobson, 2007). The exposure of the public to white sharks is probably one of the most significant contributions that wildlife tourism can make towards the conservation of sharks. Psychological theory supports the notion of exposing individuals to stimuli that can result in the enhancement of their attitudes towards it (Higham and Lück, 2007).

Whale shark-based tourism has highlighted the inherent value of live sharks (Anderson and Waheed, 2001; Cisneros-Montemayor *et al.*, 2013), with related incomes replacing those once provided by targeted fisheries (Quiros, 2005, 2007). Established tourism operations continue to expand throughout the world at known whale shark aggregation sites, such as in the Seychelles, Australia and Mexico. These tourism operators play an important role in conservation because they exemplify the economic benefits of sustainable wildlife tourism. Tourism has also been useful for whale shark researchers because photographs taken during diving operations are used to identify returning individuals (Speed *et al.*, 2007), which provides data essential for estimating abundance and other useful metrics (Meekan *et al.*, 2006; Rowat *et al.*, 2009).

Basking shark operations in the United Kingdom have also been shown to work as a successful eco-tourism option for safely viewing sharks. While the basking and whale shark watching industries are still relatively young, the large size and non-threatening character of these sharks, coupled with easily accessible snorkelling encounter opportunities, allow for a reliable and profitable industry (Gallagher and Hammerschlag, 2011). Moreover, with increasing international restrictions on the consumptive use of these species, eco-tourism is likely to benefit even further in the future.

Conclusions and recommendations for the future

Maximizing biodiversity among shark species is a key factor in their successful conservation (Faith, 1992; Witting and Loeschcke, 1995; Crozier, 1997). The importance of an individual species to a particular ecosystem may be reflected in the amount of divergence in their evolutionary history. For example, the extinction of a species from a species-poor clade[3] (i.e. white, whale and basking sharks) would result in a greater loss of biodiversity (i.e. loss of unique evolutionary history) than that of a recently evolved species with many close relatives (Isaac *et al.*, 2007, 2012). Therefore, the loss of this species would have a greater impact on the ecosystems to which it is connected. However, conserving such species may be difficult, since there is some evidence that they are more likely to be threatened with extinction than expected by chance (Purvis *et al.*, 2000). The heightened extinction risk associated with species-poor clades greatly increases the loss of biodiversity compared to a model of random extinction (Heard and Mooers, 2000) and suggests that entire shark orders may be at risk if evolutionarily distinct species are not adequately protected (McKinney, 1998). Consequently, it is possible that evolutionary history is being rapidly lost and that these distinct species are not being identified as high priorities in existing conservation frameworks (Issac *et al.*, 2007).

White, whale and basking sharks represent some of the world's most unique evolutionarily distinct shark species and, therefore, warrant protection for their diversity alone. Moreover, each of these species exhibits life history traits that make them particularly susceptible to even small levels of exploitation. According to the IUCN *Red List*, the extinction vulnerability of these three iconic species of sharks has remained unchanged since they were awarded protection by CITES and CMS. Therefore, questions have to be raised over the effectiveness of such agreements for sharks and whether or not more should be done to protect these vulnerable species. The persistent occurrence of these sharks in the fin trade and the poor recognition of their important role in ocean ecosystems continue to undermine international policy that attempts to protect them. To prioritize current shark conservation efforts, every attempt should be made to ensure the implementation of adequate protection for not only vulnerable species but also evolutionarily distinct species (e.g. white, whale and basking sharks) whose contribution to global biodiversity will safeguard a future for sharks.

International agreements for the protection of evolutionarily distinct and migratory shark species are essential to ensuring their survival, but such agreements will inevitably fail if we do not fully understand the life history of individual species. Much of the information we use to assess the vulnerability of the three iconic species (white, whale and basking sharks) was published prior to their protection and so a significant effort is needed to further our understanding to better inform law and policy. For example, a decline in whale shark sightings along the eastern coast of South Africa between 1993 and 1998 (Gifford, 2001) was originally included in the successful proposal for listing the species in Appendix II of CITES (Rohner *et al.*, 2013). However, with the benefit of hindsight, the substantial variability in sighting data from this area in the summer months (Cliff *et al.*, 2007) and seasonal changes in their oceanic distribution (Sequeira *et al.*, 2012, 2013) makes it difficult to attribute these earlier data to a genuine population decline. Similarly, a steep decline in the catches of basking sharks off Achill Island in Ireland between 1947 and 1975 was initially attributed to localized stock depletion (Parker and Stott, 1965). However, re-analysis of these data, in conjunction with the analysis of planktonic copepod abundance at this and other sites (Sims and Reid, 2002), suggests that the decrease may have resulted from a shift in prey, and hence basking shark distribution, rather than strictly due to population decline as a result of fishing (Sims, 2008; Rohner *et al.*, 2013). Thus, a complete understanding of a species' life history and global population trends is extremely valuable and necessary to determine specific international and national conservation requirements. The Galapagos shark, *Carcharhinus galapagensis*, for example, is not considered to be threatened globally, according to the IUCN. Yet a distinct population once found to be abundant around the Archipelago of St. Paul's Rocks (equatorial Atlantic) is now considered to be locally extinct as a result of a sharp decline in abundance that took place following the commencement of commercial fishing (Luiz and Edwards, 2011). Ongoing scientific research is, therefore, essential to developing appropriate conservation strategies, but scientists also need to foster interdisciplinary and international collaborations to ensure that new findings inform the appropriate law and policy, which will ultimately facilitate positive change.

Notes

1 Random mating within a breeding population.
2 The behaviour of remaining in, or returning to, an individual's birth place.
3 A phylogenetic lineage with few species.

References

Alava, M. N. R., Dolumbaló, E. R. Z., Yaptinchay, A. A. and Trono, R. B. (2002) 'Fishery and trade of whale sharks and manta rays in the Bohol Sea, Philippines', *Elasmobranch Biodiversity, Conservation and Management: Proceedings of the International Seminar and Workshop*, July 1997, pp. 132–148.

Anderson, C. and Waheed, A. (2001) 'The economics of shark and ray watching in the Maldives', *IUCN Newsletter: Shark News*, July, p. 20.

Anderson, K. M. and McCusker, R. (2005) 'Crime in the Australian fishing industry: key issues', *Trends and Issues in Crime and Criminal Justice*, April, p. 6.

Baum, J. K. and Myers, R. A. (2004) 'Shifting baselines and the decline of pelagic sharks in the Gulf of Mexico', *Ecology Letters*, vol. 7, pp. 135–145.

Baum, J. K., Myers, R. A., Kehler, D. G., Worm, B., Harley, S. J. and Doherty, P. A. (2003) 'Collapse and conservation of shark populations in the Northwest Atlantic', *Science*, vol. 299, pp. 389–392.

Blower, D. C., Pandolfi, J. M., Bruce, B. D., Gomez-Cabrera, M. C. and Ovenden, J. R. (2012) 'Population genetics of Australian white sharks reveals fine-scale spatial structure, transoceanic dispersal events and low effective population sizes', *Marine Ecology Progress Series*, vol. 455, pp. 229–244.

Bonfil, R., Meyer, M., Scholl, M. C., Johnson, R., O'Brien, S., Oosthuizen, H., Swanson, S., Kotze, D. and Paterson, M. (2005) 'Transoceanic migration, spatial dynamics, and population linkages of white sharks', *Science*, vol. 310, pp. 100–103.

Boustany, A. M., Davis, S. F., Pyle, P., Anderson, S. D., LeBoeuf, B. J. and Block, B. A. (2002) 'Expanded niche for white sharks', *Nature*, vol. 415, pp. 35–36.

Bruce, B. (1992) 'Preliminary observations on the biology of the white shark, *Carcharodon carcharias*, in South Australian Waters', *Australian Journal of Marine and Freshwater Research*, vol. 43, pp. 1–11.

Bruce, B., Stevens, J. and Malcolm, H. (2006) 'Movements and swimming behaviour of white sharks (*Carcharodon carcharias*) in Australian waters', *Marine Biology*, vol. 150, pp. 161–172.

Brunnschweiler, J. M., Baensch, H., Pierce, S. J. and Sims, D. W. (2009) 'Deep-diving behaviour of a whale shark *Rhincodon typus* during long-distance movement in the western Indian Ocean', *Journal of Fish Biology*, vol. 74, pp. 706–714.

Cailliet, G. M., Andrews, A. H., Burton, E. J., Watters, D. L., Kline, D. E. and Ferry-Graham, L. A. (2001) 'Age determination and validation studies of marine fishes: do deep-dwellers live longer?', *Experimental Gerontology*, vol. 36, pp. 739–764.

Carlson, J. K., Hale, L. F., Morgan, A. and Burgess, G. (2012) 'Relative abundance and size of coastal sharks derived from commercial shark longline catch and effort data', *Journal of Fish Biology*, vol. 80, pp. 1749–1764.

Cavanagh, R. D. and Gibson, C. (2007) *Overview of the Conservation Status of Cartilaginous Fishes (Chrondrichthyans) in the Mediterranean Sea*, IUCN Red List of Threatened Species, Mediterranean Regional Assessment No. 3.

Cavanagh, R. D., Kyne, P. M., Fowler, S. L., Musick, J. A. and Bennett, M. B. (2003) *The Conservation Status of Australasian Chondrichthyans*, Report of the IUCN Shark Specialist Group Australia and Oceania Regional Red List Workshop, 7–9 March.

Chen, C. T., Liu, K. M. and Joung, S. J. (1997) 'Preliminary report on Taiwan's whale shark fishery', *TRAFFIC Bulletin*, vol. 17, pp. 53–57.

Chen, V. Y., Phipps, M. J. and Asia, T. E. (2002) *Management and Trade of Whale Sharks in Taiwan*, TRAFFIC East Asia-Taipei.

Cisneros-Montemayor, A. M., Barnes-Mauthe, M., Al-Abdulrazzak, D., Navarro-Holm, E. and Sumaila, U. R. (2013) 'Global economic value of shark ecotourism: implications for conservation', *Oryx*, vol. 47, pp. 1–8.

CITES (2002) *Convention of International Trade in Endangered Species of Wild Fauna and Flora*, Appendix II listing of the basking shark.

CITES (2004) *Convention of International Trade in Endangered Species of Wild Fauna and Flora*, Appendix II listing of the white shark (revision 1).

Clarke, S. C., McAllister, M. K., Milner-Gulland, E. J., Kirkwood, G. P., Michielsens, C. G. J., Agnew, D. J., Pikitch, E. K., Nakano, H. and Shivji, M. S. (2006) 'Global estimates of shark catches using trade records from commercial markets', *Ecology Letters*, vol. 9, pp. 1115–1126.

Cliff, G., Dudley, S. and Jury, M. (1996) 'Catches of white sharks in KwaZulu-Natal, South Africa and environmental influences', in A. P. Klimley and D. G. Ainley (eds), *Great White Sharks: The Biology of* Carcharodon carcharias, Academic Press, San Diego, CA.

Cliff, G., Anderson-Reade, M. D., Aitken, A. P., Charter, G. E. and Peddemors, V. M. (2007) 'Aerial census of whale sharks (*Rhincodon typus*) on the northern KwaZulu-Natal coast, South Africa', *Fisheries Research*, vol. 84, pp. 41–46.

Colman, J. G. (1997) 'A review of the biology and ecology of the whale shark', *Journal of Fish Biology*, vol. 51, pp. 1219–1234.

Compagno, L. J. V. (1984) *FAO Species Catalogue. Vol. 4. Sharks of the World. An Annotated and Illustrated Catalogue of Shark Species Known to Date*, FAO, Rome.

Compagno, L., Dando, M. and Fowler, S. (2004) *Sharks of the World*, HarperCollins Publishers Ltd, London.

Crozier, R. (1997) 'Preserving the information content of species: genetic diversity, phylogeny, and conservation worth', *Annual Review of Ecology and Systematics*, vol. 28, pp. 243–268.

Davis, B. and Worm, B. (2013) 'The International Plan of Action for Sharks: how does national implementation measure up?', *Marine Policy*, vol. 38, pp. 312–320.

Dobson, J. (2007) *Shark! A New Frontier in Tourist Demand for Marine Wildlife, Marine Wildlife and Tourism Management: Insights from the Natural and Social Sciences*, CABI Publishing, Wallingford.

Dobson, J., Jones, E. and Botterill, D. (2005) 'Exploitation or conservation: can wildlife tourism help conserve vulnerable and endangered species?', *Interdisciplinary Environmental Review*, vol. 7, pp. 1–12.

Dudley, S. (2002) *Shark Catch Trends and Effort Reduction in the Beach Protection Program, KwaZulu-Natal, South Africa*, Northwest Atlantic Fisheries Organization, Scientific Council Meeting, September.

Duffy, C. A. J. (2002) 'Distribution, seasonality, lengths, and feeding behaviour of whale sharks (*Rhincodon typus*) observed in New Zealand waters', *New Zealand Journal of Marine and Freshwater Research*, vol. 36, pp. 565–570.

Dulvy, N. K. and Reynolds, J. D. (1997) 'Evolutionary transitions among egg-laying, live-bearing and maternal inputs in sharks and rays', *Proceedings of the Royal Society of London Series B: Biological Sciences*, vol. 264, pp. 1309–1315.

Dulvy, N. K., Baum, J. K., Clarke, S., Compagno, L. J. V., Cortés, E., Domingo, A., Fordham, S., Fowler, S., Francis, M. P., Gibson, C., Martínez, J., Musick, J. A., Soldo, A., Stevens, J. D. and Valenti, S. (2008) 'You can swim but you can't hide: the global status and conservation of oceanic pelagic sharks and rays', *Aquatic Conservation: Marine and Freshwater Ecosystems*, vol. 18, pp. 459–482.

Estrada, J. A., Rice, A. N., Natanson, L. J. and Skomal, G. B. (2006) 'Use of isotopic analysis of vertebrae in reconstructing ontogenetic feeding ecology in white sharks', *Ecology*, vol. 87, pp. 829–834.

Faith, D. P. (1992) 'Conservation evaluation and phylogenetic diversity', *Biological Conservation*, vol. 61, pp. 1–10.

Fallows, C., Gallagher, A. J. and Hammerschlag, N. (2013) 'White sharks *Carcharodon carcharias* scavenging on whales and its potential role in further shaping the ecology of an apex predator', *PLoS ONE*, vol. 8.

Fergusson, I., Compagno, L. J. V. and Marks, M. (2009) '*Carcharodon carcharias*', *IUCN Red List of Threatened Species. Version 2012.2*, available at www.iucnredlist.org, accessed 1 May 2013.

Ferretti, F., Worm, B., Britten, G. L., Heithaus, M. R. and Lotze, H. K. (2010) 'Patterns and ecosystem consequences of shark declines in the ocean', *Ecology Letters*, vol. 13, pp. 1055–1071.

Fleming, E. H. and Papageorgiou, P. A. (1997) *Shark Fisheries and Trade in Europe*, TRAFFIC Europe Report, March.

Fowler, S. L. (2000) *Whale Shark* Rhincodon typus*: Policy and Research Scoping Study*, Nature Conservation Bureau, June–September.

Fowler, S. L. (2005a) *Sharks, Rays and Chimaeras: The Status of the Chondrichthyan Fishes*, IUCN.

Fowler, S. L. (2005b) '*Cetorhinus maximus*', *IUCN Red List of Threatened Species. Version 2012.2*, available at www.iucnredlist.org, accessed 1 May 2013.

Francis, M. P. (1996) 'Observations on a pregnant white shark with a review of reproductive biology', in A. P. Klimley and D. G. Ainley (eds), *Great White Sharks: The Biology of* Carcharodon carcharias, Academic Press, New York.

Francis, M. and Duffy, C. (2002) 'Distribution, seasonal abundance and bycatch of basking sharks (*Cetorhinus maximus*) in New Zealand, with observations on their winter habitat', *Marine Biology*, vol. 140, pp. 831–842.

Gallagher, A. J. and Hammerschlag, N. (2011) 'Global shark currency: the distribution, frequency, and economic value of shark ecotourism', *Current Issues in Tourism*, vol. 14, pp. 797–812.

Gifford, A. (2001) *Aerial Surveys of Whale Sharks (*Rhincodon typus*) off the East Coast of Southern Africa from 1993 to 1998*, Report to Shark Research Institute, Durban, SA.

Gilmore, R. G. (1993) 'Reproductive biology of lamnoid sharks', *Environmental Biology of Fishes*, vol. 38, pp. 95–114.

Gore, M. A., Rowat, D., Hall, J., Gell, F. R. and Ormond, R. F. (2008) 'Transatlantic migration and deep mid-ocean diving by basking shark', *Biology Letters*, vol. 4, pp. 395–398.

Graham, R. T. and Roberts, C. M. (2007) 'Assessing the size, growth rate and structure of a seasonal population of whale sharks (*Rhincodon typus* Smith 1828) using conventional tagging and photo identification', *Fisheries Research*, vol. 84, pp. 71–80.

Graham, R. T., Roberts, C. M. and Smart, J. C. R. (2006) 'Diving behaviour of whale sharks in relation to a predictable food pulse', *Journal of the Royal Society Interface*, vol. 3, pp. 109–116.

Griffiths, S., Edgar, S., Wang, Y. and Salini, J. (2008) *Calculating Recent Foreign Fishing Vessel Numbers Using Established Estimators Based on Coastwatch Surveillance and Apprehension Data*, CSIRO Marine and Atmospheric Research, Melbourne.

Hanfee, F. (2001) *Trade in Whale Shark and its Products in the Coastal State of Gujarat, India*, TRAFFIC India, New Delhi.

Heard, S. B. and Mooers, A. Ø. (2000) 'Measuring the loss of evolutionary history from extinction: phylogenetically patterned speciation rates and extinction risks alter the calculus of biodiversity', *Proceedings of the Royal Society of London Series B: Biological Sciences*, vol. 267, pp. 613–620.

Herndon, A., Gallucci, V. F., DeMaster, D. and Burke, W. (2010) 'The case for an international commission for the conservation and management of sharks (ICCMS)', *Marine Policy*, vol. 34, pp. 1239–1248.

Higham, J. E. S. and Lück, M. (2007) *Marine Wildlife and Tourism Management: Insights from the Natural and Social Sciences*, CABI Publishing, Wallingford.

Hisano, M., Connolly, S. R. and Robbins, W. D. (2011) 'Population growth rates of reef sharks with and without fishing on the Great Barrier Reef: robust estimation with multiple models', *PLoS ONE*, vol. 6.

Hoelzel, R. A., Shivji, M. S., Magnussen, J. E. and Francis, M. P. (2006) 'Low worldwide genetic diversity in the basking shark (*Cetorhinus maximus*)', *Biology Letters*, vol. 2, pp. 639–642.

Hueter, R. E., Heupel, M. R., Heist, E. J. and Keeney, D. B. (2005) 'Evidence of philopatry in sharks and implications for the management of shark fisheries', *Journal of the Northwest Atlantic Fisheries Science*, vol. 35, pp. 239–247.

Isaac, N. J. B., Turvey, S. T., Collen, B., Waterman, C. and Baillie, J. E. M. (2007) 'Mammals on the EDGE: conservation priorities based on threat and phylogeny', *PLoS ONE*, vol. 2.

Isaac, N. J. B., Redding, D. W., Meredith, H. M. and Safi, K. (2012) 'Phylogenetically-informed priorities for amphibian conservation', *PLoS ONE*, vol. 7.

Jorgensen, S. J., Reeb, C. A., Chapple, T. K., Anderson, S., Perle, C., Van Sommeran, S. R., Fritz-Cope, C., Brown, A. C., Klimley, A. P. and Block, B. A. (2010) 'Philopatry and migration of Pacific white sharks', *Proceedings of the Royal Society B: Biological Sciences*, vol. 277, pp. 679–688.

Joung, S. J., Chen, C. T., Clark, E., Uchida, S. and Huang, W. Y. P. (1996) 'The whale shark, *Rhincodon typus*, is a livebearer: 300 embryos found in one "megamamma" supreme', *Environmental Biology of Fishes*, vol. 46, pp. 219–223.

Kempster, R. M. and Collin, S. P. (2011a) 'Electrosensory pore distribution and feeding in the megamouth shark *Megachasma pelagios* (Lamniformes: Megachasmidae)', *Aquatic Biology*, vol. 11, pp. 225–228.

Kempster, R. M. and Collin, S. P. (2011b) 'Electrosensory pore distribution and feeding in the basking shark *Cetorhinus maximus* (Lamniformes: Cetorhinidae)', *Aquatic Biology*, vol. 12, pp. 33–36.

Krogh, M. (1994) 'Spatial, seasonal and biological analysis of sharks caught in the New-South-Wales Protective Beach Meshing Program', *Australian Journal of Marine and Freshwater Research*, vol. 45, pp. 1087–1106.

Lack, M. and Sant, G. (2011) *The Future of Sharks: A Review of Action and Inaction*, TRAFFIC International, Cambridge, and the Pew Environment Group, Washington, DC.

Lam, V. Y. Y. and Sadovy de Mitcheson, Y. (2011) 'The sharks of South East Asia: unknown, unmonitored and unmanaged', *Fish and Fisheries*, vol. 12, pp. 51–74.

Last, P. R. and Stevens, J. D. (2009) *Sharks and Rays of Australia*, Havard University Press, London.

Li, W., Wang, Y. and Norman, B. (2012) 'A preliminary survey of whale shark *Rhincodon typus* catch and trade in China: an emerging crisis', *Journal of Fish Biology*, vol. 80, pp. 1608–1618.

Luiz, O. J. and Edwards, A. J. (2011) 'Extinction of a shark population in the Archipelago of Saint Paul's Rocks (equatorial Atlantic) inferred from the historical record', *Biological Conservation*, vol. 144, pp. 2873–2881.

McKinney, M. L. (1998) 'Branching models predict loss of many bird and mammal orders within centuries', *Animal Conservation*, vol. 1, pp. 159–164.

Malcolm, H., Bruce, B. and Stevens, J. (2001) *A Review of the Biology and Status of White Sharks in Australian Waters*, CSIRO Marine and Atmospheric Research, Melbourne.

Marshall, L. J. (2011) 'The fin blue line: quantifying fishing mortality using shark fin morphology', PhD, University of Tasmania at Hobart TAS, Australia.

Matthews, L. H. and Parker, H. W. (1950) 'Notes on the anatomy and biology of the basking shark (*Cetorhinus maximus* (Gunner))', *Proceedings of the Zoological Society of London*, vol. 120, pp. 535–576.

Meekan, M. G., Bradshaw, C. J. A., Press, M., McLean, C., Richards, A., Quasnichka, S. and Taylor, J. G. (2006) 'Population size and structure of whale sharks *Rhincodon typus* at Ningaloo Reef, Western Australia', *Marine Ecology Progress Series*, vol. 319, pp. 275–285.

Neff, C. L. and Yang, J. Y. H. (2013) 'Shark bites and public attitudes: policy implications from the first before and after shark bite survey', *Marine Policy*, vol. 38, pp. 545–547.

Norman, B. (1999) 'Aspects of the biology and ecotourism industry of the whale shark *Rhincodon typus* in North-Western Australia', MSc Thesis, Murdoch University at Murdoch WA, Australia.

Norman, B. (2005) '*Rhincodon typus*', *IUCN Red List of Threatened Species. Version 2012.2*, available at www.iucnredlist.org, accessed 1 May 2013.

NSW Fisheries (1997) *Great White Shark Protection in NSW*, Fishnote DF/68, pp. 1–2.

Pardini, A. T., Jones, C. S., Noble, L. R., Kreiser, B., Malcom, H., Bruce, B. D., Stevens, J. D., Cliff, G., Scholl, M. C., Francis, M. P., Duffy, C. A. J. and Martin, A. P. (2001) 'Sex-biased dispersal of great white sharks', *Nature*, vol. 412, pp. 139–140.

Parker, H. W. and Boeseman, M. (1954) 'The basking shark, *Cetorhinus maximus*, in winter', *Proceedings of the Zoological Society of London*, vol. 124, pp. 185–194.

Parker, H. W. and Stott, F. (1965) 'Age, size and vertebral calcification in the basking shark, *Cetorhinus maximus* (Gunnerus)', *Zoologische mededelingen*, vol. 40, pp. 305–319.

Pauly, D. (2002) *Growth and Mortality of the Basking Shark* Cetorhinus maximus *and Their Implications for Management of Whale Sharks* Rhincodon typus, Elasmobranch Biodiversity, Conservation and Management: Proceedings of the International Seminar and Workshop, July 1997.

Pepperell, J. G. (1992) 'Trends in the distribution, species composition and size of sharks caught by gamefish anglers off south-eastern Australia, 1961–90', *Australian Journal of Marine and Freshwater Research*, vol. 43, pp. 213–225.

Pratt, H. L. (1996) 'Reproduction in the male white shark', in A. P. Klimley and D. G. Ainley (eds), *Great White Sharks: The Biology of* Carcharodon carcharias, Academic Press, New York.

Presser, J. and Allen, R. (1995) *Management of the White Shark in South Australia*, SA Fisheries Management Series, May.

Purvis, A., Gittleman, J. L., Cowlishaw, G., Mace, G. M. (2000) 'Predicting extinction risk in declining species', *Proceedings of the Royal Society of London Series B: Biological Sciences*, vol. 267, no. 1456, pp. 1947–1952.

Pyle, P., Anderson, S. D., Ainley, D. G., Klimley, A. P. and Ainley, D. G. (1996) Trends in white shark predation at the South Farallon Islands, 1968–1993', *Great White Sharks: The Biology of* Carcharodon carcharias, Academic Press, New York.

Quiros, A. (2005) 'Whale shark "ecotourism" in the Philippines and Belize: evaluating conservation and community benefits', *Tropical Resources: Bulletin of the Yale Tropical Resources Institute*, vol. 24, pp. 42–48.

Quiros, A. L. (2007) 'Tourist compliance to a Code of Conduct and the resulting effects on whale shark (*Rhincodon typus*) behavior in Donsol, Philippines', *Fisheries Research*, vol. 84, pp. 102–108.

Ramachandran, A. and Sankar, T. (1990) 'Fin and finrays from whale shark (*Rhiniodon typus* Smith.)', *Fishery Technology*, vol. 27, pp. 138–140.

Reid, D. and Krogh, M. (1992) 'Assessment of catches from protective shark meshing off NSW beaches between 1950 and 1990', *Marine and Freshwater Research*, vol. 43, pp. 283–296.

Robbins, W. D., Hisano, M., Connolly, S. R. and Choat, J. H. (2006) 'Ongoing collapse of coral-reef shark populations', *Current Biology*, vol. 16, pp. 2314–2319.

Rohner, C., Pierce, S., Marshall, A., Weeks, S., Bennett, M. and Richardson, A. (2013) 'Trends in sightings and environmental influences on a coastal aggregation of manta rays and whale sharks', *Marine Ecology Progress Series*, vol. 482, pp. 153–168.

Rose, D. A. (1996) *An Overview of World Trade in Sharks and other Cartilaginous Fishes*, TRAFFIC Report.

Rowat, D. and Brooks, K. S. (2012) 'A review of the biology, fisheries and conservation of the whale shark *Rhincodon typus*', *Journal of Fish Biology*, vol. 80, pp. 1019–1056.

Rowat, D., Gore, M. A., Meekan, M. G., Lawler, I. R. and Bradshaw, C. J. A. (2009) 'Aerial survey as a tool to estimate whale shark abundance trends', *Journal of Experimental Marine Biology and Ecology*, vol. 368, pp. 1–8.

Sequeira, A., Mellin, C., Rowat, D., Meekan, M. G. and Bradshaw, C. J. A. (2012) 'Ocean-scale prediction of whale shark distribution', *Diversity and Distributions*, vol. 18, pp. 504–518.

Sequeira, A. M. M., Mellin, C., Meekan, M. G., Sims, D. W. and Bradshaw, C. J. A. (2013) 'Inferred global connectivity of whale shark *Rhincodon typus* populations', *Journal of Fish Biology*, vol. 82, pp. 367–389.

Simpfendorfer, C. A., Heupel, M. R., White, W. T. and Dulvy, N. K. (2011) 'The importance of research and public opinion to conservation management of sharks and rays: a synthesis', *Marine and Freshwater Research*, vol. 62, pp. 518–527.

Sims, D. W. (2008) 'Sieving a living: a review of the biology, ecology and conservation status of the plankton-feeding basking shark *Cetorhinus maximus*', in D. W. Sims (ed.) *Advances in Marine Biology*, Academic Press, New York.

Sims, D. and Merrett, D. (1997) 'Determination of zooplankton characteristics in the presence of surface feeding basking sharks *Cetorhinus maximus*', *Marine Ecology Progress Series*, vol. 158, pp. 297–302.

Sims, D. W. and Quayle, V. A. (1998) 'Selective foraging behaviour of basking sharks on zooplankton in a small-scale front', *Nature*, vol. 393, pp. 460–464.

Sims, D. W. and Reid, P. C. (2002) 'Congruent trends in long-term zooplankton decline in the north-east Atlantic and basking shark (*Cetorhinus maximus*) fishery catches off west Ireland', *Fisheries Oceanography*, vol. 11, pp. 59–63.

Sims, D. W., Southall, E. J., Richardson, A. J., Reid, P. C. and Metcalfe, J. D. (2003) 'Seasonal movements and behaviour of basking sharks from archival tagging: no evidence of winter hibernation', *Marine Ecology Progress Series*, vol. 248, pp. 187–196.

Smith, S. E., Au, D. W. and Show, C. (1998) 'Intrinsic rebound potentials of 26 species of Pacific sharks', *Marine and Freshwater Research*, vol. 49, pp. 663–678.

Soldo, A. and Jardas, I. (2002) 'Occurrence of great white shark, *Carcharodon carcharias* (Linnaeus, 1758) and basking shark, *Cetorhinus maximus* (Gunnerus, 1758) in the Eastern Adriatic and their protection', *Periodicum Biologorum*, vol. 104, pp. 195–201.

Speed, C. W., Meekan, M. G. and Bradshaw, C. J. (2007) 'Spot the match: wildlife photo-identification using information theory', *Frontiers in Zoology*, vol. 4, pp. 1–11.

Stevens, J. D. (2007) 'Whale shark (*Rhincodon typus*) biology and ecology: a review of the primary literature', *Fisheries Research*, vol. 84, pp. 4–9.

Stevens, J. D., Bonfil, R., Dulvy, N. K. and Walker, P. A. (2000a) 'The effects of fishing on sharks, rays, and chimaeras (chondrichthyans), and the implications for marine ecosystems', *ICES Journal of Marine Science: Journal du Conseil*, vol. 57, pp. 476–494.

Stevens, J. D., West, G. J. and McLoughlin, K. J. (2000b) 'Movements, recapture patterns, and factors affecting the return rate of carcharhinid and other sharks tagged off northern Australia', *Marine and Freshwater Research*, vol. 51, pp. 127–141.

Stewart, B. and Wilson, S. (2005) 'Threatened fishes of the world: *Rhincodon typus* (Smith 1828) (Rhincodontidae)', *Environmental Biology of Fishes*, vol. 74, pp. 184–185.

Taylor, J. G. (1994) *Whale Sharks: The Gentle Giants of Ningaloo Reef*, Angus and Robertson, Sydney.

Techera, E. J. (2012) 'Fishing, finning and tourism: trends in Pacific shark conservation and management', *The International Journal of Marine and Coastal Law*, vol. 27, pp. 597–621.

Towner, A. V., Wcisel, M. A., Reisinger, R. R., Edwards, D. and Jewell, O. J. D. (2013) 'Gauging the threat: the first population estimate for white sharks in South Africa using photo identification and automated software', *PLoS ONE*, vol. 8.

Trono, R. (1996) 'Philippine whale shark and manta ray fisheries', *IUCN Newsletter: Shark News*, vol. 7, p. 13.

Turnbull, S. D. and Randell, J. E. (2006) 'Rare occurrence of a *Rhincodon typus* (whale shark) in the Bay of Fundy, Canada', *Northeastern Naturalist*, vol. 13, pp. 57–58.

Verlecar, X. N., Snigdha, S. R. and Dhargalkar, V. K. (2007) 'Shark hunting: an indiscriminate trade endangering elasmobranchs to extinction', *Current Science*, vol. 92, pp. 1078–1082.

Vianna, G. M. S., Meekan, M. G., Pannell, D. J., Marsh, S. P. and Meeuwig, J. J. (2012) 'Socio-economic value and community benefits from shark-diving tourism in Palau: a sustainable use of reef shark populations', *Biological Conservation*, vol. 145, pp. 267–277.

Witting, L. and Loeschcke, V. (1995) 'The optimization of biodiversity conservation', *Biological Conservation*, vol. 71, pp. 205–207.

Worm, B., Davis, B., Kettemer, L., Ward-Paige, C. A., Chapman, D., Heithaus, M. R., Kessel, S. T. and Gruber, S. H. (2013) 'Global catches, exploitation rates, and rebuilding options for sharks', *Marine Policy*, vol. 40, pp. 194–204.

Chapter 12

Species at the intersection

Charlie Huveneers and William Robbins

Introduction

The previous chapter described the status, conservation efforts and threats posed to three iconic chondrichthyan species. These species have been historically difficult to study due to their relative low abundance and pelagic habitat. More recently, however, an increased understanding of their spatio-temporal distribution has allowed us to identify seasonal aggregation patterns of these species (Domeier, 2012; Rowat and Brooks, 2012). This, in turn, has facilitated an increase in the number of scientific studies investigating these animals (see also Chapter 5). White sharks, whale sharks and basking sharks are the focus of an increasing amount of scientific attention. For example, in the last six years, approximately 16 papers on *Rhincodon typus* have been published per year, compared to fewer than three papers per year between 1992 and 2005 (Sequeira *et al.*, 2013). White sharks, whale sharks and basking sharks have also been the focus of species-specific conferences (e.g. an international white shark symposium in Hawaii in 2010 (Domeier, 2012), an Isle of Man basking shark conference in 2009 and whale sharks have recently had their third conference dedicated to the species in Atlanta, United States).

There is, however, much more to the chondrichthyan fauna than these iconic species. With over 1,100 species described (White and Last, 2012), it is important to avoid directing management and research priorities based on iconic statuses or favouritism from the public. Many chondrichthyan species are the target of economically important and sustainable fisheries (Walker, 1998), but also ecologically unsustainable fisheries (Blaber *et al.*, 2009; Lack and Sant, 2009; White and Kyne, 2010). Other elasmobranch species are becoming increasingly targeted by wildlife tourism and have gained international and domestic protection in many countries and/or through international treaties (Group, 2012).

This chapter focuses on the potential effects of commercial and recreational fisheries, and wildlife tourism on a range of elasmobranch species. Reviews of shark-related tourism are examined to assess the species most targeted and the countries where such tourism is most frequent. The various management regulations used are discussed in relation to the economic status of these countries and the extent of their wildlife tourism opportunities. We then summarize the key benefits of wildlife tourism, emphasizing the economic value and ensuing influence on conservation regulations towards sharks.

Shark fisheries

Commercial fisheries

Elasmobranchs (sharks, rays and skates) have historically been considered of low economic value to large-scale fisheries (Camhi *et al.*, 1998), with commercial shark fisheries developing in the mid 1940s as a result of the wartime need for meat and vitamin A (Stevens *et al.*, 2000). More recently, fisheries have primarily targeted sharks in response to the rapidly increasing demand for fins, meat and, to a lesser extent, cartilage. There are varying estimates of world chondrichthyan or shark catches (e.g. Bonfil, 1994; Clarke *et al.*, 2006; Lack and Sant, 2006, 2009; Worm *et al.*, 2013). Global chondrichthyan catches peaked in the early 2000s at ~850,000 tonnes (Lack and Sant, 2006), representing an increase of more than four-fold from the 1947 estimate of ~200,000 tonnes (Bonfil, 1994). Catches have, however, recently experienced a slight decline, with 2007 catches being ~700,000 tonnes (Lack and Sant, 2009). Other estimates place shark catches to be much higher, with global shark catches of 1.44 million tonnes in 2000, reducing slightly to 1.41 million tonnes in 2010 (Worm *et al.*, 2013). This is comparable to the findings of Clarke *et al.* (2006), who estimated an annual median biomass from shark fin sales of 1.7 million tonnes in 2003. Reasons for the disparity in global catch estimates include under-reporting, illegal catches and lack of available shark data from domestic markets (Clarke *et al.*, 2006; Lack and Sant, 2008).

Chondrichthyans are regularly described as being highly susceptible to overfishing due to conservative life history characteristics, including slow growth, late maturity, low fecundity, long gestation periods, low natural mortality rates and long life (Holden, 1974, 1977). Yet, some chondrichthyans have life history characteristics permitting exploitation, and examples of sustainable chondrichthyan fisheries can be found around the world. For example, the Australian Southern shark fishery, which started in the 1920s, can arguably be described as one of the oldest and sustainable commercial shark fisheries in the world (see also Chapters 7 and 14). This multi-species gillnet fishery has commercially targeted gummy shark (*Mustelus antarcticus*) since the early 1970s, at which time gummy sharks were the most commonly commercially targeted shark species in southern Australia (Roach *et al.*, 2013). Commonwealth catches peaked in 1992–1993 at 2,435 tonnes, but have otherwise remained stable around 1,800 tonnes since 2001. At this level of exploitation, gummy sharks are considered to be sustainably harvested close to their maximum sustainable yield, with no signs of population depletion (Walker, 1998; Pribac *et al.*, 2005; FRDC, 2012; also see Chapter 15).

The blacktip shark (*Carcharhinus limbatus*) is part of the Large Coastal Shark complex in the US Atlantic directed shark fishery. This keystone species is a primary commercial target along the southeast coast from South Carolina to Florida and throughout the Gulf of Mexico (Branstetter and Burgess, 1996; Castro, 1996). Based on movement (Kohler *et al.*, 1998) and genetic (Keeney *et al.*, 2005) data, blacktip sharks are managed as two stocks: Gulf of Mexico and Atlantic. Multiple assessment methodologies, including surplus production, delay difference and age-structured production models, have been used to assess the stock status of both stocks (SEDAR, 2006, 2012). Blacktip sharks are a relatively productive shark species (Castro, 1996), and the combination of their life history characteristics and recent increases in the most representative abundance indices has suggested that the Gulf of Mexico blacktip stock is relatively healthy and has not experienced overfishing (SEDAR, 2012). The status of the Atlantic blacktip shark stock is, however, uncertain due to unreliable estimates of abundance, biomass or exploitation rates.

Although these examples show that some shark species can be sustainably harvested, overfishing remains a major concern for the many shark populations. Using trade auction records from Hong Kong, the estimated total number of sharks traded annually worldwide ranged between 26 million and 73 million individuals per year (Clarke *et al.*, 2006). More recently, Worm *et al.* (2013) estimated total annual shark mortality to range between 63 million and 273 million sharks per year. Comparisons between such exploitation rates and the rebound rates of shark populations has suggested that the majority of shark populations will decline under current levels of fishing pressure (Worm *et al.*, 2013). Earlier studies have already provided some evidence of population declines in several regions, with up to 99 per cent biomass reduction in some stocks (Baum *et al.*, 2003; Myers and Worm, 2003, 2005; Baum and Myers, 2004). Although some of the datasets used and conclusion from these studies have generated extensive debate (Baum *et al.*, 2005; Burgess *et al.*, 2005a, 2005b), there is a consensus that shark populations have substantially declined on a global scale (Field *et al.*, 2009), highlighting the inherent vulnerability of elasmobranchs to exploitation.

Targeted fisheries are not the only threat that chondrichthyans face from commercial fisheries. Indirect harvest or by-catch may in some situations be as great, if not a greater threat. Although poor reporting systems make it difficult to accurately quantify, by-catch rates have been estimated to represent up to 50–60 per cent of the total worldwide shark catch (Bonfil, 1994; Worm *et al.*, 2013). Indeed, by-catch was listed as a threat in ~70 per cent of shark species reported by the IUCN as facing conservation threats (Molina and Cooke, 2012). Several examples of chondrichthyan by-catch have shown signs of moderate to severe population decline (de Silva *et al.*, 2001; Campana *et al.*, 2005). In the southern Australian shark fishery, although catches of gummy shark (*M. antarcticus*) are considered sustainable, school shark (*G. galeus*), which is a by-product of the fishery, has been severely depleted (Punt and Walker, 1998; Punt *et al.*, 2000). In 2007, the stock size of school sharks was estimated at 9–14 per cent of original pup production levels (McLoughlin, 2007), leading school sharks to be considered overfished and listed as Conservation Dependent under the *Environment Protection and Biodiversity Conservation (EPBC) Act 1999*.

Although many large-scale population declines have been documented, some countries have made significant progress towards ensuring the conservation status of their fished resources. For example, a recent assessment of the status of all key Australian fish stocks identified only one shark population as currently overfished out of the five species and five stocks defined and assessed (FRDC, 2012). Additionally, 15 of the 20 countries with the highest elasmobranch catches are drafting or have a National Plan of Action for the Conservation and Management of Sharks (NPOA-Sharks) (Lack and Sant, 2011; IOTC Secretariat, 2012). Even though there is no evidence to indicate that the NPOAs are responsible for effective management of shark fisheries, the recent increase in the number of NPOAs being drafted and finalized likely reflects better resourced and informed systems of fisheries management and governance overall (Lack and Sant, 2011).

Recreational fisheries

Although commercial fisheries are often identified as being one of the main threats to shark populations, recreational catches can also have a significant impact on local shark stocks. Recreational shark catch can exceed commercial landings by a considerable margin (Stevens *et al.*, 2005), necessitating its inclusion in mortality calculations and stock assessments. For example, recreational catches of large coastal carcharhinid sharks in the Gulf of Mexico were higher for 15 of the 21 years between 1981 and 2001 than that taken by the commercial fishery (Cortés *et al.*, 2002). The collective levels of mortality were sufficient to drive a 50 per cent decline in sandbar sharks, from ~3,000,000 to ~1,500,000 sharks (Cortés *et al.*, 2002). The recreational spearfishing of grey nurse sharks (*Carcharias taurus*) during the 1960s and 1970s on the east coast of Australia, in the mistaken belief they were responsible for local shark attacks, is believed to be largely responsible for the decline in population size (Pollard, 1996). The population decline was severe enough to result in the population now being listed as critically endangered on the Australian east coast (Pollard *et al.*, 2003). Recent studies continue to identify recreational fishing as posing a risk to this population (Bansemer and Bennett, 2010; Robbins *et al.*, 2013). Recreational fishers in Tasmania were similarly responsible for declines in gummy and school sharks in the 1960s and 1970s through gillnetting for fish and sharks in nursery areas (Williams and Schaap, 1992).

The behaviour of recreational fishers has, however, improved over time, with recreational fishery data showing an increasing trend towards catch-and-release (Cowx, 2002; Stevens *et al.*, 2005; Babcock, 2008). For example, a survey in Australia saw respondents stating that ~80 per cent of line-caught sharks were released alive (Henry and Lyle, 2003), while 91 per cent of non-dogfish sharks caught in the US Atlantic and Gulf of Mexico are released alive (National Marine Fisheries Service, 2002). The condition and survival of released individuals, however, remains uncertain. Nevertheless, anglers are increasingly collaborating with scientists through tagging and release, by providing biological samples during normal angling activities or fishing competitions, or by offering scientists logistic support, e.g. to deploy satellite tags. However, in the absence of the structured arrangements under which licensed commercial fisheries operate, obtaining accurate recreational fisher data can be challenging. Although fisheries departments periodically undertake recreational fisher surveys through telephone or logbook studies (e.g. Henry and Lyle, 2003), the sporadic nature of recreational fishing, and lack of central facilities where catch is returned, largely prevents the independent verification of these activities. Although facilities such as boat ramps can be targeted for compliance searches or catch surveys, only the catch brought back to shore can be independently verified, and not the number or fate of discards.

Although robust, sharks can be vulnerable to the stress of capture and handling (Braccini *et al.*, 2012; Mandelman and Skomal, 2012), highlighting the importance of understanding the physiological impacts associated with catch-and-release and of quantifying post-release mortality rates. Although the field of post-release physiology in marine organisms has historically focused on bony fishes (Skomal and Mandelman, 2012), the increasing interest in the conservation and management of shark populations has stimulated a recent rise in studies investigating the stress response and survival rates of captured chondrichthyans (Mandelman and Skomal, 2012).

Shark-related tourism

Overview of shark-related tourism

Wildlife tourism is increasingly seen as an alternative to the extractive uses of resources such as fishing (Higginbottom and Tribe, 2004; Vianna *et al.*, 2012). Demand for wildlife tourism has blossomed in recent decades and is one of the fastest growing sectors of the tourism industry (Scheyvens, 1999; Wearing and Neil, 2009). Diving with sharks is one such venture that has experienced a marked increase in popularity (Gallagher and Hammerschlag, 2011). In 2002, Carwardine and Watterson listed over 40 countries where divers could undertake targeted shark dives. More recently, it was estimated that approximately 590,000 divers were engaged in shark-diving activities worldwide (Cisneros-Montemayor *et al.*, 2013). Nine years after Carwardine and Watterson's (2002) effort to review shark-diving sites, Gallagher and Hammerschlag (2011) used internet searches to reveal at least 376 established shark tourism operations in 83 specific locations, spanning 29 different countries, including tropical and temperate waters around the world. More recently, a new review used these sources to estimate that the global shark, ray and chimaera tourism industry may generate US$314,000,000 per annum, or approximately half the reported global shark landing value (Cisneros-Montemayor *et al.*, 2013).

Here, we use a similar approach to discuss the importance of shark-related tourism accounting for the diversity of shark species targeted, and the management regulations in place in developed and developing countries. We combine information from Carwardine and Watterson (2002) and Gallagher and Hammerschlag (2011), and add other unpublished sites to identify the species and countries most targeted by shark tourism. Only species that were listed as 'always' or 'very likely' to be sighted were included in this list, with species occasionally or rarely observed not included. The lists produced (Tables 12.1–12.2) are unlikely to be exhaustive as new shark-related tourism opportunities are continuously discovered and developed by diving businesses. It can then take some time before these new ventures are known in mainstream media or discussed within the scientific literature.

Based on the review of the data, shark-related tourism provides the opportunity to dive with 51 species across 41 countries (Tables 12.1–12.2). Eight species were listed in more than ten countries (*Triaenodon obesus*, *Carcharhinus amblyrhynchos*, *C. melanopterus*, *Sphyrna lewini*, *N. ferrugineus*, *C. albimarginatus*, *Rhynchobatus typus* and *C. leucas*), with reef-associated sharks (i.e. *T. obesus*, *C. amblyrhynchos*, *C. melanopterus*, *Nebrius ferrugineus* and *C. albimarginatus*), being the species regularly sighted during shark diving in most countries. In comparison, the 'iconic' and often protected species described in Chapter 11 were available as a targeted shark viewing attraction in only two, five and 13 countries for basking sharks, white sharks and whale sharks, respectively. While estimates of different shark-diving industries are available (Table 12.3), the global value of each species has never been estimated and we cannot quantitatively compare the economic value of more commonly seen reef sharks vs. 'iconic' pelagic sharks. It could, however, be argued that reef shark species are valuable to more countries than the 'iconic' species discussed in the previous chapter. Yet, many of these reef-associated species are commercially targeted in various locations around the world, including within the countries in which they are the focus of wildlife tourism.

Only a small proportion of countries offering shark-diving opportunities were classified as developed countries (32 per cent) (Table 12.2). The discrepancy in the distribution of shark-diving opportunities between developed and developing country is more evident when the number of species likely to be sighted is considered. Five or fewer species of sharks are likely to be sighted in the majority (62 per cent) of the developed countries listed. In comparison, most of the species-rich shark-diving opportunities are based in developing countries (75 per cent) (Table 12.2). The dichotomy between developed and developing countries' shark tourism industries means that shark-related tourism in developing countries could have a greater effect on local shark populations and economies (see below for further discussion about the value of shark-related tourism).

Table 12.1 List of species or species group that are 'always' or 'very likely' to be sighted during shark-related tourism

Common name	*Scientific name*	*Number of countries/states*
Whitetip reef shark	*Triaenodon obesus*	28
Grey reef shark	*Carcharhinus amblyrhynchos*	23
Blacktip reef shark	*Carcharhinus melanopterus*	22
Scalloped hammerhead	*Sphyrna lewini*	20
Tawny nurse	*Nebrius ferrugineus*	15
Silvertip shark	*Carcharhinus albimarginatus*	13
Whale shark	*Rhincodon typus*	13
Bull shark	*Carcharhinus leucas*	12
Nurse shark	*Ginglymostoma cirratum*	10
Silky shark	*Carcharhinus falciformis*	9
Great hammerhead	*Sphyrna mokarran*	8
Blue shark	*Prionace glauca*	8
Caribbean reef shark	*Carcharhinus perezi*	7
Shortfin mako shark	*Isurus oxyrinchus*	7
Tiger shark	*Galeocerdo cuvier*	7
Zebra shark	*Stegostoma fasciatum*	7
Blacktip shark	*Carcharhinus limbatus*	5
Bronze whaler	*Carcharhinus brachyurus*	6
Grey nurse shark	*Carcharias taurus*	5
White shark	*Carcharodon carcharias*	5
Galapagos shark	*Carcharhinus galapagensis*	5
Lemon shark	*Negaprion brevirostris*	4
Dusky shark	*Carcharhinus obscurus*	3
Oceanic whitetip shark	*Carcharhinus longimanus*	3
Angel shark	*Squatinidae* sp.	2
Basking shark	*Cetorhinus maximus*	2
Leopard shark	*Triakis semifasciata*	2
Pelagic thresher	*Alopias pelagicus*	2
Sixgill shark	*Hexanchus* sp.	2
Wobbegong	*Orectolobidae* sp.	2
Australian swell shark	*Cephaloscyllium laticeps*	2
Atlantic sharpnose shark	*Rhizoprionodon terraenovae*	1
Bamboo shark	*Hemyscylliidae* sp.	1
Bignose shark	*Carcharhinus altimus*	1
Catshark	*Scyliorhinidae* sp.	1
Epaulette shark	*Hemiscyllium ocellatum*	1
Finetooth shark	*Carcharhinus isodon*	1
Horn shark	*Heterodontus francisci*	1
Sickelfin lemon shark	*Negaprion acutidens*	1
Porbeagle	*Lamna nasus*	1
Port Jackson shark	*Heterodontus portusjacksoni*	1
Sandbar shark	*Carcharhinus plumbeus*	1
Broadnose sevengill shark	*Notorynchus cepedianus*	1
Spotted gully sharks	*Triakis megalopterus*	1
Total		272

Note
Number of countries/states represents the number of jurisdictions in which species are targeted by operators.

Table 12.2 List of countries offering shark-related tourism, along with the number of species 'always' or 'very frequently' sighted by operators

Country	*Country classification*	*Number of species*
USA	Developed	20
Australia	Developed	20
South Africa	Developing	16
The Bahamas	Developed	14
French Polynesia	Developed	11
Mexico	Developing	11
Costa Rica	Developing	9
Papua New Guinea	Developing	9
The Philippines	Developing	9
Belize	Developing	8
Egypt	Developing	8
Maldives	Developing	8
Micronesia	Developing	8
Mozambique	Developing	8
India	Developing	7
Myanmar	Developing	7
Solomon Islands	Developing	7
Cuba	Developing	6
Fiji	Developing	6
New Caledonia	Developed	6
Thailand	Developing	6
Ecuador	Developing	5
New Zealand	Developed	5
Portugal	Developed	5
Seychelles	Developing	5
Madagascar	Developing	4
Malaysia	Developing	4
Mauritius	Developing	4
Trinidad and Tobago	Developing	4
Cayman Islands	Developed	3
Colombia	Developing	3
Dominican Republic	Developing	3
Japan	Developed	3
Tanzania	Developing	3
United Kingdom	Developed	3
Brazil	Developing	2
Canada	Developed	1
Dutch Antilles	Developed	1
Honduras	Developing	1
Lebanon	Developing	1
Spain (Canary Islands)	Developed	1

Note

Country classifications as per the Australian Department of Foreign Affairs and Trade. Countries with more than five species being regularly viewed during shark tourism are considered as 'species-rich countries'.

Table 12.3 Summary of studies estimating the value of shark-related tourism

Country/location	*Species (scientific name)*	*Value (reported currency)*	*Standardized value (US$)*	*Method*	*Component/variable estimated*	*Source*
Ningaloo Reef, AU	Whale shark (*Rhincodon typus*)	AU$4,700,000	$3,636,000	Survey of divers	Primary injection of funds to the local economy	Davis *et al.* (1997)
Ningaloo Reef, AU	Whale shark (*Rhincodon typus*)	AU$2,400,000–4,600,000	$1,800,000–3,400,000	Survey of participants	Direct expenditure	Catlin *et al.* (2010)
Thailand	Whale shark (*Rhincodon typus*)	US$150,000,000	$150,000,000	Unknown	Unknown	Bennett *et al.* (2003)
Seychelles	Whale shark (*Rhincodon typus*)	US$4,990,000	$4,990,000	Unknown	Direct revenue and hotels and international flights costs	Rowat and Engelhardt (2007) from Newman *et al.* unpublished
Seychelles	Whale shark (*Rhincodon typus*)	US$1,200,000	$1,200,000	Contingent valuation study	Minimum direct revenue	Rowat and Engelhardt (2007)
Seychelles	Whale shark (*Rhincodon typus*)	US$2,800,000	$2,800,000	Contingent valuation study	Potential direct revenue	Rowat and Engelhardt (2007)
Seychelles	Whale shark (*Rhincodon typus*)	US$2,020,000	$2,020,000	Travel cost analysis	Unknown	Cesar *et al.* (2003)
Belize	Whale shark (*Rhincodon typus*)	US$3,700,000	$3,700,000	Survey of visitors	Value of whale shark tourism nationally	Graham (2003)

Maldive Islands	Reef sharks (*Carcharhinus* sp.)	US$2,300,000	$2,300,000	Survey of diving instructors and estimation of extent of shark-diving	Direct diving revenue	Anderson and Ahmed (1993)
Maldive Islands	Reef sharks (*Carcharhinus* sp.)	US$6,600,000	$6,600,000	Survey of departing tourists	Direct diving revenue estimated on the basis of willingness-to-pay	Waheed (1998)
The Bahamas	Reef sharks (*Carcharhinus* sp.)	US$78,000,000	$78,000,000	Unknown	Unknown	Cline (2008)
The Bahamas	Reef sharks (*Carcharhinus* sp.)	US$6,000,000	$6,000,000	Unknown	Unknown	Hall (1994)
Palau (Micronesia)	Reef sharks (*Carcharhinus* sp.)	US$18,000,000	$18,000,000	Self-administered questionnaires to divers, dive centres and fishers	Revenues generated by the industry and taxes paid to the government	Vianna *et al.* (2012)
Fiji	Reef sharks (*Carcharhinus* sp.)	US$42,200,000	$42,200,000	Self-administered questionnaires to divers, dive centres and fishers	Revenues generated by the industry and taxes paid to the government	Vianna *et al.* (2011)
Port St Johns, SA	Various whalers (*Carcharhinus* sp.)	R5,470,000 (Rand)	$774,000	On-site questionnaire to divers and dive centres	Direct value	Dicken (2010)

continued

Table 12.3 Continued

Country/ location	*Species (scientific name)*	*Value (reported currency)*	*Standardized value (US$)*	*Method*	*Component/variable estimated*	*Source*
Gansbaai, SA	White shark (*Carcharodon carcharias*)	R28,900,000	$4,400,000	Interview of key stakeholders (i.e. tour operators and tourists) and statistics from governmental organizations	Local business turnovers	Hara *et al.* (2003)
Neptune Islands, AU	White shark (*Carcharodon carcharias*)	AU$6,507,000	$6,825,000	RAT based on number of participants and estimation of expenditure	Combination of domestic, international and output value	Bradford and Robbins (2013)
Aliwal Shoal, SA	Tiger shark (*Galeocerdo cuvier*)	R12,405,274	$1,400,000	Semi-structured questionnaire to divers and dive centres	Direct value	Dicken and Hosking (2009)
Aliwal Shoal, SA	Tiger shark (*Galeocerdo cuvier*)	R2,080,925	$294,000	Travel cost analysis based on a questionnaire to divers and dive centres	Consumer surplus	Du Preez *et al.* (2012)
Moorea	Lemon shark (*Negaprion acutidens*)	US$5,400,000	$5,400,000	Email questionnaire and data from dive centres	Direct global revenue	Clua *et al.* (2011)

Global	Any	US$42,400,000	$42,400,000	Contingent valuation study	Willingness-to-pay to dive with sharks by US divers	White (2008)
Canary Islands, Spain	Sharks and rays	€3,600,000	$5,000,000	RAT based on number of participants and estimation of expenditure	Direct revenue	De la Cruz Modino *et al.* (2010)
Canary Islands, Spain	Sharks and rays	€17,700,000	$24,000,000	RAT based on number of participants and estimation of expenditure	Direct and indirect expenditure	De la Cruz Modino *et al.* (2010)

Note
Value of the industry is reported per season or year when diving takes place throughout the year. AU = Australia; SA = South Australia; RAT = Rapid Assessment Technique.

Shark-related management regulations

Shark management strategies and conservation actions vary considerably between, and within, these country categories. The existence of an International Plan of Action for Sharks (IPOA-Sharks), a framework in which individual countries draft and implement their own NPOA-Sharks, illustrates an area of shark management and conservation where developed countries (e.g. Australia, Canada, Japan, the United States) appear more efficient than developing countries (e.g. Indonesia, India) in the development of shark management plans (Lack and Sant, 2009). Additionally, some developing countries that have delayed the drafting of their NPOA for sharks contribute to a much higher proportion of reported global shark catches than the developed countries with NPOAs (Lack and Sant, 2011). This is a conflicting situation for developing countries where shark-based tourism forms an important revenue stream.

Shark populations in developed countries have not been managed with a view towards wildlife tourism, but instead as a component of domestic fisheries or indirectly through threatened species protection. For example, white sharks are protected in all countries where white shark cage-diving activities are carried out, not due to wildlife tourism, but because of the species' slow reproductive cycle, vulnerability to overfishing and evidence of declining populations (Malcolm *et al.*, 2001; Bruce, 2009). Similarly, although sharks have been identified as an important aspect of diving tourism on the Australian Great Barrier Reef (Ceccarelli and Ayling, 2010), reef sharks are managed through a catch quota system as part of the east coast Queensland shark fishery. This means that reef sharks can be harvested alongside tourist dive sites. Reef sharks derive some benefit from the presence of sanctuary zones within the Great Barrier Reef Marine Park (Robbins *et al.*, 2006), although these zones exist for the protection of biodiversity rather than for the benefit of the tourism industry. In the United States, shark populations are also mostly managed through fisheries regulations aimed at maintaining stocks at a sustainable level for exploitation.

More recently, several developed countries have created sanctuaries prohibiting commercial fishing of sharks throughout their exclusive economic zone, or have banned the sale of shark products (e.g. Hawaii, the Bahamas and New Caledonia). Although some of these bans have been implemented in areas where relevant management regulations were already in place (e.g. Oregon, Washington, California), their implementation in countries where species-specific management regulations were previously lacking (such as the Bahamas or New Caledonia) will likely make a tangible difference to the protection of shark populations.

Shark populations in developing countries have historically suffered from a lack of shark-related fishing regulations (Barker and Schluessel, 2005). However, thanks to the increasing scientific evidence of the ecological importance and vulnerability of shark populations, and the dissemination of scientific findings by scientists and conservation agencies, governments in developing countries are increasingly recognizing the importance of preserving shark populations. The economic evaluation of wildlife tourism in developing countries has also helped towards implementing new conservation strategies (Vianna *et al.*, 2010; Clua *et al.*, 2011). The combination of the global conservation concern of sharks and the economic impacts ensuing from the loss of sharks due to overfishing has led a number of countries or regions to grant greater protection to shark populations. Since 2009, the Republic of Palau, the Republic of the Maldives, Honduras and the Bahamas all created a nationwide shark sanctuary, while the Republic of the Marshall Islands and the territories of Tokelau, Guam and the Northern Marianas have banned commercial shark fishing and the trade of shark parts within their waters (Pew Environmental Group, 2012).

While the efficiency of such sanctuary zones has been debated (Robbins *et al.*, 2006; Heupel *et al.*, 2009; Davidson, 2012; Chapman *et al.*, 2013), the creation of these sanctuaries provides evidence that the governments from these states recognize the ecological and economic importance of sharks. Developing countries typically have much smaller fisheries management capacity and the banning of all shark products simplifies enforcement more than catch or size limits on shark-specific fisheries would (Chapman *et al.*, 2013).

Threats from wildlife tourism

Although wildlife tourism can be argued to be environmentally and economically beneficial, there are cases where it can be considered a threat to the wildlife and ecosystems it targets (Duffus and Dearden, 1990; Shackley, 1996). These can produce a range of negative effects (for reviews, see Green and Higginbottom, 2001; Orams, 2002; Green and Giese, 2004). The logistical difficulty associated with studying large marine predators has meant that the effects of shark-related tourism remain poorly understood. Nevertheless, research on the impacts of tourism and berleying on shark behaviours and health has recently emerged, with a few studies investigating the physiological impacts of provisioning sharks (Semeniuk *et al.*, 2007; Maljković and Côté, 2011), changes in seasonality, residency or abundance due to berleying or provisioning (Laroche *et al.*, 2007; Meyer *et al.*, 2009; Clua *et al.*, 2010a; Maljković and Côté, 2011; Bruce and Bradford, 2013; Brunnschweiler and Barnett, 2013; Huveneers *et al.*, 2013), changes in vertical movements (Fitzpatrick *et al.*, 2011) and the physical impacts of divers (Smith *et al.*, 2010; Barker *et al.*, 2011b; Barker *et al.*, 2011a). The lack of uniform effects across species and populations (Meyer *et al.*, 2009; Clua *et al.*, 2010a; Maljković and Côté, 2011; Bruce and Bradford, 2013) and some contentious results within a specific site (see Brunnschweiler and McKenzie, 2010; Clua *et al.*, 2010a, 2010b), suggest that findings cannot be generalized and may vary according to the frequency and types of activities, as well as the targeted species.

The potential impacts of wildlife tourism become most controversial when involving the feeding of potentially dangerous predatory species (Perrine, 1989;

Burns and Howard, 2003). In these cases, human safety issues are usually at the forefront of the wildlife tourism debate, with opponents of the practice claiming the potential for predators to learn to associate human presence and food rewards and proponents citing a lack of empirical documentation of such links (Orams, 2002). The white shark, *Carcharodon carcharias*, is a prime example where such concerns are frequently raised, particularly in the media (Muter *et al.*, 2013).

Benefits of wildlife tourism

The main arguments presented for the continuing development and justification of shark-related tourism are (in no particular order): education and improved conservation awareness, logistic support for research activities and economic value of the industry.

Education and improved conservation awareness

Wildlife tourism can help towards securing long-term management and conservation of sharks (Higginbottom and Tribe, 2004; Newsome *et al.*, 2005; Topelko and Dearden, 2005). This is achieved by influencing the conservation knowledge, attitudes and behaviour of tourists (Ballantyne *et al.*, 2007). The conservation benefits of wildlife tourism are arguably greater for potentially dangerous animals such as sharks, helping to balance out the negative public image from which they invariably suffer (Driscoll, 1995). It is important that a positive perspective on sharks, which tourism can generate, is promoted as negative perceptions about sharks and shark attack risks receive much media attention, and have been identified as one of the greatest barriers for global shark conservation efforts (Ferguson, 2006). Although scientists, conservation organizations, politicians and even fishers have expressed concerns about the conservation status of shark populations for years, shark conservation is just starting to become a global policy priority (Techera and Klein, 2011). Whether the increase in shark tourism has contributed to this change in attitude, or whether the change in attitude has produced the increased demand for shark tourism is difficult to disentangle. Nevertheless, it is likely that both are related and benefit from each other. Further details about human perceptions and attitudes are provided in Chapter 6.

Logistic support for research activities

Further details about the support that wildlife tourism operators can provide are provided in Chapter 8.

Economic value of wildlife tourism

The value of wildlife tourism is increasingly being estimated and has shown some large increases in value (Dwyer *et al.*, 2010). For example, the global expenditure on whale watching more than doubled to US$2.1 billion from over 13 million participants in the ten years preceding 2008 (O'Connor *et al.*, 2009). Several shark-related tourism industries have also been economically evaluated, with the Thai whale shark industry being valued the highest at ~US$110,000,000 (Table 12.3). Compared to whale watching, the evaluation of shark-related tourism is relatively recent, with 50 per cent of the estimations published in the last five years (Table 12.3), which is consistent with the comparatively recent increased interest in shark tourism. Even with relatively recent beginnings, the global chondrichthyan tourism industry is already evaluated at US$314 million per annum, with the value of the industry likely to at least double in the next two decades (Cisneros-Montemayor *et al.*, 2013).

The methods used to evaluate tourism vary extensively between studies, making direct comparison of shark-related tourism industries difficult. Absolute values can include distinct variables from different components of the industry. For example, two studies estimating the value of the tiger shark-diving operation off Aliwal Shoal, South Africa, varied more than four-fold, between ~US$300,000 and US$1.4 million (Dicken and Hosking, 2009; Du Preez *et al.*, 2012). Both studies were run by the same research team and based on the same surveys, with the difference being the former estimated the direct value of the industry to the region and the latter used a travel cost analysis, estimating the amount spent to travel to the site and consumer surplus. Regardless of the differences between studies, it is clear that shark-related tourism can be economically important to the regions where it is undertaken. This is especially true in developing countries where tourism can be a significant source of income. Shark diving in Palau, for example, was estimated to be the third highest contributor to the gross tax revenue of Palau, and was responsible for the disbursement of US$1.2 million in salaries to the local community (Vianna *et al.*, 2012). While the contribution of shark tourism may be relatively high in developing countries, the relative contribution of this industry is not as valuable in more developed countries because it does not match the revenues generated by other industries. Shark and ray tourism in the Canary Islands, for example, was valued at 0.11 per cent of GDP (De la Cruz Modino *et al.*, 2010) compared to 8 per cent for Palau (Vianna *et al.*, 2012). The high contribution towards the gross domestic product in Palau is likely to be extreme due to the relative low value of other industries, the demographics of the tourists likely to visit and dive in Palau and their willingness to pay more compared to other destinations.

Aside from the positive economic value of shark tourism for the region and country, several studies have also compared the value of a live shark as a tourism attraction against the value of a dead shark used for consumption. In each case, live sharks were much more valuable than dead sharks (Anderson and Ahmed,

1993; Vianna *et al.*, 2012). This is because live animals represent a reusable resource and the revenues generated through tourism far outweigh the market price for dead individuals (especially when indirect benefits are also considered). The projection of the value from tourism activity to individual animals has, however, recently been criticized due to the multitude of assumptions required and the propensity for these figures to be publicized and extrapolated widely (Catlin *et al.*, 2013). Nevertheless, the value of wildlife tourism to conservation is high and does not require embellishment (Higginbottom and Tribe, 2004). In some cases, the financial benefits of wildlife tourism over extractive activities such as fishing can instead be compared by evaluating the value of the respective industries. Such comparison, for example, showed that the shark-diving industry in the Maldives yielded twice as much as the export earnings of the three major shark-fishing industries in the country for the same period (Anderson and Ahmed, 1993). It has also been proposed that fishers can benefit from the wildlife tourism market by making greater returns by repeatedly supplying fish to restaurants feeding tourists, than by competing for and extracting the resource (Vianna *et al.*, 2012). This epitomizes the importance of wildlife tourism in the context of species at the intersection, where sharks are worth more alive than dead and emphasizes the importance and popularity of shark tourism, which are likely to increase in the future as tourists seek an interactive experience with sharks (Hall and Weiler, 1992).

What's next?

With global concerns regarding the sustainability of shark populations, well-managed shark tourism appears to provide an attractive economic alternative to extractive shark fishing. However, large-scale shifting of extractive operations towards tourism will not be a simple process. A substantial shift towards marine tourism would have deleterious effects to existing commercial fishing operations if conservation efforts result in fishing closures or blanket species protection. These effects would also affect downstream hospitality businesses reliant on commercial fisheries, and could impact the economies of small towns relying on commercial fishing income. If the target species is the focus of a long-running fishery, such a change will surely be met with strenuous objection. Any resource shift changing from extraction to viewing would also require sufficient rates of tourists to support the new market, and may not support the same number of vessels as commercial fishing. The focus species of any burgeoning tourism industry would also have to be sufficiently resident and in depths/habitats suitable to allow tourist sightings.

Nevertheless, such transitions are possible (Irvine and Keesing, 2007), and the revenues originating from shark-related tourism can benefit multiple sectors of the economy, including returns to the government. The increasing awareness of the ecological importance of sharks, their susceptibility to overfishing and the value of tourism has led to a number of countries banning commercial shark fishing and the trade of shark parts within their waters. This has especially been observed in developing countries that host the majority of the species-rich shark-diving opportunities. In some situations and countries, a shift from fishing to tourism might impact local fishing operators. However, gradual expansion of shark-related tourism may minimize the need for compensation, and provide opportunity for the local fishers to shift their business focus, if needed. Whether further expansion of shark-related tourism will result in additional management regulations, such as sanctuaries or species protection, or affect commercial fishing operations is unknown. Wildlife tourism does, however, provide an alternative non-extractive use of species that do not benefit from iconic status, such as white or whale sharks.

Acknowledgements

Charlie Huveneers was funded by Marine Innovation Southern Australia and Flinders University. William Robbins is funded by Wildlife Marine Research and Consultancy.

References

Anderson, R. and Ahmed, H. (1993) *The Shark Fisheries of the Maldives*, Ministry of Fisheries and Agriculture, Republic of Maldives and FAO, Rome.

Babcock, E. A. (2008) 'Recreational fishing for pelagic sharks worldwide', in M. D. Camhi, E. K. Pikitch and E. A. Babcock (eds), *Sharks of the Open Ocean: Biology, Fisheries and Conservation*, Blackwell Publishing Ltd, Oxford.

Ballantyne, R., Packer, J., Hughes, K. and Dierking, L. (2007) 'Conservation learning in wildlife tourism settings: lessons from research in zoos and aquariums', *Environmental Education Research*, vol. 13, pp. 367–383.

Bansemer, C. S. and Bennett, M. B. (2010) 'Retained fishing gear and associated injuries in the east Australian grey nurse sharks (*Carcharias taurus*): implications for population recovery', *Marine and Freshwater Research*, vol. 61, pp. 97–103.

Barker, M. J. and Schluessel, V. (2005) 'Managing global shark fisheries: suggestions for prioritizing management strategies', *Aquatic Conservation: Marine and Freshwater Ecosystems*, vol. 15, pp. 325–347.

Barker, S. M., Peddemors, V. and Williamson, J. E. (2011a) 'Recreational SCUBA diver interactions with the critically endangered Grey Nurse Shark', *Pacific Conservation Biology*, vol. 16, pp. 261–269.

Barker, S. M., Peddemors, V. and Williamson, J. E. (2011b) 'A video and photographic study of aggregation, swimming and respiratory behaviour changes in the Grey Nurse Shark (*Carcharias taurus*) in response to the presence of SCUBA divers', *Marine and Freshwater Behaviour and Physiology*, vol. 44, pp. 75–92.

Baum, J. K. and Myers, R. A. (2004) 'Shifting baselines and the decline of pelagic sharks in the Gulf of Mexico', *Ecology Letters*, vol. 7, pp. 135–145.

Baum, J. K., Myers, R. A., Kehler, D. G., Worm, B., Harley, S. J. and Doherty, P. A. (2003) 'Collapse and conservation of shark populations in the North Atlantic', *Science*, vol. 299, pp. 389–392.

Baum, J. K., Kehler, D. and Myers, R. A. (2005) 'Robust estimates of decline for pelagic shark populations in the northwest Atlantic and Gulf of Mexico', *Fisheries*, vol. 30, pp. 27–29.

Bennett, M., Dearden, P. and Rollins, R. (2003) 'The sustainability of dive tourism in Phuket, Thailand', in H. Landsdown, P. Dearden and W. Neilson (eds), *Communities in SE Asia: Challenges and Responses*, University of Victoria, Center for Asia Pacific Initiatives, Victoria, BC.

Blaber, S. J. M., Dichmont, C. M., White, W., Buckworth, R., Sadiyah, L., Iskandar, B., Nurhakim, S., Pillans, R., Andamari, R., Dharmadi and Fahmi (2009) 'Elasmobranchs in southern Indonesian fisheries: the fisheries, the status of the stocks and management options', *Reviews in Fish Biology and Fisheries*, vol. 19, pp. 367–391.

Bonfil, R. (1994) *Overview of World Elasmobranch Fisheries*, FAO, Rome.

Braccini, M., Van Rijn, J. and Frick, L. (2012) 'High post-capture survival for sharks, rays and chimaeras discarded in the main shark fishery of Australia?', *PLoS ONE*, vol. 7.

Bradford, R. W. and Robbins, R. L. (2013) 'Rapid assessment technique to assist management of the white shark (*Carcharodon carcharias*) cage dive industry, South Australia', *The Open Fish Science Journal*, vol. 6, pp. 13–18.

Branstetter, S. and Burgess, G. (1996) *Commercial Shark Fishery Observer Program: Characterization and Comparisons of the Directed Commercial Shark Fishery in the Eastern Gulf of Mexico and Off North Carolina Through an Observer Program*, MARFIN Award NA47FF0008.

Bruce, B. (2009) *White Shark Issue Paper*, Australian Government, Canberra.

Bruce, B. D. and Bradford, R. W. (2013) 'The effects of shark cage-diving operations on the behaviour and movements of white sharks, *Carcharodon carcharias*, at the Neptune Islands, South Australia', *Marine Biology*, vol. 160, no. 4, pp. 889–907.

Brunnschweiler, J. M. and Barnett, A. (2013) 'Opportunistic visitors: long-term behavioural response of bull sharks to food provisioning in Fiji', *PLoS ONE*, vol. 8.

Brunnschweiler, J. M. and McKenzie, J. (2010) 'Baiting sharks for marine tourism: comment on Clua *et al.* (2010)', *Marine Ecology Progress Series*, vol. 420, pp. 283–284.

Burgess, G. H., Beerkircher, L. R., Cailliet, G. M., Carlson, J. K., Cortés, E., Goldman, K. J., Grubbs, R. D., Musick, J. A., Musyl, M. K. and Simpfendorfer, C. A. (2005a) 'Is the collapse of shark populations in the Northwest Atlantic Ocean and Gulf of Mexico real?', *Fisheries*, vol. 30, pp. 19–26.

Burgess, G. H., Beerkircher, L. R., Cailliet, G. M., Carlson, J. K., Cortés, E., Goldman, K. J., Grubbs, R. D., Musick, J. A., Musyl, M. K. and Simpfendorfer, C. A. (2005b) 'Reply to "Robust estimates of decline for pelagic shark populations in the Northwest Atlantic and Gulf of Mexico"', *Fisheries*, vol. 30, pp. 30–31.

Burns, G. L. and Howard, P. (2003) 'When wildlife tourism goes wrong: a case study of stakeholder and management issues regarding Dingoes on Fraser Island, Australia', *Tourism Management*, vol. 24, pp. 699–712.

Camhi, M., Fowler, S., Musick, J. A., Brautigam, A. and Fordham, S. V. (1998) *Shark and Their Relatives – Ecology and Conservation*, IUCN/SSG Shark Specialist Group, Cambridge.

Campana, S. E., Marks, L. and Joyce, W. (2005) 'The biology and fishery of shortfin mako sharks (*Isurus oxyrinchus*) in Atlantic Canadian waters', *Fisheries Research*, vol. 73, pp. 341–352.

Carwardine, M. and Watterson, K. (2002) *The Shark Watcher's Handbook*, Princeton University Press, Princeton, NJ.

Castro, J. I. (1996) 'The biology of the blacktip shark, *Carcharhinus limbatus*, off the southeastern United States', *Bulletin of Marine Science*, vol. 59, pp. 508–522.

Catlin, J., Jones, T., Norman, B. and Wood, D. (2010) 'Consolidation in a wildlife tourism industry: the changing impact of whale shark tourist expenditure in the Ningaloo Coast Region', *International Journal of Tourism Research*, vol. 12, pp. 134–148.

Catlin, J., Hughes, M., Jones, T., Jones, R. and Campbell, R. (2013) 'Valuing individual animals through tourism: science or speculation?', *Biological Conservation*, vol. 157, pp. 93–98.

Ceccarelli, D. and Ayling, T. (2010) *Role, Importance and Vulnerability of Top Predators on the Great Barrier Reef: A Review*, Great Barrier Reef Marine Park Authority, Townsville, QLD.

Cesar, H. S. J., van Beukering, P. J. H., Payet, R. and Grandcourt, E. (2003) *Economic Analysis of Threats to Coastal Ecosystems in the Seychelles: Costs and Benefits of Management Options*, Ministry of Environment, Victoria, Seychelles.

Chapman, D., Frisk, M. G., Abercrombie, D., Safina, C., Gruber, S. H., Babcock, E. A., Feldheim, F., Pikitch, E. K., Ward-Paige, C. A., Davis, B., Kessel, S., Heithaus, M. R. and Worm, B. (2013) 'Give shark sanctuaries a chance', *Science (Letters to the Editor)*, vol. 339, p. 757.

Cisneros-Montemayor, A. M., Barnes-Mauthe, M., Al-Abdulrazzak, D., Navarro-Holm, E. and Sumaila, U. R. (2013) 'Global economic value of shark ecotourism: implications for conservation', *Oryx*, vol. 47, no. 3, pp. 381–388.

Clarke, S. C., McAllister, M. K., Milner-Gulland, E. J., Kirkwood, G. P., Michielsens, C. G. J., Agnew, D. J., Pikitch, E. K., Nakano, H. and Shivji, M. S. (2006) 'Global estimates of shark catches using trade records from commercial markets', *Ecology Letters*, vol. 9, pp. 1115–1126.

Cline, W. (2008) *Shark Diving Overview for the Islands of the Bahamas: Report of the Bahamas Ministry of Tourism*, Cline Marketing Group, Nassau, Bahamas.

Clua, E., Buray, N., Legendre, P., Mourier, J. and Planes, S. (2010a) 'Behavioural response of sicklefin lemon sharks *Negaprion acutidens* to underwater feeding for ecotourism purposes', *Marine Ecology Progress Series*, vol. 414, pp. 257–266.

Clua, E., Buray, N., Legendre, P., Mourier, J. and Planes, S. (2010b) 'Effects of provisioning on shark behaviour: reply to Brunnschweiler and McKenzie (2010)', *Marine Ecology Progress Series*, vol. 420, pp. 285–288.

Clua, E., Buray, N., Legendre, P., Mourier, J. and Planes, S. (2011) 'Business partner or simple catch? The economic value of the sicklefin lemon shark in French Polynesia', *Marine and Freshwater Research*, vol. 62, pp. 764–770.

Cortés, E., Brooks, L. and Scott, G. (2002) *Stock Assessment of Large Coastal Sharks in the U. S. Atlantic and Gulf of Mexico*, Sustainable Fisheries Division Contribution SFD-2/03-177, National Oceanic and Atmospheric Administration, National Marine Fisheries Service, Southeast Fisheries Science Center, Panama City, PL.

Cowx, I. G. (2002) 'Recreational fisheries', in P. Hart and J. Reynolds (eds), *The Fisheries Handbook*, Vol. 2, Blackwell Science, Oxford.

Davidson, L. N. K. (2012) 'Shark sanctuaries: substance or spin?', *Science (Letters to the Editor)*, vol. 338, pp. 1538–1539.

Davis, D., Banks, S., Birtles, A., Valentine, P. S. and Cuthill, M. (1997) 'Whale sharks in Ningaloo Marine Park: managing tourism in an Australian marine protected area', *Tourism Management*, vol. 18, pp. 259–271.

De la Cruz Modino, R., Esteban, A., Crilly, R. and Pascual-Fernandez, J. (2010) *Bucear con tiburones y rayas en Espana. Analisis de su potencial en Espana y en las Islas Canarias*, Instituto Universitario de Ciencias Politicas y Sociales NEF, The New Economics Foundation, Canary Islands.

de Silva, J. A., Condrey, R. E. and Thompson, B. A. (2001) 'Profile of shark bycatch in the US Gulf of Mexico menhaden fishery', *North American Journal of Fisheries Management*, vol. 21, pp. 111–124.

Dicken, M. L. (2010) 'Socio-economic aspects of boat-based ecotourism during the sardine run within the Pondoland Marine Protected Area, South Africa', *African Journal of Marine Science*, vol. 32, pp. 405–411.

Dicken, M. L. and Hosking, S. G. (2009) 'Socio-economic aspects of the tiger shark diving industry within the Aliwal Shoal Marine Protected Area, South Africa', *African Journal of Marine Science*, vol. 31, pp. 227–232.

Domeier, M. L. (2012) *Global Perspectives on the Biology and Life History of the White Shark*, CRC Press, Boca Raton, FL.

Driscoll, J. W. (1995) 'Attitude toward animals: species ratings', *Society and Animals*, vol. 3, pp. 139–150.

Du Preez, M., Dicken, M. L. and Hosking, S. G. (2012) 'The value of tiger shark diving within the Aliwal Shoal Marine Protected Area: a travel cost analysis', *South African Journal of Economics*, vol. 80, pp. 387–399.

Duffus, D. A. and Dearden, P. (1990) 'Non-consumptive wildlife oriented recreation: a conceptual framework', *Biological Conservation*, vol. 53, pp. 213–231.

Dwyer, L., Forsyth, P. and Dwyer, W. (2010) *Tourism Economics and Policy*, Channel View Publications, Bristol.

Ferguson, K. (2006) 'Submerged realities: shark documentaries at depth', *Atenea*, vol. 26, pp. 115–129.

Field, I., Meekan, M., Buckworth, R. and Bradshaw, C. (2009) 'Susceptibility of sharks, rays and chimaeras to global extinction', *Advances in Marine Biology*, vol. 56, pp. 275–363.

Fitzpatrick, R., Abrantes, K. G., Seymour, J. and Barnett, A. (2011) 'Variation in depth of whitetip reef sharks: does provisioning ecotourism change their behaviour?', *Coral Reefs*, vol. 30, pp. 569–577.

FRDC (2012) *Status of Key Australian Fish Stocks Reports 2012*, Fisheries Research and Development Corporation, Canberra.

Gallagher, A. J. and Hammerschlag, N. (2011) 'Global shark currency: the distribution, frequency, and economic value of shark ecotourism', *Current Issues in Tourism*, vol. 14, no. 8, pp. 797–812.

Graham, R. (2003) *Behaviour and Conservation of Whale Sharks on the Belize Barrier Reef*. PhD, University of York.

Green, R. and Giese, M. (2004) 'Negative effects of wildlife tourism on wildlife', in K. Higginbottom (ed.), *Wildlife Tourism: Impacts, Management and Planning*, Sustainable Tourism Cooperative Research Centre, Gold Coast, QLD.

Green, R. J. and Higginbottom, K. (2001) *Status Assessment of Wildlife Tourism in Australia Series: The Negative Effects of Wildlife Tourism on Wildlife*, Wildlife Tourism Research Report, CRC for Sustainable Tourism, Gold Coast, QLD.

Hall, C. M. and Weiler, B. (1992) *Special Interest Tourism*, Halsted Press, New York.

Hall, H. (1994) 'Jewels in the Caribbean Sea', *Ocean Realm*, January, pp. 51–54.

Hara, M., Maharaj, I. and Pithers, L. (2003) *Marine-based Tourism in Gansbaai: A*

Socio-economic Study, The Department of Environmental Affairs Programme for Land and Agrarian Studies, University of the Western Cape, South Africa.

Henry, G. W. and Lyle, J. M. (2003) *The National Recreational and Indigenous Fishing Survey*, FRDC Project No. 99/158, Australian Government Department of Agriculture, Fisheries and Forestry, Canberra.

Heupel, M. R., Williams, A. J., Welch, D. J., Ballagh, A., Mapstone, B. D., Carlos, G., Davies, C. and Simpfendorfer, C. A. (2009) 'Effects of fishing on tropical reef associated shark populations on the Great Barrier Reef', *Fisheries Research*, vol. 95, pp. 350–361.

Higginbottom, K. and Tribe, A. (2004) 'Contributions of wildlife tourism to conservation', in K. Higginbottom (ed.), *Wildlife Tourism: Impacts, Management and Planning*, Common Ground Publishing, CRC for Sustainable Tourism, Gold Coast, QLD.

Holden, M. J. (1974) 'Problems in the rational exploitation of elasmobranch populations and some suggested solutions', in F. R. Harden Jones (ed.), *Sea Fisheries Research*, Wiley and Sons, New York.

Holden, M. J. (1977) 'Elasmobranchs', in J. A. Gulland (ed.), *Fish Population Dynamics*, Wiley and Sons, New York.

Huveneers, C., Rogers, P. J., Beckmann, C., Semmens, J., Bruce, B. and Seuront, L. (2013) *A317:A339 to the Department of Environment, Water and Natural Resources Wildlife Conservation Fund and the Nature Foundation of South Australia*, South Australian Research and Development Institute (Aquatic Sciences), Adelaide, SARDI Research Report Series No. 657, SARDI Publication No. F2012/000417-1.

IOTC Secretariat (2012) *Status of Development and Implementatoin of National Plans of Action for Seabirds and Sharks*, Eighth Working Party on Ecosystems and Bycatch, Indian Ocean Tuna Commission, Cape Town, South Africa, 17–19 September 2012.

Irvine, T. R. and Keesing, J. K. (2007) *The First International Whale Shark Conference: Promoting International Collaboration in Whale Shark Conservation, Science and Management: Conference Overview, Abstracts and Supplementary Proceedings*, CSIRO Marine and Atmospheric Research, Perth, Western Australia.

Keeney, D. B., Heupel, M. R., Hueter, R. E. and Heist, E. (2005) 'Microsatellite and mitochondrial DNA analyses of the genetic structure of blacktip shark (*Carcharhinus limbatus*) nurseries in the northwestern Atlantic, Gulf of Mexico, and Caribbean Sea', *Molecular Ecology*, vol. 14, pp. 1911–1923.

Kohler, N., Casey, J. G. and Turner, P. A. (1998) 'NMFS cooperative shark tagging programme, 1962–93: an atlas of shark tag and recapture data', *Marine Fisheries Review*, vol. 60, pp. 1–87.

Lack, M. and Sant, G. (2006) *World Shark Catch, Production & Trade 1990–2003*, TRAFFIC Sydney, Australia.

Lack, M. and Sant, G. (2008) *Illegal, Unreported and Unregulated Shark Catch: A Review of Current Knowledge and Action*, Deparment of the Environment, Water, Heritage and the Arts, Canberra and TRAFFIC, Sydney.

Lack, M. and Sant, G. (2009) *Trends in Global Shark Catch and Recent Developments in Management*, TRAFFIC International, Cambridge.

Lack, M. and Sant, G. (2011) *The Future of Sharks: A Review of Action and Inaction*, TRAFFIC International, Cambridge and the Pew Environment Group, New York.

Laroche, K. R., Kock, A. A., Dill, L. M. and Oosthuizen, H. (2007) 'Effects of provisioning ecotourism activity on the behaviour of white sharks *Carcharodon carcharias*', *Marine Ecology Progress Series*, vol. 338, pp. 199–209.

McLoughlin, K. (2007) 'Shark gillnet and hook sectors', in J. Larcombe and K. McLoughlin (eds), *Fishery Status Reports 2006: Status of Fish Stocks Managed by the Australian Government*, Bureau of Rural Sciences, Canberra.

Malcolm, H., Bruce, B. D. and Stevens, J. (2001) *A Review of the Biology and Status of White Sharks in Australian Waters*, CSIRO Marine Research, Hobart, TAS.

Maljković, A. and Côté, I. (2011) 'Effects of tourism-related provisioning on the trophic signatures and movement patterns of an apex predator, the Caribbean reef shark', *Biological Conservation*, vol. 144, pp. 859–865.

Mandelman, J. W. and Skomal, G. B. (2012) 'The physiological stress response in elasmobranch fishes: selected papers from a symposium at the 26th annual meeting of the American Elasmobranch Society', *Comparative Biochemistry and Physiology Part A*, vol. 162, pp. 71–72.

Meyer, C. G., Dale, J. J., Papastamatiou, Y. P., Whitney, N. M. and Holland, K. N. (2009) 'Seasonal cycles and long-term trends in abundance and species composition of sharks associated with cage diving ecotourism activities in Hawaii', *Environmental Conservation*, vol. 36, pp. 104–111.

Molina, J. M. and Cooke, S. J. (2012) 'Trends in shark bycatch research: current status and research needs', *Review in Fish Biology and Fisheries*, vol. 22, pp. 719–737.

Muter, B. A., Gore, M. L., Gledhill, K., Lamont, C. and Huveneers, C. (2013) 'Australian and U.S. news media portrayal of sharks and their conservation', *Conservation Biology*, vol. 27, pp. 187–196.

Myers, R. A. and Worm, B. (2003) 'Rapid worldwide depletion of predatory fish communities', *Nature*, vol. 423, pp. 280–283.

Myers, R. A. and Worm, B. (2005) 'Extinction, survival or recovery of large predatory fishes', *Philosophical Transactions of the Royal Society of London B: Biological Sciences*, vol. 360, pp. 13–20.

National Marine Fisheries Service (2002) 'Marine Recreational Fisheries Statistics Survey', Fisheries Statistics and Economics Division, available at www.st.nmfs.gov/st1/recreational/index.html, accessed 8 May 2002.

Newsome, D., Dowling, R. and Moore, S. (2005) *Wildlife Tourism*, Channel View, Clevendon.

O'Connor, S., Campbell, R., Cortez, H. and Knowles, T. (2009) *Whale Watching Worldwide: Tourism Numbers, Expenditures and Expanding Economic Benefits*, Special Report from the International Fund for Animal Welfare, Yarmouth, MA.

Orams, M. (2002) 'Feeding wildlife as a tourism attraction: a review of issues and impacts', *Tourism Management*, vol. 23, pp. 281–293.

Perrine, D. (1989) 'Reef fish feeding; amusement or nuisance?', *Sea Frontiers*, vol. 35, pp. 272–279.

Pew Environment Group (2012) *Navigating Global Shark Conservation: Current Measures and Gaps*, available at www.pewenvironment.org/uploadedFiles/PEG/Publications/Report/Navigating%20Global%20Shark%20Conservation_Current%20Measures%20and%20Gaps%207%206%2012.pdf, accessed 16 May 2013.

Pollard, D. A. (1996) 'The biology and conservation status of the grey nurse shark (*Carcharias taurus* Rafinesque 1810) in New South Wales, Australia', *Aquatic Conservation: Marine and Freshwater Ecosystems*, vol. 6, pp. 1–20.

Pollard, D. A., Gordon, I., Flaherty, A. A. and Pogonoski, J. J. (2003) 'Red List Assessment', in R. Cavanagh, P. Kyne, S. L. Fowler, J. A. Musick and M. B. Bennett (eds), *The Conservation Status of Australasian Chondrichthyans*, Report of the IUCN Shark Specialist Group Australia and Oceania Regional Red List Workshop, Queensland,

Australia, 7–9 March, University of Queensland, School of Biomedical Sciences, Brisbane.

Pribac, F., Punt, A. E., Walker, T. I. and Tayler, B. L. (2005) 'Using length, age and tagging data in a stock assessment of a length selective fishery for gummy shark (*Mustelus antarcticus*)', *Journal of Northwest Atlantic Fishery Science*, vol. 35, pp. 267–290.

Punt, A. E. and Walker, T. I. (1998) 'Stock assessment and risk analysis for the school shark (*Galeorhinus galeus*) off southern Australia', *Marine and Freshwater Research*, vol. 49, pp. 719–731.

Punt, A. E., Pribac, F., Walker, T. I., Taylor, B. L. and Prince, J. D. (2000) 'Stock assessment of school shark, *Galeorhinus galeus*, based on a spatially explicit population dynamics model', *Marine and Freshwater Research*, vol. 51, pp. 205–220.

Roach, J., Noriega, R., Anthony Fowler, A., Lyle, J., McAuley, R., Rowling, K. and Walker, T. I. (2013) 'Gummy Shark *Mustelus antarcticus*', in Fisheries Research Development Coorporation (ed.), *Status of Key Australian Fish Stocks Reports 2012*, Fisheries Research Development Coorporation, Canberra.

Robbins, W. D., Hisano, M., Connolly, S. R. and Choat, J. H. (2006) 'Ongoing collapse of coral-reef shark populations', *Current Biology*, vol. 16, pp. 2314–2319.

Robbins, W. D., Peddemors, V. M., Broadhurst, M. K. and Gray, C. (2013) 'Hooked on fishing? Recreational angling interactions with the Critically Endangered grey nurse shark, *Carcharias taurus* in eastern Australia', *Endangered Species Research*, vol. 21, pp. 161–107.

Rowat, D. and Brooks, K. S. (2012) 'A review of the biology, fisheries and conservation of the whale shark *Rhincodon typus*', *Journal of Fish Biology*, vol. 80, pp. 1019–1056.

Rowat, D. and Engelhardt, U. (2007) 'Seychelles: a case study of community involvement in the development of whale shark ecotourism and its socio-economic impact', *Fisheries Research*, vol. 84, pp. 109–113.

Scheyvens, R. (1999) 'Ecotourism and the empowerment of local communities', *Tourism Management*, vol. 20, pp. 245–249.

SEDAR (2006) *SEDAR 11: Stock Assessment Report. Large Coastal Shark Complex, Blacktip and Sandbar Shark*, NOAA/NMFS, Silver Spring, MD.

SEDAR (2012) *SEDAR 29: Stock Assessment Report. HMS Gulf of Mexico Blacktip Shark*, NOAA/NMFS, Charleston, SC.

Semeniuk, C. A. D., Speers-Roesch, B. and Rothley, K. D. (2007) 'Using fatty-acid profile analysis as an ecologic indicator in the management of tourist impacts on marine wildlife: a case of stingray-feeding in the Caribbean', *Environmental Management*, vol. 40, pp. 665–677.

Sequeira, A. M. M., Mellin, C., Meekan, M. G., Sims, D. W. and Bradshaw, C. J. A. (2013) 'Inferred global connectivity of whale shark *Rhincodon typus* populations', *Journal of Fish Biology*, vol. 82, pp. 367–389.

Shackley, M. (1996) *Wildlife Tourism*, International Thomson Business Press, London.

Skomal, G. B. and Mandelman, J. W. (2012) 'The physiological response to anthropogenic stressors in marine elasmobranch fishes: a review with a focus on the secondary response', *Comparative Biochemistry and Physiology Part A*, vol. 162, pp. 146–155.

Smith, K., Scarr, M. and Scapaci, C. (2010) 'Grey nurse shark (*Carcharias taurus*) diving tourism: tourist compliance and shark behaviour at Fish Rock, Australia', *Environmental Management*, vol. 46, pp. 699–710.

Stevens, J. D., Bonfil, R., Dulvy, N. K. and Walker, P. A. (2000) 'The effects of fishing on sharks, rays and chimaeras (chondrichthyans), and the implications for marine ecosystems', *ICES Journal of Marine Science*, vol. 57, pp. 476–494.

Stevens, J. D., Walker, T. I., Cook, S. F. and Fordham, S. V. (2005) 'Threats faced by chondrichthyan fish', in S. L. Fowler, R. Cavanagh, M. Camhi, G. Burgess, S. V. Fordham, C. A. Simpfendorfer and J. A. Musick (eds), *Sharks, Rays and Chimaeras: The Status of the Chondrichthyan Fishes. Status Survey*, IUCN, Gland, Switzerland.

Techera, E. J. and Klein, N. (2011) 'Fragmented governance: reconciling legal strategies for shark conservation and management', *Marine Policy*, vol. 35, no. 1, pp. 73–78.

Topelko, K. N. and Dearden, P. (2005) 'The shark watching industry and its potential contribution to shark conservation', *Journal of Ecotourism*, vol. 4, pp. 108–128.

Vianna, G., Meekan, M., Pannell, D., Marsh, S. and Meeuwig, J. (2010) *Wanted Dead or Alive? The Relative Value of Reef Sharks as a Fishery and an Ecotourism Asset in Palau*, Australian Institute of Marine Science and University of Western Australia, Perth, Australia.

Vianna, G. M. S., Meeuwig, J. J., Pannell, D., Sykes, H. and Meekan, M. G. (2011) *The Socio-economic Value of the Shark-diving Industry in Fiji*, Australian Institute of Marine Science, University of Western Australia, Perth.

Vianna, G. M. S., Meekan, M. G., Pannell, D. J., Marsh, S. P. and Meeuwig, J. J. (2012) 'Socio-economic value and community benefits from shark-diving tourism in Palau: a sustainable use of reef shark populations', *Biological Conservation*, vol. 145, pp. 267–277.

Waheed, A. (1998) 'Economic value of "marine ecotourism" in the Maldives', *Bay of Bengal News*, vol. 12, p. 23.

Walker, T. I. (1998) 'Can shark resources be harvested sustainably? A question revisited with a review of shark fisheries', *Marine and Freshwater Research*, vol. 49, pp. 553–572.

Wearing, S. and Neil, J. (2009) *Ecotourism: Impacts, Potentials, and Possibilities*, Butterworth-Heinemann, Oxford.

White, L. 2008. *Sea the Value: Quantifying the Value of Marine Life to Divers*. Masters, Duke University.

White, W. T. and Kyne, P. M. (2010) 'The status of chondrichthyan conservation in the Indo-Australasian region', *Journal of Fish Biology*, vol. 76, pp. 2090–2117.

White, W. T. and Last, P. (2012) 'A review of the taxonomy of chondrichthyan fishes: a modern perspective', *Journal of Fish Biology*, vol. 80, pp. 901–917.

Williams, H. and Schaap, A. H. (1992) 'Preliminary results of a study into the incidental mortality of sharks in gill-nets in two Tasmanian shark nursery areas', in J. G. Pepperell (ed.), *Sharks, Biology and Fisheries*, CSIRO, Melbourne.

Worm, B., Davis, B., Kettemer, L., Ward-Paige, C. A., Chapman, D., Heithaus, M. R., Kessel, S. and Gruber, S. H. (2013) 'Global catches, exploitation rates, and rebuilding options for sharks', *Marine Policy*, vol. 40, pp. 194–204.

Part V

Tools and techniques

Chapter 13

The role of marine protected areas and sanctuaries

Erich Hoyt

Introduction

Marine protected areas (MPAs) began to emerge as an important tool for the conservation of ocean species and ecosystems in the 1990s (Kelleher *et al.*, 1995; Agardy, 1997, 2010; Hoyt, 2005, 2009a, 2011). As more has been learned about the habitat needs of marine species, it has become possible to use the place-based tool of MPAs to promote their conservation. The designation of MPAs borrows from well-established terrestrial conservation initiatives such as national parks, nature reserves and monuments which often encourage involvement by the public in conservation initiatives (Hoyt, 2011).

MPAs are defined within the larger context of protected areas (PAs). According to the International Union for Conservation of Nature (IUCN), a PA is 'a clearly defined geographical space, recognised, dedicated and managed, through legal or other effective means, to achieve the long-term conservation of nature with associated ecosystem services and cultural values' (Dudley, 2008). An MPA is a PA in the marine environment, ranging from estuarine and coastal waters to the high seas.

MPAs are a developing tool in the early stages of creation and implementation, but it is thought that for MPAs to be successful they must have well-defined goals, buy-in from local communities, legal protection with enforcement capability, research and monitoring components and be well integrated with other conservation tools (fisheries time-closures, educational programmes, monitoring and research) (Kelleher, 1999; Notarbartolo di Sciara, 2007; Hoyt, 2009a; Reeves, 2009).

Protecting habitat for highly mobile, wide-ranging species such as sharks would seem to present a formidable challenge. To some extent, these are the challenges facing those who would protect the habitat of many other pelagic fish species, as well as sea turtles, pinnipeds, sirenians and whales and dolphins. But as we study and begin to learn more about populations of these and other marine animals, we find that more and more of them have predictable habitats for some portion of their life cycle, including breeding, nursery and feeding grounds as well as, sometimes, migration routes (Hoyt, 2011).

Habitat-based conservation for sharks requires an evaluation of the distribution and range of populations of shark species, including habitat used at various life stages from juvenile to adult. Shark habitats extend from tropical coastal (e.g. Caribbean reef shark, *Carcharhinus perezi*) to wide-ranging pelagic (e.g. great white shark, *Carcharodon carcharias*), but some are found in rivers and lakes (e.g. bull shark, *Carcharhinus leucas*) and others live in cold, deep waters at the edge of the Arctic (e.g. Greenland shark, *Somniosus microcephalus*).

Most sharks, comprising the highest density and diversity, are found in warmer waters such as the various reef sharks. Comparatively few species regularly inhabit or range into cold waters within the Arctic Circle; besides the Greenland shark, these species include the blue shark (*Prionace glauca*), porbeagle (*Lamna nasus*), salmon shark (*Lamna ditropis*), basking shark (*Cetorhinus maximus*), bluntnose sixgill (*Hexanchus griseus*), spiny dogfish (*Squalus acanthias*) and Pacific sleeper (*Somniosus pacificus*). The salmon shark is also sometimes found in Antarctic waters. If water temperatures continue to increase in polar areas, however, more shark species may range closer to the Poles.

Shark species with some degree of site fidelity include Caribbean reef and nurse sharks, which may be mostly year-round residents of an area, such as in Glover's Reef Marine Reserve in Belize (Chapman *et al.*, 2005, 2011; Bond *et al.*, 2012). The sharks here have a range perhaps equivalent to inshore coastal bottlenose dolphins or the estuarine *Cephalorhynchus* dolphins in South America (Hoyt, 2011). Site fidelity can be connected to seasonal prey concentration of zooplankton, such as micronekton associated with fish spawning events. This has been documented with the whale shark (*Rhincodon typus*) at Ningaloo Reef, western Australia (Taylor, 1996) and at Gladden Spit in Belize (Heyman *et al.*, 2001).

Other species such as the juveniles of the raggedtooth shark (*Carcharias taurus*, also known as the grey nurse shark or sand tiger shark) remain in geographically distinct nursery areas for the first 4–5 years of life before joining the rest of the population (Dicken *et al.*, 2007). As adults, raggedtooth sharks range over hundreds up to a couple of thousand kilometres (Dicken *et al.*, 2007), but these distances are short compared to the travels of the great white shark and the whale shark, which range across vast distances of ocean comparable to the great migrations of humpback, grey or blue whales. Tagging and tracking studies have shown trans-oceanic movements for the great white shark between South Africa and Australasia (Pardini *et al.*, 2001) and for the whale shark between the Gulf of California, Mexico, and an area near Tonga, a 13,000 km journey undertaken over 37 months (Eckert and Stewart, 2001). The great white shark, however, has been shown not only to make these predictable long-distance migrations covering thousands of kilometres to and from defined oceanic core areas, but to return and show clear preferences for particular coastal foraging sites (Jorgensen *et al.*, 2009).

In the past few years, in response to the high number of shark finning and by-catch deaths, there has been a global trend to establish large-scale shark sanctuaries and to include sharks in MPA proposals. A distinction is drawn here between sanctuaries and MPAs, as they pertain to sharks. Shark sanctuaries – typically extending over all or a large part of a country's exclusive economic zone (EEZ) – can confer top-down blanket bans on hunting, while MPAs have the potential to achieve more comprehensive conservation goals by not only restricting fishing, but by engaging with the public in education programmes, funding research and monitoring, and by encouraging non-consumptive opportunities such as tourism. However, MPAs sometimes do allow activities damaging to sharks such as certain types of commercial fishing or catch-and-release game fishing. It is necessary to consider whether the best solution to a conservation problem is an MPA. A careful assessment of the positives and negatives of MPA or sanctuary protection, in view of the legal provisions, infrastructure support, enforcement capabilities, available budget and other factors, is necessary before considering the use of these or other conservation tools. This chapter will explore the use of both the sanctuary and the MPA tools, drawing on the lessons learned from attempts to conserve the habitat of other large, wide-ranging species such as whales and dolphins.

The rationale and process of creating effective MPAs for sharks

The process of creating an MPA starts with defining the rationale and specific goals for the proposal in view of the particular species and populations of sharks to be protected and the impacts and threats they are likely to continue facing (Notarbartolo di Sciara, 2007; Hoyt, 2011). The advantage of establishing an MPA is that it can be a mechanism for installing an adaptive management plan, a responsible management body and a legal framework to carry these goals forward within a national and sometimes in a wider regional context. MPAs can also become settings where public engagement with ocean conservation is able to develop.

After the rationale is defined, the question must then be asked: is an MPA the most effective tool – the answer or part of the answer – in terms of addressing threats to sharks and improving the conservation status? Most threats will come from fishing (overfishing, shark finning, by-catch, entanglements), but other issues may include pollution, ship collisions, and overall habitat degradation.

If habitat protection is determined to be worthwhile, the next step is identifying specific critical habitat. With marine mammals, critical habitat has been defined as those parts of a population's range 'that are essential for day-to-day well-being and survival, as well as for maintaining a healthy population growth rate' (Hoyt, 2011). According to Frias-Torres (2004), conservation of migratory marine species is most effective when the vulnerable life history stages or time periods are targeted for protection, such as when congregations occur for the purpose of breeding and feeding. Another consideration for critical habitat, apart from dense congregations, is where the animals are getting injured or killed (Reeves, 2009).

At the beginning of the above steps, stakeholders must be brought on board so that the MPA selection process ideally grows out of a community, taking into account socio-economic and other concerns. This stakeholder community includes everyone who uses or is interested in the marine area under consideration: commercial, sports and artisanal fishers; local marine researchers; members of conservation groups; Indigenous groups; representatives from tourism and other marine-based industries; and representatives from government ministries. The most effective MPAs proceed from the bottom-up; top-down approaches usually only work if they institute bottom-up procedures early in the process. Even then, it is sometimes impossible to orchestrate public participation and such MPA proposals may ultimately fail. With some of the most severe conservation problems of shark finning and overfishing, however, government mandated sanctuaries declaring no hunting over large areas, matched with a measure of education and enforcement, may be the best way to proceed, due to the urgency of the situation. Over the long-term, however, for a conservation measure to work, people need to be involved from the ground up.

Such ground-up involvement for inshore MPAs might include coastal community stakeholders with both commercial and recreational interests in an area from divers and surfers to marine eco-tourism operators, as well as recreational fishers, among others. For large offshore MPAs, the community involvement must come from commercial fishers, shipping companies and others. In all cases, those with a research and conservation interest, as well as those with an economic interest, must be involved.

The next steps are to compile bibliographic information, collect updated scientific data on the animals, human activities and the threats; and to recommend special highly protected zones or core areas within the MPA, as needed. A comprehensive proposal with maps and information on every aspect must then be presented to stakeholders of the community, as well as to authorities involved in the legal process. This is rarely a one-time process but usually involves a consultation phase during which stakeholders examine the proposal and help to shape it until conflicts are resolved and acceptable proposals can be formulated.

The process of creating a fully fledged, operational MPA can be a time-consuming and expensive business. That is why it is important to be sure that the goals and rationale are clearly articulated and agreed with stakeholders and that all recognize the commitment that will be required. Even after the MPA is established, it is only the beginning of the process.

Making an effective MPA requires the formulation of a management plan, setting up a management body, establishing research and education programmes, and monitoring. The essential steps to effective management are outlined in Box 13.1. Some MPAs begin with a management plan before formal dedication of the MPA, but most only start the process afterwards. A management plan can take a year or more to develop, and then it needs to be renewed every five or ten years as part of adaptive management and continued dialogue with stakeholders. Creating effective protected areas, whether marine- or land-based, is an iterative, participatory process, and is bound to fail if the management plan is seen as set in stone or as a fixed law imposed from the outside, or from above.

In Box 13.1, step 9, management review and evaluation, is essential to the long-term success of the MPA. Without periodic review, even MPAs that start out with considerable success may decline in value and fail. An MPA must have clearly defined objectives against which its performance is regularly checked and a monitoring programme to assess management effectiveness and recommend changes (Kelleher, 1999). Various methods are suggested for conducting an MPA management plan review by Pomeroy *et al.* (2004).

Status of shark MPA protection

The responsibility for habitat protection for marine species and ecosystems – including marine mammals, marine birds, turtles and certain fish – may be spread across various government departments, usually those charged with management of fisheries or the marine environment, as well as international agencies. Depending on the country, sharks may or may not be included. National laws prevail in the EEZs of countries, which typically extend up to 200 nautical miles (371 km) from the coastline of a country. Sharks venturing into rivers, estuaries or freshwater lakes, such as the bull shark, which ranges into the interior of Brazil, Nicaragua and other countries with large river systems or interior lakes, may fall under agricultural or forestry legislation.

Box 13.1 Steps to effective MPA management

The following are the key steps leading to effective MPA management (Notarbartolo di Sciara, 2007; Hoyt, 2009a, 2011):

1 engage stakeholder involvement from the beginning and throughout the process;
2 formulate clear management objectives for the proposed MPA;
3 create a management body;
4 develop a management plan, subject to periodic re-examination and revision;
5 offer management training;
6 conduct research for baseline numbers, inventory, status and monitoring purposes;
7 promote and offer educational programmes in the local community and to visitors;
8 develop effective enforcement regimes; and
9 conduct periodic management review, both in-house and outside evaluations, to assess whether objectives are being met.

The kind and degree of protection for species and ecosystems depends upon the legal regime in the country. In the past two or three decades, most coastal countries of the world have established MPA legislation, although as yet there is no universal mechanism for creating MPAs in areas beyond national jurisdiction, i.e. outside the EEZ on the high seas. With a mandate from the World Summit on Sustainable Development (WSSD) in Johannesburg, South Africa, held in 2002, later adjusted by the Nagoya Protocol of the *Convention on Biological Diversity* (CBD) in 2010, a goal was agreed to designate 10 per cent of the ocean in MPAs by 2020. By 2013, 2.3 per cent had been achieved, mainly in EEZ waters (Spalding *et al.*, 2013). This 2.3 per cent includes 7,000 declared marine protected areas, most of which are too small to be of relevance to sharks and other highly mobile marine animals. Of note, the top 20 largest MPAs contain about five million square kilometres, representing more than 60 per cent of global MPA coverage. This includes the Great Barrier Reef Marine Park, Papahānaumokuākea Marine National Monument, Phoenix Islands Protected Area, the Marianas Trench MPA and Chagos Marine Reserve. The top 20 largest MPAs, as well as a number of others down the list, do contain shark habitat, yet few ban shark hunting or directly protect shark habitat as part of their management plans. Many MPAs exist only on paper, while others have monitoring and enforcement but may not have specific bans against commercial fishing, much less ban shark fishing. MPAs are not a standardized tool for conservation; each MPA has to be assessed on its own merits. Yet MPAs are a potentially flexible tool to the extent that they can be tailored to meet the conservation needs of various shark species and populations which in different situations need different kinds of protection.

A number of MPAs, however, do have specific provisions or regulations for sharks. This list starts with the Great Barrier Reef Marine Park, in Australia and also includes Ningaloo Marine Park and the Coral Sea Commonwealth Marine Reserve in Australia, Marianas Trench and Papahānaumokuākea Marine National Monuments in the Pacific, the Galápagos Marine Resources Reserve in Ecuador and the Gladden Spit Marine Reserve in Belize. These are just a few examples. Of course, MPAs are created for a wide variety of purposes. Yet with the large number of sharks being subjected to by-catch and overfishing worldwide, more MPA management plans should be adding shark protection to whatever targeted actions they already have for their intended species and ecosystem protection. In addition, as new research identifies critical habitat for threatened shark populations, many more MPAs with specific protection measures will need to be created.

Shark sanctuaries

Achieving the CBD goal of 10 per cent of the world ocean in MPAs by 2020 will not make much difference to sharks if there are insufficient measures in place to conserve sharks in substantial-size areas. At the current rate of exploitation for shark fins, added to by-catch mortalities, 2020 may well be too late for some shark species. Some countries have begun to recognize this fact and, in addition to, or instead of, selected MPA protection, have awarded blanket protection from fishing for certain shark species in national waters. Such areas are being called 'shark sanctuaries'. It is roughly equivalent to a fishery closure, though the implication is that it will be permanent, whereas fishery closures may be temporary and are often seasonal.

The first large shark sanctuary covering an entire country's waters, its EEZ, was declared by Palau in September 2009 through its *Shark Haven Act of 2009*; this prohibited all fishing for sharks. Israel had protected sharks as early as 1980 and Congo-Brazzaville in 2001, but Palau's sanctuary covered a vastly larger area where sharks were being taken. Since 2009 the countries of the Maldives, Bahamas, Honduras, the Cook Islands, French Polynesia, Tokelau and Marshall Islands, among others, have created their own shark sanctuaries (Figure 13.1), the largest single one being French Polynesia at 4.8 million km^2. In 2011 the various nations and territories of Palau, Guam, Northern Mariana Islands, Marshall Islands, as well as the Federated States of Micronesia, proposed to work together to create a continuous Micronesia Regional Shark Sanctuary, which would total more than five million square kilometres (Techera, 2012) (Table 13.1).

The Cook Islands Shark Sanctuary covers the entire EEZ of the country and has some of the strongest shark conservation regulations yet established. The government directive bans the sale, trade and possession of sharks aboard all commercial fishing or transhipment vessels within its EEZ, as well as the use of

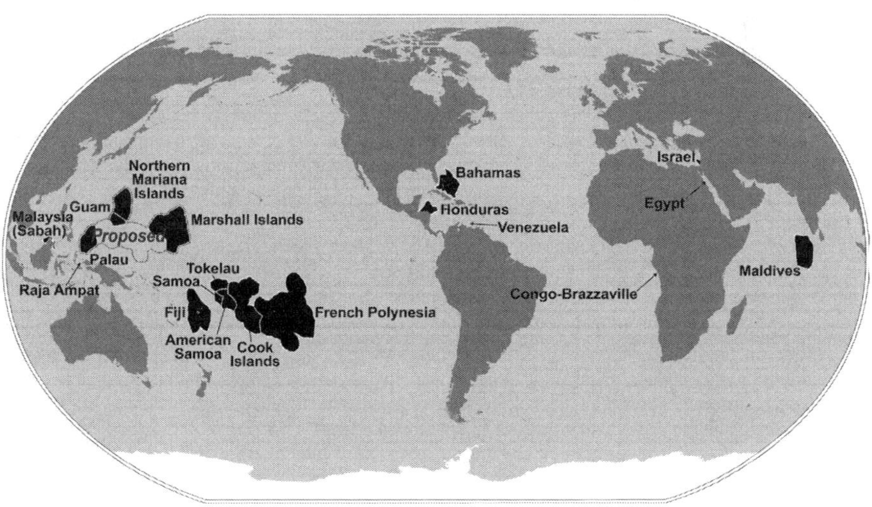

Figure 13.1 Shark sanctuaries in EEZ waters.

Table 13.1 Notable shark sanctuaries around the world

Name	*Location*	*Size*	*Date created*	*Species*	*Notes*
American Samoa	American Samoa (US)	Within 3 nm of shore	2012	Includes all sharks	Bans all shark fishing and possession of sharks within 3 nm of shore; outside fishers cannot enter territorial waters with sharks or shark parts
Bahamas	Bahamas	629,293 km^2	2011	Nurse, great hammerhead, tiger, bull, lemon, blacktip reef, silky, caribbean reef, oceanic whitetip sharks	All commercial shark fishing, as well as the sale or trade in shark products is banned in Bahamian waters
Cook Islands Whale Sanctuary	Cook Islands	1,960,135 km^2	2012	Blue, whale, oceanic whitetip, shortfin mako, pelagic thresher, lemon, scalloped hammerhead sharks, 11 others	Toughest shark conservation regulations to date; shark fishing ban covers all 18 recorded shark species in Cook Island waters
Congo-Brazzaville	Congo-Brazzaville	966 km^2	2001	All sharks	Shark fishing banned
Egypt	Egypt	Within 12 nm of shore in Red Sea	2005	All sharks	In effect a sanctuary within 12 nm territorial waters; shark fishing and trade in sharks banned

Micronesia Regional Shark Sanctuary	Federated States of Micronesia (FSM), Marshall Islands, Palau, Guam and Northern Mariana Islands	5,000,000 km^2	Proposed 2011 as a joint area with adjoining EEZs	All shark species found in the region	Would include existing shark sanctuaries in Palau, Marshall Islands, Guam and Northern Marianas to be joined by FSM
Fiji	Fiji	1,281,122 km^2	2011	All sharks	Fiji has pending legislation to ban all shark fishing and sales of shark products; to be in effect a sanctuary
French Polynesia Marine Mammal Sanctuary	French Polynesia	4,767,242 km^2	2006/2012	Whitetip, great hammerhead, lemon, oceanic whitetip, grey, thresher, blacktip reef, hammerhead sharks, 13+ others	Covers 21+ species of sharks; ban on shark fishing and trade in all sharks (but mako sharks only since 2012)
Guam	Guam (US)	221,504 km^2	2011	Shark fin ban but may extend to shark fishing in future (subsistence fishing allowed)	Bans the sale, trade and possession of shark fins; may become part of the Micronesia Regional Shark Sanctuary
Honduras	Honduras	240,240 km^2	2010	Whale, nurse, hammerhead, Caribbean reef, bull, nurse, six-gill, oceanic whitetip sharks	Includes full protection for taking sharks in Honduras waters; temporary ban while permanent shark protections under review

continued

Table 13.1 Continued

Name	*Location*	*Size*	*Date created*	*Species*	*Notes*
Israel	Israel	27,346 km^2	1980	All sharks	In effect a sanctuary in EEZ, as all sharks and rays are protected from fishing and shark finning is illegal
Malaysia (Sabah)	Malaysia (Sabah)	89,618 km^2	2011	All sharks	Shark fishing banned, as well as possessing or sale of sharks and fins
Maldives	Maldives	916,189 km^2	2010	All sharks	All shark fishing is prohibited in Maldives waters
Marshall Islands	Marshall Islands	1,992,232 km^2	2011	Blacktip reef, tiger and other sharks	Ban on all commercial fishing of sharks and sale of shark products; fines of US$25,000–200,000; sharks caught by accident must be set free
Northern Mariana Islands	Northern Mariana Islands (US)	749,268 km^2	2011	Shark fin ban but may extend to shark fishing in future	Bans the sale, trade and possession of shark fins; may become part of the Micronesia Regional Shark Sanctuary

Palau Shark Sanctuary	W. Central Pacific	604,289 km^2	2009	Whale shark and others	Declared as part of the *Shark Haven Act of 2009*
Raja Ampat Shark and Manta Ray Sanctuary	Raja Ampat, Indonesia	46,000 km^2	Created 2010, fully implemented 2013	Epaulette, silvertip, grey reef, blacktip, whitetip sharks	Bans the harvesting and trade of all sharks and manta rays; special highly protected zones
Samoa Whale, Turtle and Shark Sanctuary	Samoa	131,812 km^2	2002	Includes whales, turtles and sharks	Announced in 2002 but not yet formally declared
Tokelau Shark Sanctuary	Tokelau	319,031 km^2	2011	Tiger, leopard, whale, oceanic whitetip sharks	All shark fishing is banned in the Tokelau EEZ
Venezuela Shark Sanctuary	Venezuela	3,730 km^2	2012	Various tropical sharks	Shark finning ban in all EEZ but specific shark sanctuary outlawing commercial shark fishing in breeding area

shark-targeted fishing gear. The *Marine Resources Act* mandates a minimum US$100,000 up to $250,000 fine per offence with a repeat offence resulting in a loss of one's fishing licence (Anon, 2013).

Palau also has more intensive local management of shark and other species habitat. Local residents are responsible for managing and enforcing restrictions on the 35 protected local reefs and lagoons under Palau's *Protected Areas Network Act of 2003*. Palau's overall goal is to protect 30 per cent of the near-shore marine environment by 2020 (Schneider, 2013).

The best approach for urgent shark conservation would be something combining the blanket sanctuary in a country's waters, followed by more intensive local protection such as is found in Palau, which is in effect using the tool of MPA networks. A sanctuary, declared by a government, however, will usually present difficulties for enforcement without broad community support. With stakeholder support, such as is found with MPA conservation, there is improved compliance and the long-term educational and overall conservation goals can be more easily met.

MPA networks and ecosystem-based management

The movement of shark populations across national borders, and even to opposite ends of an ocean, dictate the necessity of creating MPA networks to ensure comprehensive protection. An MPA network can be defined as 'an organized collection of individual MPAs operating co-operatively and synergistically, at various spatial scales and with a range of protection levels, to fulfill ecological aims more effectively and comprehensively than individual sites could alone' (IUCN and WCPA, 2008). The idea of creating networks of MPAs is particularly suited to marine mammals, marine birds and turtles, and sharks. In addition to their long migrations, these animals may depend on food webs whose critical habitats are widely separated. Thus, networks are essential to create an effective conservation plan for wide-ranging species, as well as for the marine ecosystems that help to support them.

MPA networks can also be seen as a tool for facilitating ecosystem-based management (EBM). The goal of a comprehensive conservation programme should be to conserve not only the individual species and populations, but also the ecosystems that support them. EBM, or ecosystem management, is the management of the uses of ecosystems (Cortner and Moote, 1999; UNESCO, 2009; White *et al.*, 2009). An ecosystem per se needs no management. It is the escalating human interactions with ecosystems and the damaging human impacts on ecosystems and species that need to be managed (Hoyt, 2009a, 2011). Still, it has become clear that human uses must be accommodated within ecosystem capacities. EBM is a regime that recognizes that ecosystems are dynamic and inherently uncertain, yet seeks to manage the human interactions within ecosystems to protect and maintain ecological integrity and to minimize adverse impacts. EBM is widely talked about and is being attempted by some managers, but it remains at an embryonic stage, though Australia, for example, is building its regional marine planning on EBM (Smyth *et al.*, 2003).

To embark on EBM, fundamental shifts in management thinking and research must take place (Hoyt, 2009a, 2011):

- Management must move from a reactive to a proactive style. This requires ongoing scientific analysis and the ability to adapt management practice quickly when new information signals the need for a change.
- Research has to re-orient itself to view the ecosystem as a whole, using multiple components such as stability of reef or sea floor, predator presence and water quality as indicators of management success.
- Risk assessments of management choices must be reviewed regularly and adapted to new information.
- Multiple sectoral uses (e.g. commercial and sports fishing) as well as the resulting impacts (e.g. cetacean by-catch), must be viewed as cumulative rather than isolated.
- Managers, policy makers and the public must be alert to the misuse of the term EBM, particularly by those seeking to justify the culling of predators.
- The ultimate aim is to maintain the ecosystem as it naturally occurs – not to adapt it to human needs but to enable it to accommodate an acceptable level of human use.

Thus, it is important to understand more about the whole ecosystem, rather than focusing on one or other isolated area or species. More research is needed both on species and ecosystems, including large marine ecosystems (LMEs) (Sherman and Alexander, 1986, 1989; Sherman *et al.*, 2007; Hoyt, 2011). Without doubt, these are major tasks to undertake in any large marine area, but they are necessary steps to manage human involvement with marine ecosystems.

EBM as a management regime grew out of the widely acknowledged failure of single species management, primarily of fisheries (Hoyt, 2011). EBM requires an ongoing research commitment to unravel and model the complex linkages in marine ecosystems. In few species groups will this complexity be more evident than in sharks, which fulfil extremely diverse roles in ecosystems, from planktivores to apex predators. EBM is thus important in shark conservation and management. Yet shark research has lagged behind other fish and many marine mammals. Where knowledge is lacking, it is accepted that a precautionary approach should be invoked to protect ecosystems (Hoyt, 2011). Part of this precautionary approach is creating MPAs as safeguards built into the system from an early stage to secure ecosystem integrity in the absence of scientific certainty. In general, the less we know about a species and its habitat, the greater the area we must protect in order to compensate for our ignorance (Hoyt, 2009a).

Provisions for shark protection on the high seas

Both shark sanctuaries and MPAs with provisions for sharks focus on the waters *within* the EEZs. As of 2012, only 0.17 per cent of the high seas lies within declared protected areas (Spalding *et al.*, 2013). Strategies to address the problem of establishing pelagic MPAs on the high seas have focused on regional approaches through OSPAR in the Northeast Atlantic, and the UNEP *Convention on Migratory Species* (CMS) regional agreements such as in the Mediterranean, Black and Baltic Seas and western Europe, and additional agreements off West Africa and among Pacific island countries (Hoyt, 2011). These processes have recommended regional MPAs mainly for cetaceans, although sharks could in future be included. In 2010 the CMS Memorandum of Understanding (MoU) on the Conservation of Migratory Sharks tried to pull countries together to conserve sharks both on the high seas and in national waters. The conservation plan, as outlined in Annex 3 to the MoU (September 2012), stated the objective to ensure the protection of critical habitats, migratory corridors and critical life stages of sharks. To date, no MPAs have been created for sharks as a result of this MoU. However, this newly adopted conservation plan gives countries a means to work together on transboundary and high seas MPAs that could give habitat protection to the more migratory shark species.

The broadest geographic remit is set forth in the CBD. The CBD permits a process to nominate Ecologically or Biologically Significant Areas (EBSAs), which sometimes include consideration of shark habitats. The Central American Dome EBSA, for example, although it was proposed largely due to blue whale habitat, does include extensive pelagic shark habitat (Hoyt, 2011). EBSAs are not MPAs, but represent a preliminary stage of identification by experts as important habitat requiring further action. Whether these will be made into MPAs is at present unclear, although many researchers and conservation groups are working towards this goal. To achieve that goal, and by extension to obtain protection for species and ecosystems on the high seas, a specific instrument on MPAs in areas beyond national jurisdiction (ABNJ) is being sought through the UN *Convention on the Law of the Sea* (UNCLOS) (Gjerde and Rulska-Domino, 2012).

How effective are MPAs and sanctuaries for sharks?

Many MPAs remain on paper for years and are slow to put in place management provisions, including programmes of research, education, monitoring and enforcement. They may not have set up functioning management plans and management bodies and some, such as the Pelagos Sanctuary for Mediterranean Marine Mammals, may require further legislation or other measures before they can become effective (Notarbartolo di Sciara *et al.*, 2009). Protection from threats to the animals and their ecosystems may be minimal. Others, such as the

Great Barrier Reef Marine Park, one of the first MPAs to be declared in 1975, have built on their original fledgling efforts, established more highly protected zoning, developed special species conservation plans, and deepened their remit to conservation as more was learned about shark and other marine wildlife populations (Agardy, 2010). The Great Barrier Reef Marine Park Authority has also worked through other agencies to enhance protection levels. For example, the control of traffic through the park has been organized through the International Maritime Organisation (IMO) so that impact on the coral reef and other marine wildlife is minimized (Ottesen *et al.*, 1994). In 1990, the IMO designated a portion of the Great Barrier Reef as the first 'particularly sensitive sea area' (Ottesen *et al.*, 1994).

MPAs with highly protected zones or reserves (no-take areas) have been shown to be effective in rebuilding depleted fish and marine invertebrate populations. Enhancements in growth, reproduction and biodiversity in an MPA can replenish fished areas – both protected and unprotected – when young and adults move out of the MPA (PISCO, 2007). Spillover from an MPA accounts for two types of movements outside the MPA: first, adults and juvenile animals swim into adjacent areas; second, young animals and eggs can drift out from the MPA into the surrounding waters (IUCN and WCPA, 2008).

Evans *et al.* (2008) compared fished areas to the no-take zones on the Great Barrier Reef, and found increased batch fecundity, longer spawning seasons and potentially greater larval survival due to larger egg size from the larger individuals. Researchers working in other MPAs have noted fisheries that have benefited from the spillover of juveniles and export of eggs and larvae (Gell and Roberts, 2003; Halpern, 2003; Abesamis and Russ, 2005; Bartholomew *et al.*, 2007). However, it can often take years to document the benefits of spillover. The scales of spillover vary across species and ecosystems. Fish tagging and movement data from coral reefs suggest spillover may extend a few hundred metres to a few kilometres from reserves. In contrast, spillover for more mobile species in systems such as estuaries, rocky reefs and continental shelves can reach tens to hundreds of kilometres (Gell and Roberts, 2003).

Relatively few management plans for MPAs have created no-take zones for sharks in particular and few have addressed shark fishing conflicts, or pollution and habitat degradation issues, in a comprehensive way. These will need to be addressed to ensure shark populations can have the chance to recover. At present, shark protection in MPAs and sanctuaries is so new that there are as yet few data on effectiveness.

Measuring MPA effectiveness for sharks can be a complex, long-term task. As Baum *et al.* (2003) warn, MPAs, if not carefully planned, can be counterproductive for the conservation of some sharks and other species. Using simple models to analyse the implications of large-scale marine reserves for shark conservation, they ran various scenarios to protect 1–2 key species. They examined the effects of closing various areas on the overall result, finding that in some cases the fishing effort was merely redistributed to areas of higher species diversity, increasing catch rates on more species. Baum *et al.* (2003) concluded that, if marine reserves are to be effective, their placement is of critical importance, and conservation initiatives must explicitly consider impacts on the whole community of species. Emphasis on single species, without controlling effort, simply shifts pressure from one threatened species to another. Baum *et al.* (2003) suggest that carefully designed marine reserves in concert with reductions in fishing effort have the best chance of safeguarding sharks and other large pelagic predators from further declines and ecological extinction.

With any MPA, but particularly those that would protect sharks that are being fished, it is essential to involve fishers, both commercial and artisanal, in the decisions. Brunnschweiler (2010) reports on the planning, implementation and economic revenue of the Shark Reef Marine Reserve, a privately initiated reef and wildlife conservation and tourism project in Fiji. This eco-tourism project was designed to protect a small reef patch and its fauna, including bull and seven other species of sharks, while engaging local communities in a participatory business planning approach to MPA management. Income was generated through diver user fees and distributed to the local villages that exchanged their traditional fishing rights for the new source of income (Brunnschweiler, 2010).

While it is important that local initiatives, such as that in Fiji, need to be stakeholder-led, the conservation and management of sharks would still benefit from a broad UN declaration or binding agreement on high seas MPAs. This international dimension would facilitate better management of areas beyond national jurisdiction where many sharks are killed as by-catch, and also provide a means by which to control practices such as shark finning.

Shark tourism

Traditionally, sharks were unwanted visitors to coastal tourism destinations. News of the appearance of one of the larger sharks such as the great white shark at a favourite beach destination could alter traffic patterns for a season or longer. In recent years, however, shark tourism has become a growing phenomenon both within and outside MPAs and sanctuaries. It started with divers; their shift in attitudes beginning in the 1990s has led to the current popularity of shark watching (Topelko and Dearden, 2005).

The first regular shark watching dates from 1989, when visiting divers began to pay to see whale sharks in the Ningaloo Marine Park off Western Australia (Mau, 2008), although it did not become fully commercial until 1993 (Davis *et al.*, 1997). The whale sharks' sheer size and having 'whale' in the name of these sharks made them seem friendly and familiar; it was an easy step take from the already well-established whale watching to whale shark watching. Over time, shark watching spread to the carnivorous species, with feeding, or chumming, attracting the sharks close so that people could make observations from a boat or pier. Shark cages, familiar to all from the *Jaws* series of films and a long line of TV documentaries, were next to be introduced. Soon, divers, or anyone who wanted to enter the cage, could pay to have their close-up adrenalin-fuelled thrill. Thus, shark watching includes watching from the surface or underwater, swimming or floating, photographing or filming, feeding or simply observing the sharks undisturbed in their natural habitat.

In 2005 an estimated 500,000 divers per year went shark watching (Topelko and Dearden, 2005). By 2011, shark tourism companies were operating in 83 locations in 29 countries (Gallagher and Hammerschlag, 2011). The number one country for shark watching was the Bahamas, with a reported value of US$78 million (Cline, 2008). With this success in the Bahamas, tourism operators pressured government to pass a law against killing sharks or even possessing or trading shark products (Lowe, 2011).

The second most popular shark destination in terms of tourist expenditure is the Maldives, at US$38.6 million (Martin and Hakeem, 2006). Other countries with substantial shark watching industries include Australia, especially Western Australia, as well as Belize, the Philippines and the Seychelles for whale sharks, South Africa for both tiger and great white sharks, French Polynesia for lemon sharks, Palau and the Canary Islands for various sharks.

Anderson and Ahmed (1993) tried to estimate the annual value of a single grey reef shark in the Maldives and came up with US$33,500 as a total for one animal or US$603,000 for its estimated 18-year life span. More recent valuations of around US$200,000 per animal per year have been calculated in separate studies in Palau (Vianna *et al.*, 2012) and the Red Sea (Kresh, 2012). In French Polynesia, the value of an individual lemon shark was US$316,999 and multiplied by the 13 commonly observed resident sharks totalled US$5.4 million per year (Clua *et al.*, 2011).

The value or earning potential of individual animals offers a strong conservation message, stronger than a simple gross value for shark watching and stronger than indicating ecological or other reasons for protection. If each shark can be valued at levels much higher than the earnings from the fins, teeth, liver or meat, then the implications for conserving them are clearer, although there are still issues of short-term vs. long-term value and whether shark hunting and watching can coexist with the same species or other species and within the same country.

The loss of animals to tourism was felt keenly in the Maldives, as reported by Anderson and Waheed (1999). When fishers removed 20 grey reef sharks with a market value of about US$1,000, they forced the local diver operators to suspend their activity, resulting in a loss of US$500,000 per year for the local economy (Anderson and Waheed, 1999).

The global shark watching industry is still not as pervasive or valuable as whale and dolphin watching (Hoyt, 2009b; O'Connor *et al.*, 2009). Also, we must recognize that the shark watching industry is still of modest value compared to the total revenues from exploitation for fins, livers, meat and the real costs to the population from by-catch. It may be that shark tourism will work mainly to protect high-profile populations in coastal waters in countries with an interest in marine tourism and in developing a positive ecological brand or image for their destination.

'The economic value attached to shark watching has led to greater protection of sharks in some locations', conclude Topelko and Dearden (2005), 'but analysis of available data suggests that incentives do not appear large enough to encourage a significant reduction in fishing pressure appropriate to the scale of the threats facing sharks.'

In some cases, government regulations restrict the development of the shark watching industry (Topelko and Dearden, 2005) and, outside of the established whale shark industry at Ningaloo Reef, this has been the case more recently in Western Australia. Declining shark populations may also limit shark watching. Public sympathy for sharks has grown dramatically in recent decades (Ellis *et al.*, 1991; Topelko and Dearden, 2005), yet lukewarm public attitudes play a huge factor in terms of the acceptance of the need for conservation measures. People do not have to want to go shark watching, but they do need to commit to the idea that living, wild sharks must be protected in order for the industry to succeed.

Shark tourism has the potential to work well in the context of MPAs and sanctuaries to help create public sympathy. MPA managers can make sharks part of the education programme, and the MPA management plan then provides a framework for research, monitoring, public education and enforcement that improves the conservation outcomes of the animals as well as the ecosystems they depend upon (Hoyt, 2005, 2011).

Conclusion

The current situation of sharks suffering from the massive impacts of shark finning, by-catch and industrial fishing can be likened to the whaling era that culminated in the Antarctic in the 1960s with most of the great whale populations being reduced to tiny fractions of their original numbers. Following the end of commercial whaling, with many species achieving the dubious mantle of 'commercial extinction', various conservation measures have been implemented to rescue these populations, some of which are still considered endangered and several still hovering close to extinction. In a number of cases, habitat protection through MPAs has been part of the success story for whales and dolphins, including grey whales in the Baja California (Mexico) breeding lagoons, blue whales in the eastern North Pacific, and humpback whales with protection in the Pacific and Atlantic on their breeding and on some feeding grounds. Whales, like sharks, have also been given sanctuaries covering an entire country's waters.

For whales, sharks or any oceanic species, it is important to note that both MPAs and sanctuaries covering the entire waters of a country are not ends in themselves, but tools for conservation. They are only part of the larger picture of improving ecosystem management and reducing the heavy human footprint on the ocean, including considerations of noise, pollution, acidification, overfishing and the triggers to climate change.

Climate change, in particular, is certainly a confounding variable for the future of place-based protection. To adjust to possible alterations in the ranges of species, MPA managers may be able to use the tool of networks as well as larger MPAs with flexible protected zones and boundaries. Well-planned MPA networks and large MPAs may have not only a wider range of habitats, but areas that may replicate the conditions abandoned by sharks or the prey as water temperatures change.

If a country, province or state can ban shark hunting in its waters, or a portion of its waters, and is able to enforce it, either as part of a so-called 'sanctuary' or as a simple law banning hunting, that may be the single most effective spatial measure that can be taken in view of the intensive worldwide fishing and by-catch of sharks. In addition, a UN declaration, or other worldwide agreement, to ban shark finning entirely, along with spatial measures, would go a long way toward helping sharks survive the twenty-first century. Shark sanctuaries and MPAs might also become places where people go to meet and appreciate sharks, and where the tourism helps support their conservation. It has worked with marine wildlife such as whales and dolphins in 119 countries (O'Connor *et al.*, 2009), and the growing shark tourism industry in a few areas suggests that it could work at least for higher profile coastal shark populations as well.

Acknowledgements

Thanks to Giuseppe Notarbartolo di Sciara for advice and many papers, and Lesley Frampton for background research and preparation of Figure 13.1. Melanie Salmon and Global Ocean helped fund the research and writing of this chapter.

References

Abesamis, R. A. and Russ, G. R. (2005) 'Density-dependent spillover from a marine reserve: long-term evidence', *Ecological Applications*, vol. 15, no. 5, pp. 1798–1812.

Agardy, T. S. (1997) *Marine Protected Areas and Ocean Conservation*, Academic Press, London.

Agardy, T. S. (2010) *Ocean Zoning: Making Marine Management More Effective*, Earthscan, London, Washington, DC.

Anderson, R. C. and Ahmed, H. (1993) *The Shark Fisheries in the Maldives*, Ministry of Fisheries and Agriculture, Republic of Maldives and FAO, Rome.

Anderson, R. C. and Waheed, A. (1999) 'Management of shark fisheries in the Maldives', in R. Shotton (ed.), *Case Studies of the Management of Elasmobranch Fisheries*, FAO Fisheries Technical paper 378/2, FAO, Rome.

Anon (2013) 'Pacific Islands Conservation Initiative, Cook Islands Shark Sanctuary Project', available at www.picionline.org/PICI_Sharks.htm, accessed 18 September 2013.

Bartholomew, A., Bohnsack, J. A., Smith, S. G., Ault, J. S., Harper, D. E. and McClellan, D. B. (2007) 'Influence of marine reserve size and boundary length on the initial response of exploited reef fishes in the Florida Keys National Marine Sanctuary, USA', *Landscape Ecology*, vol. 23, Supp 1, pp. 55–65.

Baum, J. K., Myers, R. A., Kehler, D. G., Worm, B., Harley, S. J. and Doherty, P. A. (2003) 'Collapse and conservation of shark populations in the Northwest Atlantic', *Science*, vol. 299, pp. 389–392.

Bond, M. E., Babcock, E. A., Pikitch, E. K., Abercrombie, D. L., Lamb, N. F. and Chaptman, D. D. (2012) 'Reef sharks exhibit site-fidelity and higher relative abundance in marine reserves on the Mesoamerican barrier reef', *PLoS ONE*, vol. 7, no. 3.

Brunnschweiler, J. M. (2010) 'The Shark Reef Marine Reserve: a marine tourism project in Fiji involving local communities', *Journal of Sustainable Management*, vol. 18, no. 1, pp. 29–42.

Chapman, D. D., Pikitch, E. K., Babcock, E. A. and M. S. Shivji (2005) 'Marine reserve design and evaluation using automated acoustic telemetry: a case study involving coral reef-associated sharks in the Mesoamerican Caribbean', *Marine Technology Society Journal*, vol. 39, no. 1, pp. 42–55.

Chapman, D., Babcock, E., Abercrombie, D., Bond, M. and Pikitch, E. (2011) 'The elasmobranchs of Glover's Reef Marine Reserve', *Fisheries Centre Research Reports*, vol. 19, no. 6.

Cline, W. (2008) *Shark Diving Overview for the Islands of the Bahamas*, Report of the Bahamas Ministry of Tourism, Cline Marketing Group, Nassau.

Clua, E., Buray, N., Legendre, P., Mourier, J. and Planes, S. (2011) 'Business partner or simple catch? The economic value of the sicklefin lemon shark in French Polynesia', *Marine and Freshwater Research*, vol. 62, pp. 764–770.

Cortner, H. J. and Moote, M. A. (1999) *The Politics of Ecosystem Management*, Island Press, Washington, DC.

Davis, D., Banks, S., Birtles, A., Valentine, P. and Cuthill, M. (1997) 'Whale sharks in Ningaloo Marine Park: managing tourism in an Australian marine protected area', *Tourism Management*, vol. 18, no. 5, pp. 259–271.

Dicken, M. L., Booth, A. J., Smale, M. J. and Cliff, G. (2007) 'Spatial and seasonal distribution patterns of juvenile and adult raggedtooth sharks (*Carcharias taurus*) tagged off the east coast of South Africa', *Marine and Freshwater Research*, vol. 58, pp. 127–134.

Dudley, N. (2008) *Guidelines for Applying Protected Area Management Categories*, IUCN, Gland, Switzerland.

Eckert, S. A. and Stewart, B. S. (2001) 'Telemetry and satellite track of whale sharks, *Rhincodon typus*, in the Sea of Cortez, México, and in the North Pacific Ocean', *Environmental Biology of Fishes*, vol. 60, pp. 299–308.

Ellis, R., McCosker, J. E. and Giddings, A. (1991) *Great white shark*, HarperCollins in collaboration with Stanford University Press, New York.

Evans, R. D., Russ, G. R. and Kritzer, J. P. (2008) 'Batch fecundity of *Lutjanus carponotatus* (Lutjanidae) and implications of no-take marine reserves on the Great Barrier Reef, Australia', *Coral Reefs*, vol. 27, no. 1, pp. 179–189.

Frias-Torres, S. (2004) 'Whale sharks and marine protected areas in the tropical western Atlantic', *Current: The Journal of Marine Education*, vol. 20, no. 3, pp. 39–40.

Gallagher, A. J. and Hammerschlag, N. (2011) 'Global shark currency: the distribution and frequency, and socio-economics of shark ecotourism', *Current Issues in Tourism*, vol. 14, no. 8, pp. 797–812.

Gell, F. R. and Roberts, C. M. (2003) 'Benefits beyond boundaries: the fishery effects of marine reserves', *Trends in Ecology and Evolution*, vol. 18, no. 9, pp. 448–455.

Gjerde, K. M. and Rulska-Domino, A. (2012) 'Marine protected areas beyond national jurisdiction: some practical perspectives for moving ahead', *International Journal of Marine and Coastal Law*, vol. 27, no. 2, pp. 351–373.

Halpern, B. (2003) 'The impact of marine reserves: do reserves work and does reserve size matter?', *Ecological Applications*, vol. 13, no. 1, Supp, p. 21.

Heyman, W. D., Graham, R. T., Kjerive, B. and Johannes, R. E. (2001) 'Whale sharks *Rhincodon typus* aggregate to feed on fish spawn in Belize', *Marine Ecology Progress Series*, vol. 215, pp. 275–282.

Hoyt, E. (2005) 'Sustainable ecotourism on Atlantic islands, with special reference to whale watching, marine protected areas and sanctuaries for cetaceans', *Biology and Environment: Proceedings of the Royal Irish Academy*, vol. 105B, no. 3, pp. 141–154.

Hoyt, E. (2009a) 'Marine protected areas', in W. F. Perrin, B. Würsig and J. G. M. Thewissen (eds), *Encyclopedia of Marine Mammals*, 2nd edn, Academic Press, San Diego, CA.

Hoyt, E. (2009b) 'Whale watching', in W. F. Perrin, B. Würsig and J. G. M. Thewissen (eds), *Encyclopedia of Marine Mammals*, 2nd edn, Academic Press, San Diego, CA.

Hoyt, E. (2011) *Marine Protected Areas for Whales, Dolphins and Porpoises: A World Handbook for Cetacean Habitat Conservation and Planning*, 2nd edn, Earthscan/Routledge, London and New York.

IUCN and WCPA (2008) *Establishing Marine Protected Area Networks: Making It Happen*, IUCN World Commission on Protected Areas, National Oceanic and Atmospheric Administration and The Nature Conservancy, Washington, DC.

Jorgensen, S. J., Reeb, C. A, Chapple, T. K., Anderson, S., Perle, C., Van Sommeran, S. R., Fritz-Cope, C., Brown, A. C., Klimley, A. P. and Block, B. A. (2009) 'Philopatry and migration of Pacific white sharks', *Proceedings of the Royal Society B*, vol. 277, pp. 679–688.

Kelleher, G. (1999) *Guidelines for Marine Protected Areas*, IUCN, Gland, Switzerland, and Cambridge.

Kelleher, G., Bleakley, C. and Wells, S. (eds) (1995) *A Global Representative System of Marine Protected Areas*, Vols I–IV, Great Barrier Reef Marine Park Authority, World Bank and IUCN, Washington, DC.

Kresh, M. (2012) 'Egypt's Red Sea sharks face extinction', *Green Prophet*, 1 January.

Lowe, A. (2011) 'Shark dives bite off $78m tourism spend', *The Tribune*, 7 January, available at www.tribune242.com/business/01072011_alsharks_business_pg1-Lead, accessed 20 September 2013.

Martin, R. A. and Hakeem, A. A. A. (2006) 'Development of a sustainable shark diving ecotourism industry in the Maldives: Challenges and opportunities', *Maldives Marine Research Bulletin*, No. 8.

Mau, R. (2008) 'Managing for conservation and recreation: the Ningaloo Whale Shark experience', *Journal of Ecotourism*, vol. 7, pp. 208–220.

Notarbartolo di Sciara, G. (2007) *Guidelines for the Establishment and Management of Marine Protected Areas for Cetaceans*, Contract no 03/2007, RAC/SPA, Tunis, Tunisia.

Notarbartolo di Sciara, G., Agardy, T. and Scovazzi, T. (2009) 'Governance shift required for the world's first high seas MPA', Pelagos Sanctuary for Mediterranean Marine Mammals, Poster to the International Marine Conservation Congress, George Mason University, Fairfax, VA.

O'Connor, S., Campbell, R., Cortez, H. and Knowles, T. (2009) *Whale Watching Worldwide: Tourism Numbers, Expenditures and Expanding Economic Benefits*, Special Report from the International Fund for Animal Welfare, Yarmouth, MA.

Ottesen, P., Sparkes, S. and Trinder, C. (1994) 'Shipping threats and protection of the Great Barrier Reef Marine Park: the role of the particularly sensitive sea area concept', *International Journal of Marine and Coastal Law*, vol. 9, no. 4, pp. 518–522.

Pardini, A. T., Jones, C. S., Noble, L. R., Kreiser, B., Malcolm, H., Bruce, B. D., Stevens, J. D., Cliff, G., Scholl, M. C., Francis, M., Duffy, C. A. J. and Martin, A. P. (2001) 'Sex-biased dispersal of great white sharks', *Nature*, vol. 412, pp. 139–140.

PISCO (2007) *The Science of Marine Reserves*, 2nd edn, Partnership for Interdisciplinary Studies of Coastal Oceans, available at www.piscoweb.org, accessed 20 September 2013.

Pomeroy, R. S., Parks, J. E. and Watson, L. M. (2004) *How is your MPA Doing? A Guidebook of Natural and Social Indicators for Evaluating Marine Protected Area Management Effectiveness*, IUCN, Gland, Switzerland and Cambridge, available at http://effectivempa.noaa.gov/guidebook/guidebook.html, accessed 20 September 2013.

Reeves, R. R. (ed.) (2009) *Proceedings, First International Conference on Marine Mammal Protected Areas*, Maui, Hawaii, 30 March–3 April.

Schneider, B. (2013) 'An interconnected environment and economy: shark tourism in Palau', available at http://blogs.scientificamerican.com/expeditions/2013/06/12/an-interconnected-environment-and-economy-shark-tourism-in-palau, accessed 18 September 2013.

Sherman, K. and Alexander, L. M. (eds) (1986) *Variability and Management of Large Marine Ecosystems*, Westview Press Inc, Boulder, CO.

Sherman, K. and Alexander, L. M. (eds) (1989) *Biomass Yields and Geography of Large Marine Ecosystems*, Westview Press Inc, Boulder, CO.

Sherman, K., Aquarone, M. C. and Adams, S. (2007) *Global Applications of the Large Marine Ecosystem Concept 2007–2010*, NOAA Technical Memorandum NMFSNE-208.

Smyth, C., Prideaux, M., Davey, K. and Grady, M. (2003) *Oceans Eleven: The Implementation of Australia's Oceans Policy and Ecosystem-Based Regional Marine Planning*, Australian Conservation Foundation, Melbourne.

Spalding, M. D., Meliane, I., Milam, A., Fitzgerald, C. and Hale, L. Z. (2013) 'Protecting marine species: global targets and changing approaches', in A. Chircop, S. Coffen-Smout and M. McConnell (eds), *Ocean Yearbook*, Vol. 27, Martinus Nijhoff, Leiden, the Netherlands.

Taylor, G. (1996) 'Seasonal occurrence, distribution and movements of the Whale Shark, *Rhincodon typus*, at Ningaloo Reef, Western Australia', *Marine and Freshwater Research*, vol. 47, pp. 637–642.

Techera, E. J. (2012) 'Fishing, finning and tourism: trends in Pacific shark conservation and management', *International Journal of Marine and Coastal Law*, vol. 27, no. 3, pp. 597–621.

Topelko, K. N. and Dearden, P. (2005) 'The shark watching industry and its potential contribution to shark conservation', *Journal of Ecotourism*, vol. 4, no. 2, pp. 108–128.

UNESCO (2009) *Global Open Oceans and Deep Seabed (GOODS): Biogeographic Classification*, IOC Technical Series No. 84, UNESCO–IOC, Paris.

Vianna, G. M. S., Meekan, M. G., Pannell, D. J., Marsh, S. P. and Meeuwig, J. J. (2012)

'Socio-economic value and community benefits from shark-diving tourism in Palau: a sustainable use of reef shark populations', *Biological Conservation*, vol. 145, no. 1, pp. 267–277.

White, A., Siciliano, D. and Andersson, A. (2009) 'Communicating EBM: facing the challenge of describing a new management system to various audiences', *Marine Ecosystems and Management*, vol. 3, no. 2, pp. 1–2.

Chapter 14

Fisheries management and regulations

Boris Worm, Aurelie Cosandey-Godin and Brendal Davis

Introduction

As scientists have been documenting the decline of many shark populations (Manire and Gruber, 1990; Stevens *et al.*, 2000; Baum *et al.*, 2003; Ferretti *et al.*, 2010; Clarke *et al.*, 2013), it is now widely acknowledged that there is an urgent need to manage and regulate shark fisheries more effectively (FAO, 1999; Musick *et al.*, 2000; Ward-Paige *et al.*, 2012). Shark fisheries likely pre-date recorded history, but it is only over the last 50 years that shark catches have increased sharply and are now estimated conservatively at 1.4 million tonnes or 100 million individuals per year (Worm *et al.*, 2013). Yet, due to sharks' life history of slow growth, late maturity and limited reproduction, most species are intrinsically vulnerable to exploitation (Smith *et al.*, 1998; Musick *et al.*, 2000; Dulvy *et al.*, 2008). Compounding this problem is the lack of spatial refuges due to the global expansion and industrialization of fishing (Watson *et al.*, 2012). Today, the average annual exploitation rate of sharks is estimated to range from 6.4 per cent to 7.9 per cent of total biomass fished per year, which significantly exceeds the rebound rate of many species, averaging 4.9 per cent per year (Worm *et al.*, 2013). Hence, it is unsurprising that shark populations have declined to a fraction of their former abundance, and that many continue to decline under current exploitation rates.

There are 113 shark fishing nations, of which 20 collectively account for ~80 per cent of the global shark catch (Camhi *et al.*, 2009); 13 of these are located in the tropics (Figure 14.1). The three highest shark-producing fishing areas for 2011 were the Western Central Pacific, Eastern Central and Southwest Atlantic (Figure 14.1). Shark fisheries around the world represent a complex management problem for a number of reasons: many shark stocks are shared by several countries; few stock assessments are available; and even accurate catch statistics are lacking from many areas (FAO, 2008). As a result, two independent studies estimated that actual catches of sharks may exceed catches reported to the United Nations Food and Agriculture Organisation (FAO) about four-fold (Clarke *et al.*, 2006; Worm *et al.*, 2013). Hence, total mortality is much larger than what is accounted for by official statistics.

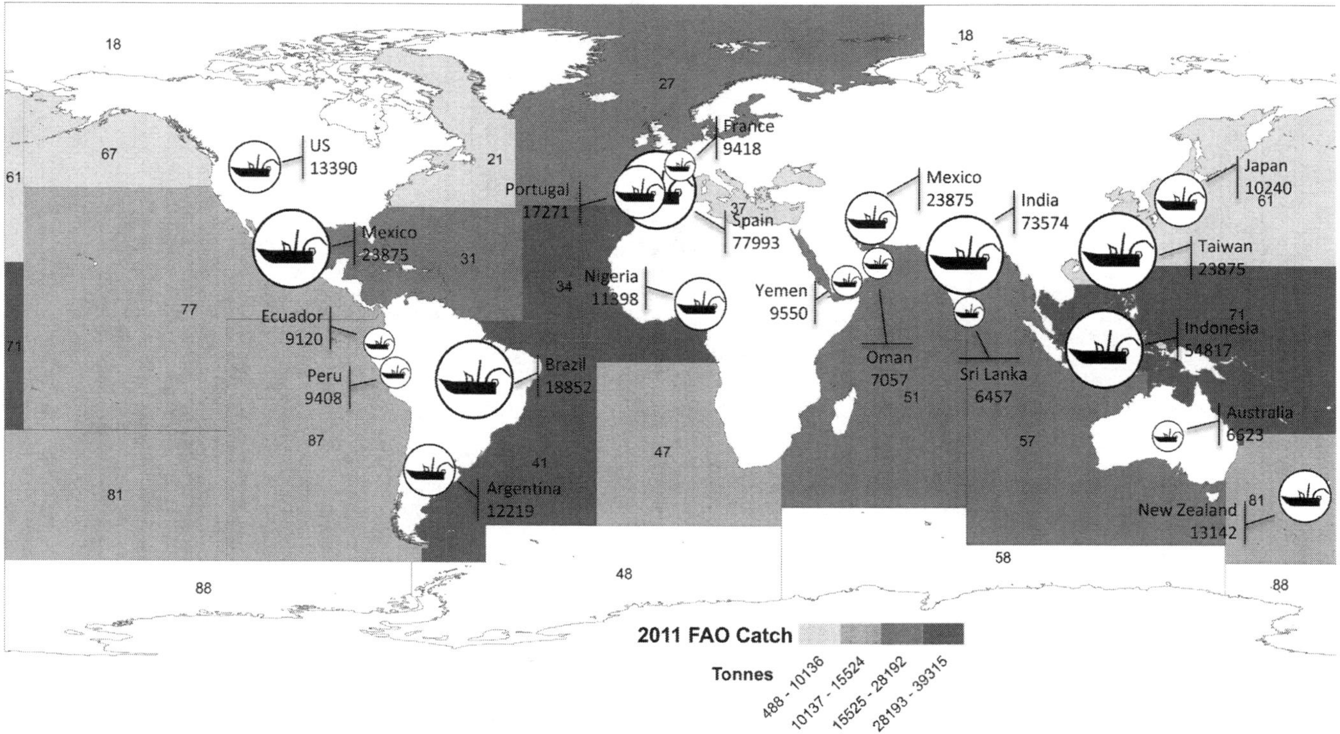

Figure 14.1 Global distribution of reported shark catches for the year 2011.

Note
Large areas refer to FAO fishery area, shaded according to their 2011 total shark catch. Circles denote top-20 shark fishing nations as seen in FAO official catch statistics.

These well-documented problems necessitate a close look at existing fisheries management measures and regulations. In this chapter, we review the state of fisheries management with respect to sharks. We identify both successes and failures, and identify priority actions that might help with the conservation and rebuilding of depleted populations. We also draw on relevant experiences with non-shark fisheries, and well-understood cases of rebuilding overexploited stocks.

Types of shark fisheries

Sharks are captured with a variety of fixed and mobile fishing gears, mainly gill-nets, hooks, and trawls (FAO, 2000). Some portion of shark fisheries is legal, as per existing fisheries regulations and, if landed, is usually reported to authorities. Another portion is illegal, unreported and unregulated (IUU) fishing, and hence does not contribute to official catch statistics, complicating any management efforts. Directed fishing refers to the catching of sharks as the main target of the fishing operation, either in a commercial, subsistence or recreational context. There is no comprehensive inventory of the total number of directed shark fisheries worldwide, but they are common throughout the world, from tropical to cold-temperate regions. However, most sharks are taken in multi-species fisheries directed at more productive bony fish (teleost) species, e.g. tuna and swordfish (FAO, 2000). Such fisheries are here referred to as 'by-catch fisheries' because sharks are not the main target species. Depending on the socio-economic and regulatory context, by-catch may be landed and used or discarded, dead or alive. Because shark fins are by far the most valuable shark-derived product, there are strong economic incentives to utilize shark by-catch for their fins (Clarke *et al.*, 2006). FAO trade statistics indicate that shark fins are imported to East Asia from 125 countries, with a total export value ranging from about US$20 million in 1976 to US$455 million in 2000, and slightly dropping to US$419 million for 2010 (Worm *et al.*, 2013). 'Shark finning', the practice of removing any of the fins of a shark (including the tail) and discarding the remainder of the shark at sea, occurs primarily in the context of by-catch fisheries, and is still widespread despite being outlawed by many jurisdictions (Clarke *et al.*, 2013). This is a classic example of 'opportunistic exploitation' (Branch *et al.*, 2013), whereas the incidental by-catch (in this case of sharks) may be more valuable than the target catch (pound by pound), but may become so rare that it would not be economical fishing for sharks alone. When subsidized by another target fishery, however, it can be economical to drive the by-catch species to extinction (Branch *et al.*, 2013). According to the International Union for the Conservation of Nature (IUCN) *Red List*, by-catch fisheries are a primary threat to shark populations, and play a major role for 67 per cent of known species threatened by extinction (reviewed in Molina and Cooke, 2012). Likewise, a recent global study estimated that sharks killed for their fins and then discarded accounted for 63 per cent of total global mortality in the year 2000, whereas reported landings comprised only 27 per cent of the total. Another 8 per cent might have been landed by illegal fisheries, and 2 per cent died from injuries after being released (Worm *et al.*, 2013).

Shark fisheries may also be classified into four species categories: (1) pelagic, (2) coastal cold-temperate or (3) tropical, and (4) deep-water (Musick and Musick, 2011). Pelagic shark fisheries are typically operated as by-catch fisheries in tuna and billfishes fleets (Pikitch *et al.*, 2008). These fisheries capture for the most part oceanic shark species, such as blue shark (*Prionace glauca*) (Musick and Musick, 2011). Because of their large size, oceanic shark species are highly valued in the shark fin trade and account for a large proportion (~70 per cent) of the fins identified in the Hong Kong market (Clarke *et al.*, 2006). Coastal cold-temperate fisheries often target smaller sharks, such as dogfish (e.g. spiny dogfish, *Squalus acanthias*), whereas the coastal tropical fisheries catch a large number of species, primarily requiem sharks and their relatives (Carcharhiniformes) (Musick and Musick, 2011). Deep-water shark species are increasingly landed as industrial fisheries move from the continental shelves to the slopes, where stocks remain more abundant (Morato *et al.*, 2006). As opposed to other shark species that are primarily used for their meat and fins, deep-water species are mainly sought for their liver oil, also called squalene, which is used in the cosmetic and pharmaceutical industries (Musick and Musick, 2011).

Types of management interventions

The main goal of contemporary fisheries management is to rebuild populations to a level that sustains their productivity, while safeguarding the structure and biodiversity of supporting ecosystems (FAO, 2003; Worm *et al.*, 2009). This is achieved through a number of management measures, such as (1) monitoring and assessment, (2) regulations on fishing capacity, effort and landings, (3) regulations on by-catch and discards, (4) regulations on fishing gear and fishing practices and (5) spatial management and protected areas. With respect to sharks, the goal is to limit overall mortality from both directed and by-catch fisheries to a level that ensures populations are sustained, or rebuilt to a prescribed level – for example, the biomass that allows for maximum productivity (Musick *et al.*, 2000). Specific measures to ensure this depend on the local context and on the state of knowledge about the population. For example, shark species caught and landed in directed fisheries or as by-catch are typically managed through some form of catch restrictions. These can take the form of quotas that are expressed as a total allowable catch (TAC) for a particular species. Setting a TAC requires some assessment of population status, and ideally a model that relates fisheries removals to population abundance or biomass. In the absence of a TAC, other measures are required. In some cases, the catch and retention of certain species is entirely prohibited, as a way of minimizing their mortality. Alternatively, certain areas that are known to harbour concentrations of threatened species could be temporarily or permanently closed to certain forms of fishing; this is spatial management. Spatial management and prohibited species are management measures that are more robust to ignorance than a TAC, which requires reasonably detailed knowledge.

Particularly for non-target (by-catch) species, changes in fishing practices can significantly help reduce by-catch rates, or at least the mortality of species caught incidentally (Lewison *et al.*, 2004). Among these, fishing gear modifications remain the most popular option to manage shark by-catch to date. The goal is to minimize the interaction between the fishing gear and the by-catch species, while maximizing the target catch. Where this works, it has obvious ecological and economic benefits. For example, in order to limit the extent of shark by-catch in pelagic longline fisheries targeting tuna and swordfish, a ban on wire leaders (the hook-bearing branchlines of the main longline) has been enacted in a number of countries, including Australia, Ecuador, South Africa and many Pacific islands (Lack and Meere, 2009). Wire leaders retain all sharks, while monofilament leaders may be bitten through by larger specimens (Ward *et al.*, 2008). Likewise, trawl fisheries have received a lot of attention for their high by-catch rates. Several by-catch reduction devices (BRDs), such as the turtle excluder device and other filter grids, were developed to increase trawl selectivity; these also reduce the capture of sharks. For example, 86–94 per cent of the larger shark species were successfully released in Australia's northern prawn fishery when trawls were equipped with different combinations of BRDs (Brewer *et al.* 2006; also see Chapter 7 for more examples). Similarly, in the Canadian Arctic shrimp fishery, by-catch of Greenland sharks (*Somniosus microcephalus*) was reduced to near zero after the introduction of a 'Nordmore' separator grate (Siferd, 2010). In some cases, persistent high by-catch rates may lead to the closure of a particular fishery or the banning of certain fishing gear; for example, Costa Rica recently banned all shrimp trawling, citing concerns about by-catch (MarViva, 2013). Similarly, high-sea driftnets have been globally banned since the 1990s due to by-catch concerns.

Recognizing the widespread problems with shark finning, many management efforts have tried to eliminate finning practices in by-catch fisheries. Regulations vary from a 5 per cent ratio rule (fins can be landed separately from carcasses, but can weigh no more than 5 per cent of carcass weight), to regulations that mandate sharks be landed with their fins naturally attached, or even a wholesale ban on commercial shark fishing. The fin-to-carcass ratio rule has proven challenging to monitor and enforce, hence there is a trend towards mandating landing sharks with their fins naturally attached; this also allows fisheries observers to record species-specific landings data (Camhi *et al.*, 2009). In some countries, shark-related eco-tourism is becoming economically more important than shark fisheries; here, regulations may disallow all forms of shark fishing (see Chapters 8 and 14 on tourism and sanctuaries, respectively).

Management of shark fisheries: from global to local

As described in detail in Chapter 5 of this volume, the FAO has long recognized the challenges associated with shark fisheries, and introduced an International Plan of Action (IPOA) framework to guide all fishing nations in the sustainable management of sharks, as well as other elasmobranch fisheries (FAO, 1999; Musick and Bonfil, 2005). Its recommendations are considered best practice for managing shark fisheries, and include data collection and research, population monitoring and a range of management measures to ensure fisheries sustainability. The IPOA and its recommendations are a good baseline against which to compare existing fishery management regimes at national and regional levels (Davis and Worm, 2013). However, implementation of these voluntary measures is poor (FAO, 2006, 2008), and many populations are currently left unmanaged and unmonitored. In addition to the IPOA, limited international measures have been instituted to control the trade of some of the most threatened sharks; eight species are now included under the *Convention on International Trade in Endangered Species* (CITES), and seven species receive limited protection under the *Convention on Migratory Species* (CMS) (see Chapter 3 for details).

At a regional level, and on the high seas, regional fisheries management organizations (RFMOs) are engaged in efforts to assess the population status of sharks, at least for some of the most commonly caught species. Based on this information, these organizations have begun implementing some management measures specifically for sharks. These include regulations introduced between 2004 and 2008 by many RFMOs that ban shark finning, or prohibitions regarding the retention of particularly threatened species such as white shark (*Carcharodon carcharias*), basking shark (*Cetorhinus maximus*), hammerhead (*Sphyrna* spp.), thresher (*Alopias* spp.) and oceanic whitetip sharks (*Carcharhinus longimanus*) (since 2010). It is not clear how well finning and retention bans are enforced at this point. For example, in the Western Pacific there is evidence that finning is still widespread, and several shark populations are declining precipitously, despite a ban that has been in effect since 2008 (Clarke *et al.*, 2013). Such research results make it clear that finning bans by themselves are not enough in limiting the mortality of commonly caught species, and additional measures are required, such as banning the retention of threatened species and introducing by-catch quotas for all sharks. Among the various RFMOs, the *Convention on the Conservation of Antarctic Marine Living Resources* (CCAMLR) goes furthest in mandating the live release of all sharks, except for scientific research.

At a local (i.e. national) level, individual shark fishing states are tasked under the IPOA framework to develop their own National Plan of Action (NPOA) for sharks, which should outline data collection, research, monitoring and management measures to ensure sustainable use of sharks, rays, skates and chimeras in national fisheries. Table 14.1 shows that of the top 20 shark fishing states only 12 (or 60 per cent) had developed an NPOA by 2013, 14 years after

Table 14.1 Major management measures in the top-20 shark-fishing nations

Country	*Catch (tonnes)*	*NPOA*	*Finning ban*	*Stock assessment*	*TAC*	*Prohibited species*	*Size restriction*	*By-catch limits*	*Protected Areas*
Spain	77,993	Yes	Full	Yes	Yes	Yes	No	No	No
India	73,574	No	Full	No	No	No	No	No	No
Indonesia	54,817	Yes	Regional	No	No	Yes	No	No	Yes
Taiwan	42,892	Yes	Full	No	No	Yes	No	No	No
Mexico	23,875	Yes	Partial	No	No	Yes	No	No	No
Brazil	18,852	No	Full	No	No	Yes	No	No	No
Portugal	17,271	Yes	Full	Yes	Yes	Yes	No	No	No
United States	13,394	Yes	Full	Yes	Yes	Yes	Yes	Yes	Yes
New Zealand	13,142	Yes	No	Yes	Yes	Yes	Yes	Regional	No
Argentina	12,219	Yes	Partial	No	Yes	No	Yes	Yes	No
Nigeria	11,398	No	No	No	No	No	No	No	No
Iran	10,292	No	Full	No	No	No	No	No	No
Japan	10,240	Yes	No	Yes	No	No	No	No	No
Yemen	9,550	No	No	No	No	No	No	No	No
France	9,418	Yes	Full	Yes	Yes	Yes	No	Regional	Yes
Peru	9,408	No	No	No	No	No	Yes	No	No
Ecuador	9,120	Yes	Full	No	No	No	No	Yes	Yes
Oman	7,057	No	Full	No	No	No	No	No	No
Sri Lanka	6,457	No	Yes	No	No	Yes	No	No	No
Australia	6,623	Yes	Partial	Yes	Yes	Yes	Yes	Regional	Yes
Total	437,592	12	15	7	7	11	5	6	5

Note
Nations were ranked according to reported annual catches for 2011 extracted from the FAO Fishstat database. The last row totals catch and the number of countries that have enacted a particular management measure. A partial finning ban refers to any finning measure that does not include landing sharks with their fins attached. Protected areas refer to spatial closures that are specifically designed to protect sharks, among other species. Information was gathered from available published sources, government reports and by directly contacting fisheries scientists in these countries

the FAO developed the international guidelines to this effect. Fifteen (75 per cent) of the top 20 states had banned shark finning in their waters, but only ten (50 per cent) of these were full bans, meaning that sharks can only be landed with their fins naturally attached. Many of these regulations are recent – for example, the EU only closed the last loopholes on shark finning in June 2013, and India banned all finning in August 2013. As such, enforcement cannot yet be evaluated at the national scale.

With respect to data collection and research, only seven (35 per cent) of the surveyed states had any dedicated stock assessments for sharks; these were all developed states with established scientific capacity (EU countries, the United States, Japan, Australia and New Zealand). The lack of scientific capacity may be a major roadblock to ensuring sustainability among many of the world's major fishing nations (Worm and Branch, 2012). As some form of scientific assessment is usually required to set a TAC, it is unsurprising that only seven states have established such a quota system for at least some of their sharks. In the absence of a TAC, however, there are some other options, such as the prohibition of landing species that are at a high risk of extinction. Eleven of the top 20 states have established such restrictions, making this the most common management measure next to finning regulations, and mirroring the actions taken by RFMOs (it is likely that some of the RFMO-prohibited species were simply adopted on a national scale as well). Other measures that may not require a detailed assessment include size limits (e.g. species above or below a certain size cannot be landed), total by-catch limits (e.g. no more than 40 per cent of landings can be elasmobranch by-catch in Argentina) or protected areas that are set up wholly or in part to protect sharks. Five states mandate size restrictions, six have some form of by-catch limit and five have established protected areas for sharks in their waters (Table 14.1). Often, these measures are regional – for example, two jurisdictions in Indonesia recently declared their own shark sanctuaries. Likewise, size and by-catch regulations in Australian shark fisheries tended to vary among different territories.

Overall, the picture emerges that even among the top shark fishing states, relevant scientific and management measures remain scattered and incomplete, with the possible exception of bans on finning and retention of prohibited species. This analysis suggests that current management measures across the top 20 shark fishing states need to be improved. Fortunately, some improvements are underway as evidenced by the recent adoptions of protective measures by major shark fishing states such as India and Indonesia. It needs to be noted, however, that this selection of 'top 20' countries is solely a reflection of reported catch data to the FAO, and considering the massive underreporting of global shark catches (Clarke *et al.*, 2006; Worm *et al.*, 2013) it may provide a very incomplete picture. On average, the situation for shark management is likely not better for the 93 other countries that are engaged in shark fisheries, but report fewer landings than those highlighted here. Yet, there are some interesting exceptions, particularly for small developing states that derive significant income from shark-related dive tourism. Several of these states have placed a complete moratorium on all shark fishing in their territorial waters, creating large shark sanctuaries (see Chapter 13). While some of these proactive measures are economically motivated (Gallagher and Hammerschlag, 2011), local culture may also play a role. In Polynesia, for example, traditional beliefs that sharks incorporate the souls of ancestors may partly motivate protective measures there (Lewis, 1980). Finally, we note that some responsibility also lies with major shark-trading states, particularly those that import a majority of shark fins. Here, it is desirable that stronger management measures be implemented and enforced, these could include stronger import controls, improved reporting on import of shark fins by species and country, enforcement of CITES-listed species and ensuring that the trade of shark products are accurately separated by their correct commodity code (e.g. shark fins, squalene, meat).

In the following, we discuss in greater detail the successes and failures of existing management measures to conserve and sustainably manage sharks at a local level. We focus on directed fisheries, but also touch on the management of shark by-catch.

Management of directed shark fisheries

Directed shark fishing requires tight monitoring and careful management of exploitation rates (Musick *et al.*, 2000). Unfortunately, the history of most directed shark fisheries around the world has followed a 'boom and bust' pattern, wherein overharvest rapidly depleted populations with no or slow recovery thereafter (Bonfil, 1994). Examples of such fisheries include the porbeagle shark off Eastern Canada (*Lamna nasus*) (Campana *et al.*, 2008), tope shark (*Galeorhinus galeus*, regionally also known as soup fin or school shark) off California and Australia (Ripley, 1946; Olsen, 1959) and dogfish *Squalus* spp. in the Atlantic and Pacific Oceans (Pawson *et al.*, 2009; Rago and Sosebee, 2009; Wallace *et al.*, 2009). The available evidence hence suggests that sustainable shark fisheries are difficult to achieve. An exception may be fisheries for some smaller, faster-growing species that are well-assessed and tightly managed, such as the gummy shark (*Mustelus antarcticus*) in Australia. Here, we review three well-documented case studies that show contrasting trends of exploited shark stocks over time (Figure 14.2).

Porbeagle shark, Atlantic Canada

The porbeagle shark is a large cold-temperate shark species (maximum length 350 cm) that occurs in the Atlantic, South Pacific, Indian and Southern Oceans. The Northwest Atlantic population is considered a single stock, and is genetically distinct from the East Atlantic populations (Campana *et al.*, 2001). Porbeagle sharks tend to concentrate in areas along the continental shelves off the Gulf of Maine and eastern Canada. Life history attributes are typical of

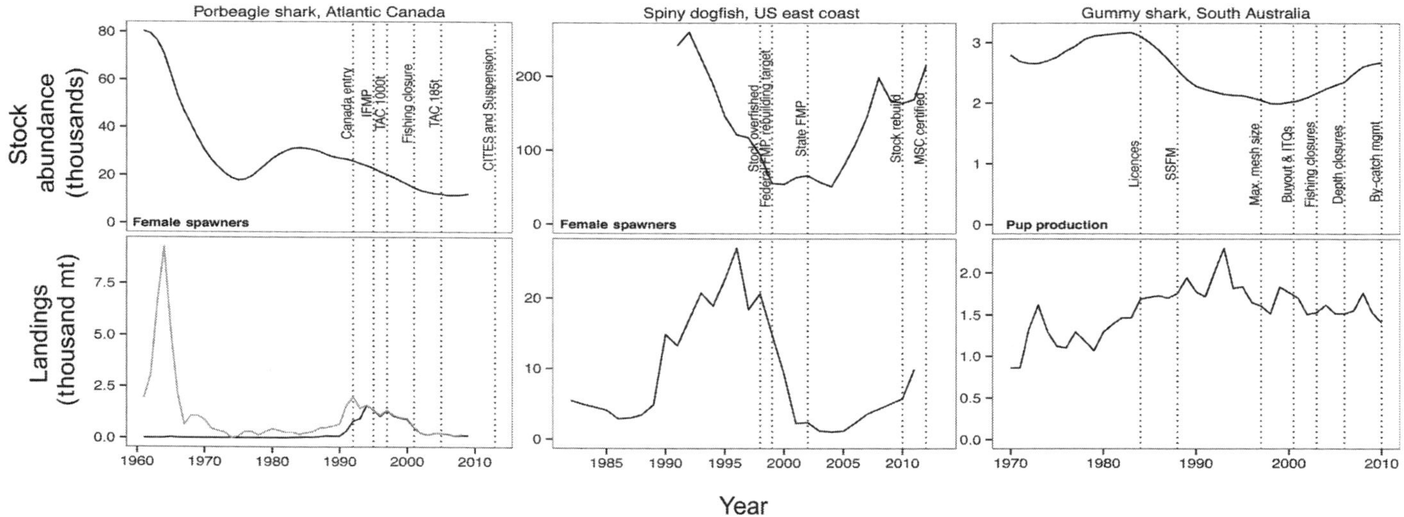

Figure 14.2 Shark fishery case studies.

Note

Shown are time trends of shark counts or biomass, and reported landings, relative to established management measures. The light grey line on porbeagle catches represents catches by foreign fleet; dark line represents Canadian catches. Spawner abundance for porbeagle in 1,000 individuals, for other stocks 1,000 tonnes.

a large species, with late maturity (at 8–13 years), low reproductive rate (1–5 pups year^{-1}), and an estimated maximum age of 26–46 years (Jensen *et al.*, 2002).

Directed fisheries in the Northwest Atlantic began in 1961, when the Norwegian fleet was looking for new profitable grounds. Vessels from the Faroe Islands also started fishing the population and in only six years the fishery collapsed (Figure 14.2). Landings dropped from over 9,000 tonnes in 1964 to less than 1,000 tonnes in 1970 and further to 500 tonnes in the late 1980s (Campana *et al.*, 2008, 2013). The year 1992 marked Canada's entry into the fishery. After the collapse and closure of eastern Canadian cod stocks that year, there was acute interest in investigating alternatives, such as directed shark fisheries. By 1994, foreign vessels were excluded from the porbeagle shark fishery, and, by that time, total landings by Canadian offshore and inshore vessels totalled 1,600 tonnes. The practice of finning was outlawed in 1994 in Canada. In 1995 the first shark fisheries management plan was introduced, which included limited entry to a fishery that was previously open-access and not managed. A number of exploratory fishing licences for porbeagle were handed out; licensees were obligated in helping to gather scientific data. In 1997, a provisional TAC of 1,000 tonnes was imposed, which was based on historic catches, in the absence of a stock assessment. Dedicated research has since been undertaken by the Canadian Department of Fisheries and Oceans (DFO), leading to the development of comprehensive stock assessments. By 2001 it was obvious that porbeagle abundance was too low to support the 1,000 tonnes quota. As a response, some licences were not renewed, a fishing closure to protect pupping females was established and the TAC was lowered to 200 tonnes to allow for recovery. Based on an improved stock assessment in 2005, the TAC was again lowered to 185 tonnes, which corresponds to a 4 per cent exploitation rate. From this, 125 tonnes were allotted to the directed fishery while 60 tonnes were reserved for domestic by-catch (Campana *et al.*, 2008, 2013). In 2004, the Committee on the Status of Endangered Wildlife in Canada designated the porbeagle as an endangered species, but failed to gain legal protection under Canadian Endangered Species Legislation (Cosandey-Godin and Worm, 2010). After several failed attempts at CITES, the proposal to limit trade on porbeagle passed in 2013. In the wake of the CITES process, market prices caved and the fishery became unprofitable. The directed fishery was officially suspended in 2013.

Management measures applied since 2002 have halted population decline and new analyses indicate that the total biomass may now be 4–22 per cent higher than it was in 2001 (Campana *et al.*, 2013). Nonetheless, stock biomass remains very low (Figure 14.2). One issue that may jeopardize further recovery is continued IUU fishing outside the Canadian EEZ and continued by-catch in domestic fisheries (Campana *et al.*, 2013).

Spiny dogfish, US east coast

The spiny dogfish is a smaller demersal shark (maximum length 160 cm) that can reach high abundance in temperate continental shelf waters of the Atlantic and Indo-Pacific. Spiny dogfish schools are regularly composed of large females found inshore, while immature and male fish are found both inshore and offshore. Females mature late at 16 years, have gestation periods between 18–22 months, produce litters ranging from 2–15 pups and live between 40–50 years (Branstetter and Burgess, 2002; Campana *et al.*, 2009a). These life history traits constrain the species to very slow population growth (Smith *et al.*, 1998), making it intrinsically vulnerable to overexploitation, particularly where groups of females are targeted.

In the Northwest Atlantic, spiny dogfish range from the Labrador Shelf to Florida, with seasonal migratory movements between US and Canadian waters (Campana *et al.*, 2009a). The stock experienced low fishing pressure up to the Second World War. Subsequently, there were two periods of overfishing, first by foreign fleets in 1962–1978, with a peak catch of 25,000 tonnes in 1974 (Kulka *et al.*, 2012). During the 1980s, trawl surveys indicated a period of stock recovery, aided by the elimination of foreign fishing from the newly declared US exclusive economic zone (EEZ); furthermore, the progressive depletion of other groundfish may have eased competition and helped dogfish recover (Fogarty and Murawski, 1998). Expanding European markets led to a second period of overexploitation, this time by the US fleet, which landed an annual average of 18,000 tonnes from 1990–1998, with a peak of 27,200 tonnes in 1996 (Figure 14.2). The situation was compounded by the deliberate targeting of large females, and by large discards in both target and non-target fisheries. Following a 1997 stock assessment, the National Marine Fisheries Service (NMFS) declared the US stock to be overfished in 1998, with particular concerns about the sharp decline of female spawners since the early 1990s (Figure 14.2).

In response to the NMFS 1998 declaration, a joint Fisheries Management Plan (FMP) was developed by the Mid-Atlantic and New England Fishery Management Councils in 1999 and implemented in 2000 (Kulka *et al.*, 2012). The plan aimed to regulate the previously unmanaged directed fishery, reduce fishing mortality of females and to rebuild the spawning stock to a target biomass of 180,000 tonnes within five years. This target was later corrected by NMFS to 200,000 tonnes, which is thought to maximize recruitment. Strict incidental catch quotas (1,820 tonnes) and restrictive trip limits were instituted, which essentially ended the directed fishery. Additional measures included a prohibition on shark finning, annual quota adjustments, standardizing by-catch reporting and the establishment of a dedicated Spiny Dogfish Monitoring Committee. Following a 2000 emergency closure in state waters, a state FMP was approved in 2002 that broadly followed the lead of the federal FMP. Restrictive quotas kept total mortality (commercial, incidental and recreational) at low levels, from 2,322 tonnes in 2001 to 1,087 tonnes in 2004, then increasing to 5,411 tonnes in 2009. NMFS declared the stock to be rebuilt in 2010, showing the success of the FMP and associated management measures. Based on this, the US Northwest Atlantic Spiny Dogfish Fishery sought Marine Stewardship Council (MSC) certification in 2010. In 2012 the certification was granted, with an additional 16 conditions aimed to further improve the fishery's sustainability record (Kulka *et al.*, 2012).

Southern Australian shark fishery: gummy shark

Directed fishing for sharks was first recorded in southern Australia in the late 1920s, but it was not before the 1940s that demand for shark liver and later for shark meat resulted in a large expansion of the fishery (Woodhams *et al.*, 2011). At the time, the main target was the school shark (*Galeorhinus galeus*). In the early 1970s, the fishing effort shifted to gummy sharks (*Mustelus antarcticus*) as school sharks were banned from sale from 1972 to 1985 due to severe population declines and concerns over mercury content (Woodhams *et al.*, 2011).

Gummy sharks are endemic to southern Australia. They are a smaller demersal species (maximum length of 175 cm) of intermediate productivity. Age of maturity may be around 4–6 years, gestation period is one year and the average litter size is 14 pups (Last and Stevens, 2009). They are generally found near shore on the shelf in shallow waters up to 80 m deep. The fishery remained under open-access until 1984, when licensing was first introduced. Total shark catch peaked at 4,226 tonnes in 1987 and in 1988 the Southern Shark Fishery Management Plan was introduced (Figure 14.2). Regulatory measures included a limit on fishing capacity by issuing maximum gear units to operators based on catch history. Each net unit permit the use of a standard gillnet (length of 6,000 m, 20 meshes deep and 150 mm mesh size) (Woodhams *et al.* 2011). A suite of measures has since been introduced in the fishery (see Figure 14.2 for a chronology of major events) and included input controls such as a reduction in gillnet length to 4,200 m, individual transferable quotas (ITQs), a reduction in the number of active vessels through buyout and other structural adjustments and, recently, in 2007, area closures. For example, areas deeper than 130 m were closed off the west coast of Tasmania. Moreover, in response to declining stocks, several measures were implemented to limit school shark by-catch, specifically an upper mesh size limit of 165 mm (6.5 inches) to protect adults, fishing closures to protect pupping areas and, recently, the TAC was further lowered to 150 metric tonnes for the 2012–2013 fishing season and a maximum by-catch–target catch ratio of 20 per cent was established (Woodhams *et al.*, 2011). The most recent stock assessment of gummy shark included both age-composition and length-frequency data and the assessment of three separate populations: the Bass Strait, South Australian and Tasmanian populations (Punt and Thomson, 2011). The current index of biomass (pup production) in the three regions is close to or above the target reference point, such that the stock is considered healthy and not experiencing overfishing.

The gummy shark has not been overfished and has remained relatively stable over the last 40 years of fishing history. This is a rare example of a sustainably managed shark fishery. A more resilient life history, size selectivity of gillnets, as well as rigorous science-based TACs played a major role in the management success of this fishery. However, there are still many challenges concerning the long-term sustainability of other shark species captured in this fishery. Despite recent effort to better protect school shark populations, current by-catch levels are unlikely to facilitate recovery within the legally required timeframe, and may thus require further restriction on the gummy shark fishery. Moreover, the fishery is undergoing significant changes to address concerns about Australian sea lion and dolphin by-catch (AFMA, 2010, 2011). For additional discussion of this fishery, refer to Chapter 8.

Summary

These case studies exemplify some of the problems that plague shark fisheries around the world, i.e. historical overfishing in data-poor situations, lack of management oversight, problems with by-catch and discarding, rapid declines in biomass and slow recovery after overfishing. It emerges that shark fisheries can only allow for very low mortality, and there is limited scope for adaptive management, as the resource may collapse within a few years of overfishing. All cases show the importance of fisheries data being collected and analysed, and the role of stock assessments to help monitor the long-term health of an exploited stock. Yet, a comprehensive analysis of 21 assessed populations showed that exploitation rates in the majority of cases exceeded the species' rebound potential, on average by 30 per cent (Worm *et al.*, 2013). This means that even assessed shark fisheries are vulnerable to progressive depletion. For shark fisheries to be considered sustainable, they require very close monitoring, stringent and precautionary management and strict enforcement. The measures used to manage shark fisheries are similar to those found in teleost fisheries. These include setting a TAC based on an assessment, modification of fishing gear, effort restrictions, trip and size limits and spatial and temporal closures, including fishing moratoria. In all three case studies, declining population trends were only halted after a stock assessment was conducted, and a very stringent TAC was implemented. Importantly, the issue of by-catch and discards was also addressed to some extent in all three species, as non-directed (by-catch) mortality was also counted against the TAC. This is more manageable for species that reside in shelf waters (such as dogfish and gummy shark), but much more challenging for pelagic species that may range widely and experience additional (often unaccounted for) fishing mortality on the high seas (such as porbeagle). All three case studies, however, show that it is possible to recover overfished shark populations if stringent management measures are enforced. Recovery time was about ten years for spiny dogfish, but could be over 100 years for porbeagle (Campana *et al.*, 2013).

Market-based approaches

Market-based incentive programmes, such as eco-labelling, have gained increasing influence over the last 15 years. Such approaches can be effective in promoting research and supporting the development of more rigorous fisheries management practices. This can affect sharks directly, where shark fisheries are proposed for certification, or indirectly, where reduction of shark by-catch is one of the objectives in certifying a non-shark fishery.

The MSC certification programme remains the most prominent and comprehensive eco-labelling scheme to date. It follows the FAO guidelines for sustainable fisheries and is based on three core principles: maintaining sustainable fish stocks, minimizing the environmental impact of fisheries and promoting effective management (MSC, 2013). By-catch species are defined based on catch size or vulnerability of species caught. A species that comprises less than 5 per cent of the total catch by weight is normally not included. However, due to their particular vulnerability, most sharks are considered a main by-catch species under MSC rules (MSC, 2013). Moreover, new rules, introduced in 2012, resolved that that fisheries engaged in shark finning would not be eligible for certification to the MSC standard for sustainable fisheries.

Directed shark fisheries

Recently, the certification of directed shark fisheries has caused significant controversy. Both the Canadian Pacific spotted spiny dogfish (*Squalus suckleyi*) and the US Atlantic spiny dogfish fishery discussed above were certified in 2012. Concerns revolve around uncertainties in stock status, and possible incentives in expanding a directed fishery. On the other hand, the rebuilding success for the US Northwest Atlantic dogfish (see the case study above) is evident, and supports the view that current management is effective in ensuring a sustainable fishery. This is less clear in the case of the Canadian fishery, where data limitations have prevented a fully analytic assessment, and catch levels were simply set close to historical levels, with the argument that the fishery is small and has not yet depleted the stock. Here, the MSC process could motivate improved data collection and research, and in fact this is mandated under the conditions issued by the certification agency.

By-catch fisheries

Likewise, there have been concerns over the certification of fisheries that have high shark by-catch. The most prominent example is the Canadian Northwest Atlantic swordfish (*Xiphias gladius*) fishery, certified in 2013. The main concern associated with the certification was related to the incidental catch of sharks and turtles. Three shark species were assessed, namely the porbeagle and shortfin mako (*Isurus oxyrinchus*) as retained by-catch, and blue shark as discards. Blue shark catch rates in particular are very high, often 2–3 times higher than swordfish catch rates (Campana *et al.*, 2009b). The first assessment report was heavily criticized by over 40 different stakeholder groups that felt the assessment failed to recognize the urgent need for improved shark conservation and the necessity for stringent discard mortality management overall. This review process resulted in additional conditions to the certification, including annual surveillance audits on discards, tagging studies to determine release mortality and improved stock assessments for sharks caught as by-catch (Devitt *et al.*, 2012). Concerns remain, however, that there is currently no effective way of reducing the overall catch of sharks in this fishery; a pilot study testing rare-earth metal deterrents on longlines did not produce any tangible results, and other options still need to be explored (Cosandey-Godin *et al.*, 2013).

Summary

Despite the vigorous debate of current MSC practices (Christian *et al.*, 2013), eco-labelling clearly has the potential to promote research, foster partnership and better communication between stakeholders, and could ultimately help support the development of sustainable practices for shark fisheries and shark by-catch. The extent to which this will happen likely depends on continued engagement by concerned stakeholders during the consultation process and MSC audits.

Lessons from other fisheries

Given the state of fisheries resources in general, and sharks in particular, there is a strong emphasis in contemporary fisheries management on rebuilding and recovery of depleted stocks. There is a rich literature documenting successes and failures both from a historical (Lotze *et al.*, 2006, 2011) and recent perspective (Caddy and Agnew, 2004; Worm *et al.*, 2009; Ward-Paige *et al.*, 2012). These analyses suggest that successful rebuilding strategies often include the following elements: (1) exploitation rate is substantially reduced in order to initiate recovery; (2) this is typically achieved by a merging of diverse management actions, including catch restrictions, gear modification and closed areas, depending on local context; (3) the 'hidden' effects of IUU fishing, incidental by-catch and discards are accounted for; and (4) other threats such as habitat destruction are addressed, where applicable. A comprehensive review of 60 case studies by Caddy and Agnew (2004) also concluded that the most successful recoveries occurred within the centre of the species' geographical range, and in favourable environmental regimes. On the governance side, success seems to depend on non-discretionary fishery control laws being applied (Caddy and Agnew, 2004), such as pre-agreed reference points that trigger certain management actions.

In terms of guiding appropriate management action in the face of considerable uncertainty (a problem endemic to most shark populations), the authors developed a consideration matrix scheme that identifies necessary management measures depending on two key variables: resource status and productivity (Table 14.2). Most shark populations fall within the bottom row of low productivity and moderate-to-collapsed stock status. Note that a fishing moratorium is typically mandated under these conditions unless the stock is considered to be in moderate condition (TAC needs to be lowered) or healthy (TAC remains stable) (Table 14.2).

Conclusion: best practices in shark fisheries management

Conceptually, fisheries management of sharks is simple: the goal is to reduce mortality rates to a level that allows depleted populations to recover, and other populations to maintain their productivity. The difficult question is what is required to achieve those low mortality rates in practice where there are large uncertainties about the status of many populations, and about the magnitude of fishing mortality. Our case studies (Figure 14.2) all show that proper monitoring and assessment are critical to achieving lower mortality rates and rebuilding depleted populations. Importantly, all case studies derive from regions that have a large and established capacity in fisheries science, management and enforcement of a hard TAC. The problem is that most regions where sharks are caught in large numbers (Figure 14.1) have a much lower capacity to perform the relevant science and enforce appropriate management measures (Mora *et al.*, 2009; Worm and Branch, 2012). In the absence of the capacity to assess and fine-tune fishing mortality rates via TAC or similar measures, 'blunter' management measures such as prohibitions on retaining certain species are important; large-scale fishing closures can play a similar role in a spatial management context. As Table 14.2 shows, a moratorium on shark fishing is in order for all those cases where populations of low productivity and low recovery potential are depleted or collapsed; arguably this is true for a majority of pelagic sharks (Dulvy *et al.*, 2008). As most sharks are threatened less so by directed fisheries but by incidental by-catch, any measures that reduce by-catch rates or discard mortality will be critical in achieving the recovery of depleted populations, particularly in pelagic environments on the high seas. Here, RFMOs and other international entities such as CITES will play a critical role in reducing, and ideally eliminating, the current threats of unregulated by-catch fisheries on pelagic shark populations.

Acknowledgements

This research was supported by grants from the National Science and Engineering Research Council of Canada (NSERC) to Boris Worm, an NSERC

Table 14.2 Consideration matrix for stock management and rebuilding

Productivity regime	*Stock condition*			
	Healthy	*Moderate*	*Poor*	*Collapsed*
High	TAC may be raised	TAC may be raised	TAC remains stable	By-catch only
Intermediate	TAC may be raised	TAC remains stable	TAC should decrease	Fishing moratorium
Low	TAC remains stable	TAC should decrease	Fishing moratorium	Fishing moratorium

Note
This scheme proposes certain harvest rules that follow an assessment of stock condition and productivity; redrawn after Caddy and Agnew (2004). Most shark species fall into low productivity (shaded areas) and poor or collapsed condition (e.g. porbeagle shark, Figure 14.2), some well-managed or recovered stocks may be considered healthy to moderate stock status (gummy shark, dogfish, Figure 14.2).

Industrial Postgraduate Scholarship and funding from WWF-Canada to Aurelie Cosandey-Godin. We acknowledge the help of students in the 2013 Elasmobranch Biology and Management class at Dalhousie University, who compiled data for Table 14.1; further information was provided by M. Erdmann (Indonesia), J. Javid and F. Kaymaram (Iran) and R. Barreto (Brazil).

References

AFMA (2010) *Australian Sea Lion Management Strategy, Southern and Eastern Scalefish and Shark Fishery (SESSF)*, Australian Fisheries Management Authority, Canberra

AFMA (2011) *Changes in the Gillnet, Hook and Trap Sector of the Southern and Eastern Scalefish and Shark Fishery to Protect Dolphins*, Australian Fisheries Management Authority, Canberra.

Baum, J. K., Myers, R. A., Kehler, D., Worm, B., Harley, S. J. and Doherty, P. A. (2003) 'Collapse and conservation of shark populations in the Northwest Atlantic', *Science*, vol. 299, pp. 389–392.

Bonfil, R. (1994) 'Overview of world elasmobranch fisheries', FAO Fisheries Technical Paper, no. 341.

Branch, T. A., Lobo, A. S. and Purcell, S. W. (2013) 'Opportunistic exploitation: an overlooked pathway to extinction', *Trends in Ecology and Evolution*, vol. 28, pp. 409–413.

Branstetter, S. and Burgess, G. (2002) 'Sharks, superorder Selachiiomorpha', in B. Collette and G. Klein-MacPhee (eds), *Bigelow and Schroeder's Fishes of the Gulf of Maine*, Smithsonian Institution Press, Washington, DC.

Brewer, D., Heales, D., Milton, D., Dell, Q., Fry, G., Venables, B. and Jones, P. (2006) 'The impact of turtle excluder devices and bycatch reduction devices on diverse tropical marine communities in Australia's northern prawn trawl fishery', *Fisheries Research*, vol. 81, pp. 176–188.

Caddy, J. F. and Agnew, D. J. (2004) 'An overview of recent global experience with recovery plans for depleted marine resources and suggested guidelines for recovery planning', *Reviews in Fish Biology and Fisheries*, vol. 14, pp. 43–112.

Camhi, M. D., Lauck, E., Pikitch, E. K. and Babcock, E. A. (2009) 'A global overview of commercial fisheries for open ocean sharks', in M. D. Camhi, E. K. Pikitch and E. A. Babcock (eds), *Sharks of the Open Ocean*, Blackwell Publishing, Oxford.

Campana, S., Marks, L., Joyce, W. and Harley, S. (2001) *Analytical Assessment of the Porbeagle Shark (*Lamna nasus*) Population in the Northwest Atlantic, with Estimates of Long-term Sustainable Yield*, CSAS Research Document, 2001/067, Department of Fisheries and Oceans, Ottawa.

Campana, S. E., Joyce, W., Marks, L., Hurley, P., Natanson, L., Kohler, N. E., Jensen, C. F., Mello, J. J., Pratt Jr, H. L., Myklevoll, S. and Harley, S. (2008) 'The rise and fall (again) of the porbeagle shark population in the Northwest Atlantic', in M. D. Camhi, E. K. Pikitch and E. A. Babcock (eds), *Sharks of the Open Ocean: Biology, Fisheries and Conservation*, Blackwell Publishing, Oxford.

Campana, S. E., Joyce, W. and Kulka, D. W. (2009a) 'Growth and reproduction of Spiny Dogfish off the eastern coast of Canada, including inferences on stock structure', in V. Gallucci, G. McFarlane and G. Bargmann (eds), *Biology and Management of Spiny Dogfish Shark*, American Fisheries Society, Bethesda, MD.

Campana, S. E., Joyce, W. and Manning, M. J. (2009b) 'Bycatch and discard mortality in commercially caught blue sharks *Prionace glauca* assessed using archival satellite pop-up tags', *Marine Ecology Progress Series*, vol. 387, pp. 241–253.

Campana, S. E., Gibson, A. J. F., Fowler, M., Dorey, A. and Joyce, W. (2013) *Population Dynamics of Northwest Atlantic Porbeagle (*Lamna nasus*), with an Assessment of Status and Projections for Recovery*, CSAS Research Document 2012/096, Department of Fisheries and Oceans, Ottawa.

Christian, C., Ainley, D., Bailey, M., Dayton, P., Hocevar, J., LeVine, M., Nikoloyuk, J., Nouvian, C., Velarde, E., Werner, R. and Jacquet, J. (2013) 'A review of formal objections to Marine Stewardship Council fisheries certifications', *Biological Conservation*, vol. 161, pp. 10–17.

Clarke, S. C., McAllister, M. K., Milner-Gulland, E. J., Kirkwood, G. P., Michielsens, C. G. J., Agnew, D. J., Pikitch, E. K., Nakano, H. and Shivji, M. S. (2006) 'Global estimates of shark catches using trade records from commercial markets', *Ecology Letters*, vol. 9, pp. 1115–1126.

Clarke, S. C., Harley, S. J., Hoyle, S. D. and Rice, J. S. (2013) 'Population trends in Pacific oceanic sharks and the utility of regulations on shark finning', *Conservation Biology*, vol. 27, pp. 197–209.

Cosandey Godin, A. and Worm, B. (2010) 'Keeping the lead: how to strengthen shark conservation and management policies in Canada', *Marine Policy*, vol. 34, pp. 995–1001.

Cosandey Godin, A., Wimmer, T., Wang, J. H. and Worm, B. (2013) 'No effect from rare-earth metal deterrent on shark bycatch in a commercial pelagic longline trial', *Fisheries Research*, vol. 143, pp. 131–135.

Davis, B. and Worm, B. (2013) 'The International Plan of Action for Sharks: how does national implementation measure up?', *Marine Policy*, vol. 38, pp. 312–320.

Devitt, S., Park, A., O'Boyle, R., Maguire, J.-J. and Sissenwine, M. (2012) *North Atlantic Swordfish (*Xiphias gladius*) Canadian Pelagic Longline Fishery: Public Certification Report*, Moody Marine, Dartmouth, Nova Scotia.

Dulvy, N., Baum, J. K., Clarhe, S., Compagno, L. J. V., Cortes, E., Domingo, A., Fordham, S., Fowler, S., Francis, M. P., Gibson, C., Martinez, J., Musick, J. A., Soldo, A., Stevens, J. D. and Valenti, S. (2008) 'You can swim but you can't hide: the global status and conservation of oceanic pelagic sharks and rays', *Aquatic Conservation*, vol. 18, pp. 459–482.

FAO (1999) *International Plan of Action for the Conservation and Management of Sharks*, available at www.fao.org/fishery/ipoa-sharks/en, accessed 26 August 2013.

FAO (2000) *Fisheries Management: 1. Conservation and Management of Sharks*, FAO, Rome, Italy.

FAO (2003) *The Ecosystem approach to Fisheries*, FAO Technical Guidelines for Responsible Fisheries. No. 4, Suppl. 2, FAO Fisheries Department, Rome.

FAO (2006) *Report of the FAO Expert Consultation on the Implementation of the FAO International Plan of Action for the Conservation and Management of Sharks*, Rome, 6–8 December 2005.

FAO (2008) *Report of the Technical Workshop on the Status, Limitations and Opportunities for Improving the Monitoring of Shark Fisheries and Trade*, Rome, 3–6 November.

Ferretti, F., Worm, B., Britten, G., Heithaus, M. R. and Lotze, H. K. (2010) 'Patterns and ecosystem consequences of shark declines in the ocean', *Ecology Letters*, vol. 13, pp. 1055–1071.

Fogarty, M. J. and Murawski, S. A. (1998) 'Large-scale disturbance and the structure of marine systems: fishery impacts on Georges Bank', *Ecological Applications*, vol. 8, Supp, pp. 6–22.

Gallagher, A. J. and Hammerschlag, N. (2011) 'Global shark currency: the distribution, frequency, and economic value of shark ecotourism', *Current Issues in Tourism*, vol. 8, pp. 797–812.

Jensen, C. F., Natanson, L. J., Pratt Jr., H. L., Kohler, N. and Campana, S. E. (2002) 'The reproductive biology of the porbeagle shark (*Lamna nasus*) in the western North Atlantic Ocean', *Fisheries Bulletin*, vol. 100, pp. 727–738.

Kulka, D., Rivard, D. and Scott, I. (2012) *MSC Certification: The United States Atlantic Fishery for Spiny Dogfish (Squalus acanthias)*, Moody Marine Ltd, Moody International Certification, Dartmouth, Canada.

Lack, M. and Meere, F. (2009) *Pacific Islands Regional Plan of Action for Sharks: Guidance for Pacific Island Countries and Territories on the Conservation and Management of Sharks*, Pacific Islands Forum Fisheries Agency, Honiara, Solomon Islands.

Last, P. R. and Stevens, J. D. (2009) *Sharks and Rays of Australia*, Havard University Press, London.

Lewis, R. E. (1980) 'The soul and the afterworld in Hawaiian myth and in other Polynesian cultures', thesis, University of Hawaii at Honolulu, HI.

Lewison, R. L., Crowder, L. B., Read, A. J. and Freeman, S. A. (2004) 'Understanding impacts of fisheries bycatch on marine megafauna', *Trends in Ecology and Evolution*, vol. 19, pp. 598–604.

Lotze, H. K., Lenihan, H. S., Bourque, B. J., Bradbury, R., Cooke, R. G., Kay, M. C., Kidwell, S. M., Kirby, M. X., Peterson, C. H. and Jackson, J. B. C. (2006) 'Depletion, degradation, and recovery potential of estuaries and coastal seas', *Science*, vol. 312, pp. 1806–1809.

Lotze, H. K., Coll, M., Magera, A. M., Ward-Paige, C. and Airoldi, L. (2011) 'Recovery of marine animal populations and ecosystems', *Trends in Ecology and Evolution*, vol. 26, pp. 595–605.

Manire, C. A. and Gruber, S. H. (1990) 'Many sharks may be headed toward extinction', *Conservation Biology*, vol. 4, pp. 10–11.

MarViva (2013) 'The use of trawling nets to capture shrimp is forbidden in Costa Rica', available at www.marviva.net/index.php/en/2011-12-15-15-50-51/notes-archive/427-the-use-of-trawling-nets-to-capture-shrimp-is-forbidden-in-costa-rica, accessed 18 September 2013.

Molina, J. M. and Cooke, S. J. (2012) 'Trends in shark bycatch research: current status and research needs', *Reviews in Fish Biology and Fisheries*, vol. 22, pp. 719–737.

Mora, C., Myers, R. A., Coll, M., Libralato, S., Pitcher, T. J., Sumaila, R. U., Zeller, D., Watson, R., Gaston, K. J. and Worm, B. (2009) 'Management effectiveness of the world's marine fisheries', *PLoS Biology*, vol. 7.

Morato, T., Watson, R., Pitcher, T. J. and Pauly, D. (2006) 'Fishing down the deep', *Fish and Fisheries*, vol. 7, pp. 24–34.

MSC (2013) *MSC Certification Requirements Version 1.3*, Marine Stewardship Council, London.

Musick, J. A. and Bonfil, R. (2005) *Management Techniques for Elasmobranch Fisheries*, FAO Technical Guidelines for Responsible Fisheries, FAO, Rome.

Musick, J. A. and Musick, S. (2011) *Sharks*, FAO Fisheries and Aquaculture Reviews and Studies, Rome.

Musick, J. A., Burgess, G., Cailliet, G., Camhi, M. and Fordham, S. (2000) 'Management of sharks and their relatives (Elasmobranchii)', *Fisheries*, vol. 25, pp. 9–13.

Olsen, A. M. (1959) 'The status of the school shark fishery in south-eastern Australia waters', *Australian Journal of Marine and Freshwater Research*, vol. 10, pp. 150–176.

Pawson, M. J., Ellis, J. and Dobby, H. (2009) 'The evolution and management of spiny dogfish (spurdog) fisheries in the Northeast Atlantic', in V. F. Gallucci, G. A. McFarlane and G. C. Bargmann (eds), *Biology and Management of Spiny Dogfish Sharks*, American Fisheries Society, Bethesda, MD.

Pikitch, E. K., Camhi, M. D. and Babcock, E. A. (2008) 'Introduction to sharks of the open ocean', in M. D. Camhi, E. K. Pikitch and E. A. Babcock (eds), *Sharks of the Open Ocean: Biology, Fisheries and Conservation*, Blackwell Publishing, Oxford.

Punt, A. and Thomson, R. (2011) 'Gummy shark (*Mustelus antarcticus*) assessment based on data up to 2009', in G. N. Tuck (ed.), *Stock Assessment for the Southern and Eastern Scalefish and Shark Fishery*, AFMA and CSIRO Marine and Atmospheric Research, Hobart, Australia.

Rago, P. and Sosebee, K. (2009) 'The agony of recovery: challenges of spiny dogfish recovery programs', in V. F. Gallucci, G. A. McFarlane and G. C. Bargmann (eds), *Biology and Management of Spiny Dogfish Sharks*, American Fisheries Society, Bethesda, MD.

Ripley, W. E. (1946) 'The soup-fin shark and the fishery', *Fisheries Bulletin*, vol. 64, pp. 7–37.

Siferd, T. (2010) *By-catch in the Shrimp Fishery from Shrimp Fishing Areas 0–3, 1979 to 2009*, CSAS Research Document 2010/037, Department of Fisheries and Oceans, Ottawa.

Smith, S. E., Au, D. W. and Show, C. (1998) 'Intrinsic rebound potentials of 26 species of Pacific sharks', *Marine and Freshwater Research*, vol. 49, pp. 663–678.

Stevens, J. D., Bonfil, R., Dulvy, N. K. and Walker, P. A. (2000) 'The effects of fishing on sharks, rays, and chimaeras (chondrichthyans), and the implications for marine ecosystems', *ICES Journal of Marine Science*, vol. 57, pp. 476–494.

Wallace, S., McFarlane, G., Campana, S. and King, J. R. (2009) 'Status of spiny dogfish in Atlantic and Pacific Canada', in V. F. Gallucci, G. A. McFarlane and G. C. Bargmann (eds), *Biology and Management of Spiny Dogfish Sharks*, American Fisheries Society, Bethesda, MD.

Ward, P., Lawrence, E., Darbyshire, R. and Hindmarsh, S. (2008) 'Large-scale experiment shows that nylon leaders reduce shark bycatch and benefit pelagic longline fishers', *Fisheries Research*, vol. 90, pp. 100–108.

Ward-Paige, C. A., Keith, D., Worm, B. and Lotze, H. K. (2012) 'Recovery potential and conservation options for elasmobranchs', *Journal of Fish Biology*, vol. 80, pp. 1844–1869.

Watson, R. A., Cheung, W. W. L., Anticamara, J. A., Sumaila, R. U., Zeller, D. and Pauly, D. (2012) 'Global marine yield halved as fishing intensity redoubles', *Fish and Fisheries*, vol. 14, no. 4, pp. 493–503.

Woodhams, J., Vieira, S. and Stobutzki, I. (2011) 'Shark gillnet and shark hook sectors', in J. Woodhams, I. Stobutzki, S. Vieira, R. Curtotti and G. Begg (eds), *Fishery Status Reports 2010: Status of Fish Stocks and Fisheries Managed by the Australian Government*, Australian Bureau of Agricultural and Resource Economics and Sciences, Canberra.

Worm, B. and Branch, T. A. (2012) 'The future of fish', *Trends in Ecology and Evolution*, vol. 27, pp. 594–599.

Worm, B., Hilborn, R., Baum, J. K., Branch, T. A., Collie, J. S., Costello, C., Fogarty, M. J., Fulton, E. A., Hutchings, J. A., Jennings, S., Jensen, O. P., Lotze, H. K., Mace, P. M., McClanahan, T. R., Minto, C., Palumbi, S. R., Parma, A. M., Ricard, D., Rosenberg, A. A., Watson, R. and Zeller, D. (2009) 'Rebuilding global fisheries', *Science*, vol. 325, pp. 578–585.

Worm, B., Davis, B., Kettemer, L., Ward-Paige, C., Chapman, D., Heithaus, M., Kessel, S. and Gruber, S. (2013) 'Global catches, exploitation rates, and rebuilding options for sharks', *Marine Policy*, vol. 40, pp. 194–204.

Chapter 15

Synergies, solutions and the way forward

Natalie Klein and Erika J. Techera

The dire situation confronting shark species should not be underestimated. With an approximate 100 million individual sharks being fished annually (Worm *et al.*, 2013), and uncertainty surrounding additional catches due to finning practices, unreported by-catch and illegal fishing, it is not surprising that so many shark species are considered as at-risk. For some species it is known that they are vulnerable or critically endangered, in other cases, as noted by Lack, we have insufficient data to be able to provide an accurate assessment. Sharks face a dual threat, as observed by Momigliano and Harcourt, in that there is a significant demand for shark products, but shark stocks are highly vulnerable to fishing pressure because they are long-lived, slow growing and late to reach sexual maturity. Compounding this, Kempster and Collin noted that 'Unprecedented declines in shark populations have revealed an inability to predict both the susceptibility of populations to collapse and their capacity for subsequent recovery.'

With this predicament, it is critical to consider a variety of solutions and the purpose of this chapter is to bring together the many issues raised throughout the book, as well as highlighting what could be done in the future. The solutions we consider have to address a range of problems, including the differing characteristics of shark species, the need for further scientific information and implementing laws designed to improve the sustainability of shark species. These are discussed in the first part of the chapter. The solutions must also take into account a diverse group of stakeholders, which are next discussed, because the differing roles and interests should be reflected in implementing conservation and management measures. In recognizing the varied actors, it is possible to assess the tools and techniques utilized for shark governance, which we do in the third part of the chapter. We then place all these issues against the levels of governance, highlighting the need for horizontal and vertical integration in proposing management measures. Finally, in determining how we might move forward, we can underline the utility of multi-disciplinary dimensions and highlight what might be done to improve the coherency and comprehensiveness of shark protection.

Key problems

While the term 'sharks' is used throughout this volume, this one label encompasses a diverse range of species. There is no agreement on the number of shark species, with some estimating over 500 whereas others suggest over 1,000. As Kiszka and Heithaus pointed out at the outset of this book, the characteristics between these species vary. Their main habitat may be the deep sea or shallow reefs; they may be highly migratory or coastal dwellers. The diets, fecundity, speed, size, behaviour and colourings can also differ. In light of these variables, it is difficult to suggest that there is a 'one size fits all' solution that can be proposed to ensure sustainable management of sharks *in toto*. Yet there are some broadbrush characteristics common to many sharks, such as slow growth, late age at maturity, low fecundity and long lives. These provide a starting point.

But we also need to take into account the human response to the varied shark species. Consumers have a preference between different types of shark meat, and the size of shark fins can have status value in the preparation of shark fin soup. Recreational fishers will have a preference for targeting the larger, more exotic looking shark species (e.g. hammerheads). Some sharks are docile in their interaction with humans, allowing for swimming and diving as part of tourism operations. The threat to human life sometimes presented by other shark species promotes a culture of fear and increases the human predatory instincts and reactions. In other contexts and cultures, however, sharks are revered (Techera, 2012). These attitudes then influence what steps are taken in regulating the full range of human interactions with sharks.

As discussed by Kempster and Collin, there are iconic species of sharks that have triggered the greatest focus. The great white shark, the whale shark and basking sharks have captured attention because of their interactions with humans and their specific characteristics. Targeting evolutionary distinct species for protection is important for global biodiversity conservation (Kempster and Collin chapter). These iconic species have been the subject of considerable scientific research, as noted by Momigliano and Harcourt. The availability of this data has allowed for greater regulation at all levels of governance. The great white shark, for example, has been seared into human psyches through the movie *Jaws*. Restrictions are now placed on the harvesting of great white sharks under international treaties, such as CITES and CMS, and these are incorporated into national and local laws. This level of attention is not mirrored across all shark species, and instead the IUCN *Red List* highlights that there is insufficient data on about 46 per cent of species (IUCN, 2012). This lack of scientific information does not assist law and policy makers seeking to support further species listings.

The need for further scientific research is a recurring theme in addressing shark conservation and management. Evident from the IUCN *Red List* is that further information is required just to identify the species that should be researched more in order to learn about their numbers, habits and habitats before determining appropriate management measures. Scientific data are a key driver in establishing fishing quotas, or fishing bans, as well as for deciding on the creation of marine protected areas (MPAs) or sanctuaries and whether species should be listed in international treaties to prohibit their trade or harvest.

Even when the scientific data are available, there must also be political will to establish the necessary management and conservation measures and then to implement and enforce those laws and regulations. It was lack of political will that prevented the listing of eight shark species under CITES in 2010, rather than a lack of scientific information. The data available clearly supported the case for these species to be listed, but resistance from countries with significant commercial fishing interests prevented the inclusion of these species in the CITES Appendices. The more immediate economic gains and the concomitant consumer demand have been among the reasons that states have failed to take action despite the evidence presented.

A failure to take action may also be attributed to the difficulties experienced by some developing states in fulfilling international obligations that require additional resources. Developing states may not have the ability to police their waters or fully monitor what catches are brought into port before being shipped to other markets. Legal regimes that require inspectors to be placed on fishing vessels or for the detailed collection of data on board fishing vessels may demand more resources than developing countries have available. Some developing states may be open registry (or flag of convenience) states and do not take the required steps to monitor vessels registered or flagged to them; such lack of diligence may contribute to the data deficiencies existing in relation to shark catches both as targeted catch and as by-catch. As Momigliano and Harcourt have demonstrated, research from developing country sites also lags behind the data available from developed countries. Lack of scientific capacity in developing countries hampers the implementation of appropriate conservation measures. Where developing countries are ahead of their more developed counterparts, Huveneers and Robbins revealed, was in the establishment of shark-related tourism, as these countries have the most species-rich shark-diving opportunities.

Implementation and enforcement issues are of course not limited to developing states. As noted in Klein's chapter, the FAO's International Plan of Action on Sharks (IPOA-Sharks) anticipates that states will adopt National Plans of Action (NPOAs). Lack has highlighted the low numbers of states that have done so, and that this is particularly problematic vis-à-vis those states that have the most fishing vessels harvesting sharks. The sheer quantity of sharks being harvested is problematic in its own right, but as noted previously, the extent of catch that is taken and not reported, as well as illegal catches and by-catch, compound the problem and underline how critical is the implementation and enforcement of laws.

Worm, Cosandey-Godin and Davis have demonstrated what difference adherence to strict fishing regulations may have on the recovery of specific shark fisheries. Their case studies show that closing fishing grounds and prohibiting the harvesting of species may be required and most effective. To this end, they note, 'Spatial management and prohibited species are management measures that are more robust to ignorance than a [total allowable catch], which requires reasonably detailed knowledge.' Implementation and enforcement of regulations are essential to ensure the effectiveness of conservation and management strategies yet are among the greatest challenges.

Another challenge in shark conservation and management is the prevalence of finning. Finning may be undertaken in an especially heinous manner, where the fin is cut off and retained while the shark is alive and the body flung back into the ocean and left to drown. This practice has enabled shark advocates to focus attention on the conservation status of shark species, leading to public pressure for regulatory change. Regional organizations as well as individual states have taken action to reduce the cruelty by requiring that carcasses be retained (even if not attached to the fin) or by outlawing finning in its entirety. Censuring this particular practice in relation to sharks has been a means to improve conservation and management measures, but, as outlined by Hepp and Griffin Wilson, controversy still surrounds the fin–carcass ratio tool, with continual calls to require that sharks be landed with fins naturally attached. Beyond such direct mechanisms it is necessary to much more effectively address the supply chain and markets for fins; although it is noted that there have been recent advances in this area, with airlines and hotels in Southeast Asia refusing to transport and stock shark fins (Cripps, 2013).

However, finning, while financially important in relation to the harvesting of sharks, is not the only concern. Finning constitutes a significant threat to shark species, but sharks are also harvested for their meat and for other products, and are taken as targeted species in some fisheries or as by-catch in other fisheries. As noted by Lawrence, as well as Huveneers and Robbins, some shark fisheries have been sustainably managed over relatively long periods of time. Again, this points to the differences between species, some of which do allow for ongoing commercial fisheries to be maintained. It is also clear that the issue of by-catch needs much greater research attention, both in terms of assessing the extent of the problem and identifying potential solutions.

Sharks are also threatened by a range of human activities, including recreational or game fishers, vessel collisions and habitat destruction, as well as shark nets around beaches as explored in the chapter by Neff. Even shark eco-tourism carries risks for the sharks, despite its benefits, as the techniques used to enhance the tourist experience may prove harmful to the sharks. Such harm can arise in terms of modifying their behaviour (a particular concern in relation to chumming/berleying/feeding) or the interactions making certain feeding or breeding grounds less desirable. These diverse problems underline the need for broad engagement in finding appropriate responses.

Stakeholder engagement

In responding to these assorted issues, there are many stakeholders who have an interest in how sharks are managed and conserved. The stakeholders include the state, the fishing community and associated industries, the tourism and other businesses dependent upon sharks, consumers, community members and organizations, as well as scientists, lawyers, economists, policy makers and potentially the media. These actors will have concerns that they want addressed and interests that they want protected. Each stakeholder has particular roles to play and may contribute to the strategies needed to improve shark conservation and management. These roles are discussed immediately below.

The state has a critical position as the key decision maker in shark governance specifically and marine governance more generally. The state has the authority to determine whether marine areas under its jurisdiction will be afforded specific protections and what restrictions or proscriptions are required. While governments have authority over the maritime areas and industries in question, the relevant government may be local, provincial or state governments, as well as federal or national governments. In some countries, local and national governments will need to work together depending on the authority each holds over sea areas. For example, in Australia, state and federal authorities have joined forces in creating marine conservation parks at Ningaloo Reef to enhance the protection of whale sharks that migrate there annually.

At the international level, the national government undertakes negotiations, consultations and discussions with other national governments to assess problems and decide on solutions. For example, it is the state that decides whether it will participate in the international regimes created under CITES or CMS and whether it will be bound by the restrictions that follow from the listing of a species in the Appendices of these treaties. Equally, a state that has fishing vessels operating in particular areas will need to determine if it will join a regional fisheries management organization (RFMO) and be bound, for example, by catch limitations and reporting requirements as part of that regime, or engage in other regional responses.

Even when a state has become party to an international treaty or regional organization, steps must usually still be taken for the state to implement the international rules and standards within its national or local (provincial) law. This step is vital in shark conservation and management when it is recalled that the main international instrument focused on sharks is the non-binding IPOA-Sharks. As discussed in the chapters by Klein and Lack, states must establish their own NPOAs following the guidelines laid out in the IPOA-Sharks. Action at the international level alone, while potentially carrying some political importance and the possibility of sanctions, is insufficient to improve the conservation status of shark species by itself.

Once implemented, states must dedicate the resources to ensure the relevant laws are enforced. While this may be possible for developed countries, for developing states with large maritime areas under their jurisdiction, ensuring that fishing vessels are adhering to fishing catch quotas may not be feasible because of the lack of available resources for monitoring and enforcement. It is essential to identify novel ways and means to enhance capability and build capacity in such nations. Palau provides an example of such innovation. Initially, Palau sought to enter into an agreement with the Sea Shepherd Conservation Fund to assist with policing its exclusive economic zone (EEZ) after declaring the entire area a shark sanctuary (Sea Shepherd, 2011). More recently it has been the subject of a pilot project involving the use of unmanned surveillance drones to monitor its vast EEZ (AFP, 2013).

Engagement with the fishing industry is another critical dimension to shark conservation and management. This industry has an economic interest in ensuring the ongoing sustainability of the fisheries in question. In the absence of a sustainable fishery, those in the industry must consider other livelihoods. In this regard, an alternative may be involvement in the tourism industry and development of shark eco-tourism sites. Again, engagement with those involved in the industry, the regulators and the scientific experts is essential.

Fishers are not limited to those engaged in commercial operations, but also include those involved in recreational fishing activities. Huveneers and Robbins have discussed how recreational shark catch can exceed commercial landings in some local shark fisheries. These recreational activities must be taken into account in devising management practices, particularly the total allowable catch and equipment requirements.

The fishing industry not only has to align activities with legal requirements relating to catch quota and equipment use, but must also properly document what catch is taken. The collection of data and reporting of those data to the FAO, as well as to RFMOs, are indispensable steps to assess the status of stocks. Scientists and economists can feed this data into their own work and provide assessments on what steps could or should be taken to maintain the longevity of a shark species. These data are then also essential for governments making decisions in setting national allocations of any particular species or in deciding whether the status of a species is so precarious that all international trade or harvesting of the species must be banned.

The fishing industry is, of course, predicated on consumer demand for what is harvested at sea. In some countries, ocean resources are a vital source of protein and fundamental to the nutrition of local populations. In other countries, the export of marine species, as well as the industries that support fishing (such as others in the supply chain, as well as bunkering and port services), are important economic activities. The fishing industry necessarily responds to consumer demand and it was clear from Lawrence's chapter how eco-labelling has proven influential and remains a potential avenue in changing fishing industry practices, as well as modifying consumer choices.

Consumer demand in relation to sharks has been most telling in relation to shark fins. Serving shark fin soup at important events has cultural significance in different Asian countries and in Asian communities living in other countries. Conservation groups have sought to bring greater awareness to the cruelty that may be associated with finning, as well as the unsustainable level at which fins are being harvested, in order to deter consumers from continuing to serve shark fin soup. Progress has been made in this regard in China, with reports that consumer demand has dropped as greater information about the status of shark species has become available (Denyer, 2013). A further example may be seen in Hong Kong, where the government has announced that it will no longer include the soup on the menus of official banquets and other functions (Wassener, 2012). This has been aided by sports and other personalities who have been enlisted to draw public attention to the issues (Thibault, 2013) and also by airline bans on the transport of fins and major hotel chain refusal to serve shark fin soup, as noted above.

Influential in consumer behaviour has been the work of diverse non-governmental organizations (NGOs) as discussed by Hepp and Griffin Wilson. The conservation groups seeking to improve shark conservation and management have been strong advocates in shifting government policy and in encouraging states to take action in setting international standards and requirements. NGOs have further been influential through their work with the fishing industry in demonstrating how changes in fishing practice may both ensure the sustainability of the industry and reduce cruelty to the animals involved. In addition, NGO networks, such as the IUCN and its Shark Specialist Group (SSG), contribute directly to shark research. The mandate of the NGO, along with its available resources, will inevitably determine what role the organization plays in relation to shark governance.

As shark eco-tourism has increased in popularity throughout the world, the stakeholders in this industry have sought greater participation in decisions relating to the regulation of shark species. The tourism operators are primary constituents in this regard, but the local communities that economically benefit from the visitors to the area also have an interest in ensuring the protection of the tourism sites and the species that are the subject of tourism ventures. Governments can take action to support these industries through engagement with the sector to develop conducive licensing and regulatory regimes, declaring MPAs and restricting fishing activities in associated areas.

Tourism can have a positive influence on consumers because of the educational role that may be inculcated into the tourism experience. Participants may become ambassadors for shark conservation and/or assist with research as suggested by Ward-Paige. Diners may be less inclined to eat shark species once aware of their conservation status, or once aware of techniques that may have been used in the production of shark fin soup. Further, an understanding of shark behaviour and appreciation of their role in the marine ecosystem may reduce demand for shark culls following attacks on swimmers and surfers.

Tourism operators may also work with scientists and provide data about shark sightings or behaviour, for example, during diving and swimming trips.

Ward-Paige demonstrated how those involved in the tourism industry could provide useful input into research through the collection of data and conduct of specially prepared surveys. Scientists may accompany tour operators for the collection of a range of information and use the results of this research to inform policy makers and government officials about steps that are necessary to sustain the industry or to better protect the shark species involved.

Scientists have a pivotal role in the governance of shark species as the information provided by scientists may form the foundations of decisions as to how to manage a particular species. As science emerges about shark biology and further data is revealed about the number of sharks, governments are provided with the impetus to reassess fishing quotas. Investigations into shark behaviour in response to tourism may also prompt changes in codes of conduct, regulations and licences. Scientific assessments will also determine how well any particular strategy is working for the recovery of any shark species.

Multiple stakeholders and actors with differing roles and interests have input into resolving these problems. Lawyers are typically at the forefront of drafting regulations, agreements and treaties that govern the rights and responsibilities of those engaged in shark management and conservation. As Techera noted at the outset of this volume, strong regulatory frameworks are essential to protect marine areas and resources, especially if a conservation ethic towards sustainable development and environmental responsibility is lacking. Lawyers particularly need to engage with scientists and economists to ensure the most effective rules may be formulated. As Hepp and Griffin Wilson rightly observed, 'even after laws or regulations were put in place, additional and consistent NGO pressure was required to bring public attention to the conservation plight of sharks and to ensure the effective enforcement of these policies'. Economists also have an important role in informing decision making and policy development. Given the financial imperatives in the fishing industry broadly and shark harvesting specifically, as well as emerging data regarding the relative financial benefits of shark tourism, ensuring that economic incentives are embedded in management plans is critical.

Finally, the role of the media should not be underestimated. As evident from Neff's chapter, the media has considerably swayed general opinion towards sharks and the responses that should be taken when humans feel threatened by sharks. The media may also prove influential in the campaigns of different advocacy and conservation groups; consumers may shift their preferences away from shark products when information is disseminated as to the status of shark species or the barbaric techniques that have been used to procure those shark products. Popular culture has progressed from the time of the ferocious great white shark portrayed in *Jaws* to the more empathetic Bruce in *Finding Nemo*, who avows 'I am a nice shark, not a mindless eating machine.' However, the broad-based public support that exists for other marine species, such as whales and dolphins, has not yet emerged for sharks.

Tools and strategies

As discussed by Techera, shark conservation and management has benefited from the variety of conservation approaches, legal principles and regulatory mechanisms that have developed over time. The many stakeholders in shark governance are engaged in different ways in relation to the tools and strategies that have been brought to bear in conservation and management efforts for different shark species. Governments are key decision makers, but those policies and decisions are informed by the work of scientists and economists, as well as by the advocacy efforts of NGOs. In making decisions, governments may draw on a range of options depending on the particular species, its habitat and behaviour, and other information available. Some of the options explored in this book are discussed in this part.

Listing species for specific protections is a key technique utilized in the international legal instruments, such as CITES and CMS, as well as at the domestic level in fisheries regulations and environmental legislation. Listing identifies a particular species and singles it out for special treatment and protection. Once listed at the international level, governments may have greater impetus (or political cover) in listing a species at the domestic level and thereby subjecting local waters to restrictions that would not have otherwise been imposed.

Listing, if it simply bans the harvesting or trade in a particular species, can be a blunt tool. Therefore, more sophisticated approaches are necessary, such as seasonal bans, restricted harvest or the use (or limitation) of particular equipment or fishing methods. For example, as noted in Klein's chapter, RFMOs have generally preferred to find alternative measures in managing a particular species rather than banning its capture outright. If a fishery can be sustainably managed, then the fishing industry and consumer markets dependent on the relevant shark product are less likely to be severely prejudiced.

An increasingly common tool, which is highlighted in Hoyt's chapter, is the use of MPAs or sanctuaries to enhance shark protection. Hoyt emphasizes that successful MPAs 'must have well-defined goals, buy-in from local communities, legal protection with enforcement capability, research and monitoring components and be well integrated with other conservation tools'. The declaration of these areas may provide protection to shark species in particular breeding or feeding grounds. Within MPAs, there may be strict quotas on the number of sharks that may be caught or, as is more commonly the case with sanctuaries, harvesting of shark species may be prohibited entirely. The use of MPAs has also fostered the development of shark eco-tourism sites, as discussed by Hoyt.

Shark eco-tourism, then, constitutes an alternative strategy around human utilization of sharks. Ward-Paige noted this potential in writing 'there is momentum to reduce anthropogenic impacts, mitigate past degradations, recover populations, and monitor environmental conditions to ensure long-term sustainable use'. Rather than primarily appreciating sharks as a food source, sharks could instead be showcased to divers and swimmers as majestic creatures requiring human protection. However, as observed in several chapters, research must still be undertaken to determine if the tourism industry is harmfully modifying shark behaviour. Best-practice standards must be developed to counter this risk.

A further advantage to shark eco-tourism is that the establishment of dive and swim tours may provide an alternative livelihood for fishers. There can be additional economic incentives to fostering shark eco-tourism in situations where the value of sharks alive is greater than when dead. In their chapter, Cisneros-Montemayor and Sumaila demonstrate that the sum of expenditures at shark watching sites is more than the total landed value of sharks in the corresponding countries. Ward-Paige noted that the worth of sharks varies depending on species and location. Yet when shark watching already generates almost half the value of global shark fisheries, there is clearly reason to foster and promote the development of shark eco-tourism. Though, as Cisneros-Montemayor and Sumaila caution, this process should be carefully managed so unrestricted competition may be avoided at the sites, as this could decrease the benefits for those involved and risk the resource upon which the industry depends.

The promotion of shark eco-tourism is not only benefited by the creation of MPAs or sanctuaries; fishing bans may also support this industry. Clearly the continual harvesting of a shark species is not feasible if it results in a decreased number of sharks then available for viewing. Kempster and Collin note that the increasing international restrictions on consumptive use of the iconic species have benefited their tourism value.

Prohibitions on fishing for certain species of sharks may ultimately be the only way to allow that species to recover. A complete moratorium on commercial harvesting has been applied in relation to all whale species since the mid 1980s and a similar blanket approach may ultimately become necessary for all sharks if numbers continue to decline. Nonetheless, it is clear from the chapters by Lawrence and Huveneers and Robbins that some shark fisheries have been sustainably managed for some decades and may provide powerful insights for the management of other fisheries involving shark species with similar characteristics. For developing countries, though, Huveneers and Robbins write, banning all shark products may be the best option as it can simplify enforcement rather than require the settling and policing of catch or size limits (see also the chapter by Worm *et al.*). Ward-Paige underlined the existing 'scientific consensus that properly managed and enforced protected areas generally increase species richness, density and average size of fish' (citing Worm *et al.*, 2009). Again, however, for some states the resources are simply not available to make this tool effective.

Better controls on fishing for sharks may be more politically feasible and sufficient than a blanket ban. A common approach in RFMOs is to set a total allowable catch (TAC) for a particular species and then allocate certain amounts to different states. However, as discussed in Klein's chapter, there is currently no shark-specific RFMO and no cooperative international forum in existence to manage migratory shark species and implement binding requirements. It is otherwise left to individual states to determine the most sustainable catch for sharks found within their jurisdiction. Beyond regulating quotas for targeted shark fisheries, by-catch issues must be addressed. In this situation, there is a need to monitor the quantities of sharks, and type of sharks, that are taken in other fisheries. Reducing by-catch will require modification of fishing methods, including the use of certain nets and other equipment such as tuna aggregation devices that indiscriminately increase the take of non-harvest species. Banning wire leaders and using turtle exclusion devices (TEDs) and other filter grids may also be required.

Targeting the shark supply chain may prompt changes in practices, including quantities fished and equipment used. Eco-labelling on the basis of certification of fisheries has prompted shifts in practices, as demonstrated in Lawrence's chapter. Improved technologies to trace products and to undertake chain of custody checks within the fishing industry will also enhance scientific understanding of the status and behaviour of sharks, as well as being embedded in management measures.

The particular tools that are utilized for shark conservation and management may need to be varied as changes occur in habitat conditions or the conservation status of a particular species, and as research reveals more about shark biology and ecology. For laws and regulations to have ongoing relevance, mechanisms should provide for the revision of those laws and regulations over time. Momigliano and Harcourt advocate for the use of adaptive management, arguing that the 'effectiveness of management policies also needs to be scientifically assessed on clear performance indicators, and revised management strategies need to be developed based on such assessment'. Hoyt similarly moots the use of adaptive management in ensuring the ongoing success of MPAs. This approach anticipates continual feedback between scientific enquiry and policy development.

Worm, Cosandey-Godin and Davis have instead questioned the feasibility of adaptive management. They cast doubt on its utility because so much damage can be done to a fish stock in a short space of time and the length of recovery time needed can be substantial. Management, irrespective of how adaptive it is, may not be sufficient, and strict regulation in the form of complete fishing bans will then become essential for stock recovery. Worm, Cosandey-Godin and Davis have argued that these blunt tools are necessary where capacity is lacking to undertake detailed assessments and devise closely honed measures to increase sustainability. It would certainly be the case that all strategies should be left on the table for consideration in any given situation.

Levels of governance

In addition to discerning what strategies should be put in place and which stakeholders need to be engaged in the process, careful consideration needs to be given to which level of governance should be targeted. In this context, the level of governance refers to the laws, principles, institutions and actors operating at a local, regional, national or international level. Some strategies and tools will work better at a particular level of governance than others. For example, where a local population of sharks has been affected by a particular pollution incident or targeted by recreational fishers, then it may be sufficient to introduce stricter licensing or harvesting laws for that specific area. Widespread regulations would not be necessary. In other circumstances, cumulative impacts on migratory or wide-ranging species may indicate a regional approach.

We have seen that steps have been taken at each level of governance so far. Necessarily, initiatives to improve the conservation status of highly migratory species have been spearheaded at the international level where inter-state cooperation is most needed. Restricting international trade in specific shark species is best agreed at the international level, although the implementation of this restriction needs to occur at the national (or perhaps local) level.

Steps taken at the national level range across a spectrum of more progressive or active engagement in management measures to regressive or non-existent policies and approaches. As has been discussed in different chapters, states have declared sanctuaries or MPAs in the ocean areas over which they have authority and highly regulated and restricted activities in those areas. Other states have moved to adopt NPOAs consistent with IPOA-Sharks, as well as other steps to implement international obligations. Other states, including the main consumer states, have prioritized commercial exploitation or failed to regulate their fishing industry at the expense of many shark species.

Multi-level governance is ultimately required to ensure greater coherence and a more comprehensive approach to conservation and management of shark species. As Kempster and Collin noted, the biological diversity among shark species is a key factor for necessitating a multi-level approach. Moreover, situations may arise where local populations are in greater need of protection than the species as a whole and targeted responses may be appropriate in this situation.

Way(s) forward

Monitoring, implementation and enforcement of existing rules are vital steps for shark fisheries to become and remain sustainable. These are areas where political support is essential from the relevant governments, and where stakeholders can usefully support and influence government initiatives in this regard. Beyond the existing rules, there remains scope for a new, binding, international agreement that can fill the gaps in existing global governance measures and seek to integrate the range of measures being taken in different regions or by individual states. While making the existing law work better is important, there is still considerable scope to improve on that law at all levels of governance. At the international level, political appetite for the development of new law may well be limited as evidenced by the history of CITES listings, for example. As opined by Lack, the national level may offer greater potential and this has been borne out by recent experiences in the Pacific (Techera, 2012).

Yet law and policy is clearly only one relevant perspective. Scientific research must move forward and fill in many of the gaps existing in our knowledge about shark species. Kiszka and Heithaus highlighted a number of areas where more research is critical: shark taxonomy; life history data; population structure and dynamics; geographic extent of stocks; patterns of habitat use; migrations; diets; and the ecological role of shark species. This knowledge is essential to ensure the sustainable use of sharks and what management strategies may prove most effective to enhance the conservation status of shark species (see also Kempster and Collin chapter). Momigliano and Harcourt have urged that research must be directed so as to be relevant to conservation strategies: 'The most powerful management incorporates science as a means of informing best practice.'

Technology and scientific techniques are always improving, and as the technology, in particular, evolves it can be utilized more broadly. Technological advances will enhance efforts to monitor marine areas and traceability and chain of custody in the fishing industry, as well as improving the collection of data from a range of sources for diverse projects. With time the prices of such tools drop and become more accessible to developing countries. In the meantime, there is a role to be played by the international community in transferring relevant technology and building capacity where it is weak. Enhancing research infrastructure will continue to be necessary and collaborative research endeavours must be fostered to facilitate dissemination of research and advance thinking on appropriate management strategies. This collaboration should occur among developing and developed countries so as to increase local research capacity.

Collaborative effort is a key requirement in improving the conservation status of shark species. Ward-Paige highlighted how the tourism industry, and tourists themselves, can usefully contribute to scientific research by supporting data collection and generating data in order to improve our understanding of sharks. She further suggested how researchers, tourists and tour operators might be able to work together to provide real-time inventories and descriptions of populations, including through dedicated online databases. Lawrence similarly underlined the importance of integrated approaches in order to reduce the pressure globally on sharks. She highlighted that many of the approaches attempted to date had not focused, or insufficiently focused, on the fishing industry and markets, hence neglecting the shark supply chains.

We also need to move beyond the focus on charismatic or iconic shark species. There may be an advantage to 'flagship' species in fostering public awareness of conservation issues, but, as Momigliano and Harcourt observed, 'focusing on flagship species is unlikely to provide major benefits to the majority of shark species'. Hoyt further comments that focus on a single-species without controlling effort may just transfer pressure from one species to another. Our efforts must be broader, particularly when operating at the international level.

Momigliano and Harcourt, as well as Lack, have argued for a 'champion', potentially from within a regulatory agency. We have seen in Hepp and Griffin Wilson's chapter that there has been success in advocacy efforts opposed to finning and, as Lawrence also discussed, changes in consumers' attitudes towards shark fin soup. Hoyt proposes that a global ban on finning, through a UN declaration or agreement, should be established, along with spatial measures. The ongoing problem, as acknowledged by Hepp and Griffin Wilson, is that insisting on an end to finning so that sharks are landed whole does not stop over-harvesting of shark species. Neff makes a similar point in commenting that it is 'not clear that the public sees a connection between support for anti-finning efforts and support for local shark conservation of dangerous species'.

The idea of a 'champion' anticipates a strong level of stakeholder support. Such support is critical in management strategies, particularly in ocean areas where implementation cannot be easily monitored and enforcement is unpredictable. Coordination must occur across non-state actors, as previously noted, as well as between the shark fishing states and the shark consuming states (which are not necessarily the same; see the chapter by Cisneros-Montemayor and Sumaila) since it is often at the state level that policies must be developed and adopted to effect change on a broad scale.

Conclusion

As Lawrence wrote,

> One thing is clear, given the scale, complexity and globalization of shark fisheries and markets, effective transformational approaches for improved shark conservation require integrated involvement and cooperation among all stakeholders that span countries and markets to develop long-term, holistic solutions that are acceptable and beneficial to all.

This statement sums up the extent of the problems and the necessary action that is needed to address them.

It is clear that while problems remain, we are in a better position today, more than ever before, to address the depletion of sharks; a problem that is almost exclusively anthropogenic. We have more sophisticated legal tools and mechanisms, better scientific data and more advanced technology than has been available in the past. It is equally clear that we must work better with what we have. In particular, we must overcome horizontal and vertical challenges. The former include tensions between different sectors and industries; including the divide between consumptive and non-consumptive utilization of sharks. In relation to the latter it is necessary to identify the level of governance best suited to the particular problem at hand and then to facilitate best practice at that level.

It would appear that the conservation and management of sharks would best be enhanced by the creation of a forum for discussion and cooperation. Whether or not such a body is given any authority or binding powers, it could facilitate the sharing of scientific, law, policy, economic and other information. It could act as a clearing house and thereby assist in the development of best-practice conservation and management. In addition, it could be a focal point for discussion and debate to ensure that experts, governments, industry and the public have the information necessary to make informed choices and participate in decision making to ensure the future of some of the oldest species on this planet.

References

AFP (2013) 'Pacific's Palau mulls drone patrols to monitor waters', *Global Post*, 4 October, available at www.globalpost.com/dispatch/news/afp/131004/pacifics-palau-mulls-drone-patrols-monitor-waters, accessed 5 March 2014.

Cripps, K. (2013) 'More airlines ban shark fin cargo', *CNN*, 25 June, available at http://edition.cnn.com/2013/06/25/travel/airline-shark-fin-ban/index.html, accessed 5 March 2014.

Denyer, S. (2013) 'In China, victory for wildlife conservation as citizens persuaded to give up shark fin soup', *Washington Post*, 19 October, available at www.washingtonpost.com/world/in-china-victory-for-wildlife-conservation-as-citizens-persuaded-to-give-up-shark-fin-soup/2013/10/19/e8181326-3646-11e3-89db-8002ba99b894_story.html, accessed 5 March 2014.

IUCN (2012) *The IUCN Red List of Threatened Species. Version 2012.2*, available at www.iucnredlist.org, accessed 14 May 2013.

Sea Shepherd (2011) 'Sea Shepherd partners with the Republic of Palau to control poaching', www.seashepherd.org/news-and-media/2011/03/31/sea-shepherd-partners-with-the-republic-of-palau-to-control-poaching-28, accessed 5 March 2014.

Techera, E. J. (2012) 'Fishing, finning and tourism: trends in Pacific shark conservation and management', *International Journal of Marine and Coastal Law*, vol. 27, no. 3, pp. 597–621.

Thibault, H. (2013) 'China's fishmongers lament waning popularity of shark fin soup', *Guardian*, 13 February, www.theguardian.com/world/2013/feb/12/shark-fishing-china-puqi-conservation, accessed 5 March 2014.

Wassener, B. (2012) 'China says no more shark fin soup at state banquets', *New York Times*, 3 July, available at www.nytimes.com/2012/07/04/world/asia/china-says-no-more-shark-fin-soup-at-state-banquets.html?_r=0, accessed 5 March 2014.

Worm, B., Hilborn, R., Baum, J. K., Branch, T. A., Collie, J. S., Costello, C., Fogarty, M. J., Fulton, E. A., Hutchings, J. A., Jennings, S., Jensen, O. P., Lotze, H. K., Mace, P. M., McClanahan, T. R., Minto, C., Palumbi, S. R., Parma, A. M., Ricard, D., Rosenberg, A. A., Watson, R. and Zeller, D. (2009) 'Rebuilding global fisheries', *Science*, vol. 325, pp. 578–585.

Worm, B., Davis, B., Kettemer, L., Ward-Paige, C. A., Chapman, D., Heithaus, M. R., Kessel, S. and Gruber, S. H. (2013) 'Global catches, exploitation rates, and rebuilding options for sharks', *Marine Policy*, vol. 40, pp. 194–204.

Index